Self-Determination in International Law

Self-Determination

in

International Law

by
UMOZURIKE OJI UMOZURIKE
LL.M., Dip. Air Law (London), D.Phil. (Oxon)

ARCHON BOOKS
1972

Library of Congress Cataloging in Publication Data

Umozurike, U   O
    Self-determination in international law.

    Bibliography: p.
    1. Self-determination, National.   I. Title.
JX4054.U6   341.26   72-000071
ISBN 0-208-01273-7

To the People of Namibia

Contents

Abbreviations

AC	Appeal Cases
Ann. Dig.	Annual Digest
AG	Attorney-General
AJIL	American Journal of International Law
ANZUS	Australia-New Zealand-United States Defence Treaty
BFSP	British and Foreign State Papers
BYBIL	British Yearbook of International Law
CENTO	Central Treaty Organisation
Cmd.	British Command Paper
CLP	Current Legal Problems
CLR	Commonwealth Law Reports
Dept. of State Bull.	Department of State Bulletin
Doc.	Document
EALJ	East Africa Law Journal
EALR	East Africa Law Review
ECOSOC	Economic and Social Council
FLN	Front de Liberation National
GA	General Assembly
GAOR	General Assembly (UN) Ordinary Reports
HC	House of Commons
ICLQ	International and Comparative Law Quarterly
Inter. Con.	International Conciliation
ICJ	International Court of Justice
ILA	International Law Association
ILC	International Law Commission
ILR	International Law Reports
JIL	Journal of International Law
JMAS	Journal of Modern African Studies
KANU	Kenyan African National Union
LQR	Law Quarterly Review
LR	Law Reports
LN	League of Nations
LNOJ	League of Nations Official Journal
LNTS	League of Nations Treaty Series
NNC	Naga National Council
NFD	Northern Frontier District
NATO	North Atlantic Treaty Organisation
OAU	Organisation of African Unity
Off. Rec.	Official Record
Off. Sess.	Official Session
Parl. Debs.	Parliamentary Debates
PCIJ	Permanent Court of International Justice
PMC	Permanent Mandates Commission
Res.	Resolution
Soc.	Society
SC	Security Council
SEATO	Southeast Asia Treaty Organisation
Supp.	Supplement
UN	United Nations
UNCIO	United Nations Conference on International Organisation
UNYB	United Nations Year-Book
YBIA	Year-Book of International Affiars
YBIL	Year-Book of International Law
YBWA	Year-Book of World Affairs
YILC	Year-Book of International Law Commission

Preface

This book is primarily intended for international lawyers. The principle of self-determination is, however, of no less interest to political scientists, students of international relations, and politicians charged with the responsibility of allowing adequate expression to the views of all sections of the population within a state.

Self-determination is an ancient political right that is cherished by every people. It connotes the right of a people to have a government of their choice. Both the American and French revolutions were based on the claim of this right and the desire of the people to be free from external or internal domination.

During the First World War President Woodrow Wilson popularised the principle and proclaimed that respect for it had become imperative and that statesmen could ignore it only at their own peril. As the war dragged on, all the belligerents, including the Central Powers, adopted as their principal war aim the self-determination of the minorities of Central Europe. The prevailing meaning of the principle at that time was the right of secession and the formation of an independent state. The oppressed minorities could therefore secede from the states of which they formed parts if they so desired. In actual fact the principle was applied to the minorities in the territories of the defeated belligerents. On coming to power in 1917, the Bolsheviks proclaimed that the oppressed nationalities of Czarist Russia were entitled to self-determination to the extent of secession and the formation of independent states; some actually gained their independence in the exercise of this right.

If independence were the only manifestation of self-determination, it would follow that the right was denied to the smaller minorities within the new states of Central Europe founded after the First World War, for it was impracticable that every conceivable minority could secede and form an independent state. The danger of this restrictive interpretation soon became apparent. It is no wonder that Secretary of State Robert Lansing warned President Woodrow Wilson that the principle was loaded with dynamite and that it was a double-edged sword that could cut both the victors and the vanquished.

Non-annexation was also a major war aim of the Allies. The subject peoples of the defeated belligerents who could not stand by themselves were placed under "the mandate," a trust imposed on the mandatory whose duty it was to advance the political, economic, and social progress of its wards. The principle of self-determination was immanent in the mandate system insofar as it was envisaged that the mandated territories would eventually become self-governing.

During the Second World War the principle again became active— this time not as a European monopoly but as having universal application. There were millions of peoples in the vast colonial world yearning for governments of their own choice, and their demands had to be accommodated in the interest of world peace. The Charter of the United Nations expressly affirms the "self-determination of peoples" as a condition for peaceful and friendly relations among nations. Express provisions are made for the "political, economic, social, and educational advancement" of peoples in trust territories; and in colonial territories the development of "self-government," taking "due account of the political aspirations of the people." The lessons of the First World War settlement had shifted the emphasis from independence to self-government, or independence as a legitimate manifestation of self-determination.

The United Nations has built an impressive corpus of practice on decolonisation which envisages that self-determination may be enjoyed through independence, association, merger, or autonomy, provided the choice accords with the wishes of the people. Colonial powers have developed techniques for accommodating the desire of their subject peoples for self-determination, which they demand as a right, not a favour. The principle has received express mention in treaties and in the declarations of international conferences and organisations.

In spite of these developments there are still doubts in some quarters that self-determination has become a principle which is not only fundamental but also a rule of international law. It is pointed out by some of the critics of self-determination that it is undefined and vague and that in fact all peoples never did, do not, and will not, enjoy self-determination.

The purpose of this book is to trace the development of the principle and to show how it has now matured into a principle of positive international law. The evidence from the practice of the United Nations, state practice, and the writings of eminent jurists from the world's main legal systems, will, it is believed, confirm that self-determination is now recognised as a fundamental principle of international law.

I wish to express my gratitude to the British Institute of International and Comparative Law, whose award made my research possible for the greater part of the period needed to prepare this work. I am also grateful to the Humanity Trust, Oxford; Africa Educational Trust, London; Walter Gordon Trust, London; and Linacre College Trust, whose grants enabled me to complete the thesis.

I owe Professor H. G. Hanbury a debt of gratitude for his encouragement before and during my stay in Oxford. I am very grateful to my supervisor, Sir Humphrey Waldock, without whose painstaking efforts the original writing might have taken much longer to complete. I have since added views and sections with which I did not trouble Sir Humphrey. My informal discussions with Dr. I. Brownlie and Mr. J. E. S. Fawcett, both of Oxford, helped to elucidate obscure points in the course of my work. I, however, claim responsibility for all the views expressed in the book. I appreciate the kindness of the principal of my college, Linacre, Mr. J. B. Bamborough. My wife was a source of encouragement at a time when news of the Nigerian civil war was particularly disconcerting.

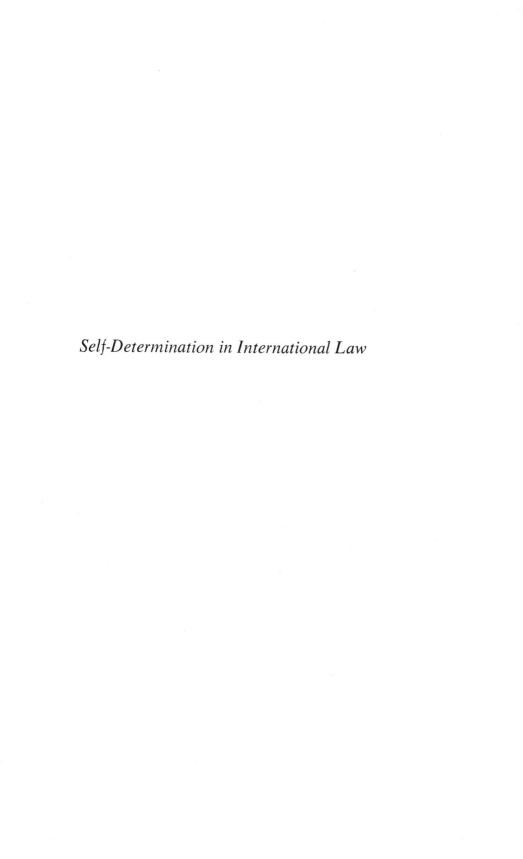

Self-Determination in International Law

I   *Self-Determination before 1919*

1. Origins of the Term "Self-Determination"

The word "self-determination" is derived from the German word *selbstbestimmungsrecht* and was frequently used by German radical philosophers in the middle of the nineteenth century. It was incorporated in a resolution of the London International Socialist Congress in 1896, which declared that "it upholds the full rights of the self-determination (*selbstbestimmungsrecht*) of all nations. . . ."[1] The Socialist Conference of Denmark, Holland, Norway, and Sweden held at Copenhagen in January 1915 called for the "recognition of the self-determination of nations."[2]

The principle was earlier regarded as the right of nations to sovereign independence. The modern meaning is not so restrictive—it is the right of all peoples to determine their political future and freely pursue their economic, social, and cultural development. Politically this is manifested through independence, as well as self-government, local autonomy, merger, association, or some other form of participation in government. It operates both externally and internally to ensure democratic government and the absence of internal or external domination. Thus the principle of self-determination is relevant to peoples in dependent and independent territories alike. A consideration of its political background, the practice of international organisations, especially the United Nations, and state practice is necessary for the proper appreciation of its legal content.

1. Lenin, *The Right of Nations to Self-determination* (New York, 1951), p. 42.
2. S. Wambaugh, *Plebiscites Since the World War* (Washington, 1933), 1:8.

2. Before the Twentieth Century

The concept of self-determination can be traced back to the beginning of government. The right has always been cherished by all peoples, although history has a long list of its denial to the weak by the strong who claimed, and often enjoyed, superiority over them.

The Greek city-states, like the earlier Mesopotamian ones, were covetous of their right to self-determination. Yet to the Greeks, non-Greeks were barbarians, born to serve them and the object of conquest if they refused to submit. Aristotle in his *Politics* regarded war against them as "just by nature," but war among the Greeks was, in words ascribed to Socrates by Plato, "disease and discord."[3] The Greeks had a common language, culture, and religion, and the predominant national sentiment probably reduced their relations to an intranational, rather than international, plane. Within the city-states individuals enjoyed rights identical with freedom of speech, equality before the law, and self-respect.[4] The Greeks had not developed the concept of the law of all nations before their independence was destroyed by Philip of Macedonia in 338 B.C., but their philosophy had profound influence on the Romans who developed the legal techniques of freedom.

The proud Romans were the classic colonisers of foreign territories. Between the Roman state and its conquered territories there was no equality, although the acceptance of *deditio* might earn them indulgent treatment. As Schwarzenberger puts it, "they were merely fit to become incorporated into the Roman world empire or to be objects of policing operations on its fringes."[5] However the Romans, unlike the Greeks, were not hostile to foreigners in their midst and developed a special law —*jus gentium*—to govern the relations between foreigners or between foreigners and the Romans. The *jus civile*, which regulated the legal relations of Roman citizens *inter se*, was rigid and therefore unsuitable for foreigners. The *jus gentium* was further developed as a law established among all people by natural reason. By the seventeenth century the term was used synonymously with the "law of nations."

The Romans also developed "natural law," an idea that is traced back to the Greeks, especially the Stoics. The philosophy had influential Roman adherents such as Cicero, who helped to popularize Greek philosophy. Natural law was the ideal law derived from right reason and was later increasingly identified with the *jus gentium*, although there

---

3. A. Nussbaum, *A Concise History of the Law of Nations* (London, 1962). chapter 1.

4. H. Lauterpacht, *International Law and Human Rights* (London, 1950), p. 4.

5. G. Schwarzenberger, *A Manual of International Law* (London, 1967), p. 6.

were some irreconcilable points between the two (e.g. slavery was common to all mankind and was, therefore, recognised by the *jus gentium;* man was by nature born free, therefore slavery was contrary to natural law.)

As long as the Roman Empire remained strong, the Romans denied to others the right to freely determine their own future. But with its breakdown, many states began to emerge. The Roman Empire was divided between the east and west, and in A.D. 476 the western part fell when Emperor Romulus Augustus was deposed by Odeacer, leader of the Germanic soldiers, who then made himself ruler. The kingdom of the Franks sprang up in Gallia in 486, the Ostrogoths in Italy in 493, the Visigoths in Spain in 456, and the Vandals in Africa (with Carthage as capital) in 429. The Saxons were established in Britannia on the western fringes of the Roman Empire. Although the western Roman Empire was partially resuscitated in 800 when Pope Leo III crowned Charlemagne as Holy Roman Emperor, it did not last, for in 843 it was divided into three parts which further disintegrated; in theory, the German emperor remained emperor of the world. By the reign of the last emperor crowned in Rome (Frederick III 1440–1493), Europe consisted virtually of independent sovereign states, each claiming and exercising the right to decide its own future.[6]

Neither Christianity nor Islam recognised the right of all peoples to self-determination inasmuch as they encouraged the subjugation of non-believers under the guise of "just wars." The church adopted the natural law doctrine and identified it with the law of God—over and above all human laws. The real importance of this doctrine is that it laid the foundation for the criticism of all human laws that were thought to offend the law of nature, including those laws that denied to people the right to determine their future.

In the development of political theory the views of Machiavelli (1469–1527), Vitoria (1480–1546), Jean Bodin (1530–96), Suarez (1548–1617), and Gentili (1552–1608) are of particular importance insofar as they tended to extend or restrict the principle of self-determination. Machiavelli, an Italian, approved of ruthlessness, devoid of political morality, on the part of a state for the attainment of its objectives. Only thus could progress be made, he believed.[7] More than any other philosopher he rationalized the tenets of positivism. Machiavellianism has been identified with the use of unscrupulous means in order to

6. *See also* L. F. Oppenheim, *International Law* (London, 1963), pp. 72–83.
7. N. Machiavelli, *The Prince* and *The First Decade of Titus Livinus,* both in 1513.

achieve ends. Vitoria, a Spaniard, was noted for his concern for the Red Indians who in his time were subjugated by the Spaniards. He compared them to children; the Spanish duty to them was like that of an adult to his ward, a duty that in no way overrides his *dominium*.[8] This idea is embodied in the mandate and trusteeship system of this century.[9] Bodin, a Frenchman, saw sovereignty as conferring on the king absolute and perpetual power over his subjects; the king enjoys the prerogative to declare peace or war. Suarez, a Spaniard, pointed to the ambiguity in the term *jus gentium*. It could mean the law that all nations should observe and it could also mean the law that all nations in fact observe in their relations with one another. This ambiguity could be applied to self-determination as a political principle. Gentilis, an Italian, reiterated the doctrine of *clausula rebus sic stantibus* in the interpretation of treaties, a doctrine that was pregnant with possibilities of changes in response to changing circumstances.

The development of modern states in Europe enhanced the status of self-determination as a political principle, but those who cherished it were inclined to deny it to others whenever necessary and possible. Influenced by Machiavellianism, European states were prone to disregard the rights of non-Europeans. The principle of self-determination did not, however, assume the definitive status of a political and constitutional principle until the American and French revolutions.

A. *The American Revolution.* The American colonists resented domination from across the seas, especially the imposition of taxes without representation. They invoked natural law and the natural rights of man and drew inspiration from the writings of John Locke (1632–1704), who taught that political societies were based upon the consent of the people who compose them, each of whom agrees to submit to the majority. Man has a natural right to life, liberty, and property. Sovereignty belongs to the people and is therefore limited by the necessity to protect the individual members.[10]

Jefferson, the greatest leader of the American Revolution, synthesised the American ideal and epitomised the republican spirit of the century. He was familiar with the works of the great philosophers and was influenced particularly by Locke and the Swiss Burlamaqui. In "An Essay

8. *See also* Eppstein, *The Catholic Tradition of the Law of Nations,* (1935), p. 397.

9. *See* chapters 2 and 5.

10. John Locke, *Treatise of Civil Government*, book 2; W. T. Jones, *Masters of Political Thought* (1960), chapter 5; C. Morris, *Great Legal Philosophers* (1959), chapter 6.

Concerning Human Understanding" Locke taught that man was the product of his environment. Thus a good environment created a good man, and the opposite the reverse. In his *Droit naturel* Burlamaqui saw happiness as the ultimate objective of existence; the pursuit of it was the key to the human system. It appeared to Jefferson that, in order to produce a man of the "high society," whose objectives would be the pursuit of life, liberty, and happiness, the proper environment had to be created and the chief ingredient of this was good government. To Niccolò Machiavelli, men were "ungrateful, voluble, dissemblers, anxious to avoid danger, and covetous of gain; as long as you benefit them they are entirely yours".[11] According to Hobbes, men were debased with vanity, lust, and avarice and in continual fear of their species; only a powerful government could control creatures so brutish if progress was to be attained.[12]

Jefferson had no grim view of human nature. Man was the product of his environment and was to be well trusted as the proper custodian of his own government: "I would say that the people, being the only safe depositary of power, should exercise in person every function which their qualifications enable them to exercise, consistently with the order and security of society."[13] He believed in the essential equality of man; not equality in social status or natural gifts, but equality before the law in the enjoyment of liberty, life, and happiness. He referred to the specially talented as belonging to "a natural aristocracy," but this only prepared them better to serve the community and was not a symbol of privilege.[14] Jefferson was first brought to the notice of the British government by his "Summary View of the Rights of British America" (1774), in which he argued that Americans, like the British, "possessed a right, which nature has given to all men" and that "God who gave us life, gave us liberty at the same time; the hand of force may destroy, but cannot disjoin them."[15]

In drafting the Declaration of Independence,[16] which followed a resolution of the Continental Congress on 7 June 1776 that "these United Colonies are and of right ought to be free and independent

11. N. Machiavelli, *The Prince*, chapter 17.

12. Thomas Hobbes, *The Leviathan* (Oxford, 1881), chapter 13.

13. Thomas Jefferson to Walter Jones, 2 January 1814, *The Writings of Thomas Jefferson* (1898), 9:447.

14. Ibid., pp. 424–429.

15. Ibid., (1894), 1:421–447.

16. In committee with John Adams, Benjamin Franklin, R. R. Livingstone, and Roger Sherman but actually the handiwork of Jefferson.

States," Jefferson embodied his fundamental philosophy of government.

> We hold these Truths to be self-evident, that all Men are created equal, that they are endowed by their Creator with certain unalienable Rights, that among these are Life, Liberty and the Pursuit of Happiness. That to secure these Rights, Governments are instituted among Men, deriving their just Powers from the Consent of the Governed, that whenever any Form of Government becomes destructive of these Ends, it is the Right of the People to alter or to abolish it and to institute new Government, laying its Foundation on such Principles and organizing its Powers in such Form, as to them shall seem most likely to effect their Safety and Happiness.[17]

He once wrote to Hartley:

> I have no fear but that the result of our experiment will be that men may be trusted to govern themselves without a master. Could the contrary of this be proved, I should conclude, either that there is no God, or that he is a malevolent being.[18]

He knew a number of men who took part in the French Revolution, and he counselled them to accept constitutional changes within the monarchy in view of France's ancient, and on the whole beloved, monarchy. Yet he was prepared to defend the extremes of the Revolution. Had it failed, he feared, the repercussions might have extended to America, the only other republic of the time. It might have resulted in bad government in France, and Jefferson was prepared to pay any price for freedom. "Were there but an Adam and an Eve left in every country and left free, it would be better than as it is now."[19] In the same way he defended Shays's Rebellion in Massachusetts (1786–87) which resulted from the government's failure to heed the grievances of certain debt-ridden farmers. He approved of rebellions as long as the objective was throwing out an autocratic government. The loss of life in the Shays's Rebellion was a worthy price: "The tree of liberty must be refreshed from time to time with the blood of patriots and tyrants. It is the natural manure."[20]

In considering the American Revolution as an outstanding example of the principle of self-determination, it is important to focus attention on Jeffersonianism in view of certain conflicting tendencies. Jefferson

17. H. S. Commanger, ed., *Documents of American History* (London and New York, 1948), p. 103.

18. Nye and Morpugo, *A History of the United States of America* (1955), p. 213.

19. Jefferson to William Short, 2 January 1793, *The Writings of Thomas Jefferson* (1898), 6:153–4.

20. Jefferson to Stephen Smith, 13 November 1787, *The Writings of Thomas Jefferson* (1894), 4:467.

was not only concerned with throwing off the foreign yoke but also with ensuring that the government was that of the people and that their will was supreme. And this involved deliberately discouraging class consciousness. In his inaugural address as President, he laid down "the creed of our political faith, the text of civic instruction," as he described it: "Though the will of the majority is in all cases to prevail, that will to be right must be reasonable; that the minority possesses their equal rights, which equal law must protect. . . ."[21]

Lincoln described Jefferson's principles as "the definitions and axioms of free society." The American experiment was to be followed by many of those who were not self-governing or who suffered from oppression.[22]

B. *The French Revolution.* French society in the eighteenth century was stratified into three estates (classes): the clergy, the nobles, and the third estate. The first two were privileged and enjoyed many advantages including exemptions from taxation. The third estate was made up of commoners—peasants, workers, soldiers, sailors, professionals, and industrialists. Some of them rose to the upper class by the grace of that class. The children of the nobility were themselves nobles.

Discontent with the order of things resulted from, *inter alia*, a rise in the standard of living among the commoners which placed them in a position to be more critical of the government, and from the teachings of the philosophers. With regard to the first, Lord Acton summarises:

> As their industry effected changes in the distribution of property, and wealth ceased to be the prerogative of a few, the excluded majority perceived that their disabilities rested on no foundation of right and justice and were unsupported by reasons of State.[23]

The philosophers had different ideas on government from what they were experiencing. Locke's hatred of arbitrary rule inspired Montesquieu to write *De l'esprit de lois*, in which he stressed the desirability of separating the powers of government in order to prevent dictatorship. Also influenced by Locke was Rousseau, who denounced inequalities in society and proposed a theory of social contract: "Since no man has natural authority over other men, and since might never makes right, it

---

21. Delivered in Washington, D.C., 4 March 1801. *See also* S. K. Padover, ed., *The Complete Jefferson* (1943), pp. 384–7.

22. *See* Padover, *Thomas Jefferson and the Foundations of American Freedom* (1965). A significant exercise of self-determination following the American example was the overthrow of Spanish and Portuguese rule in South America c.1820, giving rise to a number of independent states.

23. Lord Acton, *Lectures on the French Revolution* (London, 1916), p. 1.

follows that agreements are the basis of all legitimate authority among men."[24]

The philosophers influenced the commoners as well as the younger nobles. The commoners formed the bulk of the population in a ratio of 100 to 1; they now demanded a commensurate share in government and argued that their rulers should be their agents and not their masters. The action of the young Marquis de Lafayette, who at nineteen crossed the Atlantic as a volunteer in Washington's army of freedom-fighters, was generally admired. Later the French government declared war, but this was more out of spite for England than love of revolution against established authority. After the war, French volunteers returned home with fresh ideas of liberty and the rights of man.

France consisted of thirty-two provinces held together by the monarchy. Though they had local parliaments, only about a quarter of these were functioning. The provinces were ruled by "intendants" who were responsible to the king and his ministers who made all the laws. The General Assembly, (the Estates General) was occasionally summoned, principally to approve the taxes, but it had not been called since 1614. Government finances were worsening and the king was forced to recall the assembly to approve taxation. There were a few reforms intended to reactivate the provincial parliaments and the assembly, but these came too late and were too few to satisfy the people who had only recently witnessed a successful revolution across the seas. The General Assembly joined together and declared themselves the custodians of the public weal in 1789 and gave the country a constitution in which human rights were entrenched. The opening words of the Declaration of the Rights of Man and Citizen (*Declaration des droit de l'homme et citoyen*) embody the objective of the struggle: "All men are born and remain equal in rights." It asserts the natural rights of man and the observance of certain fundamental principles as essential for self-government. The revolt of the provincial towns and countryside ensured the defeat of the aristocracy and the administration. A revolutionary decree declared that "all men, without distinction of colour, domiciled in the French colonies are French citizens and enjoy all the rights assured by the Constitution."

The principles of the rights of man and the new emphasis on the wishes of the people led to the holding of plebiscites in the papal enclaves of Avignon and Venaissin before their annexation into the French Republic, even though the people had themselves overthrown papal rule

24. Jean Jacques Rousseau, *Les contrat social* (Paris, 1955), p. 1.

and expressed the desire to be annexed.[25] Plebiscites were also held before the annexation of Savoy in 1792 and of Nice in 1793. This early application of the plebiscite was to ascertain the wishes of the people before they joined the French Republic. Later the principle was abused, for it became an end in itself, being used to justify the annexation of territory that belonged to another sovereign. At the same time a decree of the assembly passed unanimously on 16 December 1792 reaffirmed the inviolability of French territory and imposed the death penalty on anybody attempting to cede any part of it, including the annexed portions. Thus France could annex foreign territory by way of plebiscite but could not cede its own after a plebiscite. Naturally, this interpretation of the principle of self-determination was viewed with alarm by France's neighbours.[26]

The Revolution was effected to put the ideas of liberty and equality into practice. No class of people had the inherent right to oppress another: relations between peoples were to be governed by justice and not by the favour of the privileged heredity. Being wholly an internal affair, there was no active foreign element in the French Revolution. The struggle for democracy was prolonged but was nevertheless successful in the long run.[27]

3. *The Development of Self-Determination During the First World War*

The First World War brought the principle of self-determination to the fore of international politics: it was referred to as the war of self-determination.[28] Small nationalities that were dominated by bigger ones had the opportunity of expressing their desire for freedom. The belligerents had within their own states peoples struggling for separate international personalities; both sides of the conflict appealed to the national sentiments of the minorities on the other side. Both were restrained at

25. The annexation following the plebiscite was condemned by Pope Pius VI as "a manifest violation of the law of nations." He questioned, "Will it then be permitted henceforth to everybody to choose a new master in accordance with one's pleasure? For such would be the consequence of the principle adopted by the National Assembly...." Quoted in Johannes Mattern, *The Employment of the Plebiscite in the Determination of Sovereignty* (Baltimore: The Johns Hopkins Press, 1920), p. 59.

26. *See also* Mattern, ibid, chapter 3, "The Plebiscite in The French Revolution," pp. 54–79.

27. *See also* Sydenham, *The French Revolution* (London, 1965), chapter 2; G. Ezejiofor, *Protection of Human Rights Under the Law* (London, 1964), chapter 1; F. M. Russel, *Theories of International Relations* (London, 1936), Chapter 11; E. D. Bradby, *The French Revolution* (Oxford, 1926), chapter 1.

28. Mr. Asquith's speech at Paisley on 5 February 1920, reported in the *Manchester Guardian*, 6 February 1920.

the initial stages of the war, for too much stress on self-determination might prove a boomerang. Each tried to woo allies by promising them territories and populations that did not rightly belong to them. In a speech on the war aims of the British Empire in Dublin on 25 September 1914, Mr. Asquith adumbrated on what he called "the enthronement of the idea of public right as a governing idea of European policy." He went on to say:

> First, and foremost, a clear but definite repudiation of militarism as a governing factor in the relations of States, and in the future moulding of the European world, which knows that room must be found and kept for the independent existence and free development of smaller nationalities, each for the life of its history and corporal consciousness of its own. . . . It means the final, or it ought to mean, perhaps, by a slow and gradual process, the substitution of force, for the nourishing of competing ambition, for the groupings of alliances, and the precarious equipoise of substituting for these things a real European partnership based upon the recognition of equal rights, established and enforced by common will.[29]

The Socialists of Western Europe were concerned about the minorities of Central Europe and the people of German-occupied territories. In February 1915 the British Labour Movement issued a memorandum on war aims which it communicated to Socialists in other countries including those of the enemy. It demanded, inter alia, a plebiscite for Alsace-Lorraine, restoration of Belgium, evacuation of Serbia, Montenegro, Roumania, and Albania and the reorganisation of the Balkan peoples under an international commission. It also demanded a reconstituted Poland, national independence for the Czechoslovakians and Yugoslavians if they so desired, and international administration for Armenia, Mesopotamia, and Arabia.[30] With regard to German colonies the Socialists proposed that they should be given administrative autonomy or progressive participation in local government under the control of the League of Nations. While a favourable reply was received from the Austrian Democratic party and the German "Minority" Socialists, the German "Majority" Socialists favoured the status quo insofar as Germany was concerned but demanded independence for Ireland, Egypt, India, Morocco, Finland, and Tripoli.

The Germans were the first to make the minority issue an official weapon of propaganda. They also encouraged Flemish nationalism and

29. D. L. George, *The Truth About the Peace Treaties* (London, 1938), pp. 23–24.
30. H. W. V. Temperley, *A History of the Peace Conference of Paris* (London, 1920–24), 1:217.

welcomed the meeting of oppressed nationalities, mostly Russian, which was held in Lousanne in June 1916.

It fell to President Wilson of the United States to enunciate the principle of self-determination as an honourable aim of the war. The Americans had no imperial aims and nothing to lose in Europe and prestige to gain from championing the cause of the oppressed nationalities. He defended the principle with missionary zeal and in the spirit of American anticolonial tradition which dates back to the war of independence. His statements embodied the main tenets in Lincoln's "government of the people, by the people, and for the people," the Virginian Bill of Rights ("that all power is vested in and consequently derived from the people"), the Declaration of Independence, and the United States Constitution. "He had read and re-read with a student's care and an evangelist's ardour the writings and speeches of the great men who formed the Republic and built up the splendid fabric of her political philosophy."[31]

Wilson's utterances had

> a unique significance, not only because they were taken as the legal basis of the peace negotiations, but because they form a definite and coherent body of political doctrine. This doctrine, though developed by the war, was not formed or even altered by [it]. His ideas like those of no other great statesman of the war, are capable of being worked out as a complete political philosophy. ... The tenets in themselves were few and simple, but their consequences, when developed by the war, were such as to produce the most far-reaching results.[32]

President Wilson drew no distinction between private and public morality, and this was to be the main guide in politics. Tyranny, like external aggression, was to be resisted by the people. When in Europe he visited the monument dedicated to the memory of the Italian Giuseppe Mazzini, the political leader who helped to unify the states of Italy on the basis of self-determination, and there with veneration and emulation felt delighted "to feel that I am taking some small part in accomplishing the realisation of the ideals to which his life and thought was devoted."[33] Though Wilson's ideas were not always accepted by his own people, they retained an immense historical value and have been a source of inspiration to oppressed peoples.

31. Ibid., p. 174.
32. Ibid., p. 173. *See also* G. A. Macartney, *National States and National Minorities* (Oxford, 1934), pp. 185–6.
33. Baker and Dodd, eds., *The Public Papers of Woodrow Wilson: War and Peace*, 1:371. This statement was made on 5 January 1919.

In an address to Congress in May 1917, Wilson averred, "No peace can last or ought to last, which does not accept the principle that governments derive all their just powers from the consent of the governed, and that no right anywhere exists to hand peoples about from sovereignty to sovereignty as if they were property."[34]

This was a reference to the minorities of Central Europe. He insisted that the belligerents should declare their war aims in order to clarify the main issues involved. The result was the adoption of self-determination as a principal aim of the Allies.

In the meantime the corrupt regime of the Czar of Russia was overthrown and the provisional government led by Lvov proclaimed on 10 April 1917 that Russia did not want to dominate other nations and was anxious to establish durable peace on the basis of the right of nations to self-determination. Russians exclaimed that they had voluntarily relinquished control over the Poles "in the name of the higher principles of equity."[35] They declared their readiness to observe agreements entered into with the Allies—a reference to the secret treaties—and reaffirmed this intention on 19 May 1917.[36] President Wilson declared that the United States was struggling for "the liberty, the self-government of all peoples, and every feature of the settlement that concludes the war must be conceived and executed for that purpose."[37] On 15 May 1917 the Petrograd Soviets, however, appealed to Socialists of all countries and proclaimed at the same time: "Peace without annexations and indemnities on the basis of self-determination of peoples is the formula adopted without mental reservations by the proletarian mind and heart."[38]

Pope Benedict XV on 1 August 1917 lent his influence to territorial settlements based on the aspirations of the populations involved.[39] The German Reichstag on 19 July 1917 declared that Germany was not impelled by "lust of conquest" and demanded "peace of understanding and the permanent reconciliation of the peoples" which would be inconsistent with "forced requisitions of territory and political, economic, or financial oppression."

The repudiation of self-determination by Miliukov, the Russian foreign minister, and the readiness to act in strict compliance with the secret

34.   J. B. Scott, *Official Statements of War Aims and Peace Proposals* (Washington, 1921), p. 52.

35.   Ibid., p. 96.

36.   Ibid., p. 102.

37.   Ibid., p. 105.

38.   Golder, *Documents of Russian History, 1914–1917* (New York, 1927), p. 341.

39.   Scott, pp. 129–131.

treaties gave Lenin the opportunity to make an open attack on the government.[40] The Bolsheviks took over the government and exposed the secret treaties entered into with the Allies.[41] On 15 November 1917 the Soviets issued the Declaration of Rights of the Peoples of Russia, laying down the policy for Russia's minorities. It included:

(1) the equality and sovereignty of Russia's nationalities;
(2) the right of Russia's nationalities to free self-determination up to seceding and the organisation of an independent state.[42]

The constitution of 10 July 1918 became a voluntary compact of the people. In a note to Allied embassies in Petrograd, Trotsky, the new foreign minister, proposed that peace should be made on the basis of "no annexations or indemnities and the self-determination of nations. . . ." A similar note was sent to the Central Powers. The latter accepted the offer, but the Germans maintained that self-determination would only be applied to the extent that was practicable and in any case not to the colonies. The Allies declined the offer, as they were not satisfied with the conditions for peace at that time.

On 17 December 1917 the Russians signed the Treaty of Brest-Litovsk with the Central Powers, and the cardinal principles were supposed to be the renunciation of war, and self-determination.[43] Two of the Russian proposals had been:

(1) Complete political independence to be given to those nationalities which had been deprived of it before the beginning of the war.
(2) Nationalities not hitherto in the enjoyment of political independence to be allowed the right to decide by means of a referendum whether they elect to be united to other nations or to acquire independence. The referendum should be so arranged as to ensure complete freedom of voting.[44]

The Germans coerced the Russians to recognise the independence of the Ukraine, and in the Supplementary Treaty of Berlin on 27 August 1918 forced them to renounce sovereignty over Estonia and Livonia, their future to be decided by the Central Powers in collaboration with

---

40.   Golder, pp. 329–331.

41.   R. S. Baker, *Woodrow Wilson and World Settlement* (London and New York, 1923), 1:38.

42.   M. M. Lasserson, *"The Development of Soviet Foreign Policy in Europe 1917–1942"* International Conciliation (1943), pp. 10–14. See also Norman Hill, *Claims to Territory in International Law and Relations* (London, 1945), p. 118.

43.   L. Shapiro, ed., *Soviet Treaty Series* (Washington, 1950), 1:1.

44.   George, p. 760.

the inhabitants. Russia was virtually deprived of its rights over Kurland and Lithuania. The Germans refused to withdraw their troops from the territories over which referenda were to be held and turned these nominally independent states into their satellites. This lopsided application of the principle of self-determination exposed Germany's expansionism and strengthened Allied determination to fight the war until victory was attained. The success of the Russian Revolution helped to popularise the concept of self-determination; the oppressed nationalities under the domination of the Central Powers saw that salvation for them could only come from their defeat.

The first official British pronouncement on self-determination came in 1916 when the British Foreign Office prepared a memorandum on territorial settlement in Europe. It favoured the setting up of a League of Nations and the reduction of armaments. It went on to say:

> His Majesty's government have announced that one of their chief objects is to ensure that all the states of Europe, great and small, shall in the future be in a position to achieve their national development in freedom and security. It is clear, moreover, that no peace can be satisfactory to this country unless it promises to be durable, and an essential condition of such a peace is that it should give full scope to national aspirations as far as is practicable. The principle of nationality should therefore be one of the governing factors in the consideration of territorial arrangements after the war.[45]

The same document however warned that "we should not push the principle of nationality so far as unduly to strengthen any state which is likely to be a cause of danger to European peace in the future."[46] Lloyd George notes that this was the "first official pronouncement in which what came to be known as self-determination constituted the principle of a readjustment of national boundaries."[47]

In their reply to President Wilson on their war aims, bearing in mind that this might significantly affect American attitude to the war, the Allies, in a note dated 10 January 1916 made the following demands:

> The restoration of Belgium, of Serbia, and of Montenegro, with compensation due to them for damage done by the invaders.
> The evacuation of the invaded territories of France, Russia, and Roumania, with fitting reparation.
> The reorganisation of Europe, guaranteed by a stable settlement, based alike upon the principle of nationalities, on the right which

45. Ibid., pp. 31–32.
46. Ibid., p. 32.
47. Ibid., p. 31.

all people, whether small or great, have to the enjoyment of full security and free economic development, and also upon territorial and international agreements so framed as to guarantee land and sea frontiers against unjust attacks.

The restitution of provinces or territories formerly torn from the Allies by force or contrary to the wishes of their inhabitants.

The liberation of Italians, Slavs, Roumanians, Czechs, and Slovaks from foreign domination.

The liberation of non-Turkish peoples who then lay beneath the murderous tyranny of the Ottoman Empire, and the expulsion from Europe of that Empire which had proved itself so radically alien to Western civilisation.

The implementing of the Czar's proclamation as to the emancipation of Poland.[48]

The initial objective of protecting small states from their powerful neighbours had been enlarged to include the liberation of nationalities forcefully assimilated by powerful ones. Within four months of the reply, America joined the war on the side of the Allies.

On the British side Lloyd George also proclaimed self-determination and referred specifically to German colonies. On 29 June 1917 he said in a speech in Glasgow: "When we come to settle who must be the future trustees of those uncivilised lands, we must take into account the sentiments of the peoples themselves."[49] He reasserted this in the Commons on 20 December 1917. Having consulted the dominions, the cabinet, the parliamentary opposition, and the labour leaders, he made a major statement affecting the colonies on 5 January 1918:

> With regard to German colonies, I have repeatedly declared they are held at the disposal of a conference whose decision must have primary regard to the wishes and interests of the native inhabitants of such colonies. None of those territories are inhabited by Europeans; the governing consideration, therefore, in all these cases must be that the inhabitants should be placed under the control of an administration acceptable to themselves, one of whose main purposes will be to prevent their exploitation for the benefit of European capitalists or governments. The natives live in their various tribal organisations under chiefs and councils who are competent to consult and speak for their tribes and thus represent their wishes and interests in regard to their disposal. The general principle of national self-determination is, therefore, as applicable in their cases as in those of European occupied territories.[50]

48. Ibid., pp. 57–58.
49. Temperley, 2:227; Baker and Dodd, 7:136.
50. Temperley, 2:227.

He insisted that the consent of the governed must be the basis of any territorial settlement and that genuine self-government and true democratic principles must be granted to the Austro-Hungarian nationalities and the subject territories of the Turkish Empire. He denied that the Allies had imperialistic aims or intended to rely on the secret treaties with Russia.

Similar principles were declared on behalf of Italy by its prime minister, Vittorio Orlando, on 12 December 1917[51] and on behalf of France by its foreign minister, Stéphen Pichon, on 28 December 1917 and 11 January 1918.[52] The Central Powers also adopted the principle of self-determination and in their reply to the first peace-treaty draft stated:

> In this war, a new fundamental law has arisen which the statesmen of all belligerent peoples have again and again acknowledged to be their aim: the right of self-determination. To make it possible for all nations to put this privilege into practice was intended to be one achievement of the war.[53]

On 8 January 1918 President Wilson announced his Fourteen Points programme to a joint sitting of Congress. Though the term itself was not expressly mentioned, seven of them related to self-determination:

> VI. The evacuation of all Russian territories and such a settlement of all questions affecting Russia as will secure the best and freest cooperation of the other nations of the world in obtaining for her an unhampered and unembarrassed opportunity for the independent determination of her political development and national policy and assure her of a sincere welcome into the society of nations. . . .
>
> VII. Belgium, the whole world agrees, must be evacuated and restored without any attempt to limit the sovereignty which she enjoys in common with all the other free nations. . . .
>
> VIII. All French territory should be freed and the invaded portions restored. . . .
>
> X. The peoples of Austro-Hungary, whose place among the nations we wish to see safeguarded and assured, should be accorded the freest opportunity of autonomous development. . . .
>
> XI. Roumania, Serbia, and Montenegro should be evacuated; occupied territories restored; Serbia accorded free and secured access to the sea; and the relations of the several Balkan states to one another determined by friendly counsel

51. *New York Times Current History*, vol. 7, part 2, p. 272.
52. Ibid., pp. 210–212.
53. Ibid., vol. 2, part 1, p. 5.

along historically established lines of allegiance and nationality; and international guarantees of the political and economic independence and territorial integrity of the several
Balkan states should be entered into.

XII. The Turkish portions of the present Ottoman Empire should
be assured a secure sovereignty, but the other nationalities
which are now under Turkish rule should be assured un-
doubted security of life and an absolutely unmolested opportunity of autonomous development.

XIII. An independent Polish state should be erected which should
include territories inhabited by indisputably Polish populations, which should be assured a free and secure access to
the sea, and whose political and economic independence and
territorial integrity should be guaranteed by international
covenant.[54]

President Wilson was restating the principles adopted by the First International American Conference held in Washington, D.C., in 1890,
which outlawed title to territory by right of conquest.

In later major speeches—"The Four Principles for Permanent Peace"
(11 February 1918), "The Four Objects" (Mount Vernon speech, July
1918), "The Five Particulars" (27 September 1918)—the president further reiterated his views, including the demand for a League of Nations
and the destruction of arbitrary power. Far from being a mere phrase,
self-determination was to become "an imperative principle of action
which statesmen will henceforth ignore at their peril." American involvement in the war was to bring about a revolution in the relations between
the weak and the strong, just as the American War of Independence had
brought a new era to the New World.

The war propaganda on both sides had benevolent effects on the
plight of minorities and subject peoples. The Russian Czar had promised
that the Poles would be given local autonomy in the year that he was

54. Compare the principles adopted three decades earlier in the Conference of
Washington—
    First: That the principle of conquest shall not, during the continuance
    of the treaty of arbitration, be recognised as admissible under Ameri-
    can public law.
    Second: That all cessions of territory made during the continuance of
    the treaty of arbitration shall be void if made under threat of war
    in the presence of an armed force.
    Third: Any nation from which such cession shall be enacted may de-
    mand that the validity of the cessions so made shall be submitted to
    arbitration.
    Fourth: Any renunciation of the right to arbitrate made under the
    conditions named in the second section, shall be null and void.
International American Conference, Washington, D.C., 1889–1890, "Reports of
Committees and Discussions Thereon," 2:1147–8.

overthrown. In 1915 the emir of Mecca was promised independence to take effect after the war; similarly, the Sykes-Picot agreement of May 1916 guaranteed Arab freedom over an area extending from the Red Sea to Damascus. Arabs deserted the Turkish army in large numbers and helped in the conquest of Palestine. The promise of independence to Czechoslovakia weakened the Austrian army through desertion. Liberation offers to the Roumanians of Transylvania brought Roumania to the side of the Allies. By 1918 the fight against the Central Powers had apparently become a war of self-determination for the minorities.

4. *Self-determination at the Peace Conference.* By the time of the peace conference the principle of self-determination was already generally accepted by all the belligerents of the war including the Central Powers. President Wilson's speeches reverberated throughout the conference, especially his Fourteen Points. He had no great respect for the sanctity of the secret treaties but rather conceived of a world order based on peace and the self-determination of nations. He pressed for a world organisation that would act as umpire among nations that were equal in rights.

Different groups of people converged on Paris seeking the rectification of wrongs done to them. The Ukrainians and Roumanians wanted their kith and kin in Hungary to reunite with them. The Jews wanted a Jewish state created, and the Koreans protested against Japanese rule. The Swedes demanded the return of the Aaland Islands and the Belgians the revision of the Treaty of London, 1839 [27 BSFP 1000]. The Poles wanted the historic archives removed by Austria in the eighteenth century to be returned to them, and Belgium wanted the Rubens pictures, the *Golden Fleece*, and other art objects which were removed during the American Revolution. Vienna feared that its art treasures might be despoiled by Italy, Yugoslavia, and Czechoslovakia. Albania was worried about its independence, Persia applied for self-determination, and a group of Afro-Americans were there to protect African interests. The United States president had become a world ombudsman for self-determination was what Minoque described as his "favourite panacea."[55]

France was obsessed with the fear of German militarism and revanche and did not want to see an arrangement that preserved the German threat. Lloyd George says of Clemenceau:

He did not believe in the principle of self-determination, which

55. K. R. Minoque, *Nationalism* (London, 1967), p. 137.

allowed a man to clutch at your throat the first time it was convenient to him, and he would not consent to any limitation of time
being placed upon the enforced separation of the Rhenish Republic
from the rest of Germany.[56]

Italy insisted upon its right under the secret treaties. Though the
British were not opposed to self-determination, they were hamstrung by
the possession of an extensive colonial empire.

> The most ardent British advocate of the principle of self-determina-
> tion found himself, sooner or later, in a false position. However
> fervid might be our indignation regarding Italian claims to Dal-
> matia and the Dodecanese it could be cooled by a reference, not to
> Cyprus only, but to Ireland, Egypt, and India. We had accepted
> a system for others which, when it came to practice, we should
> refuse to apply to ourselves.[57]

It was clearly impossible to satisfy all the demands made on the
peace conference. New states had arisen from the wrecks of the old
empires and in some cases were scrambling for their pieces. The conference was mainly concerned with confirming the boundaries of the
new states. From the Austro-Hungarian Empire emerged Austria,
Hungary, and Czechoslovakia, and from the Russian Empire were
separated Finland, Estonia, Latvia, Lithuania, and Poland. Yugoslavia,
Greece, and Roumania were territorially aggrandized by the breakup of
the Austro-Hungarian Empire. The conference proposed a number of
plebiscites to determine sovereignty over border territories, although
only eight of them were actually held.[58]

> But it was recognised that no matter how frontiers would be
> drawn, there will always be groups in Europe who will have to
> live in a state the majority of whose inhabitants are ethnically,
> linguistically, or religiously different. Hence the international law
> for the protection of minorities [was] a substitute in cases where
> the application of the principles of self-determination of nations
> was, for one reason or the other, not possible or not wanted. The
> international protection of minorities is, therefore, a strict and
> logical corollary of the principle of self-determination of nations.[59]

56. George, p. 286.

57. H. Nicolson, *Peace making 1919* (London, 1933), p. 193.

58. *See* Wambaugh. The Saar presents interesting changes in sovereignty; it was
joined to Germany in 1935 as a result of a plebiscite but rejoined to France in
1947 after another plebiscite and finally reunited with Germany by the Franco-
German Treaty of January 1957.

59. J. L. Kunz, "The Present Status of International Law for the Protection of
Minorities" 48 *AJIL* (1954), p. 282. *See also* on the protection of minorities:
J. Robinson, "From Protection of Minorities to Promotion of Human Rights,
1948" *Jewish YBIL* (1949), p. 115; J. L. Claude, *National Minorities, an Interna-
tional Problem* (Cambridge, 1955); Jones, "National Minorities: A Case Study in
International Protection" 14 *Law and Contemporary Problems* (1949), p. 599.

A mandate, under the administration of certain powers but subject to the supervision of the League Council, was created for the subject peoples of the Turkish Empire and German colonies who were supposedly unable to stand by themselves.[60]
Not directly concerned with the conference but influenced by it were the grant of self-government to Ireland and the initiation of constitutional progress in India; the latter had made significant contributions to the war effort and the former had been agitating for home rule.

5. Assessment of Self-determination at the Peace Conference

The peace conference paid more respect to the principle of self-determination than had any earlier conference that ended a war. The principle was manifested in several ways.

First, the conference confirmed the sovereign independence of certain territories that had been under the domination of their stronger neighbours and gave them the fullest opportunity of determining their future. There was however undue emphasis on independence as an expression of self-determination. This notion led Robert Lansing, President Wilson's secretary of state, to fear that it was "loaded with dynamite" and bound to lead to frustration from unfulfilled hopes. In his view, self-determination must yield place to consideration of economic interests, historic rights, and national security.[61] Under the same stress, President Wilson regretted that he had stretched the principle too far. He even denied that it had a general application: "It was not within the privilege of the conference of peace to act upon the right of peoples except those who had been included in the territories of the defeated empires."[62]

Far from expressing itself exclusively through independence as in the American War of Independence, self-determination also expresses itself through genuine self-government, as in the French Revolution. Had this fact been fully appreciated, more might have been done to safeguard fundamental human rights and the full participation of peoples in their governments. The new states contained minorities whose lot was often worse than it had been before separation. The Bulgars of Yugoslavia and Roumania, the Magyars of Schütt Island, the Germans of Italy, and the Albanians of Yugoslavia were apparently unhappy with the arrangements. Lloyd George remarked: "It fills me with despair, the way

---

60. *See* chapter 2 on mandates.
61. R. Lansing, *The Peace Negotiations: A Personal Narrative* (London, 1921), pp. 97–104.
62. Baker and Dodd, eds., *The Public Papers of Woodrow Wilson: War and Peace*, 2:244. Speech of 17 September 1919.

which I have seen small nations, before they have hardly leapt into the light of freedom, beginning to oppress other races than their own."[63] What the conference achieved, according to Cobban, was "national determinism" rather than self-determination.[64]

Second, national boundaries were for the first time fixed on the principle of nationality and in accordance with the wishes of the people as expressed through plebiscites. The peace treaties were a charter of freedom for millions of people who were released from foreign yoke. Although self-determination was the proclaimed principle, it was either ignored or misapplied in some cases. German territories were signed away to other powers without consultation with the populations. Thus the neutral zone of Moresnet was ceded to Belgium without a plebiscite, while Prussian Moresnet went to Belgium "in partial compensation for the destruction of Belgian forests," though its future was to be determined subsequently by the inhabitants recording their wishes in public registers. Western Prussia was ceded to Poland in order to enhance the indepe..dence of the new state. The city of Danzig, with a German majority, was made a free city partly in order to secure Poland's outlet to the sea, while t' e city and district of Memel were ceded to Lithuania to secure for it an exit to the sea. Germany was forced to renounce its rights over Kreis Leobschütz in favour of Czechoslovakia. Austria ceded South Tyrol to Italy in furtherance of the secret treaties that prompted Italy to enter the war on the side of the Allies. Austria expressed an unmistakable desire to join Germany but was prevented from exercising that right of self-determination; the peace treaty with Austria made such a union subject to the consent of the League of Nations. This was to become a major cause of German discontent in the future. Hitler considered in later years that the unification of German lands was his main duty and this was a prelude to the conquest of foreign lands.[65] He expressed much anguish at his trial in 1924 that self-determination had been denied to the Germans in some respects: "Self-determination. Yes, but self-determination for every negro tribe: and Germany does not count as a negro tribe."[66]

In general the peace conference could not be said to have laid down the general principle that sovereignty over disputed territories should be determined on the basis of self-determination, nor did it rule out

63. D. H. Miller, *Diary*, 19:98.
64. A. Cobban, *National Self-determination* (London, 1945), p. 54.
65. A. Hitler, *Mein Kampf* (Munich, 1925), p. 1.
66. N. H. Baynes, *The Speeches of Adolf Hitler, April 1922–August 1939* (1942), 1:83.

title to territory established through conquest. The victorious Allies were also concerned with diminishing German power and with ensuring that the new states would lead independent existences. "The dominant motives of the peace conference would seem to have been: first, to gratify faithful allies; secondly, to show severity to the conquered foe; and thirdly, to establish a new balance of power."[67]

Third, the peace treaties contained provisions for the protection of minorities by guaranteeing "full and complete protection of life and liberty to all inhabitants. . . . without distinction of birth, nationality, language, race, or religion." All the inhabitants were entitled to "the free exercise, whether public or private, of any creed, religion or belief, whose practices are not inconsistent with public order or morals." They also provided for "the same treatment and security in law and in fact" as the other subjects of the states.[68] While guaranteeing the enjoyment of human rights by members of the minorities, they went beyond ordinary notions of individual human rights. The equality of treatment in fact and in law sometimes demanded a more favourable treatment for the minorities. Thus in protecting the minority schools from measures that operated against other schools in Albania the international court said in an advisory opinion: "Equality in law precludes discrimination of any kind; whereas equality in fact may involve the necessity of different treatment in order to attain a result which establishes an equilibrium between the different situations."[69]

The court referred approvingly to its statement in the *German Settlers in Poland*.[70] "There must be equality in fact as well as ostensible legal equality in the sense of the absence of discrimination in the words of the law."[71]

The treaties tended to solidify the minority elements for they discouraged their assimilation into the majority. Recounting the background to the provisions and to their effect, the court explained in the *Minority Schools* case:

The idea underlying the treaties for the protection of minorities

67. P. M. Brown, "Self-determination in Central Europe," 14 *AJIL* (1920), p. 237.

68. For the peace treaties with Poland *see* 13 *AJIL* (1919), supp.; with Roumania, Bulgaria, Czechoslovakia, Serb-Croat-Slovene state, and Austria *see* 14 *AJIL* (1921) supp. 5. The treaty with Turkey omitted the phrase "whose practices are not inconsistent with public order or public morals," perhaps intending to narrow Turkey's discretion in dealing with the minorities because of its discreditable record.

69. *The Minority Schools in Albania (1935)*, ser. A/B, no. 64, p. 19.

70. PCIJ, ser. B, no. 6.

71. Ibid., p. 24.

is to secure for certain elements incorporated in a State, the population of which differs from them in race, language or religion, the possibility of living peaceably alongside that population and co-operating amicably with it, while at the same time preserving the characteristics which distinguish them from the majority, and satisfying the ensuing needs.

In order to attain this object two things were regarded as particularly necessary, and have formed the subject of provisions in these treaties.

The first is to ensure that nationals belonging to racial, religious, or linguistic minorities shall be placed in every respect on a footing of perfect equality with the other nationals of the State.

The second is to ensure for the minority elements suitable means for the preservation of their racial peculiarities, their traditions, and their national characteristics.

These two requirements are indeed closely interlocked, for there would be no true equality between a majority and a minority if the latter were deprived of its own institutions, and were consequently compelled to renounce that which constitutes the every essence of its being a minority.[72]

Who belonged to the minorities did not depend on the subjective opinion of the claimants but was to be objectively verified.[73]

Insofar as the treaties sought to protect the political, cultural, religious, and economic development of specific groups, they promoted their right to self-determination within those states of which they formed integral parts. They were not only protected against discrimination but were given preferential safeguards to protect their culture, language, and religion. Although the members of the League Council could bring any infraction, or threat thereof, to the notice of the council, the safeguards did not always prove effective in all cases; for the practice developed that only states related to the minorities through kith and kin were sufficiently interested in invoking the treaties.[74] Part of the grievances

72. Ibid., ser. A/B, no. 64, p. 17.

73. *Rights of Minorities in Upper Silesia*, PCIJ (1925), ser. A, no. 12, p. 32. Such a community was defined as "the existence of a group of persons living in a given country or locality, having a race, religion, language, and traditions, maintaining their form of worship, securing the instruction and upbringing of their children in accordance with the spirit and traditions of their race and mutually assisting one another." PCIJ, ser. B, no. 17 (1930), p. 33.

74. Of the six judgments given by the permanent court on the minority treaties five dealt with complaints by Germany against Poland on behalf of German minorities: *German Settlers in Poland*, PCIJ (1923), ser. B, no. 6; *Acquisition of Polish Nationality*, PCIJ (1923), ser. B, no. 7; *German Interests in Polish Upper Silesia* PCIJ (1926), ser. A, no. 7; *Rights of Minorities in Upper Silesia*, PCIJ (1928), ser. A, no. 15; *Access to German Minority Schools in Upper Silesia*, PCIJ (1931), ser. A/B, No. 40; and *Case Concerning the Polish Agrarian Reform and the German Minority*, PCIJ (1933), ser. A/B, no. 60.

that led to the Second World War, without in any way justifying aggression, could be traced back to the discontent of German minorities in other states.

Fourth, the mandate system was an acknowledgment of the fact that peoples who had been colonised were also entitled to self-determination, exercised for the time being as a trust to the peoples and to civilisation at large by selected powers until they were able to assume full responsibility. The opportunity existed to extend this principle to the administration of all colonies, but it was restricted to the subject territories of the defeated belligerents. The rest of the colonial world had to wait until a later period to be conceded the principle as of right. Japan was left in occupation of Korea against the wishes of the Korean people.

Though a fundamental principle of the peace conference, self-determination had no express mention in the League Covenant. The chance was thereby lost to clear some of the present doubts about its legal nature and content. President Wilson's draft of the Covenant contained the principle but the final text omitted it.[75] The failure of the United States to ratify the Covenant was a further source of weakness, for the power most responsible for the prominence of self-determination at the peace conference did not become a member of the League, thus denying the organisation some idealism in the implementation of the principle.

75. Article 3 of Wilson's draft:
   The Contracting Parties unite in guaranteeing to each other political independence and territorial integrity; but it is understood between them that such territorial adjustments, if any, as may in future become necessary by reason of changes in present racial and political relationships, pursuant to the principle of self-determination, and also such territorial adjustments as may in the judgment of three-fourths of the Delegates be demanded by the welfare and manifest interest of the people concerned, may be effected if agreeable to those peoples; and that territorial changes may in equity involve material compensation. The Contracting Powers accept without reservation the principle that the peace of the world is superior in importance to every question of political jurisdiction or boundary.

II The Mandated Territories

1. Background to Mandates

The mandate system, though not expressly providing for self-determination, was based upon that concept and upon its application to undeveloped peoples. It was the fruit of the ideas of philanthropists, idealists, statesmen, and religious leaders. The old colonial system was characterised by exploitation, expansionism, and the rule of force. The international law of the time mainly regulated the relations between Christian nations, and non-Europeans were supposed to be outside its purview. From the eighteenth century, reformers became more openly critical of the treatment given to the latter. It was urged that it would be beneficial to all concerned if they were in good physical and moral conditions.

Along with safeguarding native interest was the need to regulate relations between the European nations in those distant lands, particularly their commercial and colonising activities, in order to prevent frictions that sometimes led to wars. Where it was undesirable or impossible for a state to establish its own exclusive sovereignty, administration was delegated to a power on behalf of the nations. In the case of the Ionian Islands, Great Britain delegated control to British and Dutch chartered companies on behalf of the powers. The Treaty of Berlin, 1885[1] entrusted King Leopold of Belgium with the administration of the Congo. Prince George of Greece was requested to administer the Island of Crete

1. 76 *BFSP* (1884–5), p. 4.

in 1898. The Treaty of Algeciras[2] delegated the administration of Morocco to France; there was a Franco-Spanish police force under the control of a Swiss inspector-general. Morocco's financial organisation was entrusted to an international bank.

Of these arrangements the most elaborate was the Berlin Act of 1885, the preamble to which enumerates the following aims:

> (1) In a spirit of good and mutual accord, to regulate the conditions most favourable to the development of trade and civilisation in certain regions of Africa, and to assure to all nations the advantage of free navigation of the two chief rivers of Africa flowing into the Atlantic (Congo and Niger).
>
> (2) To obviate the misunderstanding and disputes which might in future arise from new acts of occupation on the coast of Africa.
>
> (3) "Furthering" of "the moral and material well-being of the native populations."

In Article 6:

> All the Powers exercising sovereign rights or influence in the aforesaid territories bind themselves to watch over the preservation of the native tribes, and improve their moral and material well-being, and help in suppressing slavery and especially slave trade. They shall, without distinction of creed or nation, protect and favour all religious, scientific, or charitable institutions and undertakings created and organised for the above ends, or which aim at instructing the natives and bringing home to them the blessings of civilisation. Christian missionaries, scientists, and explorers, with their followers, property, and collections, shall likewise be the objects of special protection.
>
> Freedom of conscience and religious toleration are expressly guaranteed to the natives, no less than to subjects and to foreigners. The free and public exercise of all forms of Divine worship, and the right to build edifices for religious purposes, and to organise religious missions belonging to all creeds, shall not be limited or fettered in any way whatsoever.[3]

The Berlin Treaty was confirmed by the Brussels Treaty of 1890.[4] These experiments in international colonial administration did not however achieve their purpose. The king of Belgium turned the Congo into his personal empire and the scene of the worst form of colonial exploitation. It was taken over by the Belgian government after widespread outcry in 1908. In 1912 Morocco became a French protectorate. The

2. 106 *BFSP* (1913), p. 1023.

3. The treaty became the chief legal instrument for the deprivation of sovereignty to African people and their subjugation to alien rule.

4. 82 *BFSP*, p. 55.

main weakness in these administrations was the absence of international supervision.

Early in this century Hobson advocated that the exploitation of undeveloped areas should be brought under international control in order to prevent friction.[5] He developed his ideas during the First World War with regard to native treatment: while natives were not to impede the exploitation of natural resources, they were to be well treated and only the minimal interference with their way of life was to be allowed.[6]

A memorandum on war aims of the British Labour party suggested in February 1915 that colonies should either have administrative autonomy or participate progressively in local government. The Independent Labour party proclaimed in April 1917 that "annexation of territory and people by force of arms is oppression and incompatible with international socialism." The executive committee of the party, meeting in December 1917, repudiated imperialism in Central Africa and suggested the transfer of all colonies there to a supra-national authority of a league of nations. The guiding principles were to be respect for the wishes of the natives, prohibition of exploitation and oppression, and the neutralisation of the territories from international rivalries. The Inter-Allied Socialist Conference of February, 1918 demanded:

> The natives of all Colonies and Dependencies must be protected against capitalist exploitation. Administrative autonomy should be granted to all groups sufficiently civilised, and to others a progressive participation in local government. Colonies taken by conquest must be the subject of special consideration at the Peace Conference. Those in Tropical Africa should be controlled in accordance with international agreements under the League of Nations.[7]

The International Socialist Conference at Berne repeated these sentiments. Toward the end of the war international opinion had been geared up in favour of native welfare and non-annexation of former enemy colonies as distinct from the regulation of economic enterprise in those areas.

2. The Peace Conference and Mandates

Discussions in the peace conference on mandates were based on two documents—Wilson's Fourteen Point programme and Smuts's "The League of Nations, a Practical Suggestion" (1918). Point five of Wil-

---

5. J. A. Hobson, *Imperialism* (1902).

6. J. A. Hobson, *Towards International Government* (London, 1915).

7. *The Liberal Magazine* (March 1918), pp. 87–88. *See also* "Report of the Annual Conference of the Independent Labour Party," April 1917 and April 1918.

son's programme did not directly envisage the mandates but it touched on native welfare:

A free, open-minded and absolutely impartial adjustment of all colonial claims, based upon a strict observance of the principle that in determining all such questions of sovereignty, the interests of the populations concerned must have equal weight with the equitable claims of the governments whose title is to be determined.

A subsequent interpretation of point five approved by the President explained:

It would seem as if the principle involved in this proposition is that a colonial power acts not as owner of its colonies, but as trustee for the natives and for the interests of the society of nations, that the terms on which the colonial administration is conducted are a matter of international concern and may legitimately be the subject of international inquiry, and that the Peace Conference may, therefore, write a code of colonial conduct binding upon colonial powers.[8]

His twelfth point assured the subject peoples of the Turkish Empire "undiluted security of life and an absolutely unmolested opportunity of autonomous development."

A group of American and British experts on international affairs met in November 1918 to discuss the future of German colonies. They published the *Round Table*, in which they suggested, *inter alia*, non-militarisation, trusteeship, wardship, prohibition of forced labour and liquor traffic, and the dismissal of a mandatory that broke the terms of the mandate.[9] General Smuts was already familiar with the views of this group before he published his suggestions.

Smuts stressed that the chaos resulting from the collapse of the empires could be rectified, not by a reconstruction based on subjection but on the basis of the principles of nationality and self-determination. Some of the new states—Finland, Poland, Czechoslovakia and Yugoslavia—were sufficiently advanced to bear the burden of independence with the friendship and assistance of the powers. The League could play the role of umpire seeing that justice was done to large or small states and to the minorities in them. Other areas, though civilised, needed guidance—Transcaucasia, Mesopotamia, Lebanon, and Syria. Because of their national and religious divisions, Armenia and Palestine, in his view, should be under an international commission. For these states, he suggested mandateship:

8. *Whiteman's Digest of International Law* (1965), 5:604; For. Rel., vol. 1, supp. 1, pp. 12–16, 407, and 421.
9. "Windows of Freedom," 9 *Round Table* (1918).

No State should make use of the helpless or weak condition of any of these territories in order to exploit them for its own purposes. . . . Any authority, control, or administration which may be necessary in respect of these territories and peoples, other than their own self-determined autonomy, shall be the exclusive function of and shall be vested in the League of Nations and exercised by or on behalf of it.

He proposed that the League should be regarded as

the reversionary in the most general sense and as clothed with the right of ultimate disposal in accordance with the fundamental principles. Reversion to the League of Nations should be substituted for any policy of national annexation.

As for the German colonies in Africa and the Pacific, they were "inhabited by barbarians, who not only cannot possibly govern themselves, but to whom it would be impracticable to apply any ideas of political self-determination in the European sense."[10]

President Wilson was impressed by Smuts's ideas and embodied them in his second Paris draft of the Covenant. However, he extended the principle to all colonies through mandates:

The object of all such tutelary oversight and administration on the part of the League of Nations shall be to build up in as short a time as possible a political unit which can take charge of its own policies. The League may at any time release such a people or territory from tutelage and consent to its being set up as an independent unit.[11]

A British draft differentiated between "assisted states," which were almost ready for independence and "vested-territories," which were not but were to be held by mandatories "upon trust to afford their inhabitants peace, order, and good government." It envisaged the creation of a commission or commissions which would assist the League in supervising the mandates by examining reports from them and making recommendations. It did not however lay down that self-determination was a goal for the mandates.[12]

At the conference there were advocates of internationalisation, annexation, and restoration to Germany. Independence was ruled out because the territories were supposed not to be prepared for it, although there had been promises to Arab chiefs. Annexation was barred by pre-

---

10. Smuts's pamphlet is set out in D. H. Miller, *The Drafting of the Covenant* (1928), 2:23–60.

11. Miller, 2:104. For the text of the first Paris draft see pp. 65–93 and for the second pp. 98–105.

12. For full text *see* Miller, 1:106–7.

Armistice agreements making non-annexation and self-determination the basis of peace settlements and by the public declaration of statesmen in Allied countries, although some of the territories in question were the subject of secret treaties giving them out to one or the other party.[13] As for restoration, the maltreatment of local populations in German colonies was a notorious fact. The *Cape Argus* of 1 June 1915 had critical comments to make about German colonial administration:

> The German militarist at his worst is a stupid, unteachable brute, and it was to military men of this stamp rather than to experienced men of affairs that the delicate task of governing subject races has generally been entrusted.... If instead of the unimaginative numbskulls and military pedants—men devoid alike of any sense of fair play or humanity—Germany could have commanded the services of men of the type of our own magistrates in the native territories, who have a sympathetic consideration of the native standpoint, and above all the desire to do justice, the nameless horrors of the war against the Hereros would never have disgraced the annals of German Colonial History.

The *Cape Times* and *East London Daily Dispatch* were equally critical of German colonialism.[14] Erzberger, a German reformist had said that if German plantations could be profitable only by being manured with native blood, it would be a curse both to the colonies and to the motherland.[15] Reports from the Turkish Empire disclosed acts of extreme cruelty to their subject peoples.[16] It was also believed that Germany had intended to convert its colonies into bases for aggressive military operations.

Mandates occupied the time of the conference from January 23 to 28, 1919, and almost caused its breakdown. The British dominions were curiously brought in by Lloyd George to participate in the discussions affecting German colonies. Lloyd George was not eager to extend the British Colonial Empire: "Personally I was not anxious to add any more millions to the number of square miles we already found much difficulty in garrisoning and a still greater difficulty in developing." He was, however, convinced that in a matter of choice, the people would prefer British rule to German for the former had "less rigid and more indulgent

13. Temperley, 1:429–30; 4:516–7; 6:4–9, 16–17.

14. *Cape Times* of 2 November 1914 and *East London Daily Dispatch* of 2 June 1915. *See also* W. R. Louis, "The South-West African Origins of the Sacred Trust," 66 *African Affairs* (January 1967), pp. 20–39.

15. Temperley, 2:221–2.

16. *See* Bryce's report on the treatment of the Armenians and King Crane's report on the Near East, quoted in Quincy Wright, *Mandates under the League of Nations* (Chicago, 1930), pp. 28–29.

traditions."[17] On the other hand the dominions were determined to annex their conquered territories on the grounds of their own security; France and Italy were also opposed to mandateship. President Wilson made a passionate appeal to the other delegates:

> The purpose was to serve the people in underdeveloped parts, to safeguard them against abuses such as had occurred under German administration. Further, where peoples and territories were undeveloped, to assure their development so that, when the time came, their interests as they saw them, might qualify them to express a wish as to their ultimate relations—perhaps lead them to desire their union with the mandatory power. . . . If the process of annexation went on, the League of Nations would be discredited from the beginning. Many false rumours had been set about regarding the Peace Conference. Those who were hostile to it said that its purpose was merely to divide up the spoils. If they justified that statement in any degree, that would discredit the Conference.[18]

Lloyd George disclosed: "I think it is fair to state that President Wilson and I were alone in supporting the principle of vesting the German Colonies in the League of Nations as a trustee, with mandatories nominated by the League to undertake the duties of administration."[19]

Confirming the uncompromising attitude of the dominions, he disclosed in his narrative:

> I spent a great part of the next two days in consultations with the Dominion Premiers. I urged them not to take the responsibility of wrecking the Conference on a refusal to accept a principle which Great Britain was quite ready to see applied to much more extensive and important territories in East Africa. Sir R. Borden (Canada) was as usual very helpful in abating the pugnacity of Mr. Hughes (Australia) and Mr. Massey (New Zealand). General Botha took, as he generally did, a broad conciliatory view and at last I obtained general agreement to a series of propositions. . . .[20]

17. George, p. 64.

18. Baker, *Woodrow Wilson and World Settlement*, 1:262. Secretary of State Lansing could not reconcile the doctrine of sovereignty with the idea of mandates but Wilson brushed this aside as mere "legal technicalities." Lansing, *The Peace Negotiations*, pp. 151–3. *See also* S. C. Sinha, "Role of President Woodrow Wilson in the Evolution of the Mandate System," *Indian Journal of Political Science* (1941–2), 3:424–436.

19. George, p. 515.

20. Ibid., p. 538. He described Wilson's demeanour toward the dominion premiers on that occasion as "hectoring" and to Hughes in particular as occasionally "dictatorial and somewhat arrogant." Criticising the part played by Lloyd George in the conference, R. S. Baker made the following comment: "At Paris throughout the Conference, the French were more direct and outspoken than the British. If they believed a thing they said it. One knew where Clemenceau stood and what he intended to do; one never knew where Lloyd George stood: he never stood in the same place twice." *Woodrow Wilson and World Settlement*, 1:270.

On 29 January he introduced a compromise proposal which made the
territories which South Africa, Australia, and New Zealand wanted to
annex C-mandates, to be governed as integral parts of those states and
from which the open-door policy was excluded but subject to the overriding principle of a trust in favour of the natives. The mandates system
was finally incorporated as Article 22 of the Treaty of Versailles. "It
was viewed by those on the left as a limited triumph in the cause of
internationalisation, and by those on the right as annexation in all but
name."[21]

By Article 19 of the Treaty of Versailles[22] Germany renounced in
favour of the Principal Allied and Associated Powers all its rights and
duties over its overseas possessions, but the mandatories were designated
by the League Council, which also laid down their duties. The same
effect was achieved in respect to Turkish dependent territories in Article
16 of the Treaty of Lousanne.[23]

3. The Principles of the Mandate

The mandate principle was applied to territories of the defeated
Germans and Turks which were not in a position to assume independent
statehood. The method was through the tutelage of nations who, by their
experience and propinquity, were best suited to guide them. In practice
the mandatories were the occupying powers that defeated whatever
forces the enemy had in them. The fundamental principle was that the
"well-being and development of such peoples form a sacred trust to
civilisation. . . ." They were not newly acquired colonies of the administering powers but were to be administered purely for the benefit of
the inhabitants. The system is "an attempt to translate into reality the
principles upon which European nations have always sought to defend
the authority which they have exercised over communities in what, according to their own standard, is a less advanced and, therefore, it is
assumed, less desirable stage of development."[24]

The territories were not in the same stage of development and were
divided into A-, B- and C-mandates in a descending scale of development. Article 22 of the League Covenant states the duties of the mandatory, but these are more specifically stated in the mandate agreements.
In the A-mandates the mandatory controlled foreign affairs and secured

21. Louis, "African Origins of the Mandate," 19 *International Organisation*
(1965), p. 20. For full text *see* Appendix A.
22. 13 *AJIL* (1919), supp. 157.
23. 28 LNTS, p. 196.
24. J. F. Williams, *Some Aspects of the Covenant of the League of Nations*
(London, 1934), p. 201.

the inviolability of the territory. It observed general treaties concluded with the consent of the League (e.g., the prohibition of the traffic in slaves and drugs, the freedom of aerial navigation and communications). The mandatory guaranteed freedom of worship and conscience, subject to the maintenance of public order and morality, prevented discrimination among the races, religions, or languages although communal education based on particular languages might be supported. The limitations on religions and educational institutions were only those necessary for public order and good government.[25]

The B-mandates were to be administered by the mandatories subject to conditions protecting native welfare and preventing abuses. The mandatory was obliged to secure humane labour conditions, suppress the slave trade and slavery, control the importation of arms and spirits, protect native land patrimony, and make the transfer of land to non-natives subject to official authorisation. Military training was permissible only for internal police and defence purposes with the exception of French mandates, where native military forces could be used for defence within or outside the territory, in deference to France's feeling of insecurity from Germany.[26]

"Owing to the sparseness of their population or their small size, or their remoteness from the centres of civilisation, or their geographical contiguity to the territory of the Mandatory, and other circumstances" the C-mandates could be administered as integral parts of the mandatory's territories. The supply of intoxicants was absolutely prohibited. The C-mandates enjoyed all the safeguards given to the B-mandates. Military training could be given only for police purposes and for local defence. The open-door policy was excluded, although Japan threw the doors open in its own mandates. In all the categories of mandates freedom of worship and of missionary evangelism by members of the League were secured. The policy of non-discrimination prevailed in taxation, commerce, industry, the professions, and communications.[27]

25. In the Iraq Mandate Agreement, Britain "in view of the rapid progress in Iraq, recognised an independent government therein," and was to advise and assist "until such time as it might be able to stand alone." In Palestine (and Trans-Jordan) Mandate, "The Mandatory shall, so far as circumstances permit, encourage local autonomy." In Syria and Lebanon the mandatory shall further enact measures to facilitate their progressive development toward independence. "The Mandatory shall so far as circumstances permit, encourage local autonomy."

26. "Mr. Lloyd said that so long as M. Clemenceau did not train big nigger armies for the purpose of aggression, which was all the clause (non-militarisation) was intended to guard against, he was free to raise troops." George, p. 547.

27. For the open-door policy in mandates, see The Colonial Problem (1937), chapter 5.

The phrase "as integral portions" in relation to C-mandates has caused some confusion and is sometimes used to support the theory of annexation, but it merely indicates a permissible mode of administration, for convenience sake, without in any way detracting from the fundamental purpose of creating a new class of dependent territories in which "the welfare and development" of the peoples were the raison d'être. Annexation was strenuously opposed at the peace conference to the point of risking its breakdown; the compromise proposals were intended to allow the mandatory a free hand in economic enterprise by excluding the open door and in administration within the principles of non-annexation and self-determination which dominated the conference. The sentence that provided for this special characteristic added "subject to the safeguards . . . in the interest of the indigenous population." Whatever the mode of administration, it was intended to carry into effect the "sacred trust of civilisation" placed upon the mandatory. According to the international court: "The rights of the Mandatory in relation to the mandated territory and the inhabitants have their foundation in the obligation of the Mandatory and they are, so to speak, mere tools given to enable it to fulfil its obligation."[28]

The Permanent Mandates Commission repeatedly rejected any act or suggestion that might imply that the mandatory possessed sovereignty over a mandated territory. A preamble to the Portuguese-South African Treaty relating to the boundary between South-West Africa and Angola recited in part: "the Government of the Union of South Africa, subject to the terms of the said mandate, possesses sovereignty over the territory of South-West Africa."[29] The commission questioned this assertion and in its report to the council it noted:

> Under the circumstances, the Commission doubts whether such an expression as "possesses sovereignty," used in the preamble to the above-mentioned Agreement, even when limited by such a phrase as that used in the above-quoted passage, can be held to define correctly, having regard to the terms of the Covenant, the relations existing between the mandatory power and the territory placed under its mandate.[30]

The foremost jurists are agreed on the point that a mandatory could not unilaterally annex any category of mandate. According to Bentwich,

the Mandate System marked a reaction against the policy of ac-

28.   South-West Africa Cases, ICJ Rep. (1962), p. 329.
29.   123 BFSP (1926), p. 590.
30.   PMC Minutes (1926), p. 182, Doc. C. 632 M. 248.

quisitiveness which had hitherto characterised the relations of the Great Powers to backward peoples. In that policy the natives were regarded primarily as agents in the production of raw materials and the consumption of goods; and there was a gross disregard of their material and moral welfare.[31]

Further,

> with regard to the inhabitants, the Mandatory is requested, negatively, to abstain from any action which may impair the integrity, or political status of the territory under his administration, and, positively, to carry out the administration in such a way as to secure the well-being and progress of the population. . . .[32]

Writing much later, Duncan Hall commented:

> In practice, the Mandates Commission consistently acted on the assumption that the words in Article 22 of the Covenant about the peoples of "B" and "C" mandates being "not yet able to stand by themselves" implied the goal of sovereign independence. The Commission therefore consistently challenged on every possible occasion any policy or legal text that seemed to imply directly or indirectly that the mandatory state possessed or could possess sovereignty. For the same reason it looked askance at any proposal that seemed to involve too close legal and administrative relationships between a mandate and neighbouring territories.[33]

In its advisory opinion the court found that the "competence to determine and modify the international status of South-West Africa rests with the Union of South Africa acting with the consent of the United Nations."[34] In other words, the Union could not unilaterally alter the international status of the C-mandate of South-West Africa. The advisory opinions of 1953[35] and 1956[36] and the judgment of 1962[37] were given on the basis that South-West Africa was a mandated territory. Despite its generally adverse effect, the judgment of 1966 recognised that the true intention of the peace conference excluded annexation:

> As is well known, the mandate system originated in the decision taken at the Peace Conference following upon the world war of

---

31. N. Bentwich, *The Mandates System* (London, 1930), p. 4.

32. Ibid., p. 18.

33. Duncan Hall, *Mandates, Dependencies, and Trusteeships* (London, 1948), p. 81.

34. *ICJ Rep.* (1950), p. 143.

35. The Voting Procedure Case, *ICJ Rep.* (1955), p. 67.

36. Admissibility of Hearings of Petitioners, *ICJ Rep.* (1956), p. 23.

37. South-West Africa Cases, *ICJ Rep.* (1962), p. 319.

1914–1918, that the colonial territories over which, by Article 119 of the Treaty of Versailles, Germany renounced "all her rights and titles" in favour of the then Principal Allied and Associated Powers, should not be annexed by those Powers or by any country affiliated to them, but should be placed under an international regime, in the application to the peoples of these territories, deemed "not yet able to stand by themselves," of the principle declared by Article 22 of the League Covenant, that their "well-being and development" should form "a sacred trust of civilisation."[38]

The achievement of self-determination by the peoples of the mandated territories, A-, B-, and C-mandates, was the object of the system; whether they should become independent, merge with the mandatory, or be associated with it in any form were options from which the peoples could themselves choose freely when they were politically matured to do so. It is noteworthy that only in the case of South West Africa did the mandatory seriously contend that the wording of the Article permitted annexation.[39]

Since the mandatories were acting "on behalf of the League," they rendered account to the League Council and their conduct of the mandate was scrutinised by the Permanent Mandates Commission. The principle of international accountability was a new feature that differentiated the system from earlier experiments at international administration. The compromissory clause ensured that the provisions could be judicially enforced and further strengthened that accountability.

Although the *locus* of sovereignty was a source of controversy among earlier writers, it is now generally agreed that it does not lie with the mandatory. A draft mandate agreement presented to the Sixth Committee of the League Assembly on 14 December 1920 dealt with the subject in the following manner:

> The relations between a Mandatory Power and a mandated territory differ in kind from those between a sovereign State and its dependencies. The Mandatory's status is not that of a proprietor, but of a trustee. He is not free to govern in his own interest by right of conquest. Such authority as he exercises over the inhabitants of the territory is exercised on behalf of the League of Nations; and it is conferred upon him solely with a view to serve their well-being and development and to open the territory to the trade and enterprise of all Members of the League. In accepting a Mandate

---

38. *ICJ Rep.* (1966), p. 24.

39. Both Britain and France were agreed that the use of the phrase "as integral parts" in the trusteeship agreements in no way diminished the status of their trust territories. UN, GA Doc. A/258 of 12 December 1946, pp. 5–6.

he does not acquire the right of annexation. He assumes the duty of tutelage.[40]

In 1927 and 1930 the League Council adopted resolutions to the effect that sovereignty did not lie with a mandatory power.[41] This view has since been confirmed in municipal courts.[42] The A-mandates had provisional sovereignty. The mandates were "a new form of administration— subject to foreign States which presented themselves not as conquerors but as trustees, and as trustees upon whom devolved a number of obligations in the interests of the local population for whose benefit the mandate had been created."[43] The new type of dependent territories had become not a source of profit maintained by force, but a field of disinterested service.

The territories were divided as follows:

A-mandates

Iraq	Great Britain
Trans-Jordan	Great Britain
Palestine	Great Britain
Syria and Lebanon	France

B-mandates

Cameroons	Great Britain and France
Tanganyika	Great Britain
Togoland	Great Britain and France
Ruanda-Urundi	Belgium

40. League of Nations, First Assembly, Sixth Committee (1920), pp. 353–4. *See also* J. C. Hales, "The Creation and Application of the Mandate System" 25 *Transactions of the Grotius Society* (1939), pp. 185–204.

41. *See also* F. B. Sayre, "Legal Problems Arising from the United Nations Trusteeship System" 42 *AJIL* (1948), p. 263. For a long list of references *see* Wright, *Mandates Under the League of Nations* (Chicago, 1930), pp. 319–339.

42. In *R. v. Christian*, South African LR (1924), pp. 101–137, three of the five judges held that South Africa possessed internal but not external sovereignty over South-West Africa. In *Ffrost* v. *Stevenson*, 58 CLR (1937) 528, the Australian court rejected a suggestion that sovereignty over New Guinea lay with Australia, a view confirmed by a Palestine Court in *A. G. (Palestine)* v. *Goralschwili* LR (1920–3) 353. In the *Mavromatis* case PCIJ, Ser. A, no. 2, p. 23 the court found that Britain was responsible for Palestine which therefore lacked the capacity to answer a claim. D. P. O. O'Connell in *International Law* (1965) 1:369, sees the power of the UN in regard to trust territories as being so great that it may be regarded as sharing sovereignty: "The totality of functions in the administering Powers and the UN and the ultimate interest of the beneficiaries make up the totality of sovereignty but its incidents are distributed." It was held in *De Bodined* v. *Administration de L'Enregistrement, Ann. Dig.* (1919–42), case no. 33 (1939) that French officials in the service of the A-mandates lost their status as French officials but not those in B-mandates. *See also In Re Karl and Toto*, Ibid. (1931–4) case no. 14.

43. Mirriam Mushkat, "The Process of African Decolonisation" 4 *Indian JIL* (1966), p. 489.

C-mandates

North Pacific Islands	Japan
Nauru	Great Britain, Australia, and New Zealand (Australia acting)
New Guinea	Great Britain, Australia, and New Zealand (Australia acting)
Western Samoa	Great Britain, Australia, and New Zealand (New Zealand acting)
South-West Africa	Great Britain and South Africa (South Africa acting)

4. *Evaluation of Self-determination in Mandates*

The mandates system was an international recognition of the fact that the principle of self-determination applied to all peoples regardless of their stage of development. In the case of undeveloped peoples full exercise of the right was held in trust for the people until they were politically matured to bear the responsibility. The mandate was therefore a preparatory stage and was not to last indefinitely. This is indeed implied in the words "[peoples] not yet able to stand by themselves." The alternative would have been annexation, which the conference clearly rejected. A League of Nations study noted: "It follows from this and from the very conception of tutelage that this mission is not, in principle, intended to be prolonged indefinitely, but only until the peoples under the tutelage are capable of managing their own affairs."[44]

Duncan Hall makes the following comment on the point:

> As conceived by the Peace Conference the mandate system was not merely an expedient limited to a particular situation; it was also thought of as something temporary in character. The assumption was that it would come to an end when the various mandated territories were able to stand by themselves.[45]

The inhabitants were to participate progressively in self-government until they achieved independence unless they freely chose some other rela-

44. *The Mandates System—Origins, Principles, Application* (1945), p. 23. The French text reads *non encore capables* as opposed to merely *incapables* (not able). *Conference de la Paix* (1919–20) *Recueil des Actes de la Conference*, partie 4B (1), p. 76. Note also President Wilson's emphasis: "The whole theory of mandates is not the theory of permanent subordination. It is the theory of development, of putting upon the mandatory the duty of assisting in the development of the country under the mandate, in order that it may be brought to a capacity for self-government and self-dependence which for the time being it has not reached. . . ." The Paris Peace Conference, 5 *Foreign Relations of the United States* (1944), p. 700.

45. Hall, p. 31.

tions with the mandatory. The grant of sovereignty was "provisional" in the case of A-mandates but ultimate in the case of B-mandates and C-mandates following a period of political, economic, and social advancement embodied in the "welfare and development" of Article 22 of the Covenant.

The commission gave its view on the conditions that would justify the end of the tutelage. There were two preliminary conditions:

(1) The existence in the territory concerned of *de facto* conditions which justify the presumption that the country has reached the stage of development at which a people has become able, in the words of Article 22 "to stand by itself under the strenuous conditions of the modern world."

(2) Certain guarantees to be furnished by the territory desirous of emancipation to the satisfaction of the League of Nations, in whose name the Mandate was conferred and has been exercised by the Mandatory.

The commission found that it was a question of fact observable over a sufficient period as to whether that stage has been attained. It laid down the following conditions as indicative:

(1) It must have a settled Government and an administration capable of maintaining the regular operation of essential services.

(2) It must be capable of maintaining its territorial integrity and political independence.

(3) It must be able to maintain the public peace throughout the whole territory.

(4) It must have at its disposal adequate financial resources to provide regularly for normal government requirements.

(5) It must possess laws and a judicial organisation which will afford equal and regular justice to all.

It further suggested that the new state must protect all minorities within it as well as the interests, privileges, and immunities of foreigners. It must also respect obligations entered into on its behalf by the former government.

The mandates system was undoubtedly a way of protecting the rights of undeveloped peoples in an age when Machiavellianism had a great influence in international relations. According to the "idealist school" of mandates historiography "the mandate system was a triumph of self-determination over imperialism, internationalism over nationalism, free trade over monopoly, and humanitarianism over slavery."[46] It "rested on the implicit principle of self-determination as well as the international

46. Louis, p. 22.

guarantees for free trade and native welfare."[47] In the view of Duncan Hall one of the assumptions that underlay the system was:

> the political and social system that had to be fostered. . . . as fast and as far as it could be attained by primitive peoples was the democratic way of life as it had developed historically in the English-speaking world and in France. This was the goal assumed by all; and by it, all (save Japan) understood the same thing: liberty of person, opinion, and property; the rule of law; the freedoms of Magna Carta, the Bill of Rights, and the Rights of Man; and in due course, self-government with self-determination, ending in political partnership with the mandatory state or independence.[48]

All A- and B-mandates have since attained independence. Of the C-mandates, Western Samoa is now freely associated with New Zealand, while Nauru gained independence in 1968. The North Pacific Islands are now a strategic trust territory under the United States, New Guinea is a trust territory under Australia, while South-West Africa, which the Union refused to bring under trusteeship, is now the subject of dispute between the Republic and the United Nations.[49]

Safeguards for self-determination in mandates were not always effective nor was there a consistent policy in all the territories of advancement to self-government or independence in the shortest possible time. The Permanent Mandates Commission had limited powers and restricted itself to making recommendations or polite criticism when it disagreed with a policy. It could not officially hear petitions from the natives unless they passed through the mandatory even when direct recourse to the people might have been necessary for a full appreciation of the issue.

The fact that self-determination was not expressly incorporated but only to be implied in the mandate agreements has led to political and legal disputes over the rights of the people of Namibia and the duties of the mandatory although similar provisions in other mandates achieved the desired effect, howbeit slowly. The decision of the international court that the individual members of the League could only enforce the "special interests" provisions of the mandate agreement and that

---

47. Ibid. See also Ernst Haas, "Reconciliation of Conflicting Colonial Policy Aims: Acceptance of the League of Nations System," 6 *International Organisation,* (1952), pp. 521–36. See also the statement of Nawab Yavar Jung, the Indian representative in the Fourth Committee of the United Nations on 24 November 1960: "The intention and purpose was to internationalise instead of annex, to make the principle of self-determination applicable, to keep in view the goal of self-government and, in case of abuse of the trust an appeal for redress, to exercise the international authority to the full, even to the extent of removing the mandate."

48. Hall, pp. 128–129.

49. *See also* chapter 6 on South-West Africa.

only the League Council could enforce the "conduct" provisions whittled down the legal protection contained in the mandates.[50]

Whatever the shortcomings of the mandates system, it ultimately extended the enjoyment of the right of self-determination to undeveloped peoples. By ruling out the annexation of enemy colonial territories and making their administration a "trust of civilisation" for the period necessary to train the people to assume full responsibility for their own government, it set a standard for colonial administrations. The right of self-determination merely implicit in the mandates system was developed and given a more positive bearing in Article 73 of the United Nations Charter on non-self-governing territories, the United Nations trusteeship system, and in the 1960 Declaration on the Granting of Independence to Colonial Peoples and Countries.[51]

50. For the legal issues see chapter 6.

51. In the view of Elihu Lauterpacht the idea of self-determination is reflected in mandates and trusteeship. "These revealed the emergence of the principle that territories and peoples are not mere chattels to be acquired and disposed of by and for the benefit of the proprietary state, but are instead the heritage of those who dwell within them." ("Some Concepts in Human Rights" 2 *Howard LJ* (1965), p. 271.) *See also* Bentwich, "Colonial Mandates and Trusteeship" 32 *Transactions of the Grotius Society* (1945); J. C. Hales, "Some Legal Aspects of the Mandate System: Sovereignty, Nationality, Termination, and Transfer" 23 *Transactions of the Grotius Society* (1937), pp. 85–126; A. Wilson and L. S. Amery, "The African Mandates and Their Future" 28 *United Empire* (1937), pp. 204–212; F. White, *Mandates* (London, 1926).

III

The United Nations Charter and Self-Determination as a Fundamental Human Right

1. Self-determination at San Francisco

The Dumbarton Oaks proposals of 1944 were unanimously, though tentatively, adopted by the Great Powers (Britain, China, USA and USSR) and were to be discussed at the general conference of the United Nations.[1] There was no mention of self-determination in this draft either in chapter 1(2)[2] or in chapter 9 (1)[3] which later became Articles 1(2) and 55(1).

At the Great Power consultations in San Francisco the Soviet Union introduced an amendment which included in the text of chapters 1(2) and 9(1): "Based on respect for the principle of equal rights and self-determination of peoples." Though the Americans were suspicious of Russian motives they felt unable to oppose; it was adopted unanimously and sent to the drafting committee as a sponsors' amendment. Later the Russian foreign minister emphasised in a press conference the tremendous importance his government attached to the principle which he thought was of great relevance to peoples in colonial territories and Mandates: "We must first of all see to it that dependent countries are

1. For full text *see* UNYB (1946–47) pp. 4–9.
2. "To develop friendly relations among nations and to take other appropriate measures to strengthen universal peace."
3. "With a view to the creation of conditions of stability and well-being which are necessary for peaceful and friendly relations among nations, the Organisation shall facilitate solutions of international economic, social, and other humanitarian problems and promote respect for human rights and fundamental freedoms. Responsibility for the discharge of this fnuction should be vested in the General Assembly, in an Economic and Social Council."

enabled as soon as possible to take the path of national independence."
This was to be a function of the United Nations in order to expedite
"the realisation of the principles of equality and self-determination."[4]
A member of the Soviet delegation stated in due course that the principle
was borrowed from the Russian Constitution of 1936. In his view the
United Nations must develop friendly relations, not only among states
but also among nations even when they are still fighting for independent
statehood. The equality of rights and the self-determination of nations
must be taken into consideration. He went on:

> The Organisation cannot remain indifferent to anything which
> menaces international peace and security, and consequently may
> raise the question of the self-determination of even a people which
> has no existence as a State, if its being oppressed is a factor
> affecting international peace and security.[5]

In the drafting subcommittee the Belgian delegate proposed an amendment to the draft. He pointed out that "peoples" could represent states
as well as national groups which need not be identified with the whole
population of a state. It was not possible, he argued, to determine if
the word was used in the first or the second meaning. He opined that
putting forth self-determination as the basis for friendly relations between nations rather than states might open the door to inadmissible
intervention. He therefore proposed the following amendment: "To
strengthen international order on the basis of respect for the essential
right and equality of the States, and of the peoples' right to self-
determination."[6] The amendment was rejected by more than two-thirds
majority for the following reasons: the paragraph was intended to
strengthen universal peace and friendly relations on the basis of equality
and to proclaim the equal rights of peoples, as such; the Charter extends
the right of self-determination to States, nations, and peoples.[7] The
official summary of the proceedings of the technical committee reveals
the controversy engendered by the phrase from its insertion:

> Concerning the principle of self-determination, it was strongly
> emphasised that this principle corresponded closely to the will and
> desires of peoples everywhere and should be clearly enunciated in

4. *New York Times* (May 8, 1945), p. 15.
5. S. B. Krylov, *Materials for the History of the United Nations*, vol. 1 ("Fram-
ing the Text of the UN Charter"), (1949), unpublished translation quoted in
Russel and Muther, *A History of the United Nations Charter* (1958), p. 812.
For background to the Charter *see* Goodrich and Hambro, *The Charter of the
United Nations* (London, 1949), pp. 1–18.
6. 6 UNCIO Docs., p. 300.
7. 6 UNCIO Docs., pp. 703–4.

the chapter; on the other side, it was stated that the principle conformed to the purposes of the Charter only insofar as it implied the right of self-government of peoples and not the right of secession.[8]

In his report to Commission I (the coordinating committee) the *rapporteur* laid down the drafting committee's understanding of the principle as follows:

> It was understood; that the principle of equal rights of people and that of self-determination are two component elements of one norm. That the respect of the norm is a basis for the development of friendly relations, and is in effect, one of the appropriate measures to strengthen universal peace.
> It was understood likewise that the principle in question, as a provision of the Charter, should be considered in function of other provisions.
> That an essential element of the principle in question is a free and genuine expression of the will of the people; and thus to avoid cases like those alleged by Germany and Italy. That the principle as one whole extends as a general basic conception to a possible amalgamation of nationalities if they so freely chose.[9]

The Commission approved the text with the sponsors' amendment which was also included in chapter 9(1).

The *travaux preparatoires* shows that the principle was unanimously endorsed by the consultative group and approved by more than two-thirds majority in the drafting subcommittee. The *rapporteur's* statement represents an authoritative guide to the meaning and content of the principle of self-determination. On a further request from the commission, the Ukrainian chairman of the subcommittee explained the meaning of the principle as including the capacity of a people to establish a regime of their own liking. The commission then approved the draft after a discussion of the meaning of "peoples," "nations," and "self-determination."

2. Self-determination as a Human Right

The Charter deals with human rights in very general terms: one of the principal functions of the United Nations is to promote respect for and observance of fundamental human rights without distinction as to race, sex, language, or religion.[10] Under Article 55 the United Nations

---

8. Summary Report of Committee I/I, Doc. I/I/I of 16 May 1945, 6 UNCIO Docs., p. 296.
9. Summary Report of Committee I/I, Doc. I/I/I of 16 May 1945, 6 UNCIO Docs., p. 296.
10. 6 UNCIO Docs., pp. 703–704.

shall promote "universal respect for, and observance of, human rights and fundamental freedoms for all without distinction as to race, sex, language, or religion"[11] with a view to creating peaceful and friendly relations among nations on the basis of equal rights and self-determination. An objective of trusteeship is to promote human rights, the observance of which is recognised as a condition for stability and friendly relations among nations.[12] The General Assembly may initiate studies and make recommendations for the purpose of helping to restore fundamental human rights[13] and the Economic and Social Council (ECOSOC) may make recommendations to the same effect.[14]

The Commission on Human Rights was set up in 1946 by the ECOSOC to make proposals and recommendations concerning:

(a) An international bill of rights.
(b) International declarations or conventions on civil liberties, the status of women, freedom of information, and similar matters.
(c) The protection of minorities.
(d) The prevention of discrimination on grounds of race, sex, language, or religion.
(e) Any other matter concerning human rights not covered by a, b, c, and d.[15]

The commission decided to tackle its job in three stages; (1) the preparation of a declaration embracing the maximum number of human rights and freedoms internationally acceptable and representing a common standard for all nations but imposing no legal obligations; (2) preparation of conventions which would be ratified by members and made legally binding; and (3) preparation of enforcement machineries for legal conventions.

In presenting the draft declaration on the Universal Declaration of Fundamental Human Rights, the chairman, Mrs. Roosevelt, stated that it represented a great step forward in the protection and promotion of human rights and fundamental freedoms. The declaration was not a treaty imposing obligations, but rather a statement of basic principles of inalienable rights representing a common standard of achievement for all peoples and nations. Though not binding, it would have considerable weight, and its adoption would commit members, in the words of the preamble, "to strive by teaching and education to promote respect for

11. Article 1(3).
12. Article 76c.
13. Article 13.
14. Article 62.
15. See UNYB (1946–7), p. 523.

these rights and freedoms and by progressive measures, national and international, to secure their universal and effective recognition and observance, both among the peoples of Member States themselves and among the peoples of territories under their jurisdiction."[16]

There were differences of views as to whether certain rights should be included in the declaration, such as self-determination and protection of minorities. A Russian amendment that "Every people and every nation has the right to national self-determination" and extending it to people in non-self-governing territories was rejected.[17] A British amendment that "no distinction shall be made on the basis of the political, jurisdictional, or international status of the country or territory to which a person belongs, whether it be independent, trust, non-self-governing, or under any other limitation of sovereignty" was carried. The declaration was adopted by forty-eight votes, none against, and eight abstentions.[18] At the same session the assembly requested the ECOSOC to continue its work in the preparation of a draft covenant on human rights which will be binding and the measures for implementation. In 1950 the General Assembly adopted a resolution which "calls upon the ECOSOC to request the Commission on Human Rights to study ways and means which would ensure the right of peoples and nations to self-determination, and to prepare recommendations for consideration by the General Assembly. . . ."[19]

At the sixth session, the Afro-Asian group of states took over the initiative and regretted that the commission had not studied ways and means of ensuring the right of peoples to self-determination. It was argued that the right was already stated in the Charter and its further recognition would give moral and legal support to dependent peoples struggling for freedom. It was also considered to be a valuable contribution to international peace and security and a necessary basis for the enjoyment of other human rights.[20] Others pointed out that the principle could not be enforced and that its political connotations warranted its treatment in a declaration of the rights and duties of states.[21] When

---

16. *UNYB* (1948–49), p. 526.

17. Doc. A/784. *See also* Elliot Goodman, "The Cry of National Liberation: Recent Soviet Attitudes Toward National Self-determination" 14 *International Organisation* (1960).

18. Res. 217(III). For full text see Appendix E.

19. Res. 521(V) of 4 December 1950. *See also UNYB* (1950), pp. 519–31.

20. Supporters included Afghanistan, Burma, Egypt, India, Indonesia, Iran, Lebanon, Pakistan, the Philippines, Saudi-Arabia, Syria and Yemen.

21. Proponents of this view included Australia, Belgium, Canada, France, Greece, Liberia, the Netherlands, New Zealand, Sweden, and Turkey.

the Third Committee decided to recommend that two covenants be drafted, one on political and civil rights and another on economic, social, and cultural rights, some representatives proposed that the right of self-determination should be included in both. The assembly finally adopted resolution 545(V) of 5 February 1952:

[The assembly] Decides to include in the International Covenant or Covenants on Human Rights an article on the right of all peoples and nations to self-determination in reaffirmation of the principle enunciated in the Charter of the United Nations. This article shall be drafted in the following terms: "All peoples shall have the right of self-determination," and shall stipulate that all States, including those having responsibility for the administration of Non-Self-Governing Territories should promote the realisation of that right, in conformity with the Purposes and Principles of the United Nations, in relation to the peoples of such Territories.

Opposition to the inclusion of the right persisted. It was argued that the recommendations would retard rather than advance self-determination and were an attempt to amend and extend the scope of the Charter. The recommendations, it was alleged, ignored the capacity of the people for self-government and failed to define the terms "peoples," "nations," and "the right of self-determination," all of which were complex and required much more study particularly in relation to the rights and duties of states. Limitless exercise of self-determination, it was feared, might lead to friction and anarchy. It was also claimed that the administration of dependent territories fell within the domestic jurisdiction of the administering state and that the right of self-determination must be subordinated to the maintenance of international peace and security. In rebuttal, it was argued that a non-self-governing territory was not the private property of the administering power but was held as a sacred trust, thus excluding the operation of domestic jurisdiction which did not in any case apply to a territory geographically removed from the metropolitan state. Precise definition of legal concepts before their inclusion in legal documents was unnecessary and the call for it, it was alleged, was a delaying tactic. A purely technical approach could not serve a problem that had economic, political, cultural, and social elements; moreover information regarding the exercise of self-determination in dependent territories would offer the United Nations authentic sources on which to base decisions. The following resolution was adopted:

[The Assembly] Requests the ECOSOC to ask the Commission on Human Rights to continue preparing recommendations concerning international respect for the rights of peoples to self-determination, and particularly recommendations relating to the steps which might be taken, within the limits of their resources and competence by the various organs of the United Nations and the specialised agencies to develop international respect for the right of peoples to self-determination.[22]

The two covenants were not approved by the assembly until 1966. Article 1, which is common to both, reads:

(1) All peoples have the right of self-determination. By virtue of that right they freely determine their political status and freely pursue their economic, social, and cultural development.
(2) The peoples may, for their own ends, freely dispose of their natural wealth and resources without prejudice to any obligations arising out of international economic cooperation, based upon the principle of mutual benefit, and international law. In no case may a people be deprived of its own means of subsistence.
(3) The State Parties to the Covenant, including those having responsibility for the administration of Non-Self-Governing Territories, shall promote the realisation of the right to self-determination, and shall respect that right, in conformity with the provisions of the Charter of the United Nations.[23]

The General Assembly has also discussed self-determination as an aspect of human rights in other circumstances. When in 1956 the Soviet Union intervened in Hungary to support a communist regime against the popular wishes of the people, the assembly resolved in its second emergency session:

Recalling that the enjoyment of human rights and fundamental freedoms in Hungary was specifically guaranteed by the Peace Treaty between Hungary and the Allied and Associated Powers signed at Paris on February 10, 1947 and that the general principle of these rights and these freedoms is affirmed for all peoples in the Charter of the United Nations.
Concerned that recent events in Hungary manifest clearly the desire of the Hungarian people to exercise and to enjoy fully their fundamental rights, freedom, and independence. . . .
Affirms the right of the Hungarian people to a government responsive to its national aspirations and dedicated to its independence and well-being.[24] ,

The assembly further requested that free elections be held in accordance

---

22. Res. 673C(VII). *See also UNYB* (1950), pp. 519–31.
23. Res. 2200 of 16 December 1966. *See also* "International Legal Materials" (1967); 61 *AJIL* (1967) supp.; *UN Monthly Chronicle*, vol. 4, no. 2.
24. Res. 1004(ES-II).

with the wishes of the people,[25] condemned the violation of the rights of the people by the Soviet Union[26] and called upon it to withdraw its armed forces to enable the people to re-establish their independence. In condemning the Soviet Union and the Hungarian regime, the assembly requested them "to respect the liberty and political independence of Hungary and the Hungarian people's enjoyment of fundamental human rights and freedoms."[27]

In the Declaration on the Inadmissibility of Intervention in Domestic Affairs and Protection of Their Independence and Sovereignty, the assembly affirmed:

> All States shall respect the right of self-determination and independence of peoples and nations, to be freely exercised without any foreign pressure, and with absolute respect for, human rights and fundamental freedoms. Consequently all States shall contribute to the complete elimination of racial discrimination and colonialism in all its forms and manifestations.[28]

In Resolution 2106(XX) of 12 December 1965 the assembly adopted the International Convention on the Elimination of All Forms of Racial Discrimination, and this provides:

> State Parties shall, when the circumstances so warrant, take, in the social, economic, cultural, and other fields, special and concrete measures to ensure the adequate development and protection of certain racial groups or individuals belonging to them, for the purpose of guaranteeing them the full and equal enjoyment of human rights and fundamental freedoms.[29]

Although self-determination is not expressly mentioned, the resolution, by referring to the Declaration on Independence[30] and the Universal Declaration of Human Rights, indirectly emphasises the principle of self-determination in the field of human rights.[31] In the Special Committee on Friendly Relations and Cooperation Among States the principle has been extensively discussed in relation to human rights and other principles of international law.[32]

25. Res. 1005(ES-II).

26. Res. 1131(XI).

27. Res. 1312(XIII).

28. Res. 2131(XX) of 12 December 1965.

29. Article 2(2).

30. *See* chapter 4 on non-self-governing territories.

31. *See also* I. Brownlie, *Basic Documents in International Law* (Oxford, 1967), p. 178.

32. E.g., UN Doc. A/AC. 125/L.

In general the United Nations has treated self-determination as an essential aspect of human rights which all states should observe in relation to dependent peoples. The new emphasis, spearheaded by some of the advanced nations, is that the principle has equal validity in relation to the human rights and fundamental freedoms of peoples in independent states.

3. The Effect of Self-determination in the Charter

We have traced the close connection of self-determination with fundamental human rights in order to demonstrate that it is essentially a fundamental right *sui generis*, collective in character and belonging to the group rather than to the individual. In the two articles of the Charter where the principle is mentioned, very remarkably, fundamental human rights are also mentioned. It is therefore convenient to consider the effect of the principle in relation to the Charter, the Universal Declaration of Human Rights, and the International Covenants on Civil and Political Rights and on Economic, Social, and Cultural Rights.

A. *The Charter of the United Nations.* One school of thought maintains that the provisions of the Charter on human rights including those on self-determination have no legal effect. According to Kelsen, "The language used by the Charter . . . does not allow the interpretation that the Members are under legal obligations regarding the rights and freedoms mentioned in the Preamble or in the text of the Charter."[33] He points out that the rights and freedoms referred to are not specified. It is also argued that the principles are merely exhortatory and that the United Nations can only take action when a breach of these rights are of such enormity as to constitute a danger to peace.[34]

Another school of thought, holding a more popular view, maintains that the provisions have legal effect. Lauterpacht argues forcefully that they were adopted as part of the philosophy of the new international system, the mere absence of sufficient means of implementation and the lack of definition do not detract from their legality. He supports his view with the principle of effectiveness in the interpretation of treaties, and concludes:

> There is mandatory obligation implied in the provision of Article 55 that the United Nations "shall promote respect for, and observance of, human rights and fundamental freedoms," or, in the

---

33. H. Kelsen, *The Law of the United Nations* (London, 1950), p. 29.

34. *See also* Kunz, "The United Nations Declaration of Human Rights" 43 *AJIL* (1949), pp. 316–323.

terms of Article 13, that the Assembly shall make recommendations for the purpose of assisting in the realisation of human rights and freedoms. There is a distinct element of legal duty in the undertaking expressed in Article 56.[35]

There is at least a minimum duty on the part of members of the United Nations not to obstruct the promotion of human rights, including the rights of self-determination, a minimum standard accepted by civilised nations.[36]

B. *The Universal Declaration of Human Rights.* The nonlegal status of the Declaration of Human Rights came out clearly in the statements of delegates in the General Assembly during its adoption. It was confidently asserted that the declaration would be an inspiration to "millions of men, women, and children all over the world."[37] It had "an unprecedented moral value"[38] and was a "guiding light to all those who endeavoured to raise men's material standard of living and spiritual condition . . . a moral obligation on the different countries to find ways and means of giving effect to the rights proclaimed therein."[39]

Though not in itself a lawmaking instrument the declaration is a statement of common standards applicable to all human beings, a beginning to some and an objective to others. It has been accepted by the new states although they had no hand in drafting it. The constitutions of many African states, for example, contain bills of rights which are immediately or remotely based on the Declaration.[40] It has been referred to in national courts as in the Philippines where the Supreme Court

---

35. H. Lauterpacht, *Human Rights,* p. 148.

36. For further support for the legal effect of the human rights provisions *see* H. Waldock, *Human Rights in Contemporary International Law,* pp. 9–10; Ezejiofor, *Protection of Human Rights Under the Law* (1964), p. 60; Ganji, *International Protection of Human Rights* (1962), pp. 113–5; Higgins, *The Development of International Law Through the Political Organs of the United Nations* (1963), p. 119. *See also* Jessup, *A Modern Law of Nations* (1949), p. 91 ("It is already the law, at least for members of the United Nations, that respect for human dignity and fundamental human rights is obligatory."), N. Brierly, *Law of Nations* (1963), p. 293 (". . . a pledge to cooperate in promoting at least implies a negative obligation not to undermine human rights. . . .").

37. Evatt of Australia. UN Plenary Meeting, Official Records of third session, part 1 (1948), pp. 875–876.

38. Belgian delegate, ibid, p. 880.

39. Netherlands delegate, ibid., p. 873.

40. Thus, the constitutions of French-speaking African states, Ethiopia, Kenya, Libya, Nigeria, and Tanganyika. The preamble of the OAU Charter expressly adheres to the declaration. *See also* the constitutions of Cyprus, India, and the West Indian states.

seemed to attribute to its legal force.[41] It has been aptly noted by a former chairman of the European Commission:

> This constant and widespread recognition of the principles of the Universal Declaration clothes it, in my opinion, in the character of customary law. . . . the Declaration has acquired a status inside and outside the United Nations which gives it high authority as the accepted formulation of the common standard of human rights.[42]

The most outstanding recognition of the force of the declaration is to be found in the European Convention on Human Rights, which reaffirms "profound belief in those Fundamental Freedoms which are the foundations of justice and peace in the world" and enforces "certain of the Rights stated in the Universal Declaration" among countries which are "like-minded and have a common heritage of political traditions, ideals, freedom, and the rule of law."[43] The Understanding of 5 October 1954, regarding Trieste, provides that "in the administration of their respective areas, the Italian and Yugoslav authorities shall act in accordance with the principles of the Universal Declaration of Human Rights."[44]

The declaration has influenced subsequent assembly resolutions, declarations, and conventions, such as the Genocide Convention, 1948; Suppression of Traffic in Persons and of the Exploitation of Prostitution, 1949; the Status of Refugees, 1951; Political Rights of Women, 1952; Abolition of Slavery, 1956; Rights of Child, 1959; Declaration on the Promotion Among Youth of the Ideals of Peace, Mutual Respect, and Understanding Between Peoples, 1965; the Status of Stateless Persons, 1954; Nationality of Women, 1957; Discrimination in Education, 1960; the Reduction of Statelessness, 1961; Consent for Marriage, Minimum Age For Marriage, and Registration of Marriage, 1962; and the Declaration on the Elimination of All Forms of Discrimination, 1963.

Although self-determination was not expressly mentioned in the declaration, the principle was given prominence in the Covenants on Human

---

41. *Borovsky* v. *Commissioner of Immigration and Director of Prisons; Chirskoff* v. *Commissioner of Immigration et al. See UNYB* on Human Rights (1951), pp. 289–90. *See also* J. P. Humphrey, "The UN Charter and the Universal Declaration on Human Rights," in D. Luard, ed., *The International Protection of Human Rights* (London, 1967).

42. Waldock, *Human Rights in Contemporary International Law and the Significance of the European Convention*, p. 15.

43. For the full text *see* 45 *AJIL* (1951) supp. 24–39.

44. *See also* E. Schwelb, "Trieste Settlement and Human Rights" 49 *AJIL*, p. 242.

Rights which emanated from the declaration and sought to carry its principles into legal force.[45]

C. *The International Covenants on Human Rights.* The Covenants on Human Rights are a further elaboration of the Declaration on Human Rights but, unlike it, are legal instruments. They were unanimously adopted on 16 December 1966 and constitute a milestone in the universal recognition of human rights. Welcoming their adoption, the Secretary-General U Thant recalled his speech on Human Rights Day 1966:

> I had occasion to recall that in the philosophy of the United Nations, respect for human rights is one of the main foundations of freedom, justice, and peace in the world. I pointed out that peace and respect for human rights go hand-in-hand. It is my sincere belief that our decision today will bring us nearer to the kind of world which our Organisation is committed to build. I earnestly hope that by early action, which Member States alone can take, the Covenants on Human Rights will soon become a living reality.[46]

The Covenant on Economic, Social, and Cultural Rights promotes better living conditions, education, and health and guarantees the right to work, fair wages, social security, freedom from hunger and from discrimination on grounds of "race, colour, sex, language, religion, political or other opinion, national or social origin, property, birth or other status." It guarantees the right to form and join trade unions. The Covenant on Civil and Political Rights protects people against cruel, inhumane, and degrading treatment and recognises the right to life, liberty, security, privacy, fair trial, and equality before the law. It prohibits slavery, arbitrary arrest, and detention and guarantees freedom of opinion, expression, thought, religion, and association. It preserves the cultural, religious, and linguistic heritage of the minorities. Under both covenants state parties agree to submit reports on the measures which they have adopted and the progress made in achieving the observance of the rights.

The Covenant on Civil and Political Rights goes farther in setting up a Human Rights Committee of eighteen persons of "high moral character and recognised competence in the field of human rights," preferably experts with legal experience. This committee, the members of which

---

45. In his dissenting opinion, Tanaka states that "the Universal Declaration of Human Rights adopted by the General Assembly constitutes evidence of the interpretation and application of the relevant Charter provisions." *South-West Africa cases—ICJ Rep.* (1966), p. 293.

46. *UN Monthly Chronicle* (February 1967) vol. IV, no. 2, p. 41.

will be elected for four-year periods and be eligible for re-election, will study the reports submitted by states and give their own comments to the parties. It may also transmit these reports and its comments to the ECOSOC and will receive any further comments that states may make. Under Article 41, a state that has accepted the jurisdiction of the committee may report to it that another party (which has also accepted its jurisdiction) is not fulfilling its obligation under the covenant. Such a report is made under a procedure set out in the article and includes the exhaustion of local remedies by the individuals sought to be protected. A complainant state must first try to resolve the issue directly with the state concerned. The committee may set up an ad hoc Conciliation Commission with the consent of the parties concerned if a matter is not resolved. It must submit an annual report of its activities through the ECOSOC to the General Assembly of the United Nations.

An Optional Protocol is attached to the Covenant on Civil and Political Rights; under it, individuals may address themselves directly to the committee after they have exhausted local remedies. The committee is then to forward its views to the state party concerned and include a summary of its activities in its annual report. The optional clause is inapplicable to dependent peoples but without any prejudice whatsoever to "the right of petition granted to these peoples by the Charter of the United Nations and other international conventions and instruments under the United Nations and its specialized agencies."[47]

It is feared that these instruments which authorise international probing in areas traditionally confined to the domestic jurisdiction may not attract a large number of ratifications.[48] To allow an individual to take his national state to task before an international tribunal, it is argued, "disrupts the moral and legal unity of the state's organisation" and to permit third states to seek remedy for foreign nationals "constitutes a direct or a disguised intervention." Consequently Korowicz suggested that "the respective provisions of the Draft Covenants will never be adopted."[49]

The covenants have not in fact introduced a wholly novel procedure in international law as the following precedents suffice to show:

(1) The Hague Convention XIII of 1907, which never came into force, provided for the creation of an International Prize Court where individuals could proceed against states parties.

47.   Article 7.

48.   See, e.g., C. C. Ferguson, "The United Nations Human Rights Covenants: Problems of Ratification and Implementation" Proceedings of American Society of International Law (April 1968), p. 83; W. Korey, "The Key to Human Rights Implementation," International Conciliation (November 1968).

49.   M. St. Korowicz, Introduction to International Law (Hague, 1959), p. 386.

(2) The Treaty of Washington of 20 December 1907, signed by Costa Rica, Guatemala, Honduras, and El Salvador, set up, for a period of ten years, the Central American Court of Justice before which citizens of parties asserted claims against the members. More recently the Inter-American Commission on Human Rights was set up in 1959 "to make recommendations to the governments of member states in general. . . for the adoption of progressive measures in favour of human rights."

(3) The Peace Treaties established Mixed Arbitral Tribunals which dealt with disputes between nationals of the Principal Allied and Associated Powers and nationals of the defeated powers as well as disputes between the former and the latter powers.[50]

(4) The German-Polish Convention of 15 May 1922, concluded for a period of fifteen years, set up the Upper Silesian Mixed Commission and an arbitral Tribunal both under the supervision of the League Council with the duty of settling disputes between the Polish and German nationals and between both nationals and the governments.

(5) Under the European Convention of Human Rights 1950, individuals, groups of individuals, or nongovernmental organisations claiming that their rights under the convention are violated may petition the European Commission of Human Rights provided that their national states accept its jurisdiction. The commission or member state may bring a case of breach before the European Court of Human Rights provided the defendant state recognises its jurisdiction. Although not dealing expressly with self-determination, the denial of the rights, such as the freedoms of expression and of peaceful assembly, to a defined group can have an element of self-determination.

(6) Many conventions have been concluded regulating the conduct of states toward their own subjects without necessarily giving the latter direct action but enabling other states to champion their cause if they wish. Such are the International Labour Organisation,[51] the minorities treaties, the provisions of the Charter on human rights, the non-self-governing territories and trust territories, and the Genocide Convention.

50. These tribunals were active until 1931; their decisions are recorded in *Recueil des Décisions des Tribunaux Mixtes institués par les Traités de Paix* (Paris 1922–1930).

51. Ghana lodged a complaint against Portugal in 1961 under the Abolition of Forced Labour Convention, 1957 (320 *UNTS*, p. 292) with regard to Angola, Mozambique, and Portuguese Guinea. Portugal brought a complaint against Liberia under the Forced Labour Conventions, 1930 (39 *UNTS*, p. 55). The reports of the two commissions of inquiry are in 45 *ILO Off. Bull.*, no. 2, supp. 2 (April 1962) and 46 *ILO Off. Bull.*, no. 2, Supp. 2 (April 1963) respectively. For a discussion covering the minority treaties, ILO, UN Commissioner for Refugees, International Committee of the Red Cross, the Inter-American Commission on Human Rights, and the European Convention on Human Rights *see* T. St. G. Bissell, "Negotiations by International Bodies and the Protection of Human Rights," 7 *Columbia Journal of Transnational Law* (1968), p. 90.

The Covenants on Human Rights mark the growing and inevitable recognition of the Rights of individuals in international law; human beings are the centre of all laws, national or international, the fundamental purpose of which is the preservation of man and the promotion of his health and happiness. The first article of the Covenants begins with "All peoples have the right to self-determination. By virtue of that right they freely determine their political status and freely pursue their economic, social, and cultural development." This gives weight to the statement that the principle is the basis of all other human rights. Not unnaturally governments are reluctant to ratify the covenants although the interest of their subjects demands the greater international recognition of the rights of individuals even when these are opposable to their governments. It is however in the interest of individuals that the covenants, including the protocol, should be ratified by the greatest possible number of states.

If a dispute arises under the covenants as to whether a people have been denied the right of self-determination, the criteria are provided by the article itself:

(1) Do the people in question freely determine their political status?

(2) Do they freely pursue their economic, social, and cultural development?

In answering these questions the Human Rights Committee will bear in mind that the free determination of the political status of a people does not necessarily involve secession and the declaration of independence. It may also be expressed through association, local government, autonomy, a unitary or monolithic system, or any other form that reflects the wishes of the people. The exercise of the right must have regard to other principles of international law, such as sovereignty, and to the particular circumstances of each case. The denial of the right must be sufficiently serious to attract international attention. One-man-one-vote and the enjoyment of political rights on a basis of nondiscrimination are necessary conditions for free political determination. A people within a metropolitan territory who enjoy these rights cannot make a case that they are denied the right of self-determination even though there may in fact be political agitation for a particular status, such as independence. The situation will be different if they are denied human rights and are not free to participate in government.

A further consideration of state practice and the practice of the United Nations is necessary for a proper appreciation of the principle of self-determination.[52]

52. *See also* chapter 8 on the content of self-determination and chapter 10 on self-determination in metropolitan territories.

IV Non-Self-Governing Territories

1. Before 1945

The position in customary law was that a colony was supposed to be part and parcel of its metropolitan territory.[1] That was unchanged under the League, although colonial peoples received a small measure of international attention. Member states undertook "to secure and maintain fair and humane conditions of labour. . . ."[2] The Convention of St. Germain abrogated the Berlin and Brussels treaties on Africa but committed its parties to promote the material and moral well-being of the people. Though the League Covenant did not extend the mandate provisions to "the other similar dependencies," a British Foreign Office publication in 1919 noted: "It may be hoped that the maintenance of a high standard of administration in the mandate territories will react favourably wherever a lower standard now exists, and the mandatory principle may prove to be capable of wide application."[3]

Nationalism and anti-colonialism, which had been picking up in the inter-war years, gathered momentum during the war. The stigma attached to the status of subject peoples was increasingly resented by the educated elites and the nationalists sought to take advantage of the war by demanding a promise for political advancement as a condition for

---

1. *See* e.g., S. P. Sinha, *New Nations and the Law of Nations* (Leyden, 1967), chapter 1.

2. Article 23 of the League Covenant.

3. Cmd. 151. *See also* "Commentary on the League of Nations Covenant" 14 *AJIL* (1920), 407–418 at 417.

maximising their war effort. The ease with which European colonies in the Far East succumbed to the Japanese contrasted with the resistance put up by the Philippines, to which independence had been promised. This convinced informed opinion in many parts of the world that colonialism and imperialism were evil, that their abrogation must be a major war aim and that the cooperation of the Asians must be gained if the Japanese were to be defeated. With its anti-colonial tradition, it was easy for the United States to view self-determination as a wider application of fundamental human rights which had been so grossly trampled on by the Nazis. The principle was equated to freedom, a prerogative of all peoples everywhere. It was foreseen that there would be a conflict with the traditional rules of sovereignty; so the proposed international organisation was to detract from sovereignty only to the extent that states might consent. The Soviet Union had long been vehemently opposed to European colonialism and directed its propaganda against it.

Practical steps toward the United Nations Charter can be traced back to the meeting on the cruiser *Augusta* between British Prime Minister Churchill and United States President Franklin D. Roosevelt, in which they issued the Atlantic Charter of 14 August, 1941.[4] They disavowed territorial aggrandisement, affirmed the right of all peoples to choose their own form of government, and the restoration of sovereignty and self-government to peoples forcibly denied of them. The United Nations Declaration of 1 January, 1942, signed by the United States, USSR, Great Britain, China, and twenty-one other states, recognised the obligation of members to preserve human rights and justice in their own as well as in other lands.[5] At the Moscow Conference of 1943, the foreign ministers of the United States, USSR, and Great Britain agreed to place enemy colonies under United Nations control, and in the Cairo Conference of 1943, Churchill, Roosevelt and Chiang Kai-shek announced that Japan would be deprived of its colonies and that they themselves were not anxious to make territorial acquisitions. The Institute of Pacific Relations suggested an international commission for all dependent territories, and the Conference of Hot Springs, convened under the auspices of the institute, declared that no country was in principle superior to another and that all colonies and protectorates had a right to eventual self-government or independence.

The "wind of change" was well received in the Netherlands: as early

---

4. For full text *see* 35 *AJIL* (1941), supp. 191.

5. For full text *see* M. O. Hudson, ed., *International Legislation* (New York, 1950), 9:1.

as 1941 proposals were announced for a postwar constitutional conference with its colonies in which desired changes would be effected.
Mr. Churchill was however unsympathetic toward colonial freedom
and maintained that the Atlantic Charter applied only to European
nations occupied by the Germans and not to the British Colonial Empire.[6] His government on the whole maintained a less reactionary outlook. The situation with France was complicated by the division of
authority between the Vichy government and the Free French government in exile under General de Gaulle in London.

In 1942 Undersecretary Welles made a public statement of United
States policy:

> If this was in fact a war for the liberation of peoples, it must assure
> the sovereign equality of peoples throughout the world . . . Our
> victory must bring in its train the liberation of all peoples. Dis-
> crimination between peoples because of their race, creed, or color
> must be abolished. The age of imperialism is ended. The right of
> a people to their freedom must be recognized as the civilized world
> long since recognized the right of an individual to his personal free-
> dom. The principles of the Atlantic Charter must be guaranteed
> to the world as a whole—in all oceans and in all countries.[7]

A fortnight later Secretary of State Hull was pressed to narrow down this
declaration of independence to peoples "prepared and willing to accept
the responsibilities of liberty."[8]

2. Drafting History of Chapter 11 of the Charter

Agreement on non-self-governing territories was bedevilled by their
earlier assimilation to the proposed trust territories, since they were all
dependent territories. In the belief that the Atlantic Charter had a
general application, the American State Department in 1942 formulated
plans for international trusteeship of all dependent territories, especially
those in the Far East. The aim was to lead them swiftly to independence.[9] The proposed United Nations was to be committed to "the principle of self-determination, the restoration of independence to nations

---

6. Great Britain, *Parl. Debs.* (HC) 374 cols. 67–69. He insisted that he had not
"become the King's First Minister in order to preside over the liquidation of the
British Empire" (*London Times*, 11 November 1942).

7. U.S., *Dept. of State Bulletin*, 6:488.

8. Ibid., 7:642. *See also* L. M. Goodrich, *The United Nations* (1959), pp. 296–
299; G. S. Windass, "Power Politics and Ideals: The Principle of Self-determination," *International Relations*, vol. 3, no. 3 (April 1967), pp. 177–186; J. A.
Yturriaga, "Non-Self-Governing Territories: The Law and the Practice of the
United Nations" 18 *YBWA* (1964), pp. 178–212.

9. Cordell Hull, *The Memoirs of Cordell Hull* (New York, 1948), 2:1234–38.

forcibly deprived of it, and the opportunity to achieve independence for other peoples aspiring to it." Colonial governments were "to promote education, economic, political and social advancement, and progressively to grant such measures of self-government as the various populations were equipped to maintain, and as soon as possible to fix specific dates for the achievement of independence within a system of national security." There were however certain difficulties with this plan. Submission to trusteeship was to be voluntary and France, a major colonial power, was still under German occupation and so could not technically take part in the arrangements. Portugal and Spain, also major colonial powers, were neutral in the war. Disagreements developed between the U.S. State Department and the departments of Navy and War over the administration of islands in the Pacific which the latter considered were of strategic importance to the United States.

By 1943 the State Department had a revised draft entitled "Declaration by the United Nations on National Independence."[10] It incorporated the Atlantic Charter and pledged self-determination for all nations. Governments responsible for the administration of colonies would bind themselves to advance them to independence. It proposed an international trusteeship for League mandates and territories detached from the axis powers. To deny self-determination to Italian and Japanese colonies would have been to fall below the League standard, and three mandates had already gained independence—Iraq, Syria, and Lebanon. The British however preferred international cooperation rather than administration, and the prevention of exploitation.

The final American draft in 1944 omitted the word "independence" and substituted "self-government," describing it simply as "Draft Declaration Regarding Administration of Dependent Territories." It left the question of trusteeship to states "directly concerned" and drew a distinction between strategic and nonstrategic trust territories.[11] It sought to impose minimum political, economic, and social standards in dependent territories on the assumption that administering states were accountable to the international community. The British however favoured a statement of policy on colonial administration as part of the United Nations Charter and regional cooperation based on functionaries. There was still no agreement on dependent territories. The Dumbarton Oaks proposals were silent on them; in the meantime enthusiasm for a colonial charter waned in the United States through internal differences.

10. Text in U.S., Dept. of State, "Postwar Foreign Policy Preparation 1919–45," *Publication 3580* (February 1950), pp. 470–2.

11. *See* G. V. Wolfe, "The States Directly Concerned: Article 79 of the United Nations Charter" 42 *AJIL* (1948), p. 368.

At the Yalta Conference of 1945, the subject was raised by the United States in the meeting of the foreign ministers of the United States, the USSR, and Great Britain and it was agreed to provide machinery for the administration of trust territories and to apply the system to: (1) existing mandates, (2) territories detached from the enemy as a result of the war, and (3) any other territory that might be voluntarily placed under it.[12]

The five Great Powers were to discuss the matter again before the general conference of San Francisco. Continued disagreement in the USA made it impossible to obtain an agreed policy making the five-power meeting impossible. It had to be held concurrently with the general conference.

At San Francisco the consultative group had before them draft proposals from the United States, Great Britain, and Australia concerning dependent territories. The British proposal, like the Australian one, recognised the principle of trusteeship in the administration of colonial territories and suggested "the creation of a special system of international machinery to apply to certain territories."[13] This was accepted as a basis for a Working Paper;[14] section A on general policy dealt with colonies (non-self-governing territories) and section B with trust territories. Section A applied to "territories not yet able to stand by themselves under the strenuous conditions of the modern world."[15] Although these words were understood to refer to colonies, Iraq objected to them, arguing that few countries were able to stand by themselves either economically or militarily; dependent peoples consisted not only of primitive peoples but also of peoples with a rich cultural heritage. The words were then adopted "territories whose peoples have not yet attained a full measure of self-government." France pressed for federal relationship between colonies and metropolitan territories and preferred reference merely to the development of political institutions which could include self-government or independence, as appropriate in the circumstances of each territory. It opposed the elaboration of the duties of an administering power and charged that the principle laid down at Yalta was being exceeded. "General Policy" was changed to "Declaration" to satisfy France, but its delegate insisted that acceptance was no disclaimer to resort to the domestic-jurisdiction clause. Administering powers were

12. U. S., Dept. of State, "The Conference of Malta and Yalta, 1945," *Foreign Relations of the USA*, p. 977. *See also UNYB* (1946–7), p. II.

13. For texts of British and Australian proposals *see* 3 UNCIO, pp. 538, 609.

14. For text of Working Paper, *see UNYB* (1946–7), pp. 29–30.

15. Cf. Article 22 of the League Covenant.

merely required to "accept" rather than "undertake," and "self-government" was substituted for "independence," the United States arguing that, read as a whole, self-government included independence. A Soviet attempt to include political information under Article 73e was unsuccessful.[16]

3. The United Nations Charter Provisions

According to Article 73, members of the United Nations who are administering non-self-governing territories recognise: (1) the paramountcy of the interests of the inhabitants, and (2) the sacred trust and the obligation to promote the well-being of the inhabitants. They oblige themselves to have due respect for their cultural, political, economic, social, and educational advancement, protect them from abuses, develop self-government and free political institutions according to the circumstances of each particular territory. They also agree to further international peace and security and encourage research and cooperation with a view to achieving the objectives of Article 73. Further, they agree "to transmit regularly to the Secretary-General for information purposes, subject to such limitations as security and constitutional considerations may require, statistical and other information of a technical character relating to economic, social, and educational conditions in the territories for which they are responsible."[17] Members also agree to base their policy in these territories on good-neighbourliness in relation to other states, taking due account of their interests in social, economic, and commercial matters.[18]

4. Transmission of Information

The General Assembly in a unanimous resolution during the first part of its first session drew attention to the fact that Chapter 11 of the Charter came into force on the Charter, itself becoming effective, and was not dependent upon subsequent agreements. It requested the Secretary-General to include in his annual report a summary of the information received under Article 73e. It also expressed the view that the

16. *See also* 10 UNCIO Docs., p. 622.

17. Cf. Article 22(1) of the League Covenant: "To those colonies and territories which as a consequence of the late war have ceased to be under the sovereignty of the States which formerly governed them and which are inhabited by peoples not yet able to stand by themselves under the strenuous conditions of the modern world, there should be applied the principle that the well-being and development of such peoples form a sacred trust of civilisation and that the securities for the performance of this trust should be embodied in this Covenant."

18. Article 74 of the United Nations Charter.

realisation of the objectives of Chapters 11, 12, and 13 "will make possible the attainment of the political, economic, social and educational aspirations of non-self-governing peoples."[19]

When considering which organ should examine the information submitted under Article 73e, the Cuban delegate suggested that the Trusteeship Council should be given the function, but this was opposed by the colonial powers. There was opposition to the information's being considered at all, it being argued that the Charter framers deliberately rejected any proposals for a supervisory organ, and that the document imposed no obligation to render accounts. "Report" under the article, it was argued, was of a technical character and for information purposes only, defying any consideration or examination. The obligations were unilateral and subject to security and constitutional limitations, it was claimed.

The assembly, however, set up an *ad hoc* committee consisting of an equal number of administering and non-administering powers to consider the reports on behalf of the Secretary-General with a view to making recommendations and utilising to the full the expert knowledge and experience of the specialised agencies in the interest of the colonies.[20] The committee was replaced by the Special Committee on Information and was renewed from year to year until 1949, when it was given a three-year lease of life and the frequency of information was reduced from once a year to once in three years.[21] In 1952 the name was changed to the Committee of Information from Non-Self-Governing Territories. In 1961 the assembly authorised it to continue in existence "until such time as the General Assembly has decided that the principles embodied in Chapter 11 of the Charter and in the Declaration on the Granting of Independence to Colonial Countries and Peoples have been fully implemented."[22] Its work has been taken over by the Special Committee of Twenty-four (formerly seventeen).

From the beginning, there was much controversy over the nature of the information to be transmitted. The Charter expressly requires "information of a technical nature relating to economic, social, and educational conditions" and the administering powers have sought to give this a restrictive interpretation while the anti-colonial powers give it a wide meaning. In Resolution 144(II) of 3 November 1947 the assembly recognised that voluntary transmission of political information was en-

19. Res. 9(1) of 9 February 1946.
20. Res. 66(I) of 14 December 1946.
21. Res. 218(III), 219(III), and 332(IV).
22. Res. 1700(XVI).

tirely in the spirit of Article 73. A standard form was adopted for the guidance of members giving information but was enlarged from time to time to incorporate more information. In 1948 the Communist bloc tried to make it obligatory that political information be given and argued that the absence of it was the chief cause of the economic backwardness of those territories. The colonial powers however rejected this as an attempt to circumvent the Charter. They also opposed information on the participation of the local population in local government, the receipt of petitions from local organs and individuals, and the right of the United Nations to send observers to the territories. The transmission of political information, as a matter of practice, was adopted in Resolution 144(II); the demand for political information was strengthened from time to time as the years went by and in 1954 the assembly declared that the principles and objectives of Article 73 "relate to the political as well as the economic, social, and educational advancement of the peoples concerned."[23] In 1959 it stressed that the "inextricable relationship between developments in political and functional fields" made it desirable to transmit political information.[24] In 1960 it declared that full knowledge of political and constitutional developments was essential "not only to the proper evaluation of progress of the Territories towards independence but also to that of their economic, social and cultural advancement" and called upon the powers to cooperate.[25] In 1961 the Committee on Information was empowered to examine political and constitutional information.[26] In 1963 the assembly felt able to ask for "information prescribed under Article 73e of the Charter, as well as the fullest possible information on political and constitutional development."[27] Information has been transmitted by most administering powers under the article and in implementation of the 1960 Resolution on the Granting of Independence.[28]

5. The Designation of Non-Self-Governing Territories

Because certain colonial powers unilaterally ceased giving information on certain territories which they had previously included in their reports, the assembly, on the initiative of India, adopted a resolution claiming the

23. Res. 848(IX).
24. Res. 1468(XIV).
25. Res. 1535(XV).
26. Res. 1700(XVI).
27. Res. 1970(XVIII) of 11 December 1963.
28. See also UN, Background Paper on Chapter XI, Doc ST/DP I/ser. A/73 Rev. I; R. Higgins, The Development of International Law Through the Political Organs of the United Nations (London, 1963), pp. 110–116.

right to be informed of any constitutional change that may render the transmission of information unnecessary.[29] Some states opposed it on the basis that it might lead to a definition by the assembly of a non-self-governing territory which might conflict with the view of the administering power.[30] In 1949 the assembly resolved that it was "within the responsibility of the General Assembly to express its opinion on the principles which have guided or which may in future guide the members concerned in enumerating the territories for which the obligation exists to transmit information under Article 73e of the Charter." A committee was set up to examine the factors under which a territory may be considered to be self-governing.[31]

In 1950 the assembly approved the cessation of information by the Netherlands on Indonesia,[32] but there were difficulties with Dutch Surinam and the Antilles and also with Puerto Rico under United States jurisdiction. These were cleared in due course.[33] In approving the cessation with regard to Greenland, the assembly asserted that it might send a mission with the agreement of the administering power to a territory about to attain independence in order to satisfy itself that the right of the people to self-determination was in fact assured.[34]

The list of factors was approved in Resolution 742(VIII) in which the assembly asserted that the factors were to be used as evidence in determining the propriety of the cessation of information in each case. The resolution recognised that the primary mode of self-government is the attainment of independence, although the same goal may be attained through association with another state or states provided the act was free and on a basis of absolute equality. The factors are divided into three parts, the first indicates the attainment of independence. In its international status such a territory must possess full internal and external sovereignty, be eligible for membership of the United Nations, attain a full international personality, and have the sovereign right to

29. United States on the Panama Zone, France on all its territories except New Hebrides, on the basis that they had acquired self-government within the French Union, Britain on Malta and Pitcairne Island, based on their advanced stage of self-government.

30. Res. 222(III).

31. Res. 334(IV). See also UNYB (1948–49), pp. 719–34.

32. Res. 448(V).

33. Res. 849(XI) of 22 November 1954 approved the cessation on Puerto Rico and Res. 945(X) on the federal link of the Antilles and Surinam with the Netherlands. See also Van Panhuys, "The International Aspect of Reconstruction of the Kingdom of the Netherlands in 1954," Netherlands International Law Review (1958); "The Netherlands Constitution and International Law," 47 AJIL (1953), p. 537. See also on Puerto Rico p. 155 et seq.

34. Res. 849(XI) of 22 November 1954.

provide for its own defence. In its internal status it must have a free choice of government, full legislative, executive, judicial, and administrative competence as well as economic, social, and cultural autonomy. The second part contains factors that are indicative of the attainment of other systems of self-government, and the third, factors indicative of the free association of a territory on equal basis with the metropolitan or other state as an integral part of that state, or any other form.[35]

The claims of Portugal and Spain, which both joined the United Nations in 1955, that their colonies were not in fact "territories" within the meaning of Article 73 but by their respective constitutions were integral parts of Portugal and Spain, led to a new development in regard to factors determining non-self-governing territories. A committee of six composed of an equal number of administering and non-administering states was set up "to enumerate the principles which should guide members in determining whether or not the obligation exists to transmit the information called for in Article 73e of the Charter of the United Nations."[36]

The following principles were adopted by the assembly:

(1) An obligation exists to transmit information under Article 73e on territories of the colonial type.

(2) The obligation to transmit information ceases as soon as a territory obtains "a full measure of self-government."

(3) The obligation constitutes an international responsibility.

(4) There is a *prima facie* duty to transmit in respect of a territory which is geographically separate and is distinct ethnically and/or culturally from the administering state.

(5) Additional elements, *inter alia*, administrative, political, juridical, economic, or historical may be considered; if they operate to subordinate the territory to the metropolitan State, then the obligation subsists.

(6) A full measure of self-government may be attained through a) independence, b) free association with another state, and c) integration with an independent state.

(7) Free association should be freely expressed through democratic means and freedom to change the status should be retained. The associated territory should retain autonomy over its internal constitution.

(8) Integration should be on a basis of complete equality between the peoples.

(9) Integration should be the result of the freely expressed wishes of the people in a universal adult suffrage of a people that

35. *See also UNYB* (1953), pp. 527–29.

36. Res. 1467(XIV) of 12 December 1959. The committee consisted of India, Mexico, Morocco, the Netherlands, Great Britain, and the United States.

have attained a sufficient degree of development to be capable of a responsible choice.

(10) The transmission of information is limited to constitutional propriety and security requirements but this relates to the *quantum* of information and does not relieve a member of its obligations under Chapter 11 of the Charter.

(11) The constitutional considerations are limited to those arising from the relations with the administering power.

(12) Only in exceptional circumstances can information under Article 73e have security aspect.[37]

By virtue of Article 73 of the Charter, colonies are now matters of international concern *pro tanto*; an administering power cannot legally designate them as integral parts of its territory so as to exclude proper international interest. The Twelve Principles are an important interpretation of Article 73, a significant development of international law with regard to colonies, and have been acquiesced in by the major colonial powers. In considering whether to recognise an entity as an independent state, or to admit a new member into the United Nations, or to grant internal self-government or independence to a colony, states have recourse to these principles.[38] It may be expected that colonial powers should be reluctant to lose their colonies and therefore resent outside influence that militates against the *status quo*, but it is also natural for human beings to seek fundamental human rights for themselves and for others who may not have achieved them. The international responsibility undertaken under the Charter demands the extension of freedom to all peoples including dependent ones. The tasks of the United Nations include the achievement of decolonization at the earliest possible time and a world order in which all peoples would enjoy fundamental human rights including self-determination without distinction of race, colour, sex, class or religion.[39]

6. The Resolution on the Granting of Independence to Colonial Countries and Peoples, 1960

The Resolution on Independence was originally proposed by Prime Minister Nikita Khrushchev of the Soviet Union during his address to

37. Res. 1541(XV) of 14 December 1960; voting was 69 to 2, with 21 abstentions. *See UNYB* (1960), pp. 504–510. Compare the criteria recommended by the Permanent Mandate Commission for the termination of mandates, p. 41 above.

38. *See also* Q. Wright, "Proposed Termination of the Iraq Mandate," 25 *AJIL* (1931), p. 436.

39. *See also* Q. Wright, "Self-determination and Recognition," 98 *Recueil des Cours* (1959), esp. pp. 193–5.

the General Assembly on 23 September 1960. His resolution aimed at "the complete and final liberation of peoples languishing in colonial bondage." There were bitter exchanges between the Communist and Western delegates. Welcoming the Soviet initiative, forty-three Afro-Asian delegates substituted another resolution in the hope of getting the widest consensus. Many of them pointed to the similarity of its principles to earlier declarations of conferences in Bandung (1955),[40] Accra (1958), Monrovia (1959), and Addis Ababa (1960). While appreciating the work of the United Nations in decolonisation, they thought that progress was slow and pointed to the ills of racial discrimination as manifested in the apartheid policy of South Africa, stressed the importance of economic freedom which is essential to political freedom, and resented interference in the internal affairs of former colonies. After a lively debate in which some of the colonial powers defended the progress of decolonisation, the Soviets tried to reintroduce their original resolution. The Latin-Americans supported the Afro-Asian resolution but favoured a wider application, while the United States accused the USSR of introducing a "new lethal colonialism" in its area of influence. Resolution 1514(XV) of 14 December 1960 was adopted by 89 votes, none against and 9 abstentions.[41]

The resolution reaffirms faith in the Charter, in fundamental human rights, and in the equal rights of men and women and of nations large and small. It acknowledges that stability and friendly relations must be based on the principles of equal rights and self-determination. It answers to the yearnings of dependent peoples for freedom and forewarns that conflicts may result from its denial, thus constituting a serious threat to peace. It asserts that continued existence of colonialism impedes social, cultural and economic development of dependent peoples, prevents the development of international economic cooperation, and militates against universal peace. It affirms the right of peoples freely to dispose of their

40. The Bandung Conference of April 1955 declared on the problems of dependent peoples that "the Conference discussed the problems of dependent peoples and colonialism and the evils arising therefrom, and agreed (1) in declaring that colonialism in all its manifestations is an evil which should speedily be brought to an end; (2) in affirming that the subjection of peoples to alien subjugation, domination, and exploitation constitutes a denial of fundamental human rights, is contrary to the United Nations Charter, and is an impediment to the promotion of world peace and cooperation; (3) in declaring its support of the cause of freedom and independence for all such peoples; and (4) in calling upon the Powers concerned to grant freedom and independence to such peoples." Institute of Pacific Relations, "Selected Docs. of Bandung Conference," (26 May 1955), p. 33. See also C. E. Toussaint, "The Colonial Controversy in the United Nations," YBWA (1956).

41. Australia, Belgium, Dominican Republic, Great Britain, France, Portugal, South Africa, Spain, and the United States abstained.

natural wealth and resources upon the principles of international law and proclaims "the necessity of bringing to a speedy and unconditional end colonialism in all its forms and manifestations." It then sets out seven principles:

(1) The subjection of peoples to alien subjugation, domination and exploitation constitutes a denial of fundamental human rights, is contrary to the Charter of the United Nations and is an impediment to the promotion of world peace and co-operation.

(2) All peoples have the right to self-determination; by virtue of that right they freely determine their political status and freely pursue their economic, social, and cultural development.

(3) Inadequacy of political, economic, social, or educational preparedness should never serve as a pretext for delaying independence.

(4) All armed action or repressive measures of all kinds directed against dependent peoples shall cease in order to enable them to exercise peacefully and freely their right to complete independence, and the integrity of their national territory shall be respected.

(5) Immediate steps shall be taken, in the Trust and Non-Self-Governing Territories or all other territories which have not yet attained independence, to transfer all powers to the peoples of those territories, without any conditions or reservations, in accordance with their freely expressed will and desire, without any distinction as to race, creed or colour, in order to enable them to enjoy complete independence and freedom.

(6) Any attempt aimed at the total or partial disruption of the national unity and the territorial integrity of a country is incompatible with the purposes and the principles of the Charter of the United Nations.

(7) All States shall observe faithfully and strictly the provisions of the Charter of the United Nations, the Universal Declaration of Human Rights, and the present Declaration on the basis of equality, non-interference in the internal affairs of all States, and respect for the sovereign rights of all peoples and their territorial integrity.[42]

Although the resolution seeks the immediate liquidation of colonialism, this may, for practical purposes, be delayed for a reasonable period pending the preparedness of the people to assume the responsibility for their own administration. The practical effect of the resolution is to demonstrate the intention of the United Nations to apply maximum pressure on the administering powers to expedite the training for self-rule so that the colonial peoples can take over in the shortest possible

42. *See also UNYB* (1960), pp. 44–50.

time. Further, the transfer of power must be in accordance with the wishes of the people. This rules out a transfer to a minority regime against the wishes of the majority, as in the case of Rhodesia and, at the same time, prevents the grant of independence to a people who do not want it, provided they are politically capable of making a reasoned choice. The resolution is thus a reaffirmation of Resolution 742 on Factors, which states that a full measure of self-government may be attained not only by independence but also by free association or integration with another state provided such relations accord with the freely expressed wishes of the people in a universal adult suffrage. It does not set a time limit (a Soviet amendment to that effect was defeated) but seeks to ensure that independence is not unnecessarily delayed.[43] The resolution sets up no machinery; this was taken care of in a subsequent resolution.

In answer to the criticism that the resolution demands the immediate transfer of power in colonial territories, it may be pointed out that by 1960 most of the least-developed territories were those in which the people had been denied the opportunity of participating in government, as in Portuguese and Spanish territories and in the Belgian Congo. In this respect continued colonialism was hardly a blessing. Colonial powers are prone to delay, rather than expedite, independence. Nor has the resolution the effect of pushing small territories to independence against their wishes as they can always opt for association or integration with another state. In 1965 the Cook Islanders voted to be associated with New Zealand and this was approved by the General Assembly.[44] In 1967 the island of Puerto Rico reaffirmed its association with the United States in spite of accusations of colonialism against the United States from certain quarters. The West Indian islands of Antigua, Dominica, Grenada, St. Lucia and St. Kitts, Nevis, and Anguilla, with a population of 500,000, are associated with Great Britain with a unilateral right to end the association. On the other hand, the resolution does not offer false hopes to minorities within states, for it expressly refers to "alien subjugation," an essential qualification to "peoples" in "all peoples have the right to self-determination."

The resolution warns against the disruption of national unity and the territorial integrity of the new states that may be emerging from de-

43. Contrast Bowett, *American Society of International Law* (April 1966), p. 134: "However, the striking features of the 1960 Declaration—although this accords with the general trend of practice—are its emphasis on the need for the grant of independence or self-government, and second, its emphasis on the need for the grant of independence now."

44. Res. 2064(XX) of 16 December 1965.

pendence. Even though colonial boundaries were condemned by the All African Peoples Conference of Accra in 1958 and of Tunis in 1960, the trend was reversed by the African Summit Conference of Addis Ababa in 1963 urging respect for existing colonial boundaries.[45] The origins of dependence are irrelevant for the declaration applies equally to "Trust and Non-Self-Governing Territories or other territories which have not yet attained independence." The administration of any dependent territory is a trust to civilisation and is not intended to be a source of profit or prestige.

The eradication of colonialism is classed in the highest order of priority because of its pressing evils—a breach of the Charter and a hindrance to peace and cooperation. In the view of Malacela, then of the Special Committee, the resolution was

> at once a declaration of faith, a new inspiration to peoples still under colonial rule, and an expression of the universal desire to expedite the process of the liberation of colonial peoples. Henceforth the Declaration, together with the Charter provisions, was to form the framework within which the United Nations sought to encourage the accelerated advance of dependent peoples towards the goals of freedom and independence.[46]

There had been growing international concern over the administration of colonies since the end of the First World War. The "welfare and development" combined with the international accountability of the mandates and the "humane conditions of labour" for colonial peoples, under the League, had developed into the "progressive development towards self-government or independence" for the Trust Territories, the recognition that the interests of colonial peoples was paramount in their administration and the promotion of their "well-being" under Article 73 of the Charter. The resolution, which was the high-water mark of anti-colonialism, extends to all subject peoples the right of unimpeded progress to independence unless they themselves choose some other relations with other states.

Like other resolutions of the General Assembly, it is not binding *per se*. The fact, however, that it was unopposed even by the colonial powers increases the importance of this collective opinion of states on the issue. This wide acceptance and the fact that it was unopposed by the five Great Powers have led Tunkin to conclude that it has now at-

---

45. *See* proceedings of the Summit Conference of Independent African States (Addis Ababa, 1963).
46. J. W. S. Malacela, "The United Nations and Decolonisation of Non-Self-Governing Territories," *UN Monthly Chronicle*, vol. 4, no. 8, p. 88.

tained the character of international customary law.[47] Without going so far, Sukovic maintains:

These two declarations (the Universal Declaration of Human Rights and the Declaration on Independence) are intermediate between, on the one hand, the Charter which is an international treaty and, on the other hand, recommendations of the General Assembly which have no binding force.[48]

It has, at least, acquired a high order of obligatoriness within the United Nations. This view is supported by a) its relationship with the Charter, in which it reaffirms faith and the Universal Declaration of Human Rights, all of which states should observe "faithfully and strictly," and b) the use of the word "shall" in points 5 and 7, reducing the discretion of states on the question of self-determination for subject peoples.

Although a mere majority in the General Assembly does not instantly create law binding on all members, the circumstances of the resolution and its subject matter—colonial freedom—is such that a state acting against it sooner or later comes into such conflict with the colonial peoples themselves and with the great majority of states that the probability of a breach, or threat thereof, of international peace and stability arises.[49]

The preamble which declares that "all peoples have an inalienable right to complete freedom, the exercise of their sovereignty, and the integrity of their national territory" gives the view of the United Nations on the *locus* of sovereignty in a dependent territory. The declaration applies to colonialism in "all its manifestations" and thus encompasses economic and social factors as well as political.[50]

7. The Special Committee of Twenty-four

The General Assembly set up a committee of seventeen to make suggestions and recommendations on the progress and implementation of the Declaration on Independence. It was authorised to employ "all means which it will have at its disposal within the framework of the

47. G. I. Tunkin, *Droit International Public; Problemes Theoriques* (Paris, 1965), pp. 101 *et seq.*

48. Olga Sukovic, "The Colonial Question in the Charter and in the Practice of the United Nations," *International Problems of the Institute of Politics and Economy* (Belgrade, 1966), p. 73.

49. But *see*, e.g., "If no limits are set to the process of interpretation other than the obtaining of the required majority, we may find the Assembly assuming the functions of an international legislature without having been invested with the power. If it were to be converted into a legislature it is widely thought that the voting system might have to be altered." H. Waldock, *Recueil des Cours* (1962), 106:34.

50. *See also* p. 91 on the effect of the resolutions of the General Assembly.

procedures and modalities which it shall adopt for the efficient discharge of its functions."[51] This includes visiting when and where possible and necessary, consultation with anybody, and the receipt of petitions for which a subcommittee was formed. The committee could hold its meetings anywhere within or outside the Secretariat. In 1963 its membership was enlarged to twenty-four.

As it had since 1965, the Special Committee held some of its annual meetings in African capitals near colonies in southern Africa in order to facilitate the appearance of nationalist leaders. This gave it a close experience of conditions in those territories and thus enabled it to give more effective help. It has afforded freedom-fighters a valuable platform to air their complaints and recommended that they should be given international assistance. By according them a special status, it impliedly recognises their function in the administration of areas forcefully liberated.

The committee has been mostly responsible for the large number of resolutions passed by the General Assembly in condemnation of colonialism and in crystallizing opposition to the system. The eradication of colonialism will *ipso facto* render its existence redundant unless it is given new functions such as development and the prevention of external exploitation.

8. The Application of Self-determination to Non-Self-Governing Territories

Colonialism has undergone a drastic change in the last fifty years. Whereas the old international law regulated its expansion vis-à-vis the colonial powers, the present law is directed toward its final liquidation in the interest of humanity at large.[52] From this standpoint, Chapters 11, 12, and 13 represent a transitional stage. This change was enhanced by the enlarged membership of the United Nations, about two-thirds of which consisted of former colonial territories. The few advocates of colonialism belong to "an anachronistic fringe on the right."[53]

51. Res. 1654(XVI) of 27 November 1961. *See also UNYB* (1961), pp. 44–56.

52. *See also* H. K. Jacobson, "The United Nations and Colonialism: A Tentative Appraisal," *International Organisation* (1962), p. 47. "The League was chiefly concerned with improving standards of colonial rule, while the United Nations' concern has been to liquidate colonialism."

53. Rupert Emerson, "Self-determination Revisited in the Era of Decolonisation," *Occasional Papers in International Affairs* (Harvard Center for International Affairs) no. 9 (1964), p. 5. *See also* B. V. A. Röling, *International Law in an Expanded World* (Amsterdam, 1960); Lissitzyn, "International Law in a Divided World," *International Conciliation* (1963); Higgins, *The Development of International Law*, p. 103.

The continued survival of the system is so frowned upon that every device is employed to counter the determination of reluctant colonial po ⁊ers to prolong it. A Carnegie Foundation inquiry on the United Nations received a reply from the Indian Council of World Affairs which stated: "The division of dependent areas into non-self-governing and trust territories was merely an accident of history; the former were the possessions of victors of the two World Wars and the latter those of the defeated."[54] This explains the little regard many members have for the distinction between the two categories—both are dependent territories to which self-determination is equally applicable. There were early attempts, renewed in 1953 and 1959, to assimilate the territories, but all were unsuccessful.[55] The Charter provisions have been liberally interpreted and the practice has since developed of sending visiting missions to colonies with the consent of the colonial power or visiting capitals near them if the administering power refused to cooperate. Petitions have also been received, thereby associating the people more closely with the work of the United Nations in liberating them.

The General Assembly has condemned the setting up of military bases in colonies as incompatible with the Charter and the true interest of those peoples. After a study of colonies in southern Africa, the Special Committee concluded that foreign international firms were aiding regimes which were guilty of colonial oppression and urged members to prevent their nationals from carrying on those activities that may help to perpetuate colonialism. The United Nations has since passed resolutions condemning those States that give economic support to the oppressive regimes of southern Africa.

Indonesia provided the first test case of Article 73. After the defeat of the Japanese, the Netherlands government in the Linggadjati Agreement of March 1947 recognised the Indonesian government as the *de facto* authority after it agreed to maintain federal relations with the Netherlands in the united states of Indonesia. When subsequently it rejected the proposals, the Dutch tried to impose the federation militarily. The matter was brought to the Security Council as a threat to peace in that part of the world. The Council set up a good-offices committee[56]

---

54. Indian Council of World Affairs, *India and the World* (1957), p. 101.

55. Thus a Cuban suggestion that reports under Article 73 should be dealt with by the Trusteeship Council. India tried to extend trusteeship to all non-self-governing territories, or at least to some of them. *Off. Rec. of the General Assembly*, 2nd Sess., 4th Comm. (1947), p. 217. Poland made the same proposal for the good of the inhabitants. Doc. A/c4./152 (1948), p. 10.

56. Res. S/459.

and later raised it to the United Nations Commission for Indonesia to help achieve a peaceful settlement. In this case all the permanent members acted together and brought about a speedy settlement.[57]

The question of independence for Tunisia and Morocco was brought to the United Nations in 1952 by Arab states. In Resolution 612(VII) on Morocco, the assembly expressed the confidence that France would endeavour to further the effective development of full political institutions in conformity with the purposes and principles of the Charter. It refused to allow the presence of a large French minority in Algeria to obstruct that country's independence. The French colons had the option to become citizens or remain foreigners, enjoying individual rights under international law but their presence was not to affect the self-determination of the people to choose independence, merger with France, or membership of the French Union in accordance with the freely expressed wishes of the people. Nor was the presence of a Turkish minority in Cyprus to delay its independence. The argument was rejected that self-determination was to be applied to the communities separately. Turkey could inquire into safeguards for the minority and the proper role of the United Nations was to enforce those safeguards. The ultimate goal for a minority must be its reintegration with the majority on a basis of nondiscrimination. Military and strategic considerations were not to outweigh the right of a people to self-determination.

The meaning of self-determination for West New Guinea was one of the issues discussed during the eleventh session of the assembly. Did it mean independence, reintegration with Indonesia or with the rest of the island? After a period of administration by Indonesia, the territory was integrated following consultations carried out through electoral colleges rather than plebiscites.[58]

The issue of Southern Rhodesia first arose in the United Nations in 1961 when Britain objected to submitting reports on the territory, as it had been doing. It argued that in a referendum of 1922 the people chose self-government rather than integration with South Africa and have since (1923) been self-governing, nor was that status changed by the constitution of 1961. A subcommittee set up to study the question found that Rhodesia was not self-governing within the meaning of the Charter, whereupon the assembly decided that Britain should call a

---

57. See also UNYB (1946–7), pp. 338–341; (1948–9), pp. 212–237; M. S. Rajan, The United Nations and Domestic Jurisdiction (New York, 1961), pp. 136–151.
58. See also Repertory of Practice of United Nations Organs, vol. 5, Doc. 2488C.21/64; Background Paper on Chapter XI of the Charter, Doc. ST/DP I/Ser.A/73/Rev. I.

constitutional conference on a basis of "one-man-one-vote." It pressed for the release of political prisoners,[59] warned against the transfer of power, armed forces, and military aircraft to a racialist regime that did not represent all the people,[60] reaffirmed "the inalienable right of the people of Southern Rhodesia to self-determination and independence," and urged all members to use their influence to realise the legitimate aspirations of the people.[61] When on 11 November 1965 the regime seized independence unilaterally, the assembly reacted with a series of resolutions requesting members to break economic relations with Rhodesia and imposed other sanctions.[62] The British prime minister reaffirmed that "the existence of sufficiently representative institutions would be a condition of the grant of independence."[63] This attitude was also explained as the Doctrine of NIBMAR (No Independence Before Majority African Rule). At the Lagos Prime Ministers' Conference, the British prime minister expressed the hope that sanctions would bring down the illegal regime in "a matter of weeks, rather than months," but this forecast was completely unfounded. The Security Council tightened the sanctions and reaffirmed the right of the people to self-determination.[64] Negotiations in 1968 between Harold Wilson and Ian Smith held on the 'Tiger' and 'Fearless' failed to resolve the issue.

The government of Rhodesia has continued to defy world opinion in its actions and utterances. An apartheid-type constitution was overwhelmingly endorsed by a predominantly white electorate on 20 June 1969 in a referendum that gave the green light to the declaration of a republic and the severance of the remaining constitutional links with

---

59. Res. 1745(XVI) of 23 February 1962.

60. Res. 1883(XVII) of 14 October 1963.

61. Res. 1889(XVIII) of 6 November 1963, *UNYB* (1963), pp. 469–81.

62. Res. 216(XX) of 12 November 1966; 217(XX) of 20 November 1966; and 221(XXI) of April 1967.

63. Great Britain, *Parl. Debs.* (3 November 1964), pp. 66–7.

64. Res. 232 of 16 December 1966. The Southern Rhodesian High Court gave the regime *de facto* recognition in 1967 (*Madzimbamuto* v. *Lardner-Burke, Baron* v. *Ayre*) and *de jure* recognition in 1968. See also R. S. Welsh, "The Constitutional Case in Southern Rhodesia," 83 *LQR* (1967), pp. 64–88; P. C. Rao, "The Rhodesian Imbroglio," 6 *Indian JIL* (1966), p. 233; M. S. McDougal and W. M. Reisman, "Rhodesia and the United Nations: The Lawfulness of International Concern" 62 *AJIL* (1968), p. I; Zdenek Cervenka, "Legal Effects of Non-recognition of Southern Rhodesia's Unilateral Declaration of Independence in International Law," *Casopis pro mezi narodni pravo Roenik* (1967), 2:120–9 and 3:225–38; J. L. Cefkin, "The Rhodesian Question at the United Nations," 21 *International Organisation* (1968), pp. 649–669; C. Robinowitz, "UN Sanctions and Rhodesia" 7 *Virginia JIL* (1967).

Britain. The new constitution gives Africans sixteen out of sixty-six seats in the assembly, with the remote possibility of an increase corresponding to their share of the total income tax paid. It is envisaged, in theory, that African representation will gradually increase until it reaches parity with that of the whites. Presently, the African share of the income tax collected is .5 percent; an increase to 50 percent is, therefore, a distant prospect. The democratic principle of majority rule is ruled out as a possible political and constitutional development.

According to the Security Council Committee on Southern Rhodesia, the impact of sanctions has been diluted by a combination of factors. The Rhodesian economy has been geared to domestic consumption, thus minimising the effect of reduced foreign exchange earning. Imports have been substituted by new industries and agriculture is diversified. Malawi, Portugal, and South Africa have refused to comply with the sanctions and are actively engaged in breaking them. Zambia, Botswana and Congo (Kinshasha) are unable to cut off all links with Rhodesia because of their economic dependence on it. Sanctions have been evaded by the use of forged papers and business has been carried on with countries like Japan and West Germany.[65] In its second report dated 12 June 1969 it revealed that the volume of trade with Portugal and South Africa amounted to £44m. sterling. A resolution that would have requested all states to cut off links with Salisbury failed to be adopted on 24 June 1969.

Amidst the exasperation of OAU members and the anger of the great majority of United Nations members, Rhodesia declared itself a republic on 3 March 1970 in a desperate act that forbodes ill for black and white relations in southern Africa. An Afro-Asian attempt in March 1970 to compel the United Kingdom to use force was frustrated by United Kingdom's fourth and United States's first vetoes in the Security Council. United Kingdom's fifth veto was used against a resolution that re-emphasized the doctrine of NIBMAR. However, the United Nations still has the means, if not yet the will, of positively helping to achieve the right of the people to self-determination and to avert the impending catastrophe.

The United Nations has treated colonialism as a denial of human rights and has quoted the Charter of the United Nations, the Universal Declaration of Human Rights, and the Declaration on Independence in support of its eradication. The denial of "one-man-one-vote," the imposition of a constitution contrary to the wishes of the bulk of the

---

65. UN Docs. S/8954 of 30 December 1968 and S/9252 of 12 June 1969.

population, and the denial of equal rights and liberty are treated as contrary to international law.[66]

The United Nations regards colonialism as a threat to world peace and stability. One of the preambles of the Universal Declaration of Human Rights warns that "it is essential, if man is not to be compelled to have recourse, as a last resort, to rebellion against tyranny and oppression, that human rights should be protected by the rule of law."[67] The close affinity of colonialism with what appears to be white racism and the poverty of the ex-colonial states which now constitute *le tiers monde* emphasize the global threat posed by continued colonialism.[68]

The use of force for colonial liberation has evoked some controversy. It was approved by the Conference of Jurists of Afro-Asian Countries held in Conakry in October 1964, which resolved that "All struggles undertaken by the peoples for the national independence or for the restitution of the territories or occupied parts thereof, including armed

66. *See also* J. E. S. Fawcett, "Security Council Resolution on Rhodesia" 41 *BYBIL* (1965–1966), p. 112. "But to the traditional criteria for the recognition of a regime as a new State must now be added the requirement that it shall not be based upon a systematic denial in its territory of certain civil and political rights, including in particular the right of every citizen to participate in the government of his country, directly or through representatives elected by regular, equal and secret suffrage. This principle was affirmed in the case of Rhodesia by the virtually unanimous condemnation of the unilateral declaration of independence by the world community, and by the universal withholding of recognition of the new regime which was a consequence."

67. *See also* the preamble to the draft resolution in the Committee of Friendly Relations: "Convinced that the subordination of peoples to foreign dependence, domination and exploitation constitutes a major obstacle to the promotion of international peace and security." Doc. A/AC 125/L 48 of 27 July 1967.

The last stage of colonialism in Africa has become inextricably intertwined with white racism and is more agressive to their victims and to neighbouring African states. Portuguese armed forces, acting in conjunction with European mercenaries and Guinean dissident elements, commenced an invasion of the Republic of Guinea on 22 November 1970. An investigating committee of the Security Council confirmed Portuguese complicity. The Council condemned the invasion, demanded full compensation "for the extensive damage to life and property" and warned against a repetition. (Res. 290 of 5 December 1970). The abstention of France, Spain, United Kingdom and United States was no surprise to African states.

For its own part, the OAU called a special ministerial conference in Lagos on 9–11 December 1970. A resolution was adopted which condemned "in particular the NATO powers which allow, through their complicity and assistance, various attacks by Portugal against several African territories and states." It called upon its defence commission "to study ways and means of establishing adequate and speedy defence of African States" and requested its administrative secretary to prepare a draft convention "outlawing the recruitment, training, equipment and use of mercenaries as well as prohibiting the passage of such mercenaries and their equipment." It called for increased financial and material support for the freedom-fighters.

68. *See also* K. J. Twitchett, "The American National Interest and the Anti-colonial Crusade" *International Relations* (David Davis Memorial Institute of International Studies), vol. 3, no. 4, October 1967.

struggle, are entirely legal."[69] The Conference of Non-Aligned States held in Cairo in 1964 resolved that "[t]he process of liberation is irresistible and irreversible. Colonised peoples may legitimately resort to arms to secure the full exercise of their right to self-determination and independence if colonial powers persist in opposing their natural aspirations."[70] In the Lusaka Manifesto of 1969, approved by the United Nations General Assembly in 1970, the OAU members pledge themselves to give support to the freedom-fighters as long as "peaceful progress is blocked by actions of those at present in power in the States of Southern Africa."[71]

Both the Russians and Chinese approve of the use of force in colonial liberation and give material support where possible.[72] In 1970 the World Council of Churches decided to give financial support to freedom-fighters and a working group of the British Council of Churches reported in the same year: "to urge the people to avoid violence furthers the ends of the Governments of South Africa, South-West Africa, Rhodesia, Mozambique and Angola, who habitually employ violence to repress any move that would upset the rule of the privileged minorities." It added that unconstitutional action was the only option for the liberation of the people. The trend toward approval of the use of force followed the reluctance of Portugal and Spain (although the latter has since been cooperative) to liberate their colonies, increased repression in Namibia, and the unilateral declaration of independence by a minority regime in Rhodesia. This use of force was extensively discussed in the Committee on Friendly Relations, although no agreement was arrived at. Some delegations proposed:

(1) The subjection of peoples to alien subjugation, domination and exploitation as well as any other forms of colonialism, constitutes a violation of the principles of equal rights and self-determination of peoples in accordance with the Charter of the United Nations and, as such, is a violation of international law.

69. *Le Monde* (25 October 1962).

70. 4 *Indian JIL* (1964), pp. 599, 603.

71. For the full text *see Review of the International Commission of Jurists,* no. 2 (June 1969), pp. 56–61; U. O. Umozurike, "International Law and Colonialism in Africa," 3(1) *EALR* (1970), pp. 47–82.

72. *See* R. A. Tuzmukhamedov in *Sovietskoe Gusudararstvo i Pravo,* no. 3 (1966) justifying the use of force for colonial liberation. But *see* H. W. Baade, ed., *The Soviet Impact on International Law* (New York, 1965), where Ginsburg's writing on "Wars of National Liberation and the Modern Law of Nations—the Soviet Thesis" criticises the Soviet doctrine. *See also* G. B. Starunshenko, "Abolition of Colonialism and International Law" in G. Tunkin, ed., *Contemporary International Law* (Moscow, 1967), pp. 77–96.

(2) Consequently peoples who are deprived of their legitimate right of self-determination and complete freedom are entitled to exercise their inherent right of self-defence, by virtue of which they may receive assistance from other states.[73]

Both Czechoslovakia[74] and Yugoslavia[75] proposed that "the prohibition of the use of force shall not affect . . . the right of nations to self-defence against colonial domination in the exercise of the right of self-determination."

Although the decision of the Special Committee of Twenty-four to approve the use of force in colonial liberation was primarily directed toward Rhodesia, South-West Africa, and Portuguese territories, the assembly has approved it as a general principle in all colonies where self-determination is forcefully denied.[76] The United Nations has given immense moral support and publicity to nationalists struggling for freedom and states supporting them secretly with materials feel they are fulfilling a humanitarian object which the niceties of law and the lack of effective defensive force prevents them from doing openly.[77]

In the view of Jennings, armed colonial struggle belongs to "an area where force may still be employed for the purpose virtually of bringing about a change in territorial sovereignty, without necessarily impinging upon the prohibitions on the use of force laid down by international law."[78] It has been shown that international law is increasingly recognising the rights of individuals and groups of individuals. Individuals or peoples who are forcefully subjected to colonialism have the inherent right to regain freedom through the use of force.[79] The international

73. A/AC 125/L48 of 27 July 1967 sponsored by Algeria, Cameroon, Ghana, India, Kenya, Madagascar, Nigeria, Syria, UAR and Yugoslavia.

74. A/AC 119/L6.

75. A/AC 119/L7.

76. Res. 2105(XX), 2107(XX), 2189(XXI), 2160(XXI) and 2225(XXI), 2383 (XXIII), 2465(XXIII).

77. Calling for the liberation of all Africa, President Nkrumah of Ghana asserted in an address to the 15th session of the General Assembly on 29 September 1960 that the "possession of the colonies is now quite incompatible with membership of United Nations." Welcoming the decision of African heads of state in Addis Ababa (1963) to support the struggle for liberation, Nkrumah said that no African state could be considered safe "so long as a single colonial ruler remains on African soil." *West Africa* (29 June 1963).

78. R. Y. Jennings, *The Acquisition of Territory in International Law* (Manchester, 1963), p. 80.

79. *See also* K. Skubiszewski, "Use of Force by States, Collective Security, Law of War and Neutrality" in M. Sorensen, ed., *Manual of Public International Law* (New York, 1968), p. 771. "In the relations between the government and the governed the principle of self-determination and human rights and fundamental freedoms can be vindicated through resort to physical force conducted by the latter against the former."

community cannot be indifferent to a drawn-out colonial war that involves the death of a great number of people. A colonial war is essentially an international war for various reasons. Colonialism is an alien rule imposed by a foreign nation on the indigenous people. International law prohibits colonialism and the use of force to maintain it. On the other hand, the law supports the self-determination of colonial peoples who may legally defend themselves with the help of third states. The waging of a colonial war and the defence of the victims of colonial aggression are matters of international concern to which international-law rules apply on the conduct of war (the Hague Conventions of 1899 and 1907) and on the humanitarian treatment of the victims of armed conflict (the Geneva Conventions of 1949).[80] The whole of the Geneva Conventions should apply to colonial wars and not just Article 3, which deals with armed conflicts of a non-international character, particularly if the non-signatory accepts and applies the provisions. Moreover, the principles of the conventions being part of international customary law are binding on all peoples and states.

Although reasonable assistance to freedom-fighters to enable them to regain their freedom is permissible in international law, assistance to a colonial power or to an illegal regime to enable it to suppress a people in colonial bondage is prohibited both as intervention and as contrary to the principle of self-determination. The purposes of the Charter of the United Nations include the development of friendly relations among nations based on respect for the principle of equal rights and self-determination. The Declaration on Non-intervention (Article 6) also declares "All States shall contribute to the complete elimination of racial discrimination and colonialism in all its forms and manifestations."[81]

The intimate connection of colonialism with racial discrimination makes it so explosive and presents such a threat to peace and stability that the United Nations should, as a matter of urgency, deserving the

---

80. *See also* the resolution of the UN Conference on Human Rights held in Teheran on 22 April–13 May 1968 and approved by the General Assembly in Resolution 2444 of 19 December 1968 and Resolution 18 of the International Conference of the Red Cross held in Istanbul in September 1969 on the Status of Combatants in Non-International Armed Conflicts; H. Bokor-Szego, *New States and International Law* (Budapest, 1970), pp. 47–51.

81. *See*, e.g., Res. 2160(XXI) of 30 November 1966. "Any forcible action, direct or indirect, which deprives peoples under colonial domination of their right to self-determination and freedom and independence and of their right to determine freely their political status and pursue their economic, social and cultural development constitutes a violation of the Charter of the United Nations."
It follows that the supply of arms by certain western powers to the repressive regimes of southern Africa is contrary to international law since these arms are used for the perpetuation of colonialism, apartheid, or minority rule, all of which deny human rights to sections of the population.

support of all states, promote the transition of dependent peoples from dependence to independence. The organisation should become, as it were, "an agent of progress and evolution."[82] Although Dugard condemns as illegal the support given to the freedom-fighters of southern Africa by the OAU, he regrets that the United Nations resolutions on the area have been persistently ignored by South Africa and Portugal and then warns:

> Already the situation may be beyond the reach of a peaceful settlement, but, if inter-racial violence is not to explode in Southern Africa, a concerted eleventh hour effort by the international community is vital. A peaceful settlement through the good offices of the United Nations would appear to be unlikely as both Portugal and the Republic of South Africa have revealed their dislike for the World Body. This places a heavy responsibility upon those Western States towards which Portugal and South Africa are relatively well disposed, particularly the United States, Britain and France, for a settlement which upholds the letter of the Charter but which, at the same time, ensures respect for human rights and fundamental freedoms in Southern Africa.[83]

It is unrealistic to expect the governments of Rhodesia, Namibia, and the Portuguese territories in Africa to relinquish power by gentle persuasion. The former British High Commissioner in Salisbury, Lord Alport, confessed that the Africans would have to use force to regain their rights.[84] This is a correct, though regrettable, conclusion. The essence of an international right is that the international community will support its acquisition and prevent, or at least condemn, its denial. Surreptitious or moral support to freedom-fighters in order to enable them to regain a right internationally recognised is not enough. The international community must be prepared to take effective measures, including the use of force, to end colonialism forcefully imposed provided such force is commensurate with, and not excessive to, the force illegally applied.

In order to avoid the responsibilities imposed by the Charter, Spain and Portugal, which joined the United Nations in 1955, argued that their colonies were not in fact "territories" within the meaning of Article 73e but integral parts of the respective metropolitan territories in accordance

---

82. Wolfgang Friedmann, *The Changing Structure of International Law* (London, 1964), p. 38, referring to the present role of international law and especially of the law of international organisations.

83. C. J. R. Dugard, "The OAU and Colonialism," 16 *ICLQ.* (1967), p. 190.

84. *The Standard* (Tanzania), 3 March 1970.

with their internal constitution.[85] The purpose of this argument was to frustrate the desire of the peoples for self-determination. By their incorporation, the territories not only lose their separate identity but are also deprived of their guarantee of full human rights on the basis of nondiscrimination and equality. Portuguese and Spanish presence in those territories dates back to the period when the inhabitants had the least freedom of choice. The attempt to merge colonies with metropolitan territories without first ascertaining the wishes of the people in a universal adult suffrage is contrary to modern international law and to the law of the Charter in particular and has been rightly rejected by the majority of members of the United Nations.[86] Spain has since been cooperating with the Special Committee and in 1968 granted independence to Equatorial Guinea but Portugal remains unmoved in its stand. The outbreak of rebellion in Angola brought to the surface the seething discontent that had long been suppressed. The United Nations followed up with condemnatory resolutions decrying discrimination, deprivation of freedom, forced labour, and other repressive acts.[87] Subsequent resolutions have been passed reaffirming and extending the earlier ones.

A resolution proposed in the Special Committee on Friendly Relations maintains that "territories under colonial domination do not constitute integral parts of the territory of States exercising colonial rule over them."[88] Similarly, a Czechoslovakian draft states that "territories which, contrary to the Declaration on the Granting of Independence to Colonial Countries and Peoples, are still under colonial domination cannot be considered as integral parts of the territory."[89] The assembly in Resolution 1542(XV) of 15 December 1960 and the Security Council in Resolution S/4835 of 9 June 1961 declared that Angola is a non-self-governing territory within the meaning of Article 73 and the Resolution

85. Doc. A/C. 4/385.

86. As in Res. 1747(XVI).

87. Res. 1742(XVI) of 30 January 1961 (opposed only by Spain and Portugal) and 1807(XVIII). *See also* J. S. Bains, "Angola, the United Nations, and International Law," 3 *Indian JIL* (1963), p. 63 and *Report of the Subcommittee on the Situation in Angola*, Doc. A/4978 (1962), GA, 16th sess., suppl. no. 16. "The Portuguese authorities face a historic choice: whether to continue to rely on the use of force, with the inevitable miseries, economic losses, and uncertainties; or to respond to world public opinion and take measures to reassure the population, ensure the return of refugees, and build a new relationship with the people of Angola. Much time has been lost in a critical situation, with the casualties and the bitterness mounting in Angola. What is needed is readiness to understand the new forces in the world, courage to accept change, and wisdom to formulate and pursue viable means towards an enduring peaceful solution."

89. Doc. A/AC.125/L.16, part VI.

88. Doc. A/AC.125/L.48 of 27 July 1967.

on the Granting of Independence. Referring to Portuguese colonies the Guinean delegate affirmed that "reforms aimed at assimilation are not compatible either with Resolution 1514(XV) or with the African revolutionary movement as a whole." The Ghanaian delegate, A. Quaison-Sackey, insisted:

> The events of the last few years, especially in Africa, must surely have swept away any illusions that dependent peoples are content to wait indefinitely for their freedom, or that they will be willing, unless under exceptional circumstances and by their own free will, to settle for anything short of true national independence.[90]

The lack of precision in Chapter 11 has led some to argue that the Charter envisaged self-government for colonies and that this may or may not include independence.[91] Nothing stops dependent peoples from opting for integration, association, self-government, or autonomy as long as the choice accords with the wishes of the people, but he choice certainly includes independence.

The decolonisation of Gibraltar is complicated by the claim of title to the territory by Spain which claims to be "the victim of the colonial situation." Britain, as colonial power, relies on self-determination as the mode for settlement. In Resolutions 2070(XX) and 2231(XXI) the General Assembly invited the two powers to negotiate the decolonisation of the territory. The latter resolution included the phrase "taking into account the interest of the people of the Territory." Whereas Britain took this to mean that the Gibraltarians would be allowed to express their wishes, Spain interpreted it to mean that the interest, not necessarily the wishes, of the people will be taken into account. Agreement proved difficult, so Britain decided to resort to a referendum but the Special Committee of Twenty-four pointed out that the "holding by the Administering Power of the envisaged referendum would contradict the provisions of Resolution 2231(XXI)." The referendum was nevertheless held but the assembly resolved that it contravened its earlier resolution.

90. "Progress toward Charter Aims in the World's Dependent Territories" 6 *UN Review* (5 May 1960), p. 12. *See also* A. Coret, "La Declaration de l'Assemblee Generale de l'ONU sur l'octroi de l'indépendence aux pays et aux peuples coloniaux," 15 *Revue Juridique et Politique d'Outre*, Mer 4, (October–December 1961), p. 597.

91. Kelsen, *The United Nations*, pp. 558–9. "In general usage of language the term 'self-government' is sometimes used as identical with 'independence.' The Charter, however, differentiates 'self-government' and 'independence,' 'independence' meaning—in the Charter—'sovereignty.' " *See also* Goodrich and Hambro, *The United Nations*, pp. 422–3; Hall, *Mandates, Dependencies and Trusteeship*, pp. 28–31; Ross, *The Constitution of the United Nations*, pp. 184–5.

The question arises, Why does the assembly discard the principle of self-determination in the decolonisation of Gibraltar? M. S. Esfandiary, who was the *rapporteur* of the Fourth Committee during the twenty-second session of the General Assembly gives the following reply:

Part of the answer may be found in the fact that the UN has taken into account that the people of Gibraltar have been beneficiaries of colonialism rather than victims of it. The present inhabitants of the Rock have been brought into this territory in order to serve the needs of the administering power. The present population, having through the years gradually replaced the original Spanish population of the territory and having completely changed the cultural and social makings of the society of Gibraltar to serve their own peculiar needs, is not much interested in the idea of decolonisation. If left alone, they would probably wish to retain their present status. Under the winds of change and subject to pressures for decolonisation, they have expressed their desire to opt for associated statehood with the United Kingdom.[92]

The distinction between the "victims" and "beneficiaries" of colonialism in distinguishing the inhabitants of a territory who have settled there for a long period of time appears to be artificial and unsatisfactory in the present circumstances. However the inhabitants of the Rock got there, the fact is that Gibraltar has become their home as in the case of the Falkland Islands. The right of self-determination is exercisable by the people of Gibraltar, who should be allowed freely to determine their future. A compromise proposal may be found in one that grants the territory associate status with Britain in accordance with the wishes of the people while granting Spain defence, economic, and communications facilities.[93]

9. *Ministates.* Independence might indeed prove harmful to certain small territories. A true appreciation of their own interests might lead them to choose internal autonomy, association with other states, or integration with them. In Resolution 2064 of 16 December 1965 the assembly found that the people of Cook Islands who chose to be associated with New Zealand "have attained full internal self-government" and reaffirmed the responsibility of the United Nations to assist them "in

---

92. From a discussion of the problems of ministates, *American Society of International Law* (April 1968), pp. 174–5.

93. *See also* J. E. S. Fawcett, "Gibraltar: The Legal Issues," 43 *International Affairs* (1967), p. 236; D. J. Heasman, "The Gibraltar Affair," *International Journal of the Canadian Institute of International Affairs*, vol. 22 (2) (1967), pp. 265–277.

the eventual achievement of full independence, if they so wish at a future date."[94]

The following suggestions have been made for small territories:

(1) Objective consideration should be given to the "problems arising from the small size and population, geographical location and limited natural resources"[95] of the territory.

(2) The population of the territory should be given the opportunity to exercise their right of self-determination in full freedom.

(3) The administering powers should fully cooperate with the United Nations in inviting it to supervise the processes of the exercise of the right of self-determination.

(4) The constitution of the territory should include an option for independence at any time in the future and should provide for genuine self-government in all internal matters.[96]

In the case of the West Indian Islands associated with Britain—Antigua, St. Kitts-Nevis-Anguilla, Dominica, St. Lucia, St. Vincent, and Granada—the legislature of an associated state may under Schedule 2 of the West Indian Act terminate the status as from the date set out in the law. This requires a majority of two-thirds in the legislature and in a referendum.[97] Commenting on the status of the islands, Margaret Broderick points out:

> In the eyes of Whitehall and international organisations, the Associated States are totally dependent territories, even though United Kingdom no longer reports on them to the United Nations under Article 73 of the Charter.
>
> Given a desire on the part of the Associated States themselves, some of the international organisations, and the encouragement of the Secretary-General of the United Nations, an evolution to some

94. See also P. M. Allen, "Self-determination and Independence" *International Conciliation*, no. 560 (1966), p. 29. See also on the status of the Cook Islands, Aikman, Davidson, and Wright, *A Report to Members of the Legislative Assembly of the Cook Islands on Constitutional Developments* (Rarotonga, 1963); D. Stone, "The Rise of the Cook Islands Party 1965," 74 *Journal of the Polynesian Society;* "Self-determination in the Cook Islands," 1 *Journal of Pacific History;* J. F. Northey, "Self-determination in the Cook Islands" 74 *Journal of the Polynesian Society;* S. A. de Smith, "The Cook Islands," *Annual Survey of Commonwealth Law* (1965), 1:30–35. See also P. E. Kilbride, "The Cook Islands Constitution," 1 *New Zealand Universities Law Review* (1963–5), pp. 571–6.

95. GAOR, 19th sess. (1964–5), Annexes no. 8, part I, para 164.

96. "Micro-States and the United Nations," *International Conc.* (September 1966), p. 90.

97. Criticism of the arrangements in the Special Committee of Twenty-four centered around the stringent requirements for a change in status and the absence of a plebiscite before the constitution was adopted. UN Doc. A/AC.109/SR. 491, p. 6.

degree of international personality on the part of the Associated States can be expected in time.[98]

She considers the present arrangements are fraught with problems which might produce tension and concludes:

> Perhaps a better solution to the problem of self-determination of small territories is that achieved by Western Samoa, which upon independence handed back to New Zealand a grant of power to act as its agent in matters of external affairs. No insoluble problems arise in this case; the protecting Power acts separately for the State, which alone incurs responsibility, and has sovereign status for the purposes of international personality.[99]

Probably the United Nations opposition to the arrangement might have been avoided if it had been allowed to participate in the ascertainment of the wishes of the islanders. The subsequent complaints to the Special Committee by Anguilla and St. Vincent showed that the arrangements were unpopular in certain quarters. So great was the discontent in Anguilla with the relations with St. Kitts and Nevis that it seceded in 1969. The British government crushed the rebellion using British air, sea, and land forces while declining to use force against the minority regime of Southern Rhodesia. In defence of the administering powers in cases like this, Professor de Smith suggests:

> If they had reason to believe that constructive and informed criticism of the kind made by the visiting missions of the Trusteeship Council would emerge, things might be different. But what the administering powers find at present is mounting verbal abuse and, on the part of the many delegates, a blank refusal to accept hard facts if they happen to find them unpalatable.[100]

There is a proposal to associate small territories with the United Nations without necessarily granting them independence. It is suggested that a special unit should be created in the Secretariat to serve as a clearing house for them, to advise on such things as the facilities available to them in the organisation, when they might usefully participate in United Nations activities, information on international affairs, security, and economic development. Such a relationship will be of special importance where there is no feeling of identity with the former colonial power because of remoteness, racial divergences, or other considerations. In areas like legal system and education, relations with the former

98. M. Broderick, "Associated Statehood—A New Form of Decolonisation" 17 *ICLQ* (1968), pp. 396-7.

99. Ibid., p. 403.

100. *American Society of International Law* (April, 1968), p. 183.

colonial power will be facilitated by the foundations already laid. In some cases association with the nearest mainland will be desirable. It is of the greatest importance that the choice should be freely made by the people after a thorough examination of the possible alternatives.[101]

10. *The Relevance of Article 2(7) of the Charter.* Article 2(7) of the United Nations Charter excludes from the jurisdiction of the United Nations "matters which are essentially within the domestic jurisdiction of any State." This is without prejudice to any enforcement action that the Security Council may take under Chapter 7.

Very often administering powers sought to exclude United Nations concern for non-self-governing territories under the article. The controversy ranged from the objection that mere discussion constitutes intervention to the insistence that intervention has got to be dictatorial. Just what constitutes intervention in the United Nations Order requires a delicate balance between legitimate international concern and exclusive state domain.

In the classical sense intervention "signifies dictatorial interference in the sense of action amounting to a denial of the independence of a State. It implies a peremptory demand for positive conduct or abstention—a demand which, if not complied with, involves a threat or recourse to compulsion, though not necessarily physical compulsion, in some form."[102] "The effect of this clause appears to be, first, to preclude the United Nations from penetrating actually into a State's jurisdiction, that is, usurping some of its governmental authority within its territory —unless the State itself consents; and, secondly, to preclude it from applying compulsion to a State with respect to internal matters, except in the case of enforcement action to maintain peace."[103]

As the Permanent Court stated in the Nationality Decrees in Tunis and Morocco,[104] a matter is removed from the domain of domestic jurisdiction when it becomes the subject of agreement with other states. Matters dealt with in the Charter include non-self-governing territories, fundamental human rights, and self-determination, all of which *ipso facto* and *ipso jure* are removed from the exclusive preserve of domestic

---

101. *See also* J. G. Rapport, "The Participation of Ministates in International Affairs," *American Society of International Law* (April 1968), p. 155; R. Fisher, "The Participation of Microstates in International Affairs," ibid., p. 164; P. W. Blair, *The Ministate Dilemma*, Carnegie Endowment for International Peace, Occasional Paper, no. 6 (October 1967).

102. Lauterpacht, *The International Protection of Human Rights* (1950), p. 167.

103. Waldock, *Human Rights in Contemporary International Law*, p. 11.

104. PCIJ, ser. B, no. 4 (1923).

jurisdiction. The designation of such territories, the transmission of information, and the cessation thereof are essential to the interpretation of Chapter 11 and therefore not covered by Article 2(7). Again, what is embraced within the ambit of the clause depends on the development of international relations so that matters usually covered by that clause may in fact develop beyond it.

The mere fact that a dispute is brought to an international body does not, however, constitute it a matter of international concern.[105] Vallat summarises the cases where domestic jurisdiction has been excluded as follows: a) international legal obligations under the Charter or other treaty, b) a threat or breach of international peace or security, c) human rights and fundamental freedoms, and d) non-self-governing territories and self-determination.[106]

The General Assembly has wide powers under Articles 10 and 14. Full amplitude has been given to these articles and to the principles and purposes of the organisation. A correspondingly restrictive interpretation of the domestic jurisdiction clause is permissible provided it accords with the letter and the spirit of the Charter. The essence of international agreements is to restrict and regulate individual sovereignties for the general good. The result of the United Nations involvement has been accelerated freedom for millions of people who have also acquired new concepts of government and new territorial frontiers in the exercise of the right to self-determination.

11. *The Effect of Assembly Resolutions on Non-Self-Governing Territories.* The effect of the General Assembly resolution on non-self-governing territories will be gathered from the effect of United Nations resolutions generally and of Chapter XI in particular.

Whereas some Security Council resolutions are legally binding on members, those of the assembly are not *ipso facto.* The assembly usually "requests," "urges," "takes note," "agrees to," etc., thereby indicating its limited competence.[107] Article 10 authorises the assembly to "discuss" any questions or matters within the scope of the Charter and "make recommendations," and Article 13 authorises it to initiate studies before making recommendations on matters within its scope. This contrasts

---

105. The Aaland Island Case, *LN Journal* (1921), suppl.; "Interpretation of Peace Treaties," *ICJ Rep.* (1950), p. 70; Q. Wright, "Self-determination and Recognition," 98 *Recueil des Cours* (1959) 3:171–195.

106. *Recueil des Cours* (1959), 99:242. See also M. S. Rajan, pp. 379–89; Higgins, pp. 76–130.

107. For other words habitually used by the assembly *see* F. B. Sloan, "The Binding Force of a 'Recommendation' of the General Assembly of the United Nations," *BYBIL* (1948), p. 3.

with Article 25 where members "agree to accept and carry out the decisions of the Security Council in accordance with the present Charter." At San Francisco, the Belgians proposed that the assembly should have "sovereign competence to interpret the provisions of the Charter in order to prevent a State from imposing its will by rejecting the opinion of the rest.[108] In turning down this proposal the subcommittee of Committee IV/2 thought it was undesirable to list possible modes of authoritative interpretation, but recommended that states disagreeing over the interpretation of the provisions should submit the matter to the International Court.[109] Because each organ of the United Nations is bound to interpret the Charter in carrying out its job, Vallat draws the conclusion:

> It is as a "law-applying" not as a "law-making" body that the General Assembly exercises the function of interpretation. It acts *ad hoc* in each case. Any particular interpretation adopted by the General Assembly has no more, and no less a legal effect than the decision in which it is involved.[110]

Professor Waldock points out:

> The Organisation is based on the principle of the sovereign equality of all its Members. For the chief object of this provision is to leave no doubt that, apart from the obligations to accept and carry out the decisions of the Security Council, Members retain the sovereign right of individual decision in all matter touching their own actions and interests. Thus acceptance at San Francisco of the principle of majority decision in the political organs of the United Nations did not also mean acceptance of their decisions as being binding upon individual member States, except in the case of the Security Council.[111]

Though by themselves not binding, the resolutions are of the greatest importance since they reflect, in the words of John Foster Dulles, United States representative, "the moral judgment of the conscience of the world" expressed in the "Town Meeting of the World."[112]

108.   3 UNCIO Docs., p. 339.

109.   13 UNCIO Docs., p. 668; also 9 UNCIO Docs., pp. 233–34.

110.   F. A. Vallat, "The Competence of the United Nations General Assembly," 97 *Recueil des Cours* (1959), p. 211.

111.   106 *Recueil des Cours* (1962), p. 211.

112.   UN Doc. A/C. 4/SR. 38 of 7 October 1947, p. 6. Resolutions on the internal administration of the United Nations are binding, such as resolutions dealing with budgetary matters (Article 17), the establishment of subsidiary organs (Article 22), requests for advisory opinions from the ICJ (Article 96), the suspension of rights and privileges of membership (Article 5) and the expulsion of members from the organisation (Article 6). *See also* "Certain Expenses of the United Nations," ICJ Rep. (1962), 151 at 163.

The repeated resolutions on non-self-governing territories are anti-colonialist and favour a quick end to colonial rule and the grant of self-determination to dependent peoples. These resolutions are the guidelines to United Nations practice and by their repetition and consistency constitute strong evidence of the practice of many states. Over the years they have strengthened the customary law of nations against colonialism even if hitherto its illegality was in doubt. Commenting on the interaction between state practice, United Nations practice, and customary law in the resolutions of the United Nations, Judge Tanaka said in his dissenting opinion:

> What is requested for customary international law is the repetition of the same practice; accordingly, in this case, resolutions, declarations, etc., on the same matter in the same, or diverse, organisations must take place repeatedly.
>
> Parallel with such repetition, declaration, etc., being considered as the manifestation of the collective will of the individual participant States, the will of the international Community can certainly be formulated more quickly and more accurately as compared with the traditional method of normative process. This collective, cumulative, and organic process of custom-generation can be characterised as the middle-way between the legislation by convention and the traditional process of custom making, and can be seen to have an important role from the viewpoint of the development of international law.
>
> In short, the cumulation of the authoritative pronouncements such as resolutions, declarations, decisions, etc., concerning the interpretation of the Charter by the competent organs of the international community can be characterised as evidence of the international custom referred to in Article 38, paragraph 1(b).[113]

A resolution in some cases has the effect of multilateral act of recognition of the status of a territory for the purposes of the organisation. Thus, through its resolutions the assembly recognised that territories have ceased to be non-self-governing or that territories claimed to be overseas provinces of the metropolitan territories by the administering

---

113. South-West Africa Cases *ICJ Rep.* (1966), p. 292. *See also* the separate opinions of Judges Klaestad and Lauterpacht in "Voting Procedure on Questions Relating to Reports and Petitions Concerning South-West Africa," *ICJ Rep.* (1955); Kelsen, 195–6; Johnson, "The Effect of Resolutions of the General Assembly," 32 *BYBIL* (1955–56), pp. 97–122; "Effect of Awards of Compensation by United Nations Administrative Tribunal," *ICJ Rep.* (1954), p. 47; G. R. Lande, "The Changing Effectiveness of the Resolutions of the General Assembly," in Falk and Mendlovitz, eds., *The United Nations* (1966), 3:227–35; K. Skubiszewski, "The General Assembly and Its Power to Influence National Action," ibid., pp. 238–47; O. Y. Asamoah, "The Legal Effect of Resolutions of the General Assembly," *Columbia Journal of Transnational Law*, vol. 3, no. 2 (1965); O. Y. Asamoah, *The Legal Significance of the Declarations of the General Assembly of the United Nations* (Hague, 1966), especially pp. 163–185.

powers are in fact non-self-governing territories within the meaning of the Charter. The resolutions welcoming the former colonial territories into the United Nations have the effect of recognising the international personality of the new entities, at least vis-à-vis the organisation without necessarily compelling individual recognition.[114] There has yet been no case of a member refusing to acknowledge the separate personality of a former colony, but the issue could conceivably arise if an administering power, such as Portugal, refused to acknowledge the separation of a colony that was forcefully liberated.

With regard to the effect of chapter 11, it has been argued that since it is entitled "Declaration on Non-Self-Governing Territories" it is a unilateral statement of policy imposing, at the highest, a moral obligation.[115] This view is however rejected by the great majority of members and by eminent juristic opinions. Van Asbeck maintains:

> Chapter XI contains . . . a Declaration of Duties in connection with the exercise of national Trusteeship—A Declaration, this title is somewhat misleading—which forms an integral part of the United Nations Charter, as accepted by all Members of the United Nations. The duties are international duties prescribed for the actual colonial administration by Members of the United Nations as well as for any future administration; it is therefore incorrect to assume that Chapter XI is a unilateral declaration by the 1945 colonial powers only.[116]

In the South-West Africa cases[117] the court said, concerning the mandate agreement:

> The fact that the Mandate is described in its last paragraph as a Declaration is of no legal significance. . . . Terminology is not a determinant factor as to the character of an international agreement or undertaking. In the practice of States and of international organisations and in the jurisprudence of international courts, there exists a great variety of usage; there are many different types of

114. *See also* Q. Wright, "Recognition and Self-determination," 21 *American Society of International Law* (1954–56), p. 37. "The States of the world recognise what territories have the status of independence, self-government, or non-self-government and may collectively extend such recognition through resolutions of the General Assembly." *See also* H. Waldock, 106 *Recueil des Cours* (1962), 2:26. "There are many internal constitutional matters with regard to which the decision of the Assembly or of other organs will have full legal effect because these organs are invested with the necessary constitutional powers. For example, admission to and suspension or termination of membership. . ."

115. E.g., Kaekenbeeck, *Recueil des Cours* (1947), p. 266.

116. Van Asbeck, "International Law and Colonial Administration," 29 *Transactions of the Grotius Society* (1954), p. 23.

117. *ICJ Rep.* (1962), p. 331.

acts to which the character of treaty stipulations has been attached.[118]

Though "declaration" was deliberately used to win the cooperation of colonial powers, the section is nevertheless binding like the rest of the Charter.

Twenty-five years of United Nations practice demonstrates the determination of the great majority of members that the principle of self-determination should be extended to colonial peoples and that their interests should be paramount in colonial administration. Had the assembly abstained each time an administering power objected, the story today would have been different. Under the weight of resolutions, some of the earlier objections now appear anachronistic and evasive. It will be a great victory for the organisation when the principle of self-determination is applied to the remaining colonial territories.[119]

118. *See also* "Conclusions, Entry into Force and Registration of Treaties," *ILC,* Doc. A/CN.4/148 of 3 July 1962. "Treaty means any international agreement in written form whether embodied in a single instrument or in two or more related instruments and whatever its particular designation (followed by a list of appellations including 'convention,' 'agreements,' and 'declaration') concluded between two or more States or other subjects of international law and governed by international law." *See also Harvard Research on International Law*, pp. 718–9, for declarations which have binding effect.

119. *See also* M. K. Nawaz, "Colonies, Self-Government, and the United Nations," *Indian YBIA* (1962); the separate opinion of Judge Jessup in *South-West Africa cases, ICJ Rep.* (1962), pp. 402–404. R. Emerson, "Colonialism, Political Development, and the United Nations," *International Organisation* (Summer 1965); R. Emerson, *Nations and Dependent Peoples*; A. P. Thorton, "Colonialism," 17 *International Journal* (1961–2), Canadian Institute of International Affairs.

V Trust Territories

1. At San Francisco

The peace conference of the First World War deprived the defeated belligerents of their subject territories and placed them under the guardianship of certain advanced nations until they were able to stand by themselves. It thus brought the hope for freedom to millions of people whose interests were considered to be best protected through a system of tutelage until they were fully capable of exercising the right of self-determination. This set a precedent for the Second World War, and long before it ended, discussions were held concerning the disposition of, and freedom for, enemy colonies. It was agreed at the Moscow Conference of 1943 that enemy colonies would be placed under United Nations control, and at Yalta in 1944 that trusteeship would be applied to (1) territories detached from the enemy, (2) mandate territories, and (3) any other territory that might voluntarily be placed under the system. It was also agreed that trusteeship should be subject to further consideration.

At San Francisco the "B" Section of the Working Paper on Dependent Territories dealt with trusteeship and was based on American proposals. The Consultative Group agreed that placing territories under Trusteeship should be subject to subsequent agreement. In Committee II/4, Australia and the Philippines wanted all dependent territories to be placed under trusteeship but did not press the point. Egypt opposed the "subsequent agreement" clause on the grounds of ambiguity and superfluity. It wanted the organisation to designate trust territories and thereby apply the system automatically to all enemy colonies and mandates. This suggestion was however opposed by South Africa, France, Great Britain, the Netherlands and the United States.

The "conservatory clause," which dealt with the protection of existing interests in mandates, evoked much controversy. The American delegate was anxious to apply the open-door policy but France and Britain argued that it would work against the interests of the people it was intended to protect. Arab states were concerned about the rights of Arabs in Palestine while the Jews canvassed for the non-diminution of the rights they had acquired under the Palestine mandate on emigration. A clause was adopted to the effect that until new agreements were arrived at, the rights already acquired by States and peoples remained unaltered. This also implied the right of the people to be administered under the mandate principles until other arrangements were made. The paragraph was not to be used for delaying negotiations or the conclusion of agreements for placing mandates under trusteeship.[1]

Self-government or independence, as appropriate, was agreed upon as one of the objectives of trusteeship. A Russian amendment, supported by China, to promote the development of the territories "towards self-government and self-determination with the active participation of peoples of these territories, having the aim to expedite the achievement by them of full independence" was rejected.[2] It was feared that too much stress on self-determination might create more difficulties in Palestine. A wording was adopted referring to "The basic objectives of the trusteeship system, in accordance with the Purposes of the United Nations" in which self-determination is mentioned.

The United States proposed a division into strategic and nonstrategic trust territories and this was included in Article 82 and 83. The proposal for a Trusteeship Council to function as the principal organ in respect of trust territories was adopted. All the permanent members of the Security Council were to be members of the Trusteeship Council.

China failed in its attempt at the Consultative Group to provide for action against a defaulting trustee but Egypt pressed the issue at the committee. It proposed that the organisation should have power to terminate trusteeship and declare a territory independent at the instance of the administering authority or any other state. It also proposed that trusteeship should be transferred to another state if the administering power violated the terms of trusteeship or ceased to be a member of, or was

1. 10 UNCIO Docs., p. 515.
2. 3 UNCIO Docs., p. 618 and 10 UNCIO Docs., p. 441.

suspended from, the United Nations.[3] Rejecting the proposal, Great Britain and the United States emphasised the voluntary aspect of placing a territory under trusteeship and argued that the administering power had already established physical presence: removing it would be difficult. Both presented a joint statement and on further inquiry by the chairman of the committee as to what would happen if the administering power ceased to be a member of the United Nations or was guilty of aggression, they replied that the Security Council could act in the latter event; in the former case, the administering power could continue to act provided it respected the agreement. Any other circumstance however "could only be judged by the General Assembly and the Security Council on the merits. . . . It is impossible to make provision in advance for such a situation," they concluded.[4]

2. The Charter Provisions

The International Trusteeship System provides for "the administration and supervision" of (1) territories held under the mandate, (2) territories which were detached from the enemy as a result of the Second World War, and (3) territories voluntarily placed under the system.[5] This last category was unknown under the mandate system which applied only to territories detached from the enemy as a result of the First World War and which were unable to stand by themselves. It was hoped that colonial powers would place, at least, some of their colonies under trusteeship, but this hope was never fulfilled. Each territory was brought under the system by a subsequent agreement between the administering power and the United Nations laying down the precise terms which together with amendments and alterations were approved by the General Assembly in the case of an ordinary trust territory and by the Security Council in that of a strategic trust territory.[6]

Under the League the distinction between A-, B-, and C-mandates reflected the political development of the territories and their capacity for self-government, whereas the distinction between strategic and non-strategic trust territories related to the security interests of the adminis-

---

3. 10 UNCIO Docs., p. 510.

4. Ibid. *See also* pp. 548, 601–2, and 620–21. The committee added a note that the statement "should not be regarded as an expression of the views of the committee." *See also* Russel and Muther, *A History of the United Nations* (1958), chapter 31. The calculated rejection of China's and Egypt's proposals was later to provide South Africa the opportunity of hanging on to South-West Africa in disregard of the mandate principles.

5. Article 77.

6. Article 81.

tering power. Under the mandate the administering power was simply a state; the Charter, however, provides, in addition, for a combination of states or the United Nations itself; the last was not tried out. There is no requirement that the administering power must be a member of the United Nations; Italy was already administering Eritrea before it joined the United Nations in 1955 and it participated in discussions in the Trusteeship Council affecting the territory.

The objectives of trusteeship are set out in Article 76 as: (1) *The furtherance of international peace and security.* The acquisition of colonial territories had in the past been a cause of disputes among the Great Powers. The neutralisation of the separate rights of states by setting up administrations for purposes internationally agreed, was considered to be conducive to world peace.[7] Colonialism is inherently unstable due to the desire of the people for freedom; it is a threat to world peace. Trust territories are also required to play their part in the maintenance of international peace and security for which only volunteer forces may be used as part of the international security system and not in furtherance of the aggressive designs of the administering power, as the Japanese had used their mandated Pacific territories. This contrasts with the nonmilitarisation policy of the League except for internal security and police, although in French mandates local troops could be used for defensive purposes anywhere.

(2) *The promotion of "political, economic, social and educational advancement of the inhabitants."* This compares with the "well-being and development" of the League Covenant, but goes farther in spelling out unequivocally "their progressive development towards self-government or independence as may be appropriate to the particular circumstances of each territory and its peoples and the freely expressed wishes of the peoples concerned. . . ." This leaves no room for arguing that the trust territories are integral parts of the administering state. Self-government as an alternative to independence is a choice for the people, not for the administering power. Respect for popular wishes is a very important aspect of democratic government, for there could conceivably be a discrepancy between what the people want and what the administering power thinks is good for them.

7. For colonial disputes and the strategic importance of colonies *see The Colonial Problem* (1937), pp. 23–45. "The historians of the pre-war [First World War] years, the editors of the *Grosse Politik* and the British Documents, and other writers, lay stress on the colonial quarrels as contributing to the causes of the war. . . . Colonial territories were pawns in the diplomatic game, and none of the parties to the struggle seem to have been troubled with scruples about the transfer of populations without consulting their desires and interests. It was a naked struggle for power and prestige and markets." (pp. 26–27).

(3) *The encouragement of respect for human rights regardless of sex, religion or language and the promotion of the interdependence of peoples.* The territories were intended to be models in observance of human rights to other dependent territories outside the system where administration might be of a lower standard.

(4) *Equal treatment in social, economic and educational matters for all members of the United Nations and, for their nationals, equal administration of justice subject to safeguards for the protection of the inhabitants of the territory.* The principle of equal treatment was applied to A- and B-mandates but was excluded from C-mandates. The Charter extends the principle to all nonstrategic trust territories but without prejudice to the principles of trusteeship. In respect of strategic territories equal treatment is limited to the "people of the strategic area."[8] This does not however exclude discrimination against outsiders provided the interests of the people are not thereby prejudiced.

The underlying purpose of trusteeship is to provide the instrument for the transformation of dependent peoples of a specified category to self-governing or independent status with the full enjoyment of the right to self-determination. Having drawn from the experience of the mandates, some of which had already gained independence, the trusteeship provisions were an improvement, being clearly directed toward the achievement of political freedom in the shortest possible time. The Charter expressly excludes the possibility of a member of the United Nations being placed under trusteeship. This was intended to allay Arab fears that France might renew its claim to Syria and Lebanon, whose independence had been declared in 1941 by the Free French and British governments subject to the conclusion of treaties that would define French rights.[9]

3. *The Trusteeship Council*

Chapter 13 of the Charter sets up the Trusteeship Council as the principal organ responsible for the trust territories. The council considers reports from administering powers and petitions from the inhabitants.[10]

---

8. Article 83(2). The American representative in the Security Council said, "Now I wish to state as a matter of record that the United States Government has no intention, through this clause or any other clause, of taking advantage, for its own benefits of the meagre and almost non-existent resources and commercial opportunities that exist in the scattered and barren islands." UN Doc. S/P V/124 (2 April 1947), pp. 103–5; U.S., State Dept. Publication 2784 pp. 103–5; "Draft Agreement for the Japanese Mandated Islands" (1947), p. 8.

9. The proposed treaties in favour of France never materialised.

10. Article 87 of United Nations Charter.

Unlike the Permanent Mandates Commission, it grants oral hearings to petitioners, most of whom bring before it petitions dealing with public matters. Rule 80(1) of the council's rules of procedure provides:

The Trusteeship Council may hear oral presentations in support or elaborating a previously submitted written petition. Oral presentation shall be confined to the subject-matter of the petition as stated in writing by the petitioners. The Trusteeship Council, in exceptional cases, may also hear orally petitions which have not previously been submitted in writing, provided that the Trusteeship Council and the administering authority concerned have been previously informed with regard to the subject-matter.

This has been liberally interpreted, for the council has listened to petitioners who had given no warning of their intention in writing.

Unlike the Permanent Mandates Commission, the Trusteeship Council arranges for periodic visits, on an average of one in three years, to the territories at times agreed upon with administering authorities. Such visits are usually preceded and followed by intense political activity on the part of the inhabitants. The council has gained an intimate knowledge with the problems of the trust territories and is better placed to help them than was the Permanent Mandates Commission. It formulates questionnaires on the political, economic, social, and educational advancement of the territories, on which the administering powers base their reports. The council is composed of representatives of governments, unlike the Permanent Mandates Commission, which was a committee of experts selected for their special knowledge of colonial affairs. There is a parity of Members from Administering and non-Administering Powers, the latter selected for three-year periods. Permanent members of the Security Council who are not administering powers are automatically members. The number of trust territories has dwindled to two—New Guinea and the Pacific Islands—administered by Australia and the United States respectively. Thus the number of permanent members in the Council has already exceeded the number of administering powers.[11] The president is elected annually and the practice is to alternate between the two classes of members.

The Council has cooperated with the specialised agencies in the development of the territories. Its activities have been less controversial than

---

11. For a proposal to amend the membership of the Trusteeship Council, see P. S. Lui, "The Principle of Parity in Trusteeship Council," *Annals of the Chinese Society of International Law* (1965), 2:28–36, especially 34–5. *Also* S. D. Bailey, "The Future Composition of the Trusteeship Council," 13 *International Organisation* (1959) no. 3, pp. 412–21. An amendment is however hardly necessary now in view of the fast disappearing responsibilities of the council.

those of the Special Committee of Twenty-four dealing with non-self-governing territories, being more clearly defined in the Charter. It has made a greater impact on the trust territories than did the Permanent Mandates Commission on the mandates and has successfully combined expertise with administrative and political functions. These duties are correspondingly reduced as the territories achieve self-determination.

4. Trusteeship Agreements

During the first session of the assembly Australia, Belgium, Great Britain, and New Zealand declared their intention to place their mandates under trusteeship. France vacillated in respect of its territories and South Africa stressed its special relationship with Namibia with a view to annexation.[12]

The placing of mandates under trusteeship was not made compulsory, for the Charter merely makes the system capable of application "by means of trusteeship agreements" to all mandates. Though not legally bound, a mandatory was under a high moral duty to do so. The International Court of Justice found:

> It is true that while Members of the League of Nations regarded the Mandates System as the best method of discharging the sacred trust of civilisation provided for in Article 22 of the Covenant, the Members of the United Nations considered the International Trusteeship System to be the best method of discharging a similar mission. It is equally true that the Charter has contemplated and regulated only a single system, the International Trusteeship System. It did not contemplate or regulate a co-existing Mandates System. It may thus be concluded that it was expected that the Mandatory States would follow the normal course indicated by the Charter, namely, conclude Trusteeship Agreements. The Court, is, however, unable to deduce from these general considerations any obligation for Mandatory States to conclude or to negotiate such agreements. It is not for the Court to pronounce on the political or moral duties which these considerations may involve.[13]

Until agreements were arrived at, the dominance of the principle of the "well-being and development" of the people remained unimpaired. The General Assembly welcomed the readiness of those members who were prepared to transfer the mandates to trusteeship and urged all mandatories to expedite arrangements for the transfer.[14]

Under the League only C-mandates were administered as "integral

12. See chapter 6 on Namibia.
13. *ICJ Rep.* (1950), p. 140.
14. Res. 11(1) of 9 February 1946.

portions" of the mandatory's territory. All the agreements submitted for approval in 1946, with the exception of that on Tanganyika, contained a similar phrase and these included former B-mandates. Though objections were raised on the grounds that it opened the way for annexation, the administering powers, with the exception of New Zealand, refused to accept an amendment that deleted the phrase. The trusteeship agreements were approved by majority votes. When the United States accepted the amendment, it claimed that "its authority in the trust territory is not to be considered in any way lessened thereby."[15] The agreements further permitted the establishment of military bases in spite of objections. The system was brought into being on 13 December 1946 when the assembly approved the agreements for the following administrations:

Territory	Administering Power
New Guinea	Great Britain, New Zealand and Australia (Australia acting)
Ruanda-Urundi	Belgium
Togoland	Great Britain and France
Cameroons	Great Britain and France
Western Samoa	Great Britain, New Zealand and Australia (New Zealand acting)
Tanganyika	Great Britain

Subsequent agreements were concluded for Nauru with Great Britain, Australia and New Zealand as administering powers (New Zealand acting), and for the strategic Islands of Marshall, Caroline, and Marienne under the United States. Libya was administered jointly by Britain and France, and Somaliland by Italy.[16]

The agreements define the boundaries of the territories and designate the administering authorities. They set out the basic objectives of trusteeship, emphasise the duty to develop, and promote free political institutions and protect the rights of the people in land and natural resources. Administering powers are obliged to promote educational and cultural

15. SC Official Records 23, (7 March, 1947), p. 473. In proposing the agreement for the strategic territories, the United States sent copies to all members whom in its view had special interests in the area before formally submitting it to the Security Council for approval. "State directly concerned" was also a point of controversy. Though it ended inconclusively, the Indian view that the United Nations was the party as indicated in Article 81 appears to reflect subsequent United Nations practice. *UNYB* (1946–7), p. 80.

16. For the terms of the agreements for British Togoland, *see UNYB* (1946–7), pp. 188–90; British Cameroons, pp. 190–3; Tanganyika, pp. 193–5; New Guinea, pp. 195–6; French Togoland, pp. 196–8; French Cameroons, pp. 199–201, Ruanda-Urundi, pp. 201–3; Western Samoa, pp. 203–5.

development and protect freedom of speech and religion. They have full powers of administration, jurisdiction and legislation in constituting the territories into customs, fiscal and administrative unions with adjacent territories and in establishing military, naval, and air bases. They provide for equal treatment in social and economic matters for nationals of member states, annual reports based on questionnaires formulated by the Trusteeship Council, and the approval of the terms, their alteration and amendment by the assembly in the case of ordinary trust territories, and by the Security Council for strategic trust territories. Any dispute concerning the interpretation or application of the provisions of the agreements and which could not be settled by other means were to be submitted to the International Court of Justice.[17]

5. Administrative Unions

In Resolution 224(III) the assembly took note of the clauses in the agreements that allowed for the territories to be administered as units of adjacent territories and affirmed that they must not be used to the prejudice of the separate identities of those territories. It requested the Trusteeship Council to study the situation, to seek an advisory opinion of the court if necessary, and to call for additional information from the administering powers where it thought fit. The desirability of maintaining the separate identity of trust territories was repeated in Resolutions 326(IV), 563(IV) and others.

Further to this request, the council set up a committee on Administrative Unions to study the fiscal, customs, and administrative unions and common services affecting trust territories. In Resolution 293(IV) of 17 July, 1950, the council listed safeguards to prevent prejudice to the territories. These were that administering authorities should furnish precise statistical and other data relating to such territory, visiting missions should be allowed access to necessary information, the boundaries and separate identities should be maintained and the expenditure on each territory should at least equal the revenue collected. In Resolution 649(VII) the assembly requested the administering authorities to take into account in extending the scope of administrative unions the freely expressed wishes of the population and hoped that they would consult the council in making any changes or in establishing new ones. The concern over "unions" reflects the fears of the assembly that the territories might be absorbed into metropolitan or colonial territories and the disapproval of such intent. Over trust territories the right of the United Nations is well-founded and associating them too closely with colonies

17. There is no dispute clause in the New Guinea agreement.

over which the rights of the United Nations are more controversial could prejudice the peoples' right to self-determination. United Nations practice in fact tends to assimilate colonies to trust territories rather than the other way round; the Declaration on Independence of 1960, for instance, makes no distinctions between colonies and trust territories in the aims and obligations of the parties concerned.

6. Plebiscites in Trust Territories

A. *British Togoland*. In Resolution 944(X) of 15 December 1955 the assembly decided to hold a plebiscite in British Togoland in order to ascertain whether the people wanted to join Ghana on independence or continue as a trust territory until its status came up for determination in due course. The plebiscite was conducted in May 1956 under the supervision of the United Nations Plebiscite Commissioner. The result was 93,095 in favour of union and 67,492 for separation. In only two of the six districts with a seventh of the population did the majority vote against the union.

The Trusteeship Council recommended that British Togoland should be united with Ghana on independence. Some members of the assembly had reservations arguing that the union might make reunion with French Togoland impossible, that the majority in the south favoured separation and that the plebiscite did not disclose whether the people wanted unitary or federal relations with independent Ghana. However a resolution was adopted approving the union and on 6 March 1957, British Togoland achieved independence as part of Ghana.[18]

B. *British Cameroons*. A visiting mission to the British Cameroons in 1958 reported that the question of independence should be considered in relation to the north and south separately. It found that the north wanted to become part of Northern Nigeria but that the south was divided between joining Nigeria and the Republic of the Cameroons. In Resolution 1350(XIII) of 13 March 1959 the assembly decided that Britain should organise separate plebiscites in consultation with United Nations Plebiscite Commissioner and under United Nations supervision to ascertain the wishes of the people. The questions put were:

(a) Do you wish Northern Cameroons to be a part of the Northern Region of Nigeria when the Federation of Nigeria becomes independent?
or
(b) Are you in favour of deciding the future of the Northern Cameroons at a later date?

18. Res. 1044(XI) of 13 December 1956; *see also UNYB* (1956), pp. 368–70.

Voting was by universal male suffrage and 70,546 (62 percent of the votes cast) favoured decision at a later date, 42,788 favoured the first alternative and 526 votes were rejected.

In the south the questions put were:

(a) Do you wish to achieve independence by joining the independent Federation of Nigeria?

or

(b) Do you wish to achieve independence by joining the independent Republic of the Camerun?

There was no option for a later decision nor for the two sections to form a separate state. The electorate in the south consisted of persons who had been born there or one of whose parents had been. Of the registered voters 94.75 percent participated, 233,571 favoured joining the Republic of Cameroons and 97,751, Nigeria.

In the second plebiscite in the north, the questions were:

(a) Do you wish to achieve independence by joining the independent Federation of Nigeria?

or

(b) Do you wish to achieve independence by joining the independent Republic of Camerun?

In the results, 146,296 favoured joining Northern Nigeria and 97,659 opted for the Cameroons. Inspite of certain weaknesses inherent in the administration of Northern Cameroons, the commissioner declared that he was generally satisfied with the conduct of the plebiscite, but the Republic of Cameroons expressed dissatisfaction and unsuccessfully sought a declaration from the International Court of Justice that Britain had not fulfilled its obligations in the plebiscite.[19]

The plebiscites were approved in Resolution 1608(XV) of 21 April, 1961 and the trusteeship agreement in respect of Northern Cameroons was terminated on 1 June, 1961 when it joined Nigeria as Sardauna Province and in respect of Southern Cameroons when it joined the Republic of Cameroons as its Western Province on 1 October, 1961.

C. *Ruanda-Urundi*. In the Belgian Trust Territory of Ruanda-Urundi, disturbances broke out between the Tutsis and the Hutus in November

---

19. Case Concerning the Cameroons (*Kamerun* v. *United Kingdom*) *ICJ Rep.* (1963), p. 15. The Republic sought a declaratory judgment that Britain had breached the provisions of the trusteeship agreement prior to the termination by the assembly in Res. 1608(XV). The Court held that the dispute concerned the interpretation and application of a treaty which was no longer in force, which was outside the competence of the court. *See also* D. H. N. Johnson, "The Case Concerning the Northern Cameroons," *ICLQ* (1964); *UNYB* (1960), pp. 471–7.

1959. In Resolution 1579(XV) the assembly set up a commission to supervise election and follow the political progress of the territory toward independence. In Resolution 1580(XV) it called upon Belgium to revoke the suspension of the Nwami of Ruanda, restore him to his throne and submit the question of the monarchy to a referendum under United Nations supervision.

In the meantime there was a military takeover in Ruanda, the monarchy was abolished, and a republic was established. The plebiscite on the monarchy and the legislative elections were held with a universal adult suffrage on 25 September 1961. The questions put were:

(a) Do you wish to retain the institution of the Nwami in Ruanda?
(b) If so, do you want Kigeli V to continue as the Nwami of Ruanda?

Ninety-five percent of eligible voters participated and 80 percent answered the questions in the negative. On 4 October 1961 a republican constitution was proclaimed.[20]

D. *Western Samoa.* The Samoan Constitutional Amendment Act, passed by New Zealand Parliament introduced far-reaching reforms toward the achievement of independence. The two official members of the Legislative Assembly—the attorney-general and the financial secretary—were withdrawn. A cabinet of nine was set up and charged with general direction and control. The head of state, formerly the New Zealand High Commissioner, was replaced by a Council of State consisting of the two Fautua and the High Commissioner. A working committee on self-government was set up to draft a constitution and study the problems that would result from the transition to independence, the draft constitution was then approved by the Constitution Convention in September 1960. In Resolution 1569(XV) the assembly recommended that New Zealand, in consultation with the United Nations Plebiscite Commissioner and under the supervision of the United Nations, should organise a plebiscite in which the following questions were to be put:

(a) Do you agree with the Constitution adopted by the Constitutional Convention on 28 October, 1960?
become an independent state on the basis of that Constitution?
(b) Do you agree than on 1 January 1972 Western Samoa should

In the plebiscite, held under universal adult suffrage on 22 June 1961, 37,896 (86.1 percent of the eligible voters) participated, 31,426 (83 percent of those who voted) were in favour of the Constitution and inde-

20. See *also UNYB* (1961), pp. 484–94.

pendence. In resolution 1626(XVI) of 18 October 1961 the assembly endorsed the plebiscite and approved independence for 1 January 1962 on the basis of the Constitution. In a post-independence Treaty of Friendship, Western Samoa entrusted New Zealand with the conduct of its foreign affairs and defence and denied itself separate membership of the United Nations.[21]

7. The Application of Self-determination to Trust Territories

At its first sitting the Trusteeship Council considered a petition from Western Samoa asking for self-government under the protection of New Zealand and the abolition of artificial boundaries imposed by administrative powers. A special committee was sent to investigate the petition. The placing of the territory under the trusteeship of New Zealand was therefore entirely in accordance with the wishes of the people and the friendly relations between the two have led to their voluntary association after independence.

The agreement for Italian Somaliland contained more specific terms than the others as it provided for independence at the end of ten years and an annex expressly vested sovereignty in the people, indicating the view of the United Nations on the *locus* of sovereignty in a dependent territory. In the case of Eritrea, a commission of inquiry was set up to ascertain the wishes of the people. This resulted in federal relations with Ethiopia, a solution which was approved in Resolution 390(V).[22] Libya, administered jointly by Britain and France, was to be independent in 1952 under a constitution to be determined by a national assembly aided by a United Nations commissioner and a council of ten. Independence was proclaimed by King Idris and Libya was admitted into the United Nations by Resolution 515(IV) of 1 February 1952.

The prospect of early independence in the other territories was not very bright; so in 1948 and 1949 the assembly adopted a number of resolutions intended to speed up the progress toward self-government or

21. *See also UNYB* (1960), pp. 477–81; (1961), pp. 495–8; M. Merle, "Les Plebiscites Organises Par Les Nations Unies," *Annuaire Francaise de Droit International* (1961), pp. 425–445; H. S. Johnson: *Self-determination Within the Community of Nations*, (Leyden, 1967), especially chapter 6.

22. The former Italian colony of Eritrea became a British protectorate in 1941 after the Italians were driven out. It became a region in federal relations with Ethiopia from 1952 to 1956 when its administration was further integrated. In 1962 Eritrea was made a province of Ethiopia to the dissatisfaction of elements of the largely Muslim population, whose desire for secession is backed by certain Arab States including Iraq and Syria. The experience of Biafra indicates that secession will be frustrated by military and political pressure and that the self-determination of the people can be successfully manifested in other ways than independence.

independence[23] It also demanded greater participation by the inhabitants in "profits and management of entities, public or private, engaged in the exploitation of mineral and other resources or in the production of, or trade in, raw materials and commodities basic to the economy of the Trust Territories." The assembly affirmed that the interests of the inhabitants are paramount in all economic policies and has also given special attention to the education of the people.

In 1952 Haiti, India, Lebanon, the Philippines, and Yemen introduced a joint resolution,[24] opposed by all administering powers (United States abstained), calling upon the powers to give details of measures intended to achieve self-government or independence in the shortest possible time. The final resolution invited the administering powers to include in their reports measures taken or contemplated to achieve self-government or independence, the manner of consulting the freely expressed wishes of the people, the adequacy of existing trusteeship agreements, and a rough estimate of the time when self-determination would be achieved.[25]

The association of the inhabitants with the work of the Trusteeship Council was opposed on the basis that it created subsidiary international personalities alongside the administering powers. Nevertheless, a resolution was adopted to that effect, instructing visiting missions to take the initiative in seeking out public opinion on important problems and to make recommendations for the development of free expression, to propose action on petitions and to grant hearing to representatives of public opinion, or to examine their communications if they were unable to travel. One of these missions visited Tanganyika in 1954 and set a time limit of twenty years for independence: this had the effect of activating the Tanganyika African National Union which assumed power on independence in 1961.[26]

After British Togoland attained independence as part of Ghana, the assembly resolved that administering powers should implement its previous resolutions on speedy independence,[27] and in Resolution 1274 (XIII) of 12 November 1958 it set 1960 as the dateline for independence for French Togoland, British and French Cameroons, Somaliland, and Western Samoa. In respect of the remaining territories it invited the powers to formulate "early successive intermediate targets and dates in

23. Res. 225(III), 226(III), 320(IV), and 321(IV).

24. A/C.4/L.187.

25. Res. 558(VI), followed by 752 (VIII) and 858(IX).

26. *Trusteeship Council Off. Rec.* (15th sess.) supp. no. 3, "Report on Tanganyika."

27. Res. 1207(XII) of 13 December 1957.

the fields of political, economic, social, and educational development of
these territories so as to create, as soon as possible, the preconditions for
the attainment of self-government or independence." Although the territories named did not all gain independence in 1960, yet the resolution
had a great impact which extended to colonial territories; for in that year
a large number of dependent territories gained independence and joined
the United Nations.

The holding of plebiscites is a remarkable exercise of the right of self-
determination in trust territories; whether in abolishing the monarchy or
in joining one or the other state on independence, the people have themselves made their choice. Although the question of separate independence
was not put to the British Cameroons and Togoland, it is submitted that
that was a wiser step than the possible proliferation of unviable and
inconsequential states. In Ruanda-Urundi, however, sectional enmity
made unity impossible and relations had degenerated into internecine
feuds between the Hutus and the Tutsis; the unified territory broke into
Burundi and Ruanda. The security of the peoples, in whatever territorial
units, is more important than the territorial integrity which they had no
part in creating.

The exercise of self-determination in trust territories need not lead
irresistibly to independence, for the wishes of the people may be satisfied
through association or integration with another state. Western Samoa is
a case in point; here association was decided upon by the people after
they gained independence, a variant of the British Togoland and Cameroons situation. The 4000 people of Nauru in 1968 freely chose to be
independent in spite of their small number; they were allowed to determine what was best for them in the circumstances.[28]

Following British Togoland, which gained independence as part of
Ghana in 1957, came French Togoland, French Cameroons, and Somalia,
which became independent in 1960, Tanganyika and British Cameroons
in 1961, Western Samoa, Burundi, and Ruanda in 1962, and Nauru in
1968. Progress toward independence in trust territories has, on the whole,
been smoother than in colonies, for the goal had always been assured,
thereby removing the substantial sting of dependent status. Trusteeship
has served as a yardstick for colonial administration and helped to
quicken the tempo of colonial emancipation. Of the eleven territories
originally placed under trusteeship only New Guinea[29] and the Pacific

28.   Despite its microscopic size, Nauru is among the richest communities in the
world with a *per capita* income of $4000 derived from the huge phosphate de-
posits that cover the 8.5 square miles of territory.

29.   Oala Oala Rarua, "Will New Guinea Be the Last Colonial Country?"
Australian Quarterly, vol. 39(4), (1967) pp. 21–35.

Islands trust territories are still dependent, and in these the United
Nations continues to press for early independence. The Pacific Islands
(Micronesia) have a population of 85,000 and consist of 2100 islands
spread over 3 million square miles of the Pacific. They have a budget of
$18.5 million of which the United States subsidy amounts to $17.5 million. To such scattered islands self-determination may be made meaningful through association with another state, other states, or the United
Nations itself.[30]

30. *See also* D. W. Bowett, "Self-Determination and Political Rights in the
Developing Countries," *American Society of International Law*, (April 1966),
129 at 134; J. Fletcher-Cooke, "Some Reflections on the International Trusteeship,
with Particular Reference to Its Impact on the Governments and Peoples of the
Trust Territories," 13 *International Organisation* (1959), pp. 422–37. *See also*
on ministates p. 87 *et seq.* above. *See also* G. Marston, "Termination of Trusteeship Territories," 18 *ICLQ* (1969); J. N. Murray, *The UN Trusteeship System*
(Urbana, 1957).

VI *Self-Determination in Namibia*

1. *During the League Period*

Upon Germany's defeat its former colony of South-West Africa was renounced in 1919 to the Principal Allied and Associated Powers under Article 119 of the Treaty of Versailles. The dominant principles of the peace conference were non-annexation and self-determination; it was therefore agreed in Article 22 of the Covenant that all territories detached from the enemy "which were inhabited by peoples not yet able to stand by themselves under the strenuous conditions of the modern world" should be placed under the tutelage of more advanced nations who were to advance their well-being and development as "a sacred trust of civilisation." The territories were divided into A-, B-, and C-mandates according to their stages of development in a descending order and South-West Africa was in the last group. The distinguishing feature of (this group) a C-mandate was that it could be administered as an integral portion of the administering power's territory, with modifications if necessary, but subject to overriding safeguards in favour of the "indigenous population." It was not a newly acquired colony but a territory over which the mandatory had a duty to promote political, economic, and social progress.

The mandate was conferred upon His Britannic Majesty, to be exercised on his behalf by the government of the Union of South Africa, and it gave His Majesty full powers of administration and legislation. The mandatory was to prohibit the slave trade, intoxicating drinks, and forced labour except for essential public services and with adequate remuneration. It was to desist from the militarisation of the inhabitants except for internal police and local defence, and from the erection of military and naval bases. Subject to the maintenance of public order and public morals, freedom of worship and conscience were guaranteed and in the same article freedom for missionary enterprise for League members. The mandatory was bound to make annual reports to the League Council indicating measures employed to carry out its obligations. It could not unilaterally modify the terms of the mandate without the consent of the League Council—otherwise there could be annexation through the back door. It was agreed that "if any dispute whatever should arise between the Mandatory and another Member of the League of Nations relating to the interpretation or the application of the provisions of the Mandate, such dispute, if it cannot be settled by negotiation, shall be submitted to the Permanent Court of International Justice."[1] This provision underlines the limited rights of the Mandatory.[2]

During the period of the League, South Africa submitted reports but expressed a desire to incorporate the territory on the basis of the special relations (geographical and cultural) with it and tended to treat the international arrangement as a veiled annexation. General Smuts, who contributed so much to the mandate idea, was reported to have claimed in a speech at Windhoek:

> In effect, the relations between South-West Protectorate and the Union amount to annexation in all but name. Without annexation the Union could, under the Peace Treaty, do whatever it could have done in annexed territory. . . .[3]

The attempt to incorporate the territory as the fifth province of the Union, though supported by the all-white assembly of South-West Africa,[4] was contrary to the principles of the mandate and was correctly rejected by the Permanent Mandate Commission. Sir Frederick V. Lugard of the commission noted:

> As long as the country remained under the mandate there could not be incorporation. If incorporation took place, it would be subject to the grant of complete self-government and the surrender of the mandate, with the consent of the League.[5]

1. *See* Appendix B for the full text of the mandate agreement.

2. *See* chapter 2 on mandates.

3. *Cape Times*, 18 September 1920.

4. *See* LN Doc. C. 489 M 214 (1934) 50 for the text of the resolution of the assembly.

5. PMC Minutes (1925), p. 59.

Van Rees of the commission warned:

> [I]ncorporation would imply a change in the political and interna-
> tional status of South-West Africa without this territory having yet
> reached a sufficiently high state of development to allow the Manda-
> tory to withdraw; such incorporation would amount, without doubt,
> to annexation, which would be an obvious infraction of the manda-
> tory system.[6]

He said further:

> It would be contrary to the spirit of the arrangement if upon the
> demand of some 10,000 white settlers, a mandated territory were,
> in fact, to be incorporated with the territory of the mandatory
> Power. This was not a question of degree, but of principle. The
> mandated territory of South-West Africa, though administered as
> an integral part of the territory of the Union, was administered on
> behalf of the League of Nations.[7]

The Commission questioned the claim in the preamble of the South
African–Portuguese Treaty of 1926 on the boundary with Portuguese
Angola that the Union possessed sovereign powers over the mandated
territory. It also denied the claim that the railways and harbours built by
the former German administration passed under the "dominium" of the
Union, insisting that they properly belonged to the territory, though
administered as part of the Union system. The commission generally
frowned upon any actions that conflicted with the real interests of the
people, even if they did so in mild terms. Thus it doubted whether the
practice of requiring missions in Ovamboland to assist and support the
government and encourage the people to seek jobs in the Union at low
wages was in conformity with the letter and spirit of the mandate.[8] Condemning the Colour Bar Act, which applied to employment in the railways, it said:

> The Commission considers that this Act, the effect of which is to
> limit the occupations open to native and coloured workers and thus
> place them in a disadvantage with white workers in the area under
> the mandate, is based upon considerations which are not compatible
> with the principles laid down in the mandate.[9]

6. Ibid., p. 60. On a later occasion Rappard said, "The ultimate decision [about
incorporation] rested neither with the Mandatory Power nor with the inhabitants,
or part of the inhabitants, of the Mandated territory, but with the League of
Nations." PMC Minutes (1932), p. 24. *See also* PMC Minutes (1934), pp. 50–1,
62–6 and PMC Minutes (1937), p. 192.

7. PMC Minutes (1925), p. 61.

8. PMC Minutes (1928), p. 275.

9. Ibid.

Alberto Thēodoli had earlier declared:

> The administration has pursued a policy of force rather than of persuasion, and, further . . . this policy has been conceived and applied in the interests of the colonists rather than in the interests of the natives.[10]

The League Council did not discuss the mandates at its last sitting, but the League Assembly wound up the mandates in Syria, Lebanon and Trans-Jordan "with the concurrence of all Members of the Council which are represented at its present session." All the Mandatories of the remaining territories declared their intention to continue to honour the terms of the mandates. While announcing the intention of his government to put before the General Assembly of the United Nations plans to integrate South-West Africa, the South African delegate maintained:

> In the meantime, the Union will continue to administer the territory scrupulously in accordance with the obligations of the Mandate, for the advancement and promotion of the interests of the inhabitants, as she has done during the past six years when meetings of the Mandates Commission could not be held.
>
> The disappearance of those organs of the League concerned with the supervision of mandates, primarily the Mandates Commission and the League Council, will necessarily preclude complete compliance with the letter of the Mandate. The Union Government will nevertheless regard the dissolution as in no way diminishing its obligations under the Mandate, which it will continue to discharge with full and proper appreciation of its responsibilities until such time as other arrangements are agreed upon concerning the future status of the territory.[11]

On the basis of this and other assurances from other mandatories in respect of their own territories, the League on 18 April 1946 adopted a resolution which:

> (3) Recognizes that, on the termination of the league's existence, its functions with respect to the mandated territories will come to an end, but notes that Chapters XI, XII and XIII of the Charter of the United Nations embody principles corresponding to those declared in Article 22 of the Covenant of the League;
>
> (4) Takes note of the expressed intentions of the Members of the League now administering territories under mandate to continue to administer them for the well-being and development of the peoples concerned in accordance with the obligations

10. PMC Minutes (1923), Doc. C. 522, Annex 8B.
11. *LNOJ*, special supp. no. 194 (21st ord. session), p. 33.

contained in the respective Mandates, until other arrangements have been agreed upon ,between the United Nations and the respective Mandatory Powers.[12]

The British delegate seconded the resolution introduced by the Chinese delegate: "It had been settled in consultations and agreement by all countries interested in mandates and he thought it could therefore be passed without discussion and with complete unanimity."[13] There was thus no precise transfer of mandates to trusteeship but the dominance of the theme—"well-being and development" of the inhabitants, not excluding their political development—was quite clear.

2. The United Nations and Namibia

At the first session of the General Assembly, the South African delegate claimed that because of the special relationship between his country and South-West Africa, his government intended to consult the people of the territory on the future of their government. Had this been effectively done, it would have been in the best traditions of the principle of self-determination. The General Assembly welcomed the readiness of those mandatories who were willing to place their mandated territories under trusteeship and requested all administering powers to submit agreements for approval.[14] The other mandatories yielded to this request but South Africa reiterated its desire to annex the territory on the basis of physical contiguity and ethnological kinship. It claimed that the European population had affirmed their wish to be integrated through their representatives in Parliament and that the overwhelming majority of the Africans were in favour.[15] It was also argued that the union would attract foreign capital for development and give effect to the wishes of the people —a logical application of the principle of self-determination. The majority in the Fourth Committee, however, rejected the proposal in view of the discriminatory policy of South Africa which severely restricted the political and economic rights of the Africans. Further, annexation was repulsive to the aims of trusteeship and a retrograde step. It was also doubtful if the people really understood the issues involved or were suffi-

---

12. LN, *Report of the First Committee*, (21st ord. session), doc. A. 3 (1946), pp. 5–6.

13. *LNOJ*, special supp. no. 194 (1946), p. 78.

14. Res. 2(I) of 9 February 1946. Great Britain, Australia, New Zealand, and Belgium expressed their readiness; France vacillated.

15. South Africa stated that 208,850 Africans favoured annexation, 33,520 were opposed, and 56,790 were not consulted. The population in 1960 consisted of 428,000 Africans, 73,150 Europeans and 24,000 people of mixed blood. The territory covers 318,000 square miles.

ciently informed about the advantages of trusteeship so as to make their choice a free one. The assembly then adopted an unopposed resolution in which it noted with satisfaction "that the Union of South Africa, by presenting this matter to the United Nations, recognised the interest and concern of the United Nations in the matter of the future status of territories now held under mandate" and recommended that the territory should be placed under international trusteeship.[16]

South Africa submitted reports in 1946 and 1947. Its prime minister on 4 November 1946 stated that his government would respect the status of South-West Africa. In a memorandum to the secretary-general of the United Nations on 17 October 1946, the South African delegate referred to his government's responsibility under the mandate as being "necessarily inalienable." On 14 December 1946 the South African delegate said before the assembly: "In the meantime, as our leader, the Prime Minister of the Union of South Africa, stated in the Fourth Committee, the Union Government will continue to administer the territory in the spirit of the Mandate."[17]

In a letter dated 23 July 1947 the South African delegate informed the United Nations that his government would not proceed with incorporation but would maintain the status quo and administer the territory in the mandate spirit.[18] In Resolutions 141(II) of 1 November 1947 and 227(III) of 26 November 1948 the assembly requested that the territory be placed under trusteeship. With the coming to power of the Nationalist party, South Africa began a process of retreating from its stand over the status of the territory and from its obligation to advance it toward self-determination. Apartheid was extended and rigidly enforced in disregard of the "sacred trust." The government was even claiming that the demise of the League had also extinguished its obligations and in a letter dated 11 July 1949 informed the secretary-general of the United Nations that it would not forward any more reports on the territory. In the meantime the territory was being integrated with the Union. This open challenge to the world organization dimmed the hopes for self-determination inherent in the mandate agreement.

In Resolution 338(IV) of 6 December 1949 the assembly requested the advisory opinion of the International Court of Justice on the status of South-West Africa. The court recalled in its opinion that the dominant principles of the mandate were non-annexation and the well-being and

16. Res. 65(I) of 14 December 1946.
17. UN Doc. A/334.
18. See Res. 227(II) of 26 November 1948.

development of peoples yet unable to stand by themselves. The mandatory had full powers of administration and legislation (not involving cession or transfer of territory) but was also bound to observe certain obligations under the supervision of the League Council. The mandate constituted an international regime *sui generis*, distinct from any notions of contractual relations in municipal law and was created "in the interest of the inhabitants of the territory and of humanity in general. . . . a sacred trust of civilisation." The obligation to promote to the utmost the material and moral well-being of the inhabitants as defined in Article 22 of the Covenant and Articles 2 through 5 of the mandate agreement was subjected to the supervision of the League through the submission to it of annual reports. Further, Article 80(I) of the United Nations Charter preserves the rights of the parties, including those of the people themselves, to place the territory under trusteeship until new agreements were made.[19] The argument that the mandate lapsed would also involve the lapse of the mandatory's right to administer. This view was supported by the resolution of the League on 18 April 1946 on the conduct of South Africa in regard to the mandate. If there was no binding obligation to place the territory under trusteeship, neither could South Africa alone change its status without the consent of the United Nations.

Having established the mandate subsisted, the General Assembly adopted another resolution urging the Union to place the territory under trusteeship[20] and set up a committee of five to confer with the Union on the procedural measures for implementing the Opinion of the Court. It was also to examine reports, petitions, and other matters relating to the territory.[21] The assembly subsequently passed many resolutions urging South Africa to comply with its resolutions but without any success whatsoever.

The work of the committee was facilitated by the advisory opinion on the *Admissibility of Hearings of Petitions by the Committee on South-West Africa*,[22] in which the court found that the grant of oral hearings to petitioners was consistent with the advisory opinion of 1950 provided

---

19. "Except as may be agreed in individual trusteeship agreements, made under Article 77, 79, and 81, placing each territory under the trusteeship system, and until such agreements have been concluded, nothing in this Chapter shall be construed in or of itself to alter in any manner the rights whatsoever of any States or any peoples or the terms of existing international instruments to which Members of the United Nations may respectively be parties."

20. Res. 449B of 13 December 1950.

21. Res. 449A. The committee consisted of Denmark, Syria, Thailand, United States, and Uruguay.

22. *ICJ Rep.* (1956), p. 23.

such a course of action was necessary for the maintenance of effective international supervision of the territory. Though the right was not expressly permitted as a procedure under the mandate agreement, the League Council approved of it in a resolution of January 1923. The Permanent Mandates Commission could therefore grant oral hearings, although it never really did so. The mandatory's burden was not thereby increased; rather it ensured that the people's grievances could be heard regardless of limitations on their communications with the outside world.

South Africa has not concealed its contempt for world opinion. A typical example is the statement of Prime Minister Strijdom in the Senate in 1956:

> It is well within our power, and fully within our power, to incorporate South-West Africa as part of the Union. Up to now we have declared unto the world that legally and otherwise that is the position, but that in the meantime we are prepared, although we do not for one moment recognise the right of the United Nations, even should we one day incorporate South-West Africa, to govern South-West Africa in the spirit of the old Mandate. So whether we will proceed at a later stage to carry out and put into effect what we regard as our right, over which nobody has anything to say, that will depend on how circumstances develop in the future.[23]

The large number of resolutions passed on South-West Africa imploring South Africa to submit the territory to trusteeship was intended to secure eventual independence or self-government. When these proved unavailing, the assembly, in Resolution 1060(XI) of 26 February 1957, requested the Committee on South-West Africa to study possible legal actions that were open to United Nations organs or members to ensure that the mandate obligations were fulfilled. The committee reported: "There would be little doubt that the right to invoke Article 7 of the Mandate is enjoyed, at any rate, by those former members of the League which were members at the date of the dissolution of the League and which are now members of the United Nations."[24] It revealed a sorry tale of oppression and suppression by the Union government and referred to a "continued trend in the administration of the Territory toward the deliberate subordination and relegation of the vast majority of the people to an inferior status, through the application of such measures as the forced alienation, without proper compensation of the land which they traditionally occupied." It also disclosed that there were "dominatory controls" over their movement, residence, employment, and ownership

23. South-West Africa cases, *ICJ Rep.*, Oral Proceedings (1962), p. 259.
24. UN Doc. A/3625.

of livestock.[25] It deplored the reference in labour legislations to employer and employee as "master" and "servant" and the imposition of apartheid laws with increasing rigidity in education, housing, and medical services. In the view of the committee, the mandate obligations were not being respected.

The assembly set up a Good Offices Committee[26] but this reported that there was no basis for agreement. In Resolutions 1142A(XII) of 25 October 1957 and 1361(XIV) of 17 November 1959, the assembly drew the attention of member states to the legal action provided for in Article 7 of the mandate agreement read with Article 37 of the statute of the International Court of Justice. The initiative was taken by Ethiopia and Liberia, who had been members of the League and were now United Nations members, at the Addis Ababa Conference of Independent African States in 1960. The decision to commence legal proceedings was commended by the assembly in Resolution 1565(XV) of 18 December 1960.

The main purpose of the proceedings was not so much to vindicate the rights of the applicants as to obtain an enforceable judgment of the court to secure the fulfillment of the mandate obligations and thus safeguard the right of the people to self-determination. South Africa had declared that it was not bound by the advisory opinion of 1950, whatever its influence within the United Nations order. A decision in contentious proceedings would be binding on South Africa and it was hoped that the mandate could thus be judicially enforced.[27]

The United Nations appointed a Special Committee on South-West Africa in 1961 and charged it with the responsibility of supervising the territory. The committee was authorized by the assembly to secure a visit, evacuate South African military forces, release all political prisoners, repeal apartheid laws, prepare the territory for independence after a general election based on universal adult suffrage, secure the return of political prisoners, and coordinate the assistance of specialised agencies in helping the territory. The committee was unable to achieve the desired ends because of the refusal of the South African government to cooperate with it. However in 1962 the assembly reaffirmed the right of the people

25.   *See also UNYB* (1957), pp. 307–9.

26.   Res. 1143(XII) of 25 October 1957.

27.   *See also* E. A. Gross, "The South-West Africa Cases: What Happened," *Foreign Affairs* (October 1966), p. 40. "The objective was not to resolve doubts concerning the jurisprudence of the Mandate, which has its firm foundation in the Advisory Opinion of 1950, but to transfer a dishonoured though authoritative Opinion into an enforceable Judgment." Gross, a member of the New York bar, was one of the counsel for the applicants.

to independence and urged all nations to refrain from supplying arms to the South African regime. The Odendaal Commission, set up by South Africa to study the means of closer integration on the basis of little Bantustans, was severely criticised by the committee in 1964. The practice of granting concessions to international companies that operated with labour that was closely identified with slavery was also condemned.[28]

In its 1966 judgment[29] the court held that the provisions of the mandate agreement were divisible into "special interests" and "conduct" provisions and that the dispute between Ethiopia and Liberia on the one hand and South Africa on the other related to the "conduct" provisions. While parties could enforce the "special interests" provisions, the "conduct" provisions could be enforced only by the League Council and in these provisions the applicants had no legal interest.[30]

The decision of the World Court caused much dismay in the United Nations. In Resolution 2145(XXI) of 27 October 1966 the assembly

(1) Reaffirms that the provisions of General Assembly Resolution 1514(XV) are fully applicable to the people of the Mandated Territory of South West Africa and that, therefore, the people

28. "Apartheid in South Africa and South-West Africa," *African Weekly Review* (London), 6 January 1968. "The system of recruitment of African workers operating in South-West Africa today is unique in its organised and efficient application of conditions that are akin to slavery. Workers are recruited, under contract, in the Tribal Areas by the South African Government—sponsored South-West African Native Labour Association (SWANLA), which classifies the male population into working categories A, B, and C, suitable respectively for work in the mines, on land, and on the farms of the Europeans. These letters are reproduced on the clothes of the workers, which they have to provide for themselves. . . . Once under contract, the worker may not leave the area of employment and may not cancel the contract. No African trade unions are recognised, the workers are excluded from all systems of collective bargaining and strikes are a criminal offence."

29. *ICJ Rep.* (1966).

30. Compare the dissenting judgment of Judges Spender and Fitzmaurice in *ICJ Rep.* (1962), pp. 549–50. "The Mandate . . . has two main classes of provisions. The first (which might be called the 'conduct' of the Mandate class) comprises the provisions inserted for the benefit of the territory. The other (which might be called the 'State rights and interests' class) comprises those which were inserted for the national benefit of the Members of the League and their nationals (commercial rights, open door, freedom for missionary activities)." *See also* the South-West Africa cases: Falks, "The South-West Africa Cases: An Appraisal," 21 *International Organisation* (1967), p. 7; P. C. Rao, "South West Africa Cases: Inconsistent Judgment from the ICJ," 6 *Indian JIL* (1966); Higgins, "The ICJ and South-West Africa," 42 *International Affairs* (1966); Harry Inman, C. J. Hynning, and J. Carey, "The World Court's Decision on South-West Africa," 1 *International Lawyer* (1966); C. J. R. Dugard, "The South-West Africa Cases," *South African LJ* (1966); Khan and Kaur, "The Deadlock over South-West Africa," 8 *Indian JIL* (1968), p. 179; L. C. Green, "The United Nations, South-West Africa, and the World Court," 7 *Indian JIL* (1967), p. 491; B. Cheng, "The 1966 South-West Africa Judgment of the World Court," 20 *CLP* (London, 1967), pp. 181–212.

of South West Africa have the inalienable right to self-determination, freedom and independence in accordance with the
Charter of the United Nations;

(2) Reaffirms further that South West Africa is a territory having
international status and that it shall maintain this status until
it achieves independence;

(3) Declares that South Africa has failed to fulfill its obligation in
respect of the administration of the Mandated Territory and
to ensure the moral and material well-being and security of the
indigenous inhabitants of South West Africa and has, in fact,
disavowed the Mandate;

(4) Decides that the Mandate conferred upon His Britannic Majesty to be exercised on his behalf by the Government of the
Union of South Africa is therefore terminated, that South
Africa has no right to administer the Territory and that henceforth South West Africa comes under the direct responsibility
of the United Nations.[31]

The assembly set up an *ad hoc* committee for South-West Africa to
recommend practical measures for administering the territory.[32] The
committee met during the early months of 1967 but could not arrive at
a consensus. The chairman however noted that the members, though
disagreeing on the form of a recommendation, unanimously held that the
proposal to break up the territory into small unviable units, dependent
on South Africa and reserved for different ethnic and racial groups in a
supposedly self-governing status, was both inconsistent with Resolution
2045 and designed to exacerbate tribal rivalries.[33] An eleven-member
council under a commissioner was set up to take over the administration
and enter into negotiations with the South African government for the
transfer of power. So far, no positive result has been achieved; the committee's attempt to enter the territory was frustrated by the South African
government. Though denying the United Nations the right of supervision
the government published a lengthy report in defence of its policy in
March 1967 and sent a copy to the secretary-general of the United
Nations.[34]

31. *UNYB* (1966), pp. 605–6. The resolution was opposed by South Africa and
Portugal while Britain, France, and Malawi abstained.
32. The members of the committee were Canada, Chile, Czechoslovakia, Ethiopia, Finland, Italy, Japan, Mexico, Nigeria, Pakistan, Senegal, USSR, UAR,
and the United States.
33. *See* "Report of the *ad hoc* Committee for South-West Africa," UN Doc.
A/6640 (7 April 1967), p. 49.
34. South-West Africa Survey (Pretoria, 1967).

The United Nations has repeatedly condemned the presence of South Africa in South West Africa, hereafter referred to as Namibia. In Resolution 2325(XXII) of 16 December 1967 the assembly characterized it as a breach of the territorial integrity and of the status of Namibia. It requested members to take effective measures to ensure compliance and called upon the Security Council to take appropriate actions to enable the Council on Namibia to discharge its functions. In Resolution 2403(XXII) of 16 November 1968, the assembly reaffirmed "the inalienable right of the people of Namibia to self-determination and independence."

On 28 February 1969 the president of the Council on Namibia wrote the Security Council (S/9032) pointing out the great dangers posed by South Africa's continued presence in Namibia and the risk of racial conflict in southern Africa. In its Resolution 264 of 20 March 1969 the Security Council called on South Africa "to immediately withdraw its administration from the territory" and threatened to take action if the resolution was not complied with. Further, in Resolution 269 of 12 August 1969 the council declared that South Africa's defiance "constitutes an aggressive encroachment on the authority of the United Nations, a violation of the territorial integrity and a denial of the political sovereignty of the people of Namibia." It called upon South Africa to withdraw from the territory by 4 October 1969, failing which the council would take stern measures.

South Africa has been defying all the resolutions recklessly, including those of the Organisation of African Unity, of which it is not a member.[35] The threat to world peace and of racial conflict cannot be exaggerated. The right of the Nambians to self-determination is internationally recognised; the achievement of that right in the face of forceful denial is, therefore, the concern of the international community and not just of the OAU.

3. Some Legal Issues Affecting Namibia

Neither Article 22 of the League Covenant nor the mandate agreement contained an express provision for the revocation of the mandate. The principal founding fathers of the mandate system—General Smuts and President Wilson—held the view that a defaulting mandatory could be deprived of its right to administer.[36] On many occasions the Permanent Mandates Commission discussed the circumstances that could lead to the revocation of a mandate. Thus Mme Bugge-Wicgsell of the com-

35. *See* p. 91 *et seq.* on the effect of UN resolutions.
36. *See* p. 30 *et seq.*

mission considered that both the Permanent Court and the League Council could exercise this authority "if the Mandatory Power had misused its administrative rights over the territory, to the detriment of the native population or other members of the League of Nations, to such an extent that one of the latter felt bound to petition the Council or the Permanent Court of International Justice for the transfer of the Mandate to another country."[37] In the view of Lugard, the mandate could be revoked in the event of maladministration, although he optimistically thought that such a situation was an "inconceivable contingency."[38] In his view, revocation had to be done through the court.[39]

In his Separate Opinion in the *International Status of South-West Africa* Judge Alvarez stated:

> It may happen that a mandatory State does not perform the obligations resulting from its Mandate. In that case the United Nations Assembly may make admonitions, and if necessary, revoke the Mandate. It has this right under Article 10 of the Charter.[40]

In his Separate Opinion in the *Voting Procedure on Questions Relating to Reports and Petitions Concerning the Territory of South-West Africa* Judge Lauterpacht held that the supervisory organ may give "a verdict upon the conformity of the action of the administering State with its international obligations. . . ."[41] Judge Padilla Nervo said in his Dissenting Judgment in the *South-West Africa Case* (second phase):

> Obviously the power of administration and legislation could not be legitimately exercised by methods which run contrary to the aims, principles and obligations stated in Article 22 of the Covenant, especially in paragraphs 1, 2 and 6. Nor could (it) be exercised today in violation of the United Nations Charter provisions—among others—those regarding respect for human rights and fundamental freedoms, or the prohibition to discriminate on account of race or colour.[42]

If a mandate could not be revoked under any circumstances "then the operation would appear to look like a form of chicanery practised on mankind in the name of civilisation—a subterfuge 'intended to avoid,

37. PMC Minutes (1925), p. 154.

38. PMC Minutes (1924), p. 177.

39. *See also* Q. Wright, *Mandates Under the League of Nations*, p. 521; J. C. Hales, "Some Legal Aspects of the Mandates System" 23 *Transactions of the Grotius Society* (1938), 85 at 122.

40. *ICJ Rep.* (1950), p. 182.

41. *ICJ Rep.* (1955), p. 99.

42. *ICJ Rep.* (1966), p. 467.

through its operation, the appearance of taking enemy territory as spoils for war.' "[43] This could not have been the intention either of the peace conference or the League of Nations. The fact of accountability implied that the mandatory retained its powers for only so long as it, in the opinion of the supervisory organ, carried out its duties. Lord McNair denied that international law imported municipal law analogies holus-bolus but he also stressed that attention must be paid to "any features or terminology which are reminiscent of the rules and institutions of private law as an indication of policy and principles. . . ."[44] In some ways the mandate was based on the ideas of trust, mandate, and tutelage, which are all revocable in municipal law. The very concept of "sacred trust" implied revocability in the event of abuse, neglect, *mala fides*, or fulfill-ment. The mandate agreement was an international agreement between the members, the League, and the mandatories. According to the 1950 Opinion the General Assembly took over the supervision of the mandates from the League Council. The law of treaties permits denunciation by a party in the event of a fundamental breach by another party.[45]

The unanimity rule of the League Council could not have prevented revocation; for a mandatory could not have been judge in its own case. In the *Voting Procedure Case* Sir Hersch Lauterpacht said:

> Insofar as the principle *nemo judex in re sua* is not only a general principle of law, but also a principle of good faith, it is particularly appropriate in relation to an instrument of a fiduciary character such as a mandate or trust in which equitable considerations acting upon the conscience are of compelling application. This, too, is a general principle of law recognised by civilised States.[46]

South Africa could have been expelled for a breach of the mandate under Article 16 of the Covenant and thereafter deprived of the powers of a mandatory.[47] It follows that its consent for the revocation of the mandate was not necessary under the League, nor is it now under the United Nations.

43. *ICJ Rep.* (1966), p. 491–2, *per* Judge Mbanefo.
44. "International Status of South-West Africa," *ICJ Rep.* (1950), p. 148.
45. *See* McNair, *The Law of Treaties* (Oxford, 1961), p. 553. *See also* "The Law of Treaties" (1969) Art. 60: "A material breach of bilateral treaty by one of the parties entitles the other to invoke the breach as a ground for terminating the treaty or suspending its operation in whole or in part." A material breach is defined as "the violation of a provision essential to the accomplishment of the object or purpose of the treaty."
46. *ICJ Rep.* (1955), p. 105. *See also* the Mosul case, PCIJ (1925), ser. B., no. 12 at 32.
47. *See also* Dugard, "The Revocation of the Mandate for South-West Africa," 62(1) *AJIL* (1968), p. 78.

Although the General Assembly had not requested an advisory opinion on whether the mandate had been violated, some of the issues in the contentious proceedings between Liberia and Ethiopia on the one hand and South Africa on the other were that the Union had violated Article 2 of the mandate agreement and Article 22 of the Covenant by the implementation of apartheid and "impeded opportunities for self-determination by the inhabitants of the Territory." The court declined to pronounce on the merits of the case but reverted to the issue of an "antecedent character"—the question of their legal interest in the subject matter of the dispute.[48] However five of the seven dissenting judges (Forster, Koo, Mbanefo, Nervo, and Tanaka) condemned the policy on the evidence before them and held in law that it was contrary to the principle of the sacred trust.[49] Judge Koo said:

> From the undisputed facts presented in the written and oral pleadings of the Parties and the testimony and cross-examination of the witnesses and experts before the Court, it appears that this policy, as constituted in the said laws, regulations and measures applied or applicable to South West Africa, consecrates an unjustifiable principle of discrimination based on grounds of race, colour or ethnic origin in establishing the rights and duties of the inhabitants of the Territory. It is applied to the life, work, travel and residence of a non-White or a Native in the Territory. It is enforced in matters relating, for example, to the ownership of land in the so-called Police Zone, mining and the mining industry, employment in the Railways and Harbours Administration, vocational training and education.[50]

Judge Tanaka found that

> the practice of apartheid is fundamentally unreasonable and unjust, the unreasonableness and injustice do not depend upon the intention or motive of the Mandatory, namely its *mala fides*. Distinction on racial basis is in itself contrary to the principle of equality which is one of the characters of natural law, and accordingly illegal.[51]

Further "the observance of the principle of equality before the law must be considered as a necessary condition of the promotion of the material and moral well-being and the social progress of the inhabitants of the territory."[52]

48. *ICJ Rep.* (1966), p. 18.

49. Judges Jessup and Koretsky, the other dissenting judges, found that the court should have pronounced on the compatibility of the policy of apartheid with the principles of the mandate.

50. *ICJ Rep.* (1966), pp. 233–4.

51. Ibid., p. 314.

52. Ibid.

The deliberate policy of denying fundamental human rights to a section of the population (in this case the majority) is contrary to international law, the mandate agreement, and Article 22 of the League Covenant. The mandate was created primarily for the benefit of the Africans of South-West Africa in order to prepare them for independence or self-government according to their choice. Apartheid is so repugnant to the human personality that its implementation in the territory, along with the policy of impeding the political and economic progress of the people, legally justifies the revocation of the Republic's rights to administer the territory. The argument that apartheid means separate development and that this protects the traditions of the indigenous population is a subterfuge intended to cloak illegal actions that those applying them would vigorously resent being applied to themselves.

The steps taken by the United Nations to restore the rights of the people have not yet been effective. From 1946 to 1965 it passed seventy-three resolutions on the territory calling upon the Union government to place the territory under trusteeship, discontinue the policy of apartheid, make regular reports in accordance with the mandate agreement, and implement policies designed to achieve self-determination for the people. Although these resolutions are not in themselves binding they represent the abhorrence of the international community for the policy of apartheid and for the disregard of the interest of the people. These resolutions relating to the obligations of South Africa under the Charter and mandate agreement were so consistent and obtained with such overwhelming majorities that to ignore them amounts to a breach of international law and the law of the Charter.[53]

The attempt to enforce the mandate provisions through the International Court has so far failed. One of the consequences of the Judgment is to allow South Africa to entrench itself further in the territory in spite of its repeated challenges to the authority of the United Nations and in spite of its large-scale denial of human rights including self-determination. The Judgment upholds the view that only the League Council could have enforced the "conduct" provisions. Admitted that the General Assembly assumed the supervisory function of the League Council, the former cannot be a party to contentious proceedings. The result would then be that the mandate provisions could not be legally enforced in respect of the "conduct" provisions, which could not have been the intention of the negotiators seeking for peace at the conference.

In the mandate agreement only the freedom of missionary enterprise

---

53. But see the view of a South African jurist: Dugard, "The Legal Effect of United Nations Resolutions on Apartheid," 83 *South African LJ* (1966), p. 44.

could conceivably be classified as a special interest; the valuable open-door economic policy was excluded from all C-mandates. Evangelism is more to the benefit of the recipient than of the evangelist or his state. The compromissary clause could not have been meant to be evoked by members individually only in the protection of their special interests, leaving the legal enforcement of the "conduct" provisions exclusively to the League Council. Although states tend to invoke multilateral treaties mainly in respect of their special interests, some treaties totally lack this individual element. Such was the Genocide Convention about which the court said:

> The contracting States do not have any interest of their own; they have, one and all, a common interest, namely the accomplishment of these high purposes which are the *raison d'être* of the Convention. Consequently, in a convention of this type one cannot speak of individual advantages or disadvantages to States, or of the maintenance of a perfect contractual balance between rights and duties. The high ideals which inspired the Convention provide, by virtue of the common will of the parties, the foundation and measure of all its provisions.[54]

Rosenne deals with the question of legal interest in the following manner:

> Another form of legal interest which it is believed is recognised automatically is that which is based upon participation by the applicant State in a treaty to which the respondent State is also a party, at all events so long as the treaty is still in force. . . . Where such a treaty contains a compromissary clause, the jurisdiction may be invoked in accordance with that clause even if material interests of a concrete character cannot be shown by the applicant State. . . . This principle, which appears to be incontestable, is leading to two developments. The first is recognition of a treaty situation in which the contrasting States do not have any interests of their own but a common interest, the accomplishment of the purpose of the convention. Any party to such a treaty has a legal interest sufficient to entitle it to invoke the compromissary clause against any other party.[55]

The mandate system was specifically designed to help a category of undeveloped peoples. It was fundamentally a humanitarian innovation

---

54. "Reservations to the Genocide Convention," *ICJ Rep.* (1951) 23. In the *SS Wimbledon*, ser. A, no. 1 the court recognised the legal interest of the applicants in enforcing the provisions of the Treaty of Versailles relating to the Kiel Canal even though they adduced no evidence of financial prejudice. *See also Mavromatis Jerusalem Concessions (Merits)* (1925) ser. A, no. 5.

55. S. Rosenne, *The Law and Practice of the International Court of Justice* (1965), pp. 519–20. *See also* C. W. Jenks, *The Prospects of International Adjudication* (1964), pp. 523–24.

in the field of colonialism which, though not yet applicable to all colonies, was applied to the subject territories of the defeated enemy. The members of the League were therefore legally interested in the political, economic, and social development of the wards of civilisation, without any proof of their own special interest in the fulfillment of the sacred trust.[56]

The court's finding that humanitarian considerations alone do not constitute rules of law in themselves appears controversial in this age of human rights and in view of the Nuremberg Trials of 1946,[57] the Genocide Convention of 1948, and the Universal Declaration of Human Rights, which now constitute rules of International Law.[58] The court may yet have the opportunity of pronouncing on one of the many-sided issues affecting the territory, especially that of the jurisdiction.[59] To the people of the territory the most relevant decision would be one that promotes their right of self-determination since from that the benefits of other rights would readily flow.[60]

4. The Present Status of Namibia

Unfortunately the 1966 Judgment did not say whether the mandate was in existence or not but rather held that the decision was made "without pronouncing upon, and wholly without prejudice to, the question whether that Mandate is still in force."[61] It went on to say that the 1962

---

56. The 1962 judgment in fact spelled it out clearly: "the manifest scope and purport of the provisions of this Article [7 of the mandate] indicate that the Members of the League were understood to have a legal right or interest in the observance by the Mandatory of its obligations both toward the inhabitants of the Mandated Territory, and toward the League of Nations and its Members." *ICJ Rep.* (1962), p. 343.

57. Cmd. 6964 (1946).

58. In the Corfu Channel (Merits) case *ICJ Rep.* (1949), p. 4, the court held that Albania was liable for the destruction of British warships and lives through the failure to notify the presence of mines. It held that the obligation to notify was based "on certain general principles," *inter alia*, "elementary considerations of humanity, even more exacting in peace than in war." p. 22.

59. For possible ways of revising the 1966 judgment, *see* W. Reisman, "An Analysis of the Grounds of Nullity in the Decision of 18 July 1966 and Methods of Revision," 7 *Virginia JIL* (1966).

60. *See also* J. F. Crawford, "South-West Africa: Mandate Termination in Historical Perspective," 6 *Columbia Journal of Transnational Law* (1967); W. R. Louis, "South-West Africa, Origins of the Sacred Trust," *African Affairs* (1967), pp. 20–39; P. Calvocoressi, "South-West Africa," 65 *African Affairs* (1966), pp. 223–232; W. G. Friedmann, "The Jurisprudential Implications of the South-West Africa Case," 6 *Columbia Journal of Transnational Law* (1967); B. Fleming, "South-West Africa Cases," *Canadian YBIL* (1967).

61. *ICJ Rep.* (1966), p. 19. It however acknowledged the fact that the peace conference ruled out the annexation of a mandate territory either by the Principal Allied and Associated Powers or by any country affiliated with them. (p. 24.)

Judgment was also without prejudice to the question of the mandate. The 1950 Opinion however stated that the mandate survived the League and this was confirmed by the Opinions of 1955 and 1956[62] and the Judgment of 1962 which spelled out:

> [The] essential principles of the Mandate System consist chiefly in the recognition of certain rights of the peoples of the underdeveloped territories; the establishment of a regime of tutelage for each of such peoples to be exercised by an advanced nation as a "Mandatory" 'on behalf of the League of Nations'; and the recognition of a 'sacred trust of civilisation' laid upon its Member States. This system is dedicated to the avowed object of promoting the well-being and development of the peoples concerned and is fortified by setting up safeguards for the protection of their rights.[63]

Self-determination was not expressly written into the mandate agreement but, along with the principle of non-annexation, dominated the Peace Conference of the First World War. The concept of mandates for peoples "not yet able to stand by themselves" implied that they would ultimately enjoy the right to self-determination after a process of political, social, and economic development. Whatever doubts may exist about the right of self-determination under the mandates system as it existed at the time of the League are made irrelevant by present international law which extends the principle to all peoples. Fundamental human rights, including the right of self-determination, have become generally recognised in the international law of today. The interpretation of a mandate agreement must therefore now have regard to the changed state of international law today on this question. Support for this view is to be found in what Judge Huber called "intertemporal law" in the *Island of Palmas* case,[64] a dispute between the United States and the Netherlands concerning sovereignty over the island. Although the effect of Spain's discovery of the island in the early part of the sixteenth century was to be determined by the international law of the time, the title in 1898 when it

---

62. For the value of advisory opinions, see Rosenne: *The Law and Practice of the International Court of Justice* (1965), p. 747. "It is practically authoritative as that of a judgment in contentious proceedings." Dugard, "The South-West Africa Cases," p. 460. The 1950 opinion was accepted by the assembly in Res. 449A(V) of 13 December 1950 and whatever may be its binding effect, it is "the law recognised by the United Nations. It continues to be so although the Government of South Africa has declined to accept it as binding upon it and although it has acted in disregard of the international obligations as declared by the Court in that Opinion"—per Judge Lauterpacht in the "Admissibility of Hearings of Petitions," *ICJ Rep.* (1956), p. 23.

63. *ICJ Rep.* (1962), p. 329.

64. Permanent Court of Arbitration (1928), no. 19; Green: International Law Through the Cases (1951), pp. 350–369.

passed to the United States was to be determined by the international law of the latter period.

> The same principle which subjects the act creative of a right to the law in force at the time the right arises, demands that the existence of the right, in other words its continued manifestation, shall follow the conditions required by the evolution of the law. International law in the nineteenth century, having regard to the fact that most parts of the globe were under the sovereignty of States members of the community of nations, and that territories without a master had become relatively few, took account of a tendency already existing and especially developed since the middle of the eighteenth century, and laid down the principle that occupation, to constitute a claim to territorial sovereignty, must be effective. . . . For these reasons, discovery alone, without any subsequent act, cannot at the present time suffice to prove sovereignty over the Island of Palmas.[65]

The principle of intertemporal law is a complement of the principle of effectiveness and is applied when it reasonably conforms with the general climate of international law.[66] Judge Padilla Nervo referred to it in his dissenting judgment:

> The Court cannot be indifferent to the fact that the Mandate operates under the conditions and circumstances of 1966, when the moral and legal conscience of the world, and the acts, decisions and attitudes of the organised international community, have created principles, and evolved rules of law which in 1920 were not so developed, or did not have such strong claims to recognition.[67]

Applying Judge Huber's principle, a mandate agreement has now to be interpreted and applied in the light of the principle of self-determination, especially so when the mandatory is a member of the United Nations. The obligation under Articles 1, 55, and 56 of the Charter "to develop friendly

---

65. Green, p. 357. For the disturbing implications of the theory of "intertemporal law" *see* P. C. Jessup, "The Palmas Island Case," 22 *AJIL* (1928), p. 740. The US contention that the Spanish title established in the sixteenth century must be evaluated by the international law of the late nineteenth century was generally conceded by the Netherlands which also stated, "a title to territory is not a legal relation in international law whose existence and elements are a matter of one single moment . . . the changed conception of law developing in later times cannot be ignored in judging the continued legal value of relations which, instead of being consummated and terminated at one single moment, are of a permanent character." Netherlands Counter-Memorandum, p. 21.

66. *See also* C. de Visscher: *Problems d'Interpretation Judiciare en Droit International Public* (1966), p. 166; McNair, p. 468; Friedmann: *The Changing Structure of International Law* (London, 1964), pp. 130–1.

67. *ICJ Rep.* (1966), p. 467. *See also Nationality Decrees of Tunis and Morocco,* PCIJ (1923), ser. B, no. 4: "The question whether a certain matter is or is not solely within the jurisdiction of a State is an essentially relative question; it depends upon the development of international relations." (p. 24)

relations based on respect for the principle of equal rights and self-determination of peoples" extends to a mandated territory which the mandatory refused to place under the trusteeship system of the United Nations.[68]

Having regard to the mandate agreement, the League Covenant, or the Charter of the United Nations, the Union has not only failed to carry out the sacred trust but has also displayed much contempt for the agreement and for the organisation.

A resolution of the League Council revoking the mandate would have been legally binding by itself but this is not the case with Resolution 2145(XXI) of 27 October 1966 in which the General Assembly declared that the mandate was "terminated" and conferred the administration of the territory directly on the United Nations. Though not in itself legally binding, it represents, at least, the views of the great majority of states on the status of Namibia, and members of the United Nations have a minimum duty of considering the resolution in good faith. The Security Council Resolution 269 of 12 August 1969 asking the Republic to quit Namibia by 4 October 1969 confirms the revocation by the General Assembly and is legally binding on South Africa which, however, feels able to flout the resolutions.

Apartheid, forced labour, deprivation of the rights of movement, denial of voting rights, and land patrimony are some of the scourges the eradication of which is demanded by the communal interests of the international community, including those of South Africa in the long run. The Security Council found that the regime of apartheid in South Africa constitutes a threat to international peace and stability and banned the sale or shipment of arms to South Africa.[69] The extension of the system to Namibia poses a similar threat which is now aggravated by the refusal of the Republic to accept the direct responsibility of the United Nations over the territory. The Republic has not hidden its intention to maintain its authority over the territory by force, if necessary. If the Security Council considers that the situation constitutes a "threat to the peace" under Article 39 of the Charter, it may take the appropriate measures

---

68. *See also* the dictum of Oppenheim that international law is "conditioned by the milieu of the age." "The Science of International Law: Its Task and Method," *AJIL* (1908), 314 at 318.

69. Security Council Res. 4300 of 1 April 1960, 5386 of 7 August 1963, and 5471 of 4 December 1963. In the last resolution, it called on all states "to cease forthwith the sale and shipment of equipment and materials for the manufacture and maintenance of arms and ammunition in South Africa." These resolutions have since been repeated and extended by the council and by the assembly but have been broken by France and some other Western powers.

either of a military character under Article 42, or "not involving the use of armed force" under Article 41 "to maintain or restore international peace and security." The restoration of peace and security in the area should have as one of its objectives the preservation of the right of the people to self-determination.

5. The Bantustans of Namibia

While the proceedings of the South-West Africa cases were in progress, the South African government in 1962 set up a commission of inquiry to investigate the progress of the inhabitants of the territory and to recommend plans for future development. The main intention was to devise a plan for integration which maintains a facade of self-determination for the people. The report, published on 27 January 1964, was accepted by the government and is already being implemented despite its repudiation by the General Assembly.[70]

The Odendaal Commission prescribes the separation of races in order, it is claimed, to prevent discrimination and conflict.[71] It divides the mandated territory into areas for natives, Europeans, and "coloureds." The unallocated areas are controlled by the Government of the Republic, in which the non-whites have no say. Ten of these allocated areas constitute the "homelands" for the non-whites—Ovamboland, Tswanaland, Namaland, Eastern Caprivi, Damaraland, Rehobeth, Gebiet, Okavangoland, Hereroland, Bushmanland, and Kaokveld, with an additional three townships for the coloureds. Each homeland will have a Legislative Council which will gradually take over the powers of the Department of Bantu Administration. The largest is Ovamboland with a population of 240,000 and the smallest is Tswanaland whose population is a mere 2632. It is argued that the policy will lead to "political independence" coupled with "economic interdependence" with the white areas as opposed to a policy of multiracialism which is supposed to be explosive. Thus Prime Minister Verwoerd told the South African Club in London in 1961 that the Bantustans would follow "the model of nations, which in this modern world means political independence coupled with economic interdepend-

---

70. Res. 2074(XX) of 17 December 1965. "(5) [The assembly] Considers further that any attempt to partition the Territory or to take any unilateral action, directly or indirectly, preparatory thereto constitutes a violation of the Mandate and of Resolution 1514(XV); (6) Considers further that any attempt to annex part or the whole of the Territory of South-West Africa constitutes an act of aggression." The scheme has so far been implemented in Ovamboland and Okavangoland.

71. See also South Africa: Racial Affairs, Integration or Separate Development? (Stellensbosch, 1952).

ence.[72] If this assertion is true, the Bantustan solution opens the way to self-determination.[73]

On examination, the Bantustan policy reveals anomalies and inconsistencies that militate against the principle of self-determination. The populations of the Africans, whites and coloureds are in the proportion of 18:3:1,[74] but the division of the land gives them an average of .74, 6.74, and .62 square kilometres per Africans, white, and coloured respectively. The non-whites had no say in the division of the land. It has been suggested that "a fair procedure might consist of having representatives of the Natives divide the territory into twenty-two parts, and then let the Coloured representative choose one part and the European representative choose three parts."[75] In fact the Europeans have been allocated 13/22 of the land as against their population which is 3/22 of the total. The whites—be they English, German, Boer, French or other—are treated as a single group that must dominate, while the Africans are split into their language groups. The coloureds are herded into separate areas.

None of the Bantustans has an outlet to the sea and four of the ten are isolated from others. The minerals—copper, zinc, gold, and diamond —are located in lands that are either allocated to the whites or are unallocated and so belong to the Central Authority in which the non-whites have no say. The developed areas including the factories, railways, banks, and commercial firms and harbours are in the Police Zone and outside the Bantustans.

It is a remote probability, or indeed possibility, that the Bantustans could ever achieve political or economic independence. Under cross-examination before the International Court of Justice, P. J. Collie, editor of the influential *Die Burger*, said:

> Some of those units (Bantustans) could obviously not be independent states in any accepted sense. . . . Some of them are so small and the numbers (of the population) are so low that obviously you cannot speak of all those smaller areas as viable states; you cannot envisage that, not for the foreseeable future.[76]

72. Union of South Africa, Fact Paper 91 (Cape Town, April 1961) p. 14.

73. For a summary of the Odendaal Report, *see* P. Mason, "Separate Developments and South West Africa: "Some Aspects of the Odendaal Report," *Race* (London, 4 April 1964), 5:83–97; UN Secretariat Working Paper, 8 April 1964, 109/L. 108.

74. 424,047: 23,965: 73,464 in 1960. See Odendaal Report Tables A, B, and C, pp. 109 and 111.

75. A. A. D'Amato, "The Bantustan Proposals for South-West Africa," 4 *JMAS*, no. 2 (1966), pp. 177–92.

76. *ICJ Verbatim Record*, CR 65/66 p. 14.

Speaking of the economy, Professor J. P. van S. Bruwer, who served in the Odendaal Commission, said that the Bantustans "would not be able to thrive or possibly survive" without the use of white labour, although they might be [able to] at some time in the future in the next 300 years.[77] Although they would have their own Legislative Councils, their legislations would be subject to the approval of the President of the Republic while the South African Supreme Court and the Appeal Court would be the highest courts. Important subjects such as defence, mines, electricity, and internal and external security belong to the South African government.

There is no genuine intention to grant the South-West Africans full self-determination either immediately or in the future. Dr. Verwoerd's answer in Parliament in 1951 with regard to a plan for the Africans in South Africa, a predecessor of the present Bantustans, epitomises the South African idea of self-determination for the non-whites.

> Now a Senator wants to know whether the series of self-governing areas would be sovereign. The answer is obvious. It stands to reason that White South Africa must remain their guardian. We are spending all the money on these developments. How could small scattered states arise? The areas will be economically dependent on the Union. It stands to reason that when we talk of the Natives' right of self-government in these areas we cannot mean that we intend by that to cut large slices of South Africa and turn them into independent States.[78]

In 1964 Mr. Van Der Merwe referred in Parliament to the "normal evolution of the centuries" during which time the Bantustans would obtain their independence,[79] and Dr. Verwoerd revealed that the ideal of total separation could not be attained in a few years or even for a long time.[80] Another member of Parliament assured his constituents that freedom for the Bantustans would not come in two hundred years.[81]

In spite of the fanfare with which the Republic launched the Bantustan scheme, it is clear that it is not intended to foster the progress toward self-determination. It is rather intended to split the territory into small unviable units that would be heavily dependent on South Africa and this would amount to annexation in name and in fact. This contravenes a

---

77. Ibid., 65/56, pp. 22 and 25.
78. South Africa, Parl. Deb., Senate (1951), cols. 2893–4.
79. Parl. Deb., House of Assembly (1965), col. 5481.
80. Ibid., (1958) col. 3805 .
81. J. Lelyveld, "Apartheid Wins New Mandate," *New York Times*, 3 April 1966.

vital principle of the mandate. Genuine self-determination will enable the people to choose their form of government and the form of association, if any, with South Africa. They may choose independence, integration, or autonomy. The exercise of political power will be enjoyed by all the people according to their numbers and capabilities. They will enjoy fundamental human rights without discrimination as to race or colour: a policy that restricts the movement of nationals and confines a section of the population of undeveloped parts is to be severely condemned. The fruits of the land should be enjoyed by all sections of the population and measures calculated to impede such benefits are contrary to fundamental human rights as generally understood by the civilised world. The imposition of the Bantustan homelands on the mandate territory reflects a negation of the principle of self-determination and an affront to the international community and the United Nations in particular.[82]

82. D'Amato warns that "a belated discovery that the Bantustans are not a solution, but rather an aggravation, of the problem of racial discrimination can lead to more violent repercussions at the expense of all the inhabitants of Southern Africa than a careful assessment of the plan at the present time." 4(2) *JMAS* (1966), p. 19.

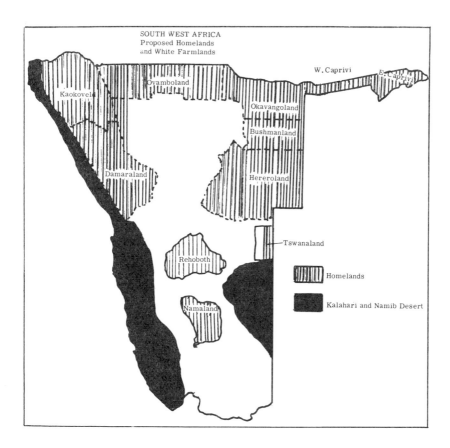

Proposed Homelands and the White Farmlands. Outside the Homelands, the Namib Desert and the Game Reserves, almost all the rest of the territory is White Farmland.

VII The State Practice of Four Major Powers as Significant Factors in the Recognition of Self-Determination in International Law

The recognition of self-determination as a fundamental principle of international law is comparatively recent. Primary factors in this development have been the policies of the major colonial powers, the United States and the Soviet Union.

Modern colonialism can be traced back to the sixteenth century when adventurers from Western Europe sailed to distant lands for varying purposes. The love of adventure, the search for raw materials, new markets, new commodities, and suitable areas for settlement were among the main reasons for overseas expansion. The conversion of heathen lands to Christianity and the control of the slave trade, as religious and humanitarian reasons, were secondary. As distant colonies were acquired, the need arose to maintain intermediate and strategic posts on the main routes. It became a matter of national prestige to expand colonies and areas of influence and to maintain the balance of power among competing nations. By the end of the nineteenth century most of the world was occupied or controlled by peoples of European stock.

The reverse process of the return to independence in modern times started with the American War of Independence. Early in the nineteenth century, the South American states overthrew Spanish and Portuguese rule and were actively supported by the Monroe Doctrine, which aimed at preventing further European colonisation of the Americas, especially

South America. The twentieth century witnessed the independence of states inhabited by coloured peoples.[1] During the process of administering colonies, states have evolved practices to accommodate the demand for self-determination, intensified by nationalism in the dependent territories. Where decolonisation was already state policy, it was speeded up; some states aimed at self-determination through assimilation, while others paid at least lip service to local autonomy or independence as appropriate. At the end of the Second World War there were eleven administering powers—United States, Great Britain, Belgium, France, Holland, Denmark, South Africa, Portugal, Spain, Australia, and New Zealand. Italy joined the group when it was invested with the trusteeship of Somalia in 1948.

Our discussion will be centered on Great Britain, France and the United States, which have worked out a clear policy of self-determination in their dependent territories. The USSR, though not an administering power within the Charter, has a distinctive outlook on the subject which deserves consideration.

1. Great Britain

A. *The Old Commonwealth States.* Britain had the largest colonial empire; its practice is thus important as evidence of state practice. Having lost the American colonies, Britain tried to learn from the mistake of refusing to concede the right of self-determination to a colony. It became the official policy to advance the colonies to independence. They were like fruits which, when ripe, fell from the parent tree. Britain regarded its role as watching over the process of ripening in an orderly form and protecting all the interests concerned, particularly its own. An important characteristic of British practice is that each colony was treated, not as part of the metropolitan state, but as a separate and distinct territory, a state in an embryo stage owing allegiance to the British Crown. It was natural to introduce the familiar Westminster form of Parliamentary Democracy, the principal characteristics of which are the supremacy of Parliament, separation of the judiciary, executive, and legislative powers, periodic elections, and the recognition of an official opposition party.

The progress toward the goal of self-determination was smooth in settled colonies. The colonists had carried on their backs the English common law and legal system. Following Durham's Report of 1839,

---

1. Ethiopia has always been independent except for the period 1936–42 when it was under Italian occupation. From the foundation of the settlement for freed slaves in 1847, Liberia has been independent though relying heavily on the United States at the early stages. Despite capitulation treaties and a few colonial enclaves, China maintained its independence.

self-government was granted to Ontario and Quebec in 1840 and to Prince Edward Island in 1851. Newfoundland became self-governing in 1855. In 1867 Ontario, Quebec, New Brunswick, and Nova Scotia formed the Federation of Canada and were subsequently joined by the other provinces. In 1847 New Zealand received a constitution that provided for ten provincial assemblies, but these gave way to a national legislature established by the Imperial Statute of 1852. New South Wales, South Australia, Tasmania (all of which received self-government in 1856), Victoria, Queensland, and Western Australia (which achieved theirs in 1855, 1859, and 1890 respectively) combined to form the Commonwealth of Australia in 1900. The Cape Province and Natal achieved responsible government in 1872 and 1893 respectively and formed the Union of South Africa in 1910.

The white population of these territories achieved a measure of self-determination when they enjoyed responsible government. Their laws were however subject to the repugnancy rule whereby any law contrary to imperial law applicable to them was void *pro tanto*.[2] The king's dominions were represented by the British monarch in their international relations since the crown was indivisible.[3] The *inter-se* doctrine emphasized that relations between members were, by their nature, so intimate that they were outside the purview of international law.[4]

It is impossible to say precisely when the dominions became international persons. From the beginning of the century there was a gradual accretion of international personality which reached a considerable degree during the Peace Conference of the First World War, enabling them to participate as members of the British Empire. In 1923 Canada established a separate legation in Washington and was soon followed by others. The Inter-Imperial Relations Committees set up by the Imperial Conference in 1926 reported that the dominions were: "autonomous communities within the British Empire, equal in status, in no way subordinate one to another in any aspect of their domestic or external affairs, though united by a common allegiance to the Crown and freely associated as members of the British Commonwealth of Nations."[5] The Statute of

2. Colonial Laws Validity Act 1865, ser. 2.

3. Thus in *Theodore v. Duncan 1919 AC 696*, it was held "The Crown is one and indivisible throughout the Empire." The crown is however limited by the relevant constitutional instrument for there may be a conflict in the exercise of its powers.

4. For the *inter-se* doctrine, *see* Fawcett, *The British Commonwealth in International Law* (1963), p. 144; Fawcett, *The Inter-se Doctrine in Commonwealth Relations* (1958).

5. Cmd. 2768.

Westminster in 1931—which removed the application to the dominions of the Colonial Laws Validity Act and any future act of the British Parliament, unless by the express consent or request of the dominion— acknowledged a situation that already existed *de facto* and is generally regarded as a landmark in the progress toward full self-determination.

B. *The New Commonwealth States.* Progress in the colonies occupied by the coloured races was not so smooth and orderly. It was complicated by a low standard of development, by the political, social and religious differences of their multiple societies, the comparative conservatism in political advancement, in some cases by the presence of a considerable number of settlers who feared and opposed the rule of the majority, and by the desire to prolong colonial exploitation as long as possible. Constitutional advancement usually followed periods of nationalist pressure and unrest which took the form of nonviolence in most colonies but occasional violence in India, and Mau Mau guerrilla warfare in Kenya. In West Africa, the pressure took the form of agitation, especially in the nationalist press. The Zik's Group of Newspapers built up a popular challenge to colonial rule, especially in Southern Nigeria.

The principle was in theory clear: the advancement of native peoples to self-determination. Thus in 1824, Thomas Munro of Madras said that the British aim was "to train Indians to govern and protect themselves."[6] Henry Lawrence of Punjab and Rajputana in 1844 expressed the same view. Secretary of State Earl Grey, who implemented self-government in Canada and Australia, expressed hopes for similar guidance for West African territories "until they shall grow into a nation capable of protecting themselves and of managing their own affairs."[7] This was confirmed by the West African Royal Commission in 1865. The report of the Parliamentary Commission on East Africa regarded the government of those territories as a threefold trusteeship:

> *Firstly,* for the moral and material development of the native inhabitants. *Secondly,* for humanity as a whole (the duty here being to develop the vast economic resources of those territories for the benefit of the whole world—a duty the conception of which has been made familiar by Lord Lugard in his doctrine of the Dual Mandate).[8] *Thirdly,* for the immigrant communities, whose initia-

6. Quoted in Duncan Hall, *Mandates, Dependencies and Trusteeships,* (1948), p. 95.

7. Ibid.

8. As trustees for the development of the resources for the benefit of civilisation and for the welfare of the natives. For the inherent incompatibilities of this policy see L. Barnes, *The Duty of Empire,* pp. 151 *et seq.*

tive, knowledge, and material resources are necessary instruments in the fulfillment of the first two tasks.[9]

An earlier white paper stated in relation to Kenya:

> Primarily Kenya is an African territory, and His Majesty's Government think it necessary definitely to record their considered opinion that the interests of the African natives must be paramount, and that if, and when, those interests and the interests of the immigrant races conflict, the former should prevail.[10]

More recently the secretary of state, in Oxford University Summer School on Colonial Administration, posed the question in August 1938:

> What is the main purpose of the British Colonial Empire? I suggest that it is the gradual spread of freedom among all His Majesty's subjects, in whatever part of the Empire they live. . . . Even among the most backward races of Africa, our main effort should be to try and help these people to stand a little bit more securely on their own feet. . . . We can see the process going on, and we can say confidently that the trend is towards the ultimate establishment of the various colonial communities as self-supporting and self-reliant members of a great Commonwealth of free peoples and nations.[11]

Speaking in Leeds in January 1944, another secretary of state, Colonel Stanley, said, "Politically, our declared aim is gradually to bring the Colonies to a position of self-government within the British Empire."[12] Oliver Lyttleton, as secretary of state for the colonies repeated:

> First, we all aim at helping the Colonial Territories to attain self-government within the British Commonwealth. . . . Second, we are all determined to pursue the economic and social development of the Colonial Territories so that it keeps pace with their political development.[13]

In spite of the clarity of the principle, there were difficulties in its implementation revolving around gradualism favoured by colonial civil servants and speedy progress, advocated by the nationalists. It was really a question of timing.

C. *Indirect Rule.* The British watchword was to interfere as little as possible with the ordinary lives of the people. Native law and custom

9. East African Commission Cmd. 2397 of 1925.
10. Cmd. 3234 of 1929, pp. 40–1.
11. W. R. Crocker, *Self-government for the Colonies* (1948), p. 135.
12. Ibid.
13. 493 HC Deb., 5th ser. col. 984, 12 November 1951.

were allowed to continue except where they conflicted with a statute applicable to the territory or were contrary to good morality and good conscience. Thus the caste system was allowed in India but widow-burning was outlawed. Polygamy was allowed in Africa and other places but the killing of twins was banned. Indigenous governmental institutions were not abolished but were employed under the supervision of advisers.

Indirect rule was applied to Ceylon, India, Malaya, and Fiji during the second half of the eighteenth century. In 1862 Moshesh, king of the Basutos, wrote the following letter to Queen Victoria:

> What I desire is this; that the Queen Victoria send a man to live with me, who will be her ear and eye, and also her hand to work with me in political matters. My "House" is Basutoland. So that the Queen rules only through me. The man whom I ask from the Queen to live with me will guide me and direct me and communicate between me and the Government. I wish to govern my own people by native law, by our own law; but if the Queen wish (sic) after this to introduce other laws into my country, I would be willing; but I should wish such laws to be submitted to the Council of the Basutos; and when they are accepted by my Council, I will send to the Queen and inform her that they have become law.[14]

Moshesh's understanding of indirect rule was subjecting applicable British law to the acceptance of the Basuto king-in-council, but he was soon to realise that the colonisers were not so democratic.

Sir Frederick Lugard introduced the system in Uganda toward the end of the nineteenth century and, at the beginning of the twentieth century, elaborated its theory and practice in Northern Nigeria after he conquered the vast territory ruled by the Emirs. Having proved its success, the system was extended to the south and to other colonies.

Indirect rule kept the society intact and only allowed innovations in graduated measures. There was an official to advise the native authority and he could only take over the administration when it broke down or fell out of the favour of the colonial master. He transmitted orders, not directly, but through the native authority. The system was a principle of

> government by which the controlling power encourages among its dependent peoples the fullest possible use of their dynamic institutions as instruments of local self-government on lines consistent with modern requirements. By the system of "Indirect Rule" native societies are enabled to continue their corporate life, to retain and speak, and to be consulted through their own familiar institutions. . . . It was framed indeed on one belief that if a backward people is sud-

14. Cited by R. L. Buell, *The Native Problem in Africa* (New York, 1928), 1:165.

denly confronted by a powerful modern State and is not given the time and assistance necessary to enable it to face the new situation, it is liable to lose its stability, and indeed its soul. Its political and social organisation is likely to break, and what was before a well-ordered community, in which all the members had a definite series of obligations to one another, may become nothing but a disorganised rabble of self-seeking individualists.[15]

In Lugard's own words, it was intended "to promote the evolution and adaptation of native institutions as opposed to Europeanisation and assimiliation."[16] Thus in *Eshugbayi-Eleko* v. *Government of Nigeria*,[17] the Privy Council rejected the view that the governor could appoint, depose, and deport indigenous rulers contrary to customary law and in *Laoye* v. *Oyetunde*,[18] the board set aside the appointment of a chief that was contrary to native law and custom.

Indirect rule restricted the free hand of the traditional rulers since they could be overruled by their political advisers who were often much younger people. Traditional rulers looked back to the "good old days" when they ruled both in theory and in practice. The system operated as a bulwark against modernisation and ensured the prolongation of the feudal and colonial status quo. A former colonial civil servant has criticised the system in Northern Nigeria, where it was most developed and applied:

And it is indisputable that the policy of the discredited Lieutenant-Governors of Northern Nigeria in the twenties who discouraged, sometimes they banned, the teaching of English and of modern trades and techniques and who insulated the people from all outside contacts and knowledge in the holy name of Indirect Rule, put the North back a generation or more. That is why in the North today most of the clerks in the Government and commerce and most of the technicians and employees in the Post and Telegraph, the Public Works Department, and the Railways, are not Northerners but Southerners.[19]

15. C. K. Meek: *Law and Authority in a Nigerian Tribe* (Oxford, 1937), p. 332.

16. Quoted in *Colonial Problem* (1937), p. 258.

17. AC (1931), p. 662.

18. AC (1944), p. 170.

19. Crocker, p. 59. *See also* Edward Feit, "Military Coups and Political Development," 20 *World Politics* (January 1968): "So by their common working the administrative and the traditional system served to legitimise each other. The administrators protected traditional systems from change and made their preservation acceptable to the governments at home. The traditional rulers, in turn, helped to make colonial practices institutional among their followers." (p. 181). "Furthermore, through the system. . . . chiefs became tools, and in many cases paid agents, of the colonial administration." K. Nkrumah, *Class Structure in Africa* (London, 1970), p. 14.

The native ruler, often old-fashioned and feudalistic, was able to extract obedience from his subjects with the powerful machinery of the new administration. He was hardly a favourite of the young progressive elements of the society, outside of his immediate family, for they were impatient with the rate of advancement. The extension of the system to chiefless societies necessitated the creation of "warrant chiefs" and these were often an unpopular class of government henchmen who were sometimes at variance with traditional functionaries with more limited authority. In terms of modern nation-building, indirect rule tended to emphasise the diversities of the peoples under the same colonial administration by creating pockets of loyalties at the expense of nationalism at the state level. The drawbacks became very evident on the attainment of independence.[20] However it was a sensible expedient in the light of a dearth of administrative personnel over vast territories, undeveloped economic resources, and poor communications. It was a stopgap, preceding the era when the generality of people gradually came to participate in government.[21]

D. *Constitutional Steps Toward Self-determination.* There was at first a governor vested with legislative, executive, and judicial powers. The separation of powers was at the early stages impracticable and the *fons et origo* of both justice and laws was subject only to the home government.

A council was then established consisting of officials and local Britishers with the duty of advising the governor, whose discretionary powers were unlimited.

The local people were introduced into the government in stages, usually beginning with the traditional rulers and local persons nominated by the governor. A few elected members were then introduced; their strength was increased until, with the nominated members, they formed the majority in the legislative council. Local people were also gradually introduced into the executive council and worked in cooperation with British heads of government departments. Eventually they formed the majority in the council. The penultimate stage was a wholly elected legislature with full executive powers while defence, foreign affairs, and finance were retained by the governor, assisted by civil servants.

When independence came, the governor became a constitutional head

20. *See also* K. W. Post, "Is There a Case for Biafra?" 44 *International Affairs* (1968), p. 28: "Far from creating any sense of transcending loyalties, it even emphasised differences within ethnic groups."

21. *See also* Nwabueze, *Constitutional Law of the Nigerian Republic* (1964), pp. 27–31; J. E. Flint, "Nigeria: The Colonial Experience" in Gann and Duignan, eds., *Colonialism in Africa* (Cambridge, 1969), pp. 252–3.

and was appointed by the British monarch with the consent of the local executive. The constitutional head at this stage represented the queen and acted, not on the advice of the British executive, but on that of the new state whose membership in international organisations was usually sponsored by Britain.

There was no defined duration for each stage of constitutional development; it all depended upon the circumstances of each territory. India was the first of the new states to achieve independence in 1947; Ghana blazed the trail for Africa in 1957, and Jamaica for the West Indies in 1962.

E. *The Sudan.* No territory exemplifies the progress toward full self-determination better than the Sudan. From about 1820 it was ruled by a Turko-Egyptian government which was overthrown in a religious revolt in 1885. Independence was sustained until 1898 when the Sudan was captured by Anglo-Egyptian forces. The first constitutional charter was the Anglo-Egyptian Agreement of 1898, which provided for a partnership, Britain being the dominant member.[22] Supreme military and civil command was vested in the governor-general, who was recommended by the British government and appointed by a decree of the Khedive of Egypt. British consent was required for his removal.

After a period of dispute between the co-domini, following Egypt's desire to annex Sudan, the agreement of 1898 was confirmed in a Treaty of Alliance in 1936[23] which stated the primary aim of the administration to be the welfare of the Sudanese. In 1945 Egypt renewed its pressure for annexation but Britain favoured a decision on the issue by the Sudanese after they had attained self-government, the demand for which divided the country into pro-Egyptian and pro-Sudanese factions.

A council composed of officials had been created in 1910 and in 1943 an advisory council was set up for Northern Sudan. Fuller participation came in 1949 with the creation of executive and legislative councils having extensive powers but subject to the governor-general's veto. A motion in the Parliament in 1950 requested the governor to approach the condominium powers on the issue of self-government and a constitution amendment commission was set up to study changes in the constitution. Egypt, however, was dissatisfied with the steps taken and announced a unilateral abrogation of the treaties of 1898 and 1936 while at the same time asserting Egypt's claim over the Sudan. This only encouraged separatism in the Sudan and led the assembly to record its warm

22. *See* text in de Martens, *Nouveau Recueil Général de Traités* 3e serie IV, 791; 91 *BFSP* (1898–99), p. 10.
23. 173 LNTS, p. 401.

appreciation of the British government's stand on self-government for the Sudan. The commission came to a standstill on the issue of the *locus* of sovereignty during the transitional period and was dissolved after the resignation of some of its members. The chairman's report, however, formed the basis for the Self-Government Statute of 21 March, 1953. Mr. Eden, the British foreign secretary stated in the House of Commons on 15 November 1951:

> Having attained self-government it will be for the Sudanese people to choose their own future status and relationship with the United Kingdom and with Egypt. His Majesty's Government consider that the attainment of self-government should immediately be followed by active preparations for the ultimate goal of self-determination. They will support the Governor-General in his efforts to ensure that the Sudanese people shall be able to exercise their choice in complete freedom and in the full consciousness of their responsibilities.[24]

In the meantime King Farouk of Egypt was overthrown in a military revolution. The new Egyptian prime minister, General Neguib, initiated a new policy of recognition of the right of the Sudanese to self-determination. Negotiations were resumed with the British and the result was an agreement on self-determination for the Sudan.[25] The preamble of the agreement recited the firm belief of the parties in "the right of the Sudanese people to self-determination and the effective exercise thereof at the proper time and with the necessary safeguards." The agreement provides for a transitional period of a maximum of three years, from the time of an election, during which time "the sovereignty of the Sudan shall be kept in reserve for the Sudanese people until self-determination is achieved."[26] The governor-general was the supreme constitutional authority and was assisted by a commission of five (two Sudanese, one Egyptian, one Briton, and one Pakistani).[27] He was responsible for foreign affairs and had to endorse resolutions of the commission that were inconsistent with its powers before they became effective. Any requests for changes in the constitution were to be made by him to the British and Egyptian governments. A Sudanisation committee was set up to provide "the free and neutral atmosphere requisite for self-determination" within a period of three years. At the end of the transitional period, Parliament was to

---

24. Winter, *Blueprints for Independence* (Djabbatan N.V., 1961), p. 231.

25. Agreement Between the Egyptian Government and the Government of the UK of Great Britain and Northern Ireland, Concerning Self-government and Self-determination for the Sudan, *Government Press* (Cairo, 1953):161 *UNTS*, p. 157.

26. Article 2.

27. Article 8.

pass a resolution "expressing their desire that arrangements for self-determination shall be put in motion."[28] This was to be followed by the drawing up of a constituent assembly which, after the withdrawal of British and Egyptian troops would decide on (1) independence for the Sudan or link with Egypt, and (2) Sudanese Constitution as well as the electoral law for Parliament.

Toward the end of the transitional period, the desire of some of the political parties to link the Sudan with Egypt became less evident. The Parliament expressed the desire to determine the future status of the country, not by a constitutional assembly as laid down in the agreement, but by a plebiscite. This led to a mutiny of Southern troops based on the deep suspicion of the North by the South, the latter preferring federal relations. Independence came, in fact, by a unanimous resolution of the assembly and not by a plebiscite. The co-domini acquiesced and recognised Sudanese independence on 1 January 1956. The amended self-government statute became the transitional constitution.[29]

The participation of two powers was probably a blessing for the Sudan, for each kept a watch on the other in the fulfillment of its responsibilities. The problem of plural societies showed up in the schism between the South and the North, the former claiming for itself the right to self-determination which was enjoyed by the country as a whole. Unfortunately the problem was not resolved before independence and was followed by a civil war. With such religious and cultural diversities, federalism might have provided the answer to the problems of the Sudan.

The military government that came to power on 25 May 1969 pledged itself to grant the South "regional self-autonomy" which it considered to be "a scientific basis for facing one of our major domestic problems, and finding a solution to safeguard our unity and to guarantee the rights of each of our two groups to develop its culture and heritage and emphasize the entity of each of those co-existing groups."[30]

F. *The Commonwealth Today*. The Commonwealth today is a voluntary, interracial and intercontinental association of states with the common experience of the tutelage of one of its members—Britain—and is designed to further cooperation and understanding among the members

---

28. Article 9.

29. *See also* Winter, pp. 224–237, 244–249; L. A. Fabunmi, *The Sudan in Anglo-Egyptian Relations* (1960).

30. *A Revolution in Action, Regional Autonomy for the South*, Government Printing Press (Khartoum, 1970.)

while at the same time allowing each full freedom in its domestic and international policy. Addressing the English-speaking union in San Francisco in 1962, the Duke of Edinburgh said that the Commonwealth was "an amalgamation of forces and ideas, partly sentiment, partly historical, partly language, partly economic, partly that it does not involve political unity, and partly because the roots of its existence strike deep into the life of the people of its member countries."[31] Mr. Frazer of New Zealand said it meant "independence with something added, and not independence with something taken away."[32]

Far from restricting the self-determination of its members, the Commonwealth aids its full exercise and enjoyment especially during the early years of independence. The older members provide aid, assistance, investment, and training opportunities for the new members without restricting their opportunities to seek aid elsewhere.

Although at their foundation the Westminster model of parliamentary democracy was the imported system of government, members have been free to change to other systems. Pakistan had the first military government within the Commonwealth and in 1966 all the West African members had military regimes, with the exception of Gambia, which had no army. The one-party system operated for a time in Kenya and in Ghana and still does in Tanzania. More than a third of the Commonwealth states are republics; though not having the queen as head of state, they recognise her as "the symbol of the free association of its independent member nations and as such the head of the commonwealth of nations."

The Westminster system has not always thrived on foreign ground. This is accounted for by the many props that support it on its home ground, *inter alia*, free press, high standard of living, homogeneous society, and a common language. The opposition in Britain are not the mortal enemies of the government and conduct their business with a certain minimum standard of decorum. Nor are their constituencies denied of social services because their representatives in Parliament oppose the government. Opposition candidates do not find themselves behind the prison walls on the eve of elections. In Britain there is always a good chance of the opposition forming the government and this avoids the frustration of being perpetually in opposition and encourages a sense of responsibility. The habits of Westminster parliamentary democracy were cultivated over the centuries and are not readily exportable holus-bolus.

31. *Times* of London, 12 November 1962.
32. *The Commonwealth Association in Brief*, British Information Services (1958), pp. 2–5.

However, it provides a model to compare and contrast other manufactures.[33]

In a demonstration of their independence, some members (Eire was first to do so in 1937) have changed the ultimate source of their constitutional power from the British act of Parliament granting independence to an instrument asserting that it derives its authority from the wishes of the people. This is said to make the constitution autochthonous. Dr. Wheare states that this is the result of a people wishing to have "a constitution [which] has the force of law, and if necessary, of supreme law within their territory through its own native authority and not because it was enacted or authorised by the parliament of the United Kingdom; that it is, so to speak 'home grown,' sprung from their own soil, and not imported from the United Kingdom."[34]

The element of autochthony is said to be a "break in legal continuity" since the constitution can no longer be traced to the original act of Parliament granting independence. It may be said in another sense that a constitution is autochthonous if it has fundamental features that are indigenous to the member state and alien to the Westminster model. Such features must be so dominant in the constitution as to give it a special character. Thus the employment of the plebiscite, the vesting of extraordinary powers on the person of the president, as in the Ghana constitution of 1960, and the one-party system are so indigenous, and alien to Westminster, as to be autochthonous in their home grounds.[35] This character remains whether or not there is a breach in legal continuity. The decisive legal fact is that a new state has come into existence having a separate legal personality from the mother country. Its constitution may adapt imperial trappings to its circumstances, it may incorporate special features reflecting its peculiar conditions, or it may incorporate mechanisms alien to Westminster. The features are the manifestations of the right of the people to self-determination.[36] A member may quit

33. *See also* N. W. Manley, "The Role of the Opposition in a Young Nation, *The Parliamentarian IL* no. 1 (January 1968), pp. 1–4.

34. K. C. Wheare: *Constitutional Structure of the Commonwealth* (Oxford, 1960), p. 89.

35. For the Ghanaian Constitution *see* Peaslee, *Constitutions of Nations* (1965), 1:213–228.

36. *See also* K. Robinson, "Constitutional Autochthony in Ghana," *Journal of Commonwealth Political Studies* (1961–4), vols. 1–2, p. 41. Perhaps no Commonwealth constitution has a better claim to autochthony than Tanzania's. There is a one-party socialist system that includes the civil service, the army and police in the political party. The philosophy of *ujamaa* for villagization is directed toward the communalisation of the thinly spread population of the hinterland. The merger between Tanganyika and Zanzibar is neither federal nor confederal. It is *sui generis*, for the former submits jurisdiction wholly to the Union while the latter, needing protection, retains certain powers for itself.

the Commonwealth; Ireland in 1949 and South Africa in 1961 exercised this right. Upon attaining independence, Burma, Sudan, and Cyprus did not join the Commonwealth, although Cyprus did so six months later. All the members are also members of the United Nations and meet regularly in New York to harmonise their policies on a purely optional basis. Some belong to organisations that others do not; thus Britain and Canada are members of NATO; Britain, New Zealand, Australia, Malaya, and Singapore joined SEATO; Britain and Pakistan belong to CENTO; New Zealand and Australia joined with the United States in ANZUS (Pacific Security Agreement 1951) and all African members belong to the OAU. Nor are relations between members always harmonious.[37] The *inter se* doctrine is now virtually restricted to matters members treat as such on a bilateral basis and is excluded from the large area of multilateral treaties to which non-members also belong. The treatment of Indians in South Africa was brought to the United Nations in 1946 when South Africa was still a member of the Commonwealth. South Africa's objection was not on the basis of the *inter se* doctrine but on domestic jurisdiction. Kashmir has been discussed by the Security Council on India's complaint without Pakistan's pleading the doctrine.

It has, so far, been advantageous for members to belong to the Commonwealth; neither the coups, the autochthony of some of the constitutions, nor some serious divergencies in politics have yet caused the other members of the Commonwealth to quit, for membership in no way impairs their right to self-determination. However, a breach of the fundamental principles of the Commonwealth by Britain could compel the non-whites to abandon an organization that critics have identified with British and Western imperialism or neocolonialism.

Sir Cecil Hurst described the evolutionary process to Commonwealth membership as a movement

from a position of dependence to one of freedom from control. These great communities have all the time been climbing a ladder. Now they have reached the top; but the climbing process is common

37. "There has been a rapid increase in the number of independent states represented. An assertive new nationalism, denunciation of colonialism and of racial discrimination and, in the recent past, some resort to sanctions have marked relations between communities in the Commonwealth." R. R. Wilson, "International Law and the Commonwealth" 60 *AJIL* (1966), p. 777. To underline their independence, Tanzania and Ghana broke diplomatic relations with Britain over the latter's handling of the Rhodesian UDI (resumed in 1968 and 1966 respectively) and President Kaunda of Zambia reportedly threatened to call for the expulsion of Britain from the Commonwealth if it did not bring down the Smith's regime. *New York Times*, 23 May 1966. The expressed intention of Britain in 1970 to supply arms to South Africa threatened to break up the Commonwealth. India and Pakistan have gone to war over a boundary dispute while relations between Ghana and Nigeria under civilian regimes were not always cordial.

to all communities which form part of the Empire. Each of them, whether the population is predominantly white or predominantly coloured, is gradually, as it develops strength and capacity, passing upward from the stage in which the community is wholly subject to control exercised from London to that in which the measure of control diminished, and so on to that in which the control has ceased entirely. The dominions of today were but the crown colonies in the past. The crown colonies of today will be the dominions in days to come.[38]

Written in 1928, this statement remains substantially true of the remaining colonies. For the small territories that are too small in population, size, or resources to carry the burden of independence, the status of associated state was created to accommodate the desire for self-determination. In such cases Britain assumes the responsibility for foreign affairs and defence while internal self-government is conducted by each state.[39] All British trust territories have gained independence. The Commonwealth exemplifies the application of the principle of self-determination by an administering power to its dependent territories and, within the Commonwealth, the interdependence of states which is essential for progress.[40]

2. The United States of America

A. *Colonial Objectives*. The attitude of the United States to self-determination for colonies is influenced by its anti-colonial tradition which tends to regard colonialism as evil *per se*. In the view of John Quincy Adams:

Colonial establishments cannot fulfill the great objectives of governments in the just purpose of civil society. . . . [They are] incompatible with the essential character of our [American] institutions, [and as] engines of wrong [it would in time be] the duty of the human family to abolish them, as they are now endeavouring to abolish the slave trade. . . .[41]

The United States was "the first colony in modern times to have won

38. C. Hurst, *Great Britain and the Dominions* (1928), p. 12.

39. For the associated states of the West Indies, see p. 88 above.

40. *See also* on the Commonwealth, de Smith, *The Vocabulary of Commonwealth Relations* (1965); Fawcett, *The British Commonwealth in International Law* (1963), especially chapter 3; "The Commonwealth in the United Nations," *Journal of Commonwealth Political Studies* (1961–4) Vol. 1–2, pp. 123–135; R. R. Wilson, "The Commonwealth as Symbol and Instrument" 53 *AJIL* (1959); T. B. Millar, "The Commonwealth and United Nations," *International Organisation* (1962); J. Holmes, "The Impact on the Commonwealth of the Emergence of Africa," ibid.

41. R. Godwin, ed., *Readings in American Foreign Policy*, part 10, chapter 4, "The American Tradition in Foreign Relations" by Frank Tannebaun (1959).

independence."[42] The natural wealth of the country and its extensive territory have reduced the importance of emigration, foreign trade, and foreign acquisitions.

On the fall of the Spanish Empire in the western hemisphere in 1898, the United States gained colonial control of Guam, Puerto Rico, and the Philippines and enjoyed quasi-suzerainty over Cuba, from which it withdrew in 1903, though reserving certain rights for itself. Thus, "the government of Cuba consents that the United States may exercise the right to intervene for the preservation of Cuban independence, the maintenance of a government adequate for protection of life, property and individual liberty, and for discharging the obligations with respect to Cuba imposed by the Treaty of Paris on the United States, now to be assumed and undertaken by the government of Cuba."[43]

Elihu Root, the secretary of state for war, warned the Taft Commission to the Philippines in 1898 that the proposed arrangements for the government of the islands were designed "not for our own satisfaction or for the expression of our theoretical views, but for the happiness, peace, and prosperity of the people."[44] In his message to Congress on 3 December 1900, President McKinley stressed a "moral as well as a material responsibility toward those millions we have freed from oppressive yoke. Our obligation as guardian was not lightly assumed."[45]

The latter part of the nineteenth century and the first decade of the present witnessed the United States' intervention in the South American republics in the interest of American business. "American imperialism and dollar diplomacy" were the cause of disquiet in the republics:

> In the previous fifty years before 1933, the United States had intervened some sixty times in the affairs and territories of its Latin American neighbours—especially in the Caribbean. . . . How could one speak of inter-American solidarity, or good-neighborliness when the stumbling block in the path of the good relations was nothing less than the most powerful republic of the hemisphere? The situation could change only if and when the United States decided to abandon once and for all its imperialistic intervention.[46]

Yet the independence of those states was not taken away from them.

42. John F. Dulles, *U.S. Dept. of State Bull.* of 21 June 1954, p. 936.

43. Known as the Platt Amendment, being part of the appropriation bill for the army for the fiscal year ending 30 June 1902, 31 Statute 897. The 1903–4 Treaty which granted independence is to be found in 1 *Malloy's Treaties* (1910), p. 364.

44. Baker, *Woodrow Wilson and World Settlement*, p. 263.

45. Ibid.

46. L. Quintanille, *A Latin American Speaks* (1943), p. 156.

In 1912 President Taft announced: "We are seeking to arouse a national spirit, and not, as under the older colonial theory, to suppress such spirit."[47] President Wilson was even more scrupulous in his respect for the self-determination of South American republics. In a major statement of policy at Mobile, Alabama, he renounced the economic domination of the republics and in a message to Congress in December 1915 declared: "All the governments of America stand, so far as we are concerned, upon a footing of genuine equality and unquestioned independence."[48]

After the bitter attack on its policy of intervention at the Havana Conference of 1928, the United States reiterated the policy of nonintervention and gave expression to this in the Montevideo Convention of 1934. In the same year the military occupation of Haiti was withdrawn and the remaining restrictions on Cuban independence were removed. The Buenos Aires Conference of 1936 declared that intervention in any form—military, economic, or political—was inadmissible.[49] The target date for the independence of the Philippines was set as 1946. Alaska and Hawaii authorised constituent conventions to draft constitutions which, having been approved by their electorates, were approved by the American House of Representatives and the Senate before they were admitted into the Federation as the forty-ninth and fiftieth states respectively.

In the 1950s American support for anticolonialism became more pragmatic partly because of the support of communism for early colonial freedom (and the fear of communism) and partly because of the pressure on the United States by its Western allies who were also colonial powers. Secretary of State Dulles described the American role in colonial problems in the international sphere as:

> To try to see that the process (progress from colonial status to independence) moves forward in a constructive evolutionary way and does not either come to a halt or take a violent revolutionary turn which would be destructive of very much good. . . . To try to aid that process, without identifying itself 100% either with the so-called colonial powers or with the powers which are primarily and uniquely concerned with the problem of getting their independence as rapidly as possible.[50]

47. Baker, 263–4.

48. Baker and Dodd, *The New Democracy*, 1:408.

49. *See also* Cobban, *National Self-determination* (1945), pp. 90–100.

50. News Conference on 2 October 1956, *U.S. Dept. of State Bull. 35* no. 903 of 15 October 1956, p. 577. In reply to the Dalai Lama of Tibet on 5 January 1960 Secretary of State, Herter wrote, "As you know, while it has been the historical position of the United States to consider Tibet as an autonomous country under the suzerainty of China, the American people have also traditionally stood for the principle of self-determination." *42 Bull.* 1082 of 2 March 1960, p. 443.

Addressing the American Academy of Political and Social Science in April 1956, Assistant-Secretary G. V. Allen demonstrated the American dilemma:

> Because of our origins and traditions, we are basically in sympathy with the desire for independence and nationhood of the emerging States, but we are also friends and allies of the Powers who must help to shape this new status. This places us in a position from which we hope and believe our influence can be exerted to make the trans-formation of Africa a process of orderly evolution and not of violent revolution.[51]

United States policy in the colonial field has sometimes evoked resent-ment among its Western allies, as in the hastening of the British with-drawal from India, the refusal to support British retaliation for the Iranian oil nationalisations and the subsequent formation of an interna-tional consortium in which the Americans owned 40 percent of the shares, and the replacement of American influence for the French in the former French Indo-China, and for the Belgian in the Congo (Kinsha-sha).[52]

B. *Puerto Rico*. Puerto Rico occupies a position *sui generis*: unlike the Philippines, it is not an independent state; unlike Hawaii and Alaska, it has not been merged with the United States. It was ceded by Spain in the Treaty of Paris in 1898,[53] which concluded the Spanish-American War, and was for two years under military rule. The first civil constitu-tion of 1900 provided for an elected lower house and an upper house of heads of departments and five nominated members. The American gov-ernor was appointed by the President of the United States with the advice and consent of the Senate. Puerto Rico was represented in Washington by an elected resident commissioner who had a seat in the House of Representatives where he had a say but not a vote.

In 1917 both houses of assembly were elected but the United States president still appointed the governor, the judges of the Supreme Court and the heads of the departments of justice, education, and audit, the others being appointed by the governor on the advice of the upper house. Puerto Ricans became citizens of the United States and the Bill of Rights was extended to them. The legislature could repass a bill rejected by the

51. *U.S. Dept. of State Bull.* of 30 April 1956.

52. *See also* Kenneth J. Twitchett, "The American National Interest and the Anti-colonial Crusade," *International Relations* (The Journal of the David and Davis Memorial Institute of International Studies) vol. 3, no. 4 (October 1967). There is increasing American influence in Kenya, a former British colony.

53. 90 *BFSP* (1897–98), p. 382.

governor, but if he again rejected it, the bill required the consent of the president to become law.

In 1946 a Puerto Rican was for the first time appointed governor and in 1948 the office became elective. The governor then appointed all the members of the cabinet and heads of departments, including the attorney general and the commissioner for education. The governor, the resident commissioner, and a majority of the members of the legislative assembly in 1948 won on the platform of continued association with the United States, whereas others who wanted independence were defeated. In accordance with the wishes of the representatives, a bill (Public Law 600) was enacted for the organisation of a constitutional government. The law was then approved in a referendum[54] and a Constitutional Convention was elected to draft the constitution which was approved in another referendum,[55] the election and referenda being on the basis of a universal adult suffrage.[56] The constitution was approved by the Constitutional Convention and the Commonwealth of Puerto Rico was established on 25 July 1952.[57]

Article 1(I) of the Puerto Rican Constitution proclaims: "[P]olitical power emanates from the people and shall be exercised in accordance with their will, within the terms of the compact agreed upon between the people of Puerto Rico and the United States of America." The constitution provides for the separation of powers, a popularly elected governor, and a bicameral legislature. A bill rejected by the governor may be re-enacted by two-thirds of the membership of each House. Amendments may be proposed by the legislature and voted upon in a referendum provided they are consistent with:

(1) the act approving the constitution,
(2) the applicable law of the federal constitution,
(3) the Puerto Rican Relations Act,
(4) the act of Congress authorising the drafting, and
(5) adoption of the constitution.

---

54. Referendum of 4 June 1951. 506,185 (65.08 percent of 777,675) voters participated and 76.5 percent approved the law.

55. 81.84 percent of those who voted.

56. Property qualification was removed in 1906 and literacy in 1935. Universal adult suffrage was introduced in 1929.

57. Commonwealth is translated in Spanish as *Estado libre asociado* and defined as "a state which is free of superior authority in the management of its local affairs but which is linked to the USA and hence is a part of its political system in a manner compatible with its Federal structure" and which "does not have an independent and separate existence." Resolution 22 of the Constitution Convention.

Judges of the Supreme Court are appointed by the governor on the advice of the Puerto Rican Senate. Final appeals lie to the United States Court of Appeals but the United States courts have worked out the rule not to set aside a judgment unless it is "inescapably wrong" or "patently erroneous." A federal court exercises the same functions as in the United States. Foreign relations and defence are conducted by the United States and a resident commissioner still resides in Washington. United States currency is used and United States laws that are not inapplicable· are enforced. There is free trade with the United States and the proceeds of the local customs and excise go to the local treasury. United States internal revenue laws do not apply.

The USSR and Cuba have often accused the United States of colonialism in Puerto Rico. This is not however borne out by the constitutional position. The Constitutional Convention itself declared that the compact was entered into "by mutual consent, which is the basis of our union with the United States," and that "the last vestiges of colonialism having disappeared in the principle of compact, and we enter into an era of new developments in democratic civilization."[58] Puerto Ricans are United States citizens; though they do not vote in presidential elections, they participate in the activities of the Republican and Democratic parties, which have local chapters on the island.

Welcoming the cessation of information on Puerto Rico, the General Assembly expressed its satisfaction:

(2) [T]he people of the Commonwealth of Puerto Rico, by expressing their will in a free and democratic way, have achieved a new constitutional status. . . .
(4) [W]hen choosing their constitutional and international status, the people of the Commonwealth of Puerto Rico have effectively exercised their right to self-determination. . . .
(5) [I]n the framework of their constitution and of the compact agreed upon with the United States, the people of the Commonwealth of Puerto Rico have been invested with attributes of political sovereignty which clearly identify the status of self-government attained by the Puerto Rican people as that of an autonomous political entity. . . .[59]

On the eve of the Seventh Meeting of Consultation of Foreign Affairs Ministers of the American Republics in 1960, the Puerto Rican governor rejected charges of colonialism made against the United States.[60] The

---

58. *U.S. Dept. of State Bull.*, no. 721 of 20 April 1953, pp. 585–7.
59. Res. 748(VIII) of 27 November 1953.
60. M. S. Dept. of State, file 371. 04/8–2660 CS/MDR.

governor also addressed a letter to the United States representative in the United Nations for circulation to members on the eve of the discussion of the Russian resolution on independence for colonial countries in 1960.[61] It read in part:

> The people of Puerto Rico strongly adhere to the democratic way of life, based on the respect of minority rights, the protection and furtherance of individual freedoms, and the effective exercise of the right to vote in free, unhindered elections. There can be no genuine self-determination unless these conditions are met.
>
> Puerto Rico has truly and effectively met them and it has freely chosen its present relationship with the United States. The people of Puerto Rico are a self-governing people freely associated to the United States on the basis of mutual consent and respect. The policies regarding the cultural and economic development of Puerto Rico are in the hands of the people of Puerto Rico themselves for them to determine according to their best interests.[62]

It stated further that a law that became effective in 1960 authorised a vote on the status of the island whenever 10 percent of the electors request it.

The association with the United States was again approved on 23 July 1967 in a plebiscite in which the people were asked to choose between independence, merger with the United States as fifty-first state, or dominion status in association with the United States. The present relationship provides vast opportunities for a duty-free market and emigration. The absence of federal tax makes it possible to keep local tax at a high level, whereas merger would revert 52 percent of the corporation tax to the United States.[63] The island has achieved a rapid economic growth (9.4 percent in 1959), made possible by the attraction of American capital through exemption from tax for stipulated periods. The right to dissociate from the United States constitutes an important safeguard for the peoples' right to self-determination.

C. *Self-determination and Communism in the Americas.* American state practice supports the principle of self-determination in colonial territories. This took the form of independence in the Philippines, merger in Hawaii and Alaska, and association in Puerto Rico. The strategic trust territories of the North Pacific Islands are still dependent but are making steady progress toward self-determination.

61. Draft resolution Doc. A/4501.

62. Doc. A/4519, 29 September 1960.

63. *See also* an article in the *London Financial Times* of 24 May 1967 by its Mexican correspondent. Whiteman, *Digest of International Law* (1965), 1:392–406; 5:60–66.

The pursuit of anti-communism in the Americas raises pertinent questions. The Monroe Doctrine has been an old strategy with which the United States keeps out outside influence it considers undesirable while securing the dominance of its own influence. The Rio Treaty on Reciprocal Assistance of 1947 provides for collective action both in the case of armed attack and "if the inviolability or the integrity of the territory or independence of any American state should be affected . . . by any . . . fact or situation that might endanger the peace of America. . . ."[64] At the Tenth Inter-American Conference held in Caracas in 1954 the United States secured the adoption of a Declaration of Solidarity for the Preservation of the Political Integrity of the American States Against International Communist Intervention:

> [T]he domination or control of the political institutions of any American State by the international communist movement extending to this hemisphere the political system of an extra-continental power, would constitute a threat to the sovereign and political independence of the American States, endangering the peace of America . . . and would call for a meeting of consultation to consider the adoption of appropriate action in accordance with existing treaties.[65]

Official American policy considers international communism as inimical to the independence of American states, the right of each state to develop its political, economic, and cultural life, and the peace and security of the hemisphere. Thus Dulles describes international communism as "an aggressive, tough, political force, backed by great resources, and serving the most ruthless empire of modern times" and demanding unquestioned obedience from members, over and above "every other obligation including love of country, obligation to family, and the honor of one's own personal conduct."[66] It is also feared that once a state falls under a communist regime, it not only loses its independence in its domestic and external policy but also becomes an "operational base for the propagation of communist ideas, for infiltration, subversion, and interference in the internal affairs of all the Americas, designed in the last analysis to overthrow by force every government in this hemisphere."[67]

Relying on the Monroe Doctrine, the Rio Treaty, and the Declaration

64. See articles 3 and 6 of the Rio Treaty in 43 *AJIL* (1943), supp. 53.

65. *U.S. Dept. of State Bull.* 26 April 1954 at 634.

66. Press Release no. 121 of 8 March 1954.

67. Secretary of State Herter at the Seventh Meeting of Consultation of the American Foreign Ministers at San Jose, Costa Rica; Press Release no. 486 of 24 August 1960.

of Caracas, the United States claims the right to keep communism out of the American states. In furtherance of this policy it intervened in Guatemala in 1954 and was instrumental in unseating the incumbent government. The Bay of Pigs invasion of Cuba in 1961 was an abortive attempt to unseat the socialist and popular government of Fidel Castro. When disturbance broke out in the Dominican Republic in 1965, the United States intervened purportedly to protect its nationals but later extended its action to include the occupation of the capital Santo Domingo. President Johnson said on 2 May 1965: "What began as a popular democratic revolution that was committed to democracy and social justice moved into the hands of a band of communist conspirators."[68]

If it is the aim of international communism to overthrow all non-communist governments by force and replace them with communist ones against the wishes of the people, then it contradicts the principle of self-determination and its exclusion from the continent becomes a legitimate endeavour.[69] A distinction must however be drawn between this brand of communism and communism fashioned in the nature of a peaceful political philosophy. Under the latter view of communism, the United States would be denying the right of its own people to the freedoms of thought and expression and *a fortiori* the right of other American states to choose a government of their choice by opposing it. The stratification of the society in South America into "haves" and "have-nots" instinctively associates the demand for political and social changes with the left wing. In these circumstances external support for the governments may mean the preservation of the status quo and the prolongation of corruption and

68. *See also* on the Dominican Intervention: C. G. Fenwick, "The Dominican Republic: Intervention or Collective Self-defense," 60 *AJIL* (1966), p. 44; R. T. Bohan, "The Dominican Case; Unilateral Intervention," 60 *AJIL* (1966), p. 809. D. Horowitz, *From Yalta to Vietnam* (Penguin, 1967), esp. part 2.

69. For the view that international communism is contrary to international law, *see* "Both major forms of 20th century totalitarianism, fascism and communism, represent a new type of social order which has deliberately set itself apart from other States of the world. Both are based on the concept that a totalitarian State has a right to destroy the rights of all other States in pursuit of what it deems to be the ultimate end of mankind. Under such a view the fundamental rights and duties of nations and the fundamental rights and duties of individuals which fall under the scope of established rules of international law are no longer legal rights and duties, but rather are mere privileges to be enjoyed upon sufferance according to the view of expediency held by those in power. A nation based upon such a philosophy refuses, of necessity, to recognise that general international law are binding on it, for its goal is not the goal of other nations. It is not seeking order under the law of nations, but rather order based on autocratic power." Thomas and Thomas, *Non-intervention* (1956), p. 104. For an article that indicates that the "Soviet Union has lowered its sights and now aims for more modest but more realistic goals" see H. S. Dinestein, "Soviet Policy in Latin America," *The American Political Science Quarterly,* vol. 61, no. 1 (March 1967), pp. 80–90.

inefficiency. The Communist world, including China, considers that United States imperialism is the greatest threat to world peace and stability. United States direct and indirect military interventions to install governments of its own choice in other states only serve to confirm the accusation.

The principle of self-determination guarantees the right of a people to "freely determine their political status and freely pursue their economic, social, and cultural development." A communist government in an American republic would however be contravening the principle if it sought forcefully, as by guerrilla action, to impose a communist regime on another state even though it could legitimately propagate its political philosophy in a democratic manner.

3. The Soviet Union

A. *Background to Self-determination in the USSR.* Soviet attitude toward self-determination is conditioned mainly by the thoughts of Lenin and Stalin who were themselves inspired by Marx and Engels. In their Communist Manifesto published in 1848, Marx and Engels divided the world into exploiters and exploited. This twofold division cuts through nationalism, which in turn divides the world into separate nationalities. Nationalism must give way to internationalism for, with the growth of international capitalism, the workers of the world could only win back their rights by forming a workers international. When hopes of immediate revolutions in the Western countries receded, the communists became more tolerant of nationalism and paid special regard to the traditions, customs, and institutions of the different nationalities. A resolution of the London International Congress in 1896 proclaimed "the full right of self-determination (*selbstbestimmungsrecht*) of all nations. . . ."[70] Under Lenin's influence the Second Congress of the Russian Social-Democratic Labour party in 1903 adopted as the ninth article of their programme "the right of self-determination for all nations forming part of the State." The demand of the Jewish Bund party for national cultural autonomy in furtherance of self-determination was rejected.[71]

70. *See* Lenin, *The Right of Nations to Self-determination* (New York 1951), p. 42. An interesting footnote gives the following inaccurate criticism: "A Russian pamphlet has been published containing the decisions of the International Congress, in which the word 'self-determination' is wrongly translated as 'autonomy' " Ibid.

71. Solomon Schwarz, *The Jews of the Soviet Union* (Syracuse University Press, 1951), p. 25. The Bund was in turn accused of encouraging the Congress "to support even those nationalities on the point of dying out"—a veiled reference to the Jews.

Interpreting the principle of self-determination as related to nationality in his article "The Socialist Revolution and the Right of Nations to Self-determination" written in March 1916, Lenin made a threefold division of countries: (a) the advanced countries of the West which had advanced economies but in which the workers were oppressed; (b) countries of Eastern Europe, including Austria, the Balkans, and Russia where the problem of nationality was still acute and whose main task was to co-ordinate the efforts of the workers in a and b; and (c) the rest of the world whose economies were not developed but whose revolutionary elements required the help of socialists.

Every self-determining entity passed through three stages—the period of mobilisation with occasional peasant struggle for political liberties and national rights, the period of conflict between the labour movement and international capital, and the moment of victory of the proletariat in a great nation. The Russian Revolution of 1917 proved the falsity of communist forecasts that the revolution would begin with the advanced countries of the West, for the Bolsheviks found themselves in control of a country that was more backward but which became the centre of communist activities.

B. *Declarations on Self-determination.* The provisional government of Russia proclaimed through Lvov, president of the council, that Russia did not want to dominate other nations but was rather anxious to establish "a durable peace on a basis of the rights of nations to decide their own destiny."[72] It referred to the voluntary termination of domination over the Poles as an act "in the name of the higher principles of equity." The autonomy of the Poles was proclaimed "on the basis of self-determination of peoples." The repudiation of this principle and the readiness of the government to honour treaties entered into with the Allies by the czarist government occasioned Lenin's attack on it and the eventual takeover by the Bolsheviks. The first act of the Soviet authority issued on 25 October/7 November 1917 by the Second All-Russia Congress of Soviets was an address to workers, soldiers, and peasants promising "guarantees to all the nations dwelling in Russia and the genuine right to self-determination."[73] Trotsky, the new commissioner for foreign affairs proposed to the Allies that peace should be made immediately on the basis of "no annexations of indemnities and the self-determination of nations. . . ."[74] The first constitutional act is to be found in the

72. Baker, *Woodrow Wilson and World Settlement*, p. 95.

73. Lenin, (Russian ed.), 22:2.

74. Baker, *Woodrow Wilson*, p. 95; Golder, pp. 329–31; M. M. Lasserson, "The Development of Soviet Foreign Policy in Europe, 1917–42," *International Conciliation* (1943), p. 10.

Declaration of Rights of the Peoples of Russia, 2/15 November 1917, when Lenin and Stalin laid down the principles for the liberation of peoples under the bondage of the czar as follows: (a) the equality and sovereignty of Russia's nationalities; (b) the right of Russia's nationalities to free self-determination up to the point of secession and the organisation of an independent state; (c) the abrogation of all privileges and limitations upon nationalities and national religions; and (d) the free development of national minorities and ethnographical groups located within Russia.[75] Russian delegates (Joffer and Trotsky) to the peace conference at Brest Litovsk pleaded that the terms should be on the basis of self-determination. They were however compelled to accept a treaty which deprived Russia of some of its territories while at the same time bringing them under German influence.[76] A decree of 13 November 1918 denounced the Brest Litovsk Treaty and called upon "the toiling masses of Russia . . . to decide their own fate."[77] The declarations of self-determination and the opportunity offered by the 1918 constitution to the workers to decide independently whether they wished to associate with the Russian Soviet and on what terms was seized upon by certain sections of the former empire. Thus Lithuania, Ukraine, and Finland proclaimed their independence in 1917 while Transcaucasia, Estonia and Latvia followed suit in 1918. A declaration of 24 November/7 December assured self-determination for the Persians, the abrogation of the czar's treaties dismembering Turkey, and the inviolability of religions. Religious freedom was extended to Moslems of the East and to the Arabs and Hindus.[78] Where there were strong communist cadres, recognition came readily from Moscow but not for Georgia and the Transcaucasia, which had strong anti-Bolshevik and anti-revolutionary elements.

The treaty of 16 March 1921[79] with Turkey recognised the right of

75. Ibid., p. 11; also Vyshinsky, *The Law of the Soviet State* (New York, 1948), pp. 249–250.

76. The treaty "while pretending to free Russia's border provinces really transforms them into German provinces and deprives them of the right of free self-determination." (Lasserson, p. 17.)

77. T. A. Taracouzio, *The Soviet Union in International Law* (New York, 1935), p. 250.

78. Lasserson, pp. 12–13.

79. Shapiro, ed., *Soviet Treaty Series* (Washington, 1958), 1:100. Article IV reads "The Contracting Parties, establishing the national movement for the liberation of the Eastern peoples and the struggle of the workers of Russia for a new social order, solemnly recognise the right of these nations to freedom and independence, also their right to choose a form of government according to their own wishes."

the peoples of the Middle East to self-determination and the treaty of 26 February 1921[80] acknowledged the sovereignty of Persia. The policy for areas that had made strong demands for local autonomy was "to build this autonomy on the basis of the local Soviets; only then can authority be popular and truly belong to the masses—that is to say, it is necessary only that autonomy guarantees authority, not for the apex but for the nether parts of a given nation."[81]

The Soviet Union today consists of autonomous republics and regions and national republics and regions.

C. *Plebiscites Under the Soviets.* In its early years, the Soviet government relied on plebiscites to determine title over disputed territories and entered into treaties providing for the consultation of the people on these matters. Thus Article 15 of the Treaty of 1 March 1918 with Finland[82] provided that Pechanga should be ceded to Finland if approved in a plebiscite. In the Treaty of 24 February 1921 with Poland[83] (later embodied in the Treaty of Riga[84]), of 28 February 1921 with Afghanistan,[85] of 13 September 1920 with Khorezm[86] and of 4 March 1921 with Bukhara,[87] provisions were made for plebiscites. No limitations were placed on the electorate except for the attempt to restrict the voting to workers and peasants. Where no agreements were arrived at to hold plebiscites, boundary commissions were set up and in some cases their findings were to be confirmed in plebiscites.[88] The principle of self-determination underlies the use of plebiscites in determining sovereignty over territory. The people themselves decide who shall exercise supreme authority over them.[89]

D. *The Formation of the USSR.* In December 1917 Stalin issued a document from the Commissariat of Nationalities declaring that the

80. Ibid., p. 92.

81. Policy of Soviet Authority on the National Question During Three Years 8, an address signed by Stalin to be delivered by the Commissars of Nationalities to the Soviets of Sasan, Ufa, Orenburg, Yekaterinburg, etc., quoted in Vyshinsky, p. 258.

82. Shapiro, 1:2.

83. Ibid., p. 87.

84. Ibid., p. 105.

85. Ibid., p. 96.

86. Ibid., p. 59.

87. Ibid., p. 98.

88. As in treaties with Estonia, Latvia, and Lithuania.

89. *See also* Taracouzio, pp. 58–60.

Council of People's Commissars was "ready to acknowledge the federative organisation of the political life of our country in the style, let us say, of the United States if the toiling population of the Russian regions shall demand it."[90] The principle of federalism was chosen and this was later extended to most of the areas of the former empire. When the Soviet Ukrainian government was established, it entered into federal relations with the Russian Soviet government on specified matters. This example was followed by other Soviets and the areas of cooperation were extended from time to time. The Third All-Russian Congress of Soviets adopted, on 28 January 1918, a resolution which provided for "separate regions distinguished by a special way of life and a national structure" and also "the delimitation of spheres of activity of federal and regional institutions of the Russian Republic."[91]

Closer relations were necessitated by foreign interventions which encouraged the demand for complete separation from Russia, by the fear of armed attack from hostile countries, and by the increasing strength of the anti-revolutionaries in certain parts of the federation. Thus after the suppression of anti-Sovietism in Georgia, Armenia, and Azerbaijan, and the reconquest of Ukraine from the Germans and White Russia from the Poles, there were moves for greater integration with Soviet Russia and Transcaucasia was unified. The Constitution of 1923 was adopted on the principles of equal rights and self-determination. It provided for a Congress of Soviets, a Central Executive Committee, and a Council of Peoples' Commissars. A period of reorganisation of multinational republics into national republics followed before they became members of the Union.

E. *The Soviet Meaning of Self-determination.* Self-determination has found a permanent place in the Constitution of the USSR, in the autonomy of the republics and regions, and in the right of secession and the founding of an independent state. The state is formed by the willing consent of the working class of the nationalities that form the Union. There is no conflict within the working class whose interest is international as there is between the proletariat and the bourgeoisie, according to Marxist philosophy.

The Bolsheviks recognised that suppression under the czarist regime and the chauvinistic nationalism of Greater Russia encouraged separate nationalism in the empire. In 1920 they set up a Commissariat for Nationalities under Stalin to protect, and act as intermediaries between, the

90. *Pravda,* no. 213, 13–26 December 1917, quoted in Vyshinsky, p. 251.
91. Gazette of the temporary Worker-Peasant Government, no. 11 (56), 18–31 January 1918, quoted in Vyshinsky, p. 251.

nationalities and at the same time propagate communism. The duties of the commissariat included "the study and execution of all measures guaranteeing the fraternal collaboration of the nationalities and tribes of the Russian Soviet Union; the study and execution of all measures necessary to guarantee the interests of national minorities on the territory of other nationalities and tribes of the Russian Soviet Federation; and the settlement of all litigious questions arising from the mixture of nationalities."[92] As the principle of federalism was extended, so were the responsibilities of the commissariat. It became one of the chambers of the Central Executive Committee in 1923.

The czar's policy of Russification was abandoned and instead national cultures and languages were encouraged though Russian has been a second language in schools in non-Russian areas since 1938. The new policy was to reanimate traditional culture and "bring them into a synthesis, consistent with the development of future world cultures national in form and international in content."[93]

The economy of backward areas is developed in order to ensure a good standard of living. Economic self-determination or self-sufficiency is recognised as essential for meaningful self-determination.

Within a large state, self-determination demands a measure of local autonomy. Stalin defined autonomy as "an organisation of local organs or authority, of local, social, political and educational institutions, with a guarantee of the completeness of the right of the local language—native to the toiling masses of the country—in all spheres of socio-political work."[94] Nor is autonomy a rigid concept for "it permits of the case of the USSR, the liberation of oppressed nationalities was a necessary prelude to their fusion into a large state on a truly democratic and internationalist basis which is incompatible without the freedom of secession. . . ."[95] The Soviet Union is a political, economic, and military unit, secession of any part is bound to affect the others. Stalin said in 1921: "Central Russia is in no position to maintain her military and economic power without fuel, raw materials and agricultural assistance of the border territories."[96]

92. W. R. Batsell, *Soviet Rule in Russia* (New York, 1929), p. 119.

93. A. Phinney, "Racial Minorities in the Soviet Union," 8 *Pacific Affairs*, no. 3 (September 1935); *see also* D. J. R. Scott, *Russian Political Institutions* (1965).

94. Policy on National Question, quoted in Vyshinsky, p. 258.

95. Lenin, *Marx, Engels, Marxism* (1934), p. 147.

96. Stalin, *Marxism i Natsional'no Kolonial'nyi Vopros*, p. 87. *See also* Lenin, *Selected Works*, vol. 1, part 2: "The mass of the population knows perfectly well from daily experience the value of geographical and economic ties and the advantages of a big market and of a big State. They will, therefore, resort to secession only when national oppression and national friction make joint life absolutely intolerable and hinder all and any economic intercourse." (p. 349.)

Self-determination is not an absolute right but is subject to the dictatorship of the proletariat. The principle "ought to be understood as the right of self-determination, not of the bourgeoisie but of the toiling masses of a given nation."[97] Lenin wrote:

> The various demands of democracy, including self-determination, are not absolute, they are a particle of the general democratic (at present socialist) world movement. In the individual concrete case a particle may contradict the whole; if it does it must be rejected.[98]

Further,

> The right of self-determination cannot and must not serve as an obstacle to the exercise by the working class of its right to dictatorship. The former must give way to the latter. That, for instance, was the case in 1920, when in order to defend the power of the working class, we were obliged to march on Warsaw.[99]

During the Second World War, East European countries fell to, and have since been under, communist influence. Hundreds of thousands of people were deported from the western part of USSR to Siberia to prevent the groups from seeking secession and were only repatriated by a Supreme Soviet decree of 1957. A ruthless method was employed to ensure the permanence of the communist regime.[100] The use of force to keep the communist regime in power where it is threatened with substitution by a non-communist government is an approved policy. This was the case in Bukhara, Khorezm, and Armenia in 1920, Georgia in 1921, and the Ukraine in 1923. Anti-communist revolts in East Germany in 1953 and in Hungary in 1956 were ruthlessly suppressed with the aid of Russian troops.[101] In 1968 the Soviet Union, along with East Germany, Poland, Bulgaria, and Hungary, intervened militarily in Czecho-

---

97.   Stalin, *Marxism and the National and Colonial Question* (1936), p. 147.

98.   Lenin, p. 147.

99.   Stalin, p. 168. *See also* Lenin, *Collected Articles on the National Question* (Moscow-Leningrad 1925).

100.   *See also* Ginsburgs, "A Case Study of Soviet Use of International Law," 52 *AJIL* (1958).

101.   *See also* Samad Shaheen, *The Communist Bolshevik Theory of National Self-determination* (The Hague, 1956): "It was clear that whenever the interests of nationality and that of the proletariat conflicted, the former had to yield to the latter, and the right to separation had to go overboard. Furthermore, he (Lenin) sponsored the right of self-determination as a general democratic right, much as he favoured the right to divorce without actually advocating for divorce in a particular case. Those whose right to secede was recognised had still to make the decision whether secession was desirable or not." (p. 106.) Assessing the Bolshevik use of the principle of self-determination before the October Revolution 1917, Shaheen concludes that "in the grand strategy of Bolshevism, the formula of 'self-determination' turned out to have almost exclusively tactical significance—useful in fanning the forces of minority unrest and winning their support in the fight for the cause." (p. 147.)

slovakia, a member of the Warsaw Pact, because they feared that the liberalisation policy of the Dubcek regime tended to be anti-communist and pro-capitalist and forced it to discontinue some of its proposed changes. This intervention was contrary to the principle of self-determination, which in this case supplemented the principles of sovereignty and non-intervention in domestic affairs.

Subjectivity colours communist thinking on self-determination. During their Asian tour in 1955, Bulganin and Khrushchev assured Afghan leaders in Kabul that they supported the demand of the Pathans to join Afghanistan and declared: "We regard as just and correct Afghanistan's demand that the population of neighbouring Pushtunistan be granted an opportunity of freely expressing their will to national self-determination as any other people."[102] In India they supported India's claim to Kashmir even though India declines to settle the Kashmir dispute by reference to the wishes of the people.

In international organisations, the Soviets traditionally advocate the principles of equality and self-determination as a basis for universal peace and coexistence among nations with different social, political, and economic backgrounds.[103] They champion the cause of self-determination in colonies and dependencies and are inclined to recognise them as international persons which have no governments of their choice. They insist that they may engage in all activities, including the use of force, to win back their independence. Their right to self-determination takes effect from the time they claim it.[104] Briefly, in the communist sense, self-determination involves a free choice of government and freedom from oppression. In Soviet internal policy, it requires the dictatorship of the proletariat organised through autonomous republics and regions.[105]

---

102. *Pravda*, 30 December 1955. *See also* Y. Y. Barsegov, "The Durand Line and the Question of Self-determination of Pushtunistan in Afghanistan-Pakistan Relations," *Soviet YBIL* (1959), p. 398; E. Goodman, "The Cry of National Liberation: Recent Soviet Attitudes Towards National Self-determination," 14 *International Organisation* (1960).

103. As early as 1922, Chicherin, addressing the League of Nations in Geneva, 10 April 1922, said "universal peace could only be achieved by a universal congress meeting on the basis of the equality of all peoples and the recognition of the right of every people to self-determination." Stenogramma Peregovorov, lsd. NKID, 1920, quoted in Taracouzio, p. 32.

104. *See* Sobakin, *Public International Law* (1964), pp. 121–139.

105. *See also* Cobban, *National Self-determination* (1945), pp. 101–120; K. M. Stahl, *British and Soviet Colonial Systems*; G. Starushenko, *The Principle of National Self-determination in Soviet Foreign Policy* (Moscow, 1963). For consideration of International communism and self-determination (in the South American Republics), *see* p. 158.

4. France

A. *Before the Second World War.* The French tried out a policy of indirect rule in those colonies which had recognised and influential rulers. Thus after the dethronement of the last Hova Queen in Madagascar, Marshal Gallieni, the military governor of the territory, carried out a form of indirect rule. Marshal Lyautey, once under him, introduced the system in Morocco after the Protectorate Treaty of 1912.[106]

After the retirement of Gallieni in 1905, the policy was changed to "assimilation" in Madagascar and elsewhere, with the exception of Morocco, which had a longer spell of the indirect system. Writing about assimilation, in contradistinction to the extermination of natives or absolute respect for their primitive customs, Joubert describes it as connected with "the intention of bringing the native populations up to the level of the civilising power, by placing them under the same laws and giving them a similar education."[107] What was in fact achieved was the conversion of a small educated elite into semi-Frenchmen while the vast majority lived under tribal customs and traditions. At best they spoke a certain amount of French, though they were expected to be frenchified in the fullness of time. The policy of "association" was then evolved to demonstrate the mutuality of benefits in their colonial system. At the opening of the session of the Government Council of French West Africa on 7 December 1934, M. Brevie described assimilation as follows:

> The colonial settler brings his superior knowledge, directive talent, moral sense, financial resources and technique of improvement. The native populations represent, at least at the beginning, only potential labour; their goodwill must be directed, their soil must be improved; the hidden resources of the mines, agriculture and stock-raising must be exploited by persistent effort.
>
> But let us remember that, since an agreement for association has been concluded, it imposes particular duties on the representative of the trustee nations, because moral considerations are mixed with material interests. It implies a fair division of the benefits of the enterprise in proportion to the efforts of each party. It not only excludes all idea of exploiting the natives, but imposes on the superior associate the duty of granting generously to his less-endowed partner a share in those moral and material developments which will later be translated into imponderables of confidence and sympathy by which the enterprise will be the gainer in the end.[108]

106. 106 *BFSP* (1913), p. 1023.

107. M. Gabriel de Joubert, "L'Empire Colonial Francais," quoted in the *Colonial Problem* (1937), p. 113.

108. Ibid., p. 114.

This policy is similar to the "dual mandate" of the British—the development of colonial resources in the interest of the British and of the native populations. The policy of association was essentially a partnership between indigenous population and the officials for whom a special training school was established in 1899. In constitutional terms, it meant government by a governor-general who was nominated by and responsible to Paris and assisted by advisory councils in which indigenous inhabitants were represented.[109]

Colonial administration was much more centralised than in the British territories and native rulers were deliberately eliminated to the advantage of the educated elite. During the Second World War, the colonies were divided on a regional basis for administrative convenience, each of the regions associating with France. Dahomey, Guinea, Ivory Coast, Mauretania, Niger, Sudan, Senegal, and Upper Volta were centrally administered from Brazzaville. Madagascar was under another governor-general who was responsible to the French minister for colonies. Not all French laws applied to the colonies, but only specific statutes (*lois*) and other laws promulgated by a governor of a colony and published in it.[110] The French Parliament could legislate for all colonies on all subjects.

B. *Progressive Autonomy up to 1956.* The defeat and occupation of France by the Germans, the rivalry between the Vichy and Gaulist governments, and the active participation by the colonies in the effort to win the war had far-reaching effects on the French colonial system. In the Brazzaville Conference of Governors (and observers from North Africa) in 1944, de Gaulle promised constitutional reforms in order to allow for greater autonomy. He announced that "France has chosen to lead sixty million men who are associated with forty-two million children on the road to a new age." Addressing the conference, he maintained:

> We are sure that there is and will be no progress of men who live in their own native land, in the shade of our flag, who are not to profit from it morally and materially, if this development did not lead them to such a standard of life that they could one day be associated in their own land in the management of their own affairs. That is the duty of France, the goal towards which we must march.[111]

The objective here was greater participation by local people in govern-

---

109.   *See also* James, *Legal Aspects of the Transfer of Power to Dependent Territories in Tropical Africa,* Unpublished thesis for the Oxford B. Litt. (1966), p. 94.

110.   Kenneth Robinson, *The Public Law of Overseas France Since the War,* p. 4.

111.   General de Gaulle's speech to Brazzaville Conference on 20 January 1944.

ment within the French Empire; autonomy outside the empire was ruled out.[112]

African leaders were later invited to participate in constitution-framing. There was more decentralisation and more deliberative powers were given to local assemblies. An era was ushered in of closer coopera-tion between the French and African leaders but with overtones of assimilation. Citizenship was extended to a wider category by law on 7 May 1946 and new governmental organs were created.[113] In the 1946 constitution:

> France forms with the people of its overseas territories a union based upon equality of rights and duties without distinction of race or religion. . . . Faithful to her traditional mission, France pro-posed to guide the peoples for whom she has assumed responsibility towards freedom to govern themselves and democratically to man-age their own affairs; putting aside any system of colonisation based upon arbitrary power, she guarantees to all equal access to public office and the individual or collective exercise of the rights and liberties. . . .[114]

The arrangement aimed at solidarity with overseas territories in a constitution that allowed for diversity in unity and equal rights and duties for all citizens in the union. Though local autonomy was enhanced, France still had dominant powers and the president of the union (who was also the president of the Republic of France) had extensive powers over all the territories. He presided in the council, prorogued and dis-solved the assembly, enacted decrees, and appointed the cabinets and government representatives in all the territories.

By 1956 the attempts to create semi-federal relations with Indo-China, Morocco, and Tunisia had failed and all three had become independent states. The Loi Cadre of that year provided for greater autonomy especially in predominantly local matters and transferred the governor-general's powers to the respective territorial councils which were now partially responsible to elected bodies and could legislate in specified fields. Universal adult suffrage was introduced and the common electoral roll was extended to Madagascar and Equatorial Africa. Africanisation was intensified in the civil service. The French government was repre-sented in each group of provinces by a high commissioner who had power

112. *Encyclopedie Politique de la France et du Mond.*, 2nd ed. (Paris, Editions de l'Union Francaise, 1948), 2:12.

113. *See also* T. Hodgkin, *Nationalism in Colonial Africa* (1956), p. 96; K. Robinson, "Constitutional Reform in French Tropical Africa," *Political Studies,* vol. 6, no. 1 (February 1955), p. 45; James, p. 100.

114. Preamble to the Constitution, A. J. Peaslee, *Constitutions of Nations* (1950), 2:9.

over thirty-two legislative heads including internal and external security, foreign affairs, justice, and higher education. He was advised by a local council of five in each territory.

The 1956 constitution marked the end of direct rule and went a long way in providing for internal self-government. It also provided the basis for the split into multiple states, some of them rather scanty in population and resources. On becoming the president, de Gaulle transferred the presidency of councils to elected members, former vice-presidents.

C. *The French Community.* In its preamble, the Constitution of the Fifth Republic (1958) refers to the "rights of man" and "national sovereignty." It states:

> In accordance with these principles and the principle of self-determination of peoples, the Republic offers to those overseas territories which express the will to adhere to it new institutions based on the common idea of liberty, equality, and fraternity and conceived with a view to democratic evolution.

Article 1 reiterates: "The Republic and the peoples of the overseas territories adopting the present constitution by an act of free determination for a Community. . . ." Sovereignty belongs to the people and is exercised through the representatives of the people and by way of referendum.[115] It provides for full autonomy: "In the Community instituted by the present Constitution, the States shall enjoy autonomy; they shall administer themselves and, democratically and freely, manage their own affairs.[116]

The constitution offered three alternatives for the territorial units: (a) retaining the status quo; (b) becoming overseas departments, or (c) seeking membership of the Community. Rejection of all three meant automatic independence and severance of all ties with France. Guinea chose independence while the other African territories chose membership of the Community.[117] By an amendment of 1960, a member could be-

115. Article 3.

116. Article 77.

117. Chad, Congo, Dahomey, Gabon, Ivory Coast, Niger, Mauretania, Senegal, Sudan, Ubangi-Shari, Upper Volta and Malagasy. The Republic of France consisted of France, Algeria (including the two Saharan departments formed in 1957), the four overseas territories—Guadeloupe, Martinique, Reunion, and Guiana, and the five small overseas territories which voted to retain their status quo—St. Pierre-et-Minquelon, the Comoro Archipelago, French Somaliland, Polynesia, and New Caledonia.

France's vengeance for Guinea's independence vote included the withdrawal of all French civil servants who, before they departed, burnt records and removed everything they could lay hands on like typewriters and electric bulbs. Guinea's self-reliance was enhanced by Ghana and some socialist states that went to its rescue.

come independent and thereby cease to belong to the Community; a State could however continue its membership after independence, just as an independent state could join without losing its independence. Thus membership was purely optional.

Although the states within the Community had full internal autonomy, they were not fully independent, for France controlled foreign affairs, defence, currency, external trade, and strategic raw materials. The president could decide on over-all policy, the Cour de Cessation was the highest court of appeal, and French civil servants, mostly paid by France, were made available to the states.

> The Republic and the Member States are not placed on a footing of absolute equality; first, because the Republic alone has external sovereignty and ensured the internal representation of the Community; and second, the Republic has a preponderant voice in the management of common affairs. . . . Subject to these two reservations, the Member States have internal sovereignty.[118]

Through France, members were associated with the Common Market under the Treaty of Rome 1956, imports from them being treated as imports from France.

The next phase was the advance to full independence. In September 1959, Mali decided to be fully sovereign and was soon followed by the rest. Senegal, Madagascar, and the Entente countries (Gabon, Chad, Central African Republic, and Congo [Brazzaville]) are still members of the Community, but the rest have left it. All of them, inside and outside the Community, concluded agreements of cooperation with France in foreign, economic and financial policies, higher education, and defence (with the exception of Upper Volta in defence). Each is associated with the Common Market by a separate agreement.[119]

The high hopes of the Community have not been fulfilled. The Senate was abolished in 1959 and the meeting of heads of governments is now virtually the only link. However, the political ties with France are close and African heads of state pay frequent visits to France, which gives extensive economic aid to its former colonies.[120] Guinea, though cut off

118. Duverger, *Droit Constitutionel et Institutions Politiques* (1955), p. 702.

119. In 1959, the Entete States (Ivory Coast, Dahomey, Niger, and Upper Volta) formed a union for economic cooperation while Chad, Gabon, Congo, Central African Republic, and Cameroons formed a customs union. Following conferences in Brazzaville, Dakar, and Younde, all the French African countries, with the exception of Guinea and Mali formed the union de africaine et malgache for cooperation in economic and foreign policies on a basis of equality.

120. In 1959 French aid to Africa was a higher percentage of French gross national product (1.96) than that of any other great Power, over 70 percent was supplied by the government and 80 percent went to Africa, quoted from Pickles, *The Fifth Republic* paperback ed. (1965), p. 164.

from this benefit, continues to send its students to France while ties with it are being slowly resuscitated. Decolonisation in the French Empire passed through the stages of assimilation, association, self-government, membership of the French Community, and finally independence, which came with remarkable speed and smoothness.

D. *Algeria.* French intervention in Algeria began in 1827 and France dispatched a military expedition to set up an administration in 1830. By 1848 the whole country was virtually conquered and colonisation began. Algeria was sometimes assimilated to France and at other times ruled separately. The 1947 constitution gave financial autonomy and a measure of home rule but these fell far short of nationalist demands. The National Liberation Front declared a war of independence on 1 November 1954 and set up a revolutionary government in exile based in Cairo.

In 1959 President de Gaulle offered a settlement on the basis of self-determination in one of three forms—secession, complete Francisation, or independence with French aid. He repeated his offer in 1960 and urged the nationalists to come to the conference table to discuss "an honourable end to the fighting."[121] His request from France for the approval of his decolonisation plans for Algeria, whereby "the Algeria of tomorrow, then will be Algerian"[122] was granted in the referendum of 8 January 1961. The result was the Evian Agreement signed by French and Algerian representatives on 18 March 1962.[123]

The agreement provides:

> The self-determination consultation will permit the electors to make known whether they want Algeria to be independent and in that case whether they want France and Algeria to cooperate in the conditions defined by the . . . declarations.

The genuineness of the consultation was guaranteed and in the meantime a provisional executive was set up. The French high commissioner retained defence, and in the last resort, law and order. It was agreed:

> The guarantees relative to the application of self-determination and the organisation of public powers in Algeria have been defined in common agreement.
>
> The formation after self-determination, of an independent and sovereign State appearing to conform to the realities of the Algerian situation, and in these conditions co-operate between France and

121. Address of 14 June 1960, *New York Times*, 15 June 1960.

122. Service de Presse et d'Information, New York, French Affairs, no. 108, December 1960.

123. For Evian Agreement *see AJIL* (1962), p. 716 *et seq.*

Algeria corresponding to the interests of the two countries, the French consider, together with FLN, that the solution of the independence of Algeria in co-operation with France is the one which corresponds to this situation.

The Government and the FLN have therefore defined this solution, in common agreement, in the declaration which will be submitted to the approval of the electors at the time of the self-determination vote.

The Evian Agreement was approved in a referendum on 8 April 1962 in France, overseas departments, and overseas territories.[124] It was also approved in Algeria on the "day of self-determination" (1 July 1962) and independence was announced two days after.

E. *Conclusion.* French policy in colonies has been greatly influenced by the threat of German militarism. Whether during the period of indirect rule, assimilation, association, or full internal autonomy, it predicates the fact that the colonies were expected to play an active part in sharing the burdens of France, for which in return, they were offered nondiscrimination and development in keeping with French "civilising mission." Writing in 1923, M. A. Sarraut referred to the sight of transport bringing resources, native soldiers, and workers to France so that its security depended, not on 40 million French people, but on 100 million people.[125] French colonial subjects in fact played an active part during the wars against Germany. In those circumstances self-determination for colonies was expected to develop along the lines of self-government and local autonomy, since they formed part of the multiracial "family."

The resurgence of nationalism during the war in the colonial world did not fail to affect French territories. Indian independence and the defined goal for British colonies stimulated the desire for fuller self-determination. Increasing powers over local matters were granted until the territories attained membership of the French Union, and later, the Community. There was a revival of African culture in the form of *négritude*,[126] as opposed to French culture, and philosophers like Senghor

124. Voting was 17,866,423 in favour, 1,809,074 against, with 6,802,769 abstentions.

125. Albert Sarraut, *La Mise-en-Valeur des colonies francaises* (Paris, Payout, 1923), pp. 17–18, quoted in the *Colonial Problem* (1937), pp. 19–20.

126. In a sharp criticism, K. Nkrumah describes *negritude* as a "bogus conception" and adds "the pseudo-intellectual theory serves as a bridge between the African-dominated middle class and the French cultural establishment. It is irrational, racist, and non-revolutionary. It reflects the confused state of mind of some of the colonised French African intellectuals, and is totally divorced from the reality of the African Personality." K. Nkrumah, *Class Struggle in Africa* (London, 1970) pp. 25–26.

made significant contributions in this field. It was clearly impossible to turn Africans into Frenchmen but, rather, each culture could influence the other toward fuller development.

The unexpected survival of Guinea, which instantly cut its links with France, showed the others as being feeble-minded. The independence of Ghana and the progress toward full nationhood in British West Africa, the pride in membership of the United Nations, made subordination to France within the French Community less compatible with the "wind of change."

With the exception of Algeria and Indo-China, the progress toward full nationhood in French territories has been smooth. In these two cases violence was required to bend French attitude toward satisfying nationalist demands. Since 1960, self-determination to the point of independence has marked French relations with the colonies. The principle found express mention in the constitutions of the Fifth Republic (1958) and of some of the former colonies, and in the Evian Agreement with Algeria,[127] thus making it a fundamental principle of the policy of those states.

The great intimacy between the leaders of former French colonies and of France and the inability of the former to criticise the latter when their actions are inimical to African interests (as in the explosion of the atomic bomb in the Sahara in 1961 and the supply of arms to South Africa in breach of UN resolutions) have led to accusations of French neocolonialism and African subservience. Post-independence agreements confer on France free military movement in the former colonies and French economic domination is very much evident. These unequal relations should, in time, disappear when the masses of the people become more conscious of the rights guaranteed by independence. The apparently smooth relations between the leaders perhaps reflect the social character of the French and a more sophisticated colonial policy which critics consider to be more politically, economically, and culturally debilitating than appears to be the case on the surface.

---

127. The Constitution of the Central African Republic proclaims in its preamble "the Ubangi people solemnly proclaims its attachment to the principle of democracy and of self-determination of peoples. . . ." The Constitution of Congo (Brazzaville) "proclaims its attachment to the principles of self-determination and the free will of peoples." Gabon: "By virtue of these principles (Rights of Man 1789, Universal Declaration of Human Rights 1948) and of the self-determination of peoples. . . ." See Peaslee, Constitutions of Nations (1965), 1:50, 85, 194.

VIII The Content of Self-Determination

1. Juristic Opinion

Juristic opinion is divided on the status of the principle of self-determination and arguments have been advanced both for and against its existence in international law. Thus G. Schwarzenberger holds the view that "the principle of national self-determination is a formative principle of great potency, but not yet part and parcel of international customary law."[1] Speaking of the principle, L. C. Green said:

> It is not a right under international law. Customary law certainly does not recognise such a right, and as yet, there are but few treaties that concede it.[2]

Rupert Emerson was "bewitched and bewildered" by the prospects of self-determination, "bewitched because of the illimitable vastness of the claims and promises which it appears to be making, and bewildered because of the drastic limitations which are imposed. . . . on any resort to self-determination."[3] In his view the principle introduces "an incalculably explosive and disruptive element which is incompatible with the maintenance of stable and organised society."

> What emerges beyond dispute is that all peoples do not have the right to self-determination; they have never had it; and they will

---

1. Schwarzenberger, *A Manual of International Law* (1960), p. 74.
2. Report of the 47th Conference of the ILA (1956), p. 58.
3. Proceedings of the American Society of International Law, 60th Annual Meeting (1966), p. 135.

never have it. The changing content of natural law in the era of decolonisation has brought no change in the basic proposition.[4]

Communist writers have no doubt at all about the legal nature of the principle of self-determination and consider it a right that belongs to all nationalities and essential for peaceful coexistence.[5] Levin maintains that "the principle of self-determination of nations, expressing the law consciousness of the masses, has become a primary international legal principle."[6] Lachs maintains that the Charter of the United Nations merely declared an already existing principle of law: "All they [Charter provisions] did was to confirm and lay down in writing a principle that had long been growing and maturing in international society until it gained general recognition," thus giving expression to "one of the elements of international law of the time."[7] In a previous article, he insists that self-determination is "a definite legal principle and it is laid down in the Charter of the United Nations, the most solemn document which is binding on . . . states of the world today. On this very principle, other elements are built. From it flow consequences which are both rights and duties in international relations."[8] In the view of R. L. Bobrov, self-determination, "though established in international law relatively recently, has already expanded and democratised the content of a number of other basic international law institutions."[9] D. I. Baratashvili maintains that "[r]ecognition of the moral and international legal nature of the principle of equality and self-determination derives from the fact that it is part of the code of modern legal norms like the United Nations Charter. In turn this means recognition of the right of all nations to

4. Emerson, "Self-determination Revisited in the Era of Decolonisation," *Occasional Papers in International Affairs*, no. 9 (December 1964), Harvard Center of International Affairs, pp. 63–4. *See also* Emerson, *From Empire to Nation* (1960), p. 307: "The right of self-determination has as yet found no stable place in the international legal structure nor has it been accepted by states as a policy to be applied consistently and across the board. Indeed, I would suggest that it is essentially miscast in the role of a legal right which can be made as an operative part of either domestic or international systems."

5. *See* e.g., Vyshinsky, *The Law of the Soviet State* (1948), p. 249; Taracouzio, *The Soviet Union and International Law* (1935), p. 26.

6. Levin, "The Principle of Self-determination of Nations in International Law," *Soviet YBIL* (1962), p. 48. *See also* Rudolf Arzinger, *Das Selbstbestimmungrecht un allgemeinen Volkerrecht der Gegenwart* (Staatsverlag Der Deutschen Demokratischen Republik, Berlin, 1966).

7. M. Lachs, "The Law in and of the United Nations Organisation," *Indian JIL* (1961), p. 432.

8. M. Lachs, "Some Reflections on the Problem of Self-determination," *Review of Contemporary Law* (1957), p. 2.

9. R. L. Bobrov, "Basic Principles of Present-day International Law," in G. Tunkin, ed., *Contemporary International Law* (Moscow, 1969), p. 51.

demand and secure the right to self-determination and independence. At the same time this makes it incumbent on the United Nations members to do all they can to facilitate the implementation of this principle."[10]

The present trend in the West is toward the acknowledgment of the principle as one of international law in spite of the difficulty of precise definition. Writing in 1920, P. M. Brown admitted that self-determination was a "fundamental principle of international law and order," though undefined and though no rules for its application had been formulated. Whatever the difficulty involved in its application, he concluded, only in self-determination characterized by "common consent," rather then coercion, is to be found the freedom, prosperity, and happiness of Central Europe and the whole world.[11] Quincy Wright views it as a new principle resulting from the modern sentiment of internationalism directed chiefly at decolonisation, and respect for which is an obligation undertaken under the Charter. He adds, "Whether it can be reduced to rules of law sufficiently precise to admit of judicial application is doubtful. . . ."[12] Ross acknowledges the principle, although in his view it is "quite impossible to define by any precise or national criterion the group to which this right should belong."[13] Korowicz "finds little reason to doubt that the principle of self-determination is recognised by the Charter as a principle of international law, all the more since it is combined with equal rights of the peoples, and the principle of equal rights of states and nations certainly is a principle of international law affirmed as such in many multilateral treaties, and in the writings of publicists."[14] In his view Articles 1 and 55 of the Charter made the principle "an integral part of positive international law." Elihu Lauterpacht maintains that international customary law acknowledges the principle of self-determination, thus providing "the meeting point of customary law and democratic principle. . . . Indeed, it is in this area of self-determination that so far the development of human rights in the international sphere, as governed by customary international law, has made its greatest progress."[15] Higgins points out that it is inescapable "that self-determination has devel-

---

10. D. I. Baratashvili, *International Law and the States of Asia and Africa* (Moscow, 1968), p. 35.

11. P. M. Brown, "Self-determination in Central Europe," 14 *AJIL* (1920), p. 235.

12. Q. Wright, *The Role of International Law* (1961), p. 28.

13. Ross, *Constitution of the United Nations* (1950), p. 135.

14. Korowicz, *Introduction to International Law: Present Concepts of International Law* (Hague, 1959), p. 285.

15. E. Lauterpacht, "Some Concept of Human Rights," 11 *Howard LJ* (1965), pp. 270–1.

oped into an international legal right, and is not an essentially domestic matter. The extent and scope of the right is still open to some debate."[16] Starke acknowledges that there is now a "wider general recognition of the right of self-determination, and of the correlative duty of states, administering dependent territories, to transfer full powers to the peoples thereof."[17] In his treatise, Ian Brownlie states unequivocally, "The present position is that self-determination is a legal principle. . . ."[18]

Opinions of writers in the non-aligned states favour the legal status of self-determination. Thus Nawaz calls it "one of the modern principles of international law."[19] It can then be said with confidence that the legal nature of the principle of self-determination, though rejected by some, is receiving a wider acknowledgement by text writers in all parts of the world.

2. Judicial Decisions

The *Aaland Islands* case,[20] was a dispute between Sweden and Finland as to whether the islanders who were under Finnish jurisdiction could opt to join Sweden in the exercise of the right of self-determination, especially in view of the fact that Finland itself obtained independence from Russia in recognition of that right. Sweden wanted the people to decide their future in a plebiscite but Finland resisted the demand as interfering with its domestic jurisdiction. The committee of jurists appointed by the Council of the League to investigate the matter found that a question of international law was involved and that the League could appropriately concern itself with it. The committee found:

> The recognition of the principle in a certain number of treaties cannot be considered as sufficient to put it upon the same footing as a positive rule of the Law of Nations. . . . Positive International Law does not recognise the right of national groups, as such, to separate themselves from the State of which they form part by the simple expression of a wish, any more than it recognises the right of other States to claim such a separation.[21]

16.   R. Higgins, *The Development of International Law Through the Political Organs of the United Nations* (1963), p. 103.

17.   Starke, *An Introduction to International Law* (1967), p. 116.

18.   Brownlie, *Principles of International Law* (1966), p. 484.

19.   M. K. Nawaz, "The Meaning and the Range of the Principle of Self-determination," *Duke University LJ* (1965), p. 99. *See also* Mensah, *Self-determination under the United Nations Auspices* (Unpublished dissertation for J. S. D. Yale Law School. 1963).

20.   *LNOJ*, no. 3 (October 1920).

21.   Ibid., p. 5.

The grant or refusal of the right to a section of the population to decide the sovereignty over a piece of territory by plebiscite or other means, the committee held, was an act of sovereignty and a matter within that state's internal jurisdiction. The committee went on to say that its decision

> does not give an opinion concerning the question as to whether a manifest and a continued abuse of sovereign power, to the detriment of a section of the population of a State, would, if such circumstances arose, give to international dispute arising therefrom, such a character that its object should be considered as one which is not confined to the domestic jurisdiction of the State concerned.[22]

Even where there is no abuse of sovereignty, the committee recognised that revolutions create situations of fact which must be recognised in law: "[t]ransition from a *de facto* situation to a normal situation *de jure* cannot be considered as one confined entirely within the domestic jurisdiction of a State."[23]

In his dissenting opinion in the *Right of Passage* case (Portugal and India), Judge Moreno Quintana maintained that the Charter sets about to end colonialism in response to the mood of the present period which he described as the "age of national independence."[24]

More recently, Judge Nervo said in the *South-West Africa* cases that concepts of equality and freedom regardless of colour "will inspire the vision and the conduct of peoples the world over until the goal of self-determination and independence is reached."[25] He stated further:

> The sacred trust of civilisation (the Mandate System) is a legal principle and a mission, where fulfillment was entrusted to more civilised nations until a gradual process of self-determination makes the people of the mandated territories able to "stand by themselves in the strenuous conditions of the modern world."[26]

The importance of these judicial pronouncements must neither be exaggerated nor underestimated. The committee's decision on the *Aaland Islands* case, though bearing directly on self-determination, was given in 1920. There have since been developments in international customary law. The treaties referred to were those concluded between Russia and neighbouring States after the coming into power of a government that was unpopular in the West and was not yet recognised by them. The

---

22. Ibid., p. 5.

23. Ibid., p. 6. For a discussion of the case *see* 33 *AJIL* (1939), pp. 465–87, by N. J. Padelford.

24. *ICJ Rep.* (1960), p. 95.

25. *ICJ Rep.* (1966), p. 457.

26. Ibid., pp. 465–6.

committee expressly denied making a pronouncement that might cover a situation where the abuse of sovereignty to the detriment of a section of the population was cause for international dispute. It follows that the committee today would have taken into consideration that self-determination is a principle of the Charter of the United Nations, that denial of it, especially in the colonial context, is a source of discord among nations, that it has since been recognised in state practice and that eminent juristic opinions from different parts of the world representing the major legal systems regard the principle as a rule of international law.

Judges Moreno Quintana and Nervo were delivering dissenting judgments; it is difficult to assess the exact weight of their opinions. However, Judge Nervo demonstrates the intimate nexus between self-determination and fundamental human rights which are the chief objective of all governments. The purpose of human rights is to enhance the human personality. The mandate system and trusteeship were designed to guide peoples who were too weak to stand by themselves until they were able to do so through a process of political, social, economic, and cultural development. Judge Moreno's "age of independence" typifies the present preoccupation of the United Nations with colonialism. This is not an exhaustive exposition of the manifestation, nor the inflexible goal of self-determination.

It is argued by some that a court is incapable of applying the principle of self-determination because it is undefined. The difficulty involved in its application is not however insuperable nor is the principle necessarily any more imprecise than, for instance, domestic jurisdiction or sovereignty. The court is expected to play its part in evolving a world community ruled by world law and should not shy away from a dispute arising from the exercise or denial of self-determination.

3. *The Practice of International Organisations*

Through its resolutions the United Nations has expounded and developed the principle of self-determination enshrined in the Charter. It has passed innumerable resolutions on self-determination for dependent peoples; the high-water mark was the 1960 Resolution on the Granting of Independence to Colonial Peoples and Countries, demanding the immediate liquidation of colonialism.[27] It has passed resolutions on Cyprus, Morocco, Tunisia, and other territories which ultimately made their impact on the administering powers. It has also passed resolutions, on Portuguese territories and on South-West Africa, which have been

27. Res. 1514 of 14 December 1960.

ignored. It has set up committees on specific territories when the question of their independence involved special difficulties, such as the United Nations Commission on Indonesia, the Committee on South-West Africa, Portuguese Territories, Angola, and Rhodesia. The implementation of the resolutions on colonial territories is now the special responsibility of the special Committee of Twenty-four. There is almost a consensus in the United Nations that dependent peoples are entitled to self-determination.[28]

The United Nations has organised plebiscites, with the cooperation of the administering authorities, to determine the true wishes of the people in choosing which state shall exercise sovereign authority over them. This has not been by way of disintegration, a characteristic derisively attributed to self-determination, but with a view to forming larger states with the consent of the people. Plebiscites were held in the British Cameroons, North and South, before mergers with Nigeria and the Republic of Cameroons respectively and in British Togoland before the merger with Ghana; in Ruanda the plebiscite was on the future of the monarchy. In Sabah and Sarawak the United Nations consulted the legislatures and the electorates of the territories on the question of joining the Federation of Malaysia.[29]

Where the decolonisation of a territory is complicated by rival claims of sovereignty, as in Gibraltar and the Falkland Islands, the organisation has regrettably deviated from a strict adherence to self-determination. In such cases, it recommends that decolonisation should be effected through negotiations between the contending parties and tends to favour the party it considers to be the "victim" of colonialism trying to regain sovereignty over all its territory.[30]

Certain resolutions on self-determination are a corollary to the principle of non-interference in the domestic affairs of member states. In Resolutions 1004–1008(ES–II), 1120–1124(XI), and 1312(XIII), the United Nations affirmed the right of the Hungarian people to have a government of their choice and condemned the intervention of Russia with troops, even though it was claimed that the troops were requested by the legal government. The organisation also referred to self-determination in resolutions that urged respect for the independence of

28. *See also* chapter 4 on colonies.
29. For plebiscites held under the United Nations' supervision, *see* p. 000 *et seq.*
30. For a criticism of the United Nations' application of the principle of self-determination, *see*, e.g., Fawcett, "The Role of the United Nations in the Protection of Human Rights—Is It Misconceived?" in A. Eide and A. Schou, eds., *International Protection of Human Rights* (Uppsala, 1968), p. 95.

Korea (112[II]), China (291[IV]), and Yugoslavia (509[VI]) and stressed that respect for the principle was essential for peace—290(IV), 1514(XV), etc. The Uniting for Peace Resolution (377[V]) also referred to it.[31]

In its desire to expound and implement human rights, the United Nations has given prominence to the principle of self-determination by including it in the very first articles of the International Covenants on civil and political rights and on economic and cultural rights: "All peoples have the right of self-determination." This is undoubtedly coloured by the present anti-colonial emphasis but it also lends weight to the assertion that individual human rights are truly meaningful in the context of a people enjoying self-determination.[32]

The United Nations recognises the importance of self-determination for peoples within metropolitan states, although some members are opposed to this aspect of the principle. Speaking before the Economic and Social Council in 1956, British representative Creech Jones reminded members that Chapter XI of the Charter did not dispose of all the problems affecting non-self-governing peoples. "There were subject peoples within sovereign States, for whom the United Nations must care as it had for peoples under the control of imperial Powers."[33] In 1952 the Belgian delegate criticised members who evaded their obligations under Chapter XI because they had non-self-governing peoples within their sovereign states but refused to extend the rights guaranteed in the Charter to them.[34] During the debate that preceded the Independence Resolution of 1960, the United States accused the Soviet Union of perpetrating the worst form of colonialism in its area of influence. In the Special Committee on Friendly Relations and Cooperation Among States, established under Resolution 1966(XVIII) of 16 December 1963, the

31. See also Repertory of Practice of United Nations Organs, supp. no. 2, vol. 5, 2488 c.21/64.

32. See also D. A. Kay, "The Politics of Decolonisation: The New Nations and the United Nations Political Process," 21(4) International Organisation (1967), pp. 786–811. "Thus, the shift after about 1955 in the primary emphasis of the Organisation away from collective security and toward decolonisation efforts is a natural result of the hyperdependency on the attitudes of the Member States.

In connection with this phenomenon it seems also to be a characteristic of the United Nations politics that secondary concerns either are recast in terms similar to the predominant emphasis or else gradually atrophy. Thus the traditional human rights activities of the Organisation have become to a considerable extent only an adjunct to the decolonisation struggle." (p. 811). While pointing to the present emphasis in the United Nations the comment goes too far in submerging human rights under anti-colonialism.

33. Off. Rec., 1st part, 1st sess. 4th Committee (1946), p. 34.

34. 7th sess., 4th Committee (1952), p. 23.

delegates of Great Britain and the United States emphasised that the principle of self-determination did not become redundant on the attainment of independence but operated beyond it. Thus a British proposal to the committee maintains:

(1) Every State has the duty to respect the principle of equal rights and self-determination of peoples and to implement it with regard to the peoples within its jurisdiction. . . .

(4) States enjoying full sovereignty and independence, and possessed of a representative government, effectively functioning as such to all distinct peoples within their territory, shall be considered to be conducting themselves in conformity with this principle as regards those peoples.[35]

Indeed, members of the United Nations whose peoples are enjoying self-determination through democracy are in a strong position to demand the extension of the principle to peoples under undemocratic regimes. This is likely to be a major preoccupation of the United Nations in the future when colonies, as they are known today, may have ceased to exist.

Other organisations have also emphasized the importance of the principle. The International Commission of Jurists, which seeks to influence the development of the law in response to changes in human relations, has in conferences held in different parts of the world arrived at resolutions which not only clarify difficult points of law but also serve as guidelines. Thus in the Congress of Athens 1955 it resolved:

(9) The recognition of the right to self-determination being one of the greatest achievements of our era and one of the fundamental principles of international law, its non-application is emphatically condemned.

(10) Justice demands that a people or an ethnic or political minority be not deprived of their natural rights and especially of the fundamental rights of man and citizens or of equal treatment for reasons of race, colour, class, political conviction, caste or creed.[36]

35. A/AC.125/L44, part VI (1967). And also United States proposal: "The principle is *prima facie* applicable in the case of the exercise of sovereignty by a State over a territory geographically distinct and ethnically or culturally diverse from the remainder of that State's territory, even though not as a colony or other Non-Self-Governing Territory." A/AC.125/L.32 (1967). *See also UNYB* (1965), p. 628. *See also* on the Committee on Friendly Relations, G. W. Haight in 1 *International Lawyer* (1967), pp. 122–126; R. Starr, " 'Friendly Relations' in the United Nations," 2 *International Lawyer* (1968), pp. 519, 534–536.

36. Committee on Public Law, Resolution 3. *See also* the Rule of Law and Human Rights: Principles and Definitions (International Commission of Jurists, Geneva, 1966).

The principle was affirmed by the Pacific Charter of September 1954,[37] and by the Conference of Non-aligned States held in Belgrade in September 1961 (twenty-five states), and in Cairo in October 1964 (forty-seven states).[38] The First World Conference of Lawyers on World Peace Through Law, in their Declaration of General Principles for a World Rule of Law, adopted a resolution to this effect:

> In order to establish an effective international legal system under the rule of law which precludes resort to force, we declare that. . . . a fundamental principle of the international rule of law is that of the right of self-determination of the peoples of the world as proclaimed in the Charter of the United Nations. . . .[39]

In the Addis Ababa Conference of African heads of state in 1963, the OAU proclaimed "the inalienable right of all peoples to control their destiny."[40] The organisation has repeatedly affirmed the right of colonial peoples to self-determination and independence and goes so far as to give them material and moral aid in the fight for freedom. This commitment is in accordance with the resolutions of the United Nations approving the use of force by liberation movements and requesting states to give them all possible material and moral aid.[41] It is also in accordance with present international law, which recognises the right of self-determination and condemns colonialism.

The OAU resolutions on the Nigerian Civil War,[42] emphasized the principle of territorial integrity at the expense of self-determination. The Charter of the OAU reaffirms the territorial integrity of African states but it also refers to "the inalienable right of all people to control their own destiny" and to "freedom, equality, justice and dignity" being essential objectives for the achievement of the legitimate aspirations of the African people. It specifically reaffirms faith in the Universal Declara-

---

37. U.S. Dept. of State Bull. 31 of 1954. The charter was proclaimed in Manilla by Australia. France, New Zealand, Pakistan, the Philippines, Thailand, United Kingdom and United States of America. They agreed to "uphold the principle of equal rights and self-determination of peoples and they will earnestly strive by every peaceful means to promote self-government and to secure the independence of all countries whose peoples desire it and are able to undertake its responsibility."

38. 4 Indian JIL (1964), p. 599.

39. 58 AJIL (1964), pp. 138–151, at 143.

40. Africa Report (1963), pp. 9–10.

41. As in Res. 2105(XX), 2107(XX), 2189(XXI), 2160(XXI), 2225(XXI), 2383(XXIII), and 2465(XXIII).

42. Passed in conferences held in Kinshasha, September 1967, Algiers, September 1968, and Addis Ababa, September 1969.

tion of Human Rights and in the Charter of the United Nations in which the principle of self-determination is enshrined.[43]

A proper interpretation of the charter of the OAU requires the recognition of both the principles of self-determination and of territorial integrity and not the subjugation of the former to the latter. President Nyerere warned against this tendency in the Nigerian/Biafran conflict at the OAU meeting of September 1969 held at Addis Ababa:

> The OAU is not a trade union of African Heads of State. Therefore, if it is to retain the respect and support of the People of Africa, it must be concerned about the lives of the people of Africa. We must not just concern ourselves with our survival as Heads of State; we must even be more concerned about peace and justice in Africa than we are about the sanctity of the boundaries we inherited.[44]

If the principle of territorial intergrity is clearly incompatible with that of self-determination, the former must, under present international law, give way to the latter. Self-determination can, however, be manifested in several ways other than independence. The practice of the OAU indicates little tolerance for secession from member states as an exercise of the right of self-determination; on the other hand, it encourages unity and merger on which a bright future for the continent depends. There is little disposition to investigate the question of human rights and self-determination within a member state; the lethargic attitude toward the Sudan, where a civil war had been raging and to Lesotho, where the ruling Basutoland National party seized power after losing the election held in January 1970 are recent examples.

Including the concept of *jus cogens* in the Draft Law of Treaties (i.e., "a peremptory norm of general international law from which no derogation is permitted and which can be modified only by a subsequent norm of general international law having the same character"),[45] the International Law Commission gave as examples of prohibited treaties those that permit the unlawful use of force contrary to the Charter of the United Nations, the commission of acts such as the trade in slaves, piracy, or genocide or the performance of any other act criminal under international law. It also stated, "[o]ther members expressed the view that . . . treaties

---

43. For the full text *see* 58 *AJIL* (1964), pp. 873–880.

44. *The Nigeria-Biafra Crisis*, Government printer (Dar es Salaam, 1969), p. 12.

45. Article 37 of the Draft Law of Treaties. For the final text *see International Legal Materials*, Vol. 8, no. 4, (July 1969). Article 53: "For the purposes of the present convention a peremptory norm of general international law is a norm accepted and recognised by the international community of States as a whole as a norm from which no derogation is permitted and which can be modified only by a subsequent norm of general international law having the same character."

violating human rights or the principle of self-determination were mentioned as other possible examples."[46] International organisations which are concerned with human rights and world peace have given full recognition to the fact that respect for self-determination is a condition for world peace. Fundamental human rights are meaningful in the context of a people enjoying self-determination.

4. State Practice

It is now a distant cry from 1920 when the committee of jurists said it knew only of "a certain number of international treaties" that embodied the principle of self-determination. The Franco-Algerian Treaty of Evian (1962),[47] though concluded with a dependent territory, had the character of an international treaty and was regarded as such by the parties. It dealt with self-determination for Algeria with a view to creating a new state that would be "Algerian Algeria." The Anglo-Egyptian Treaty[48] on the Sudan guaranteed self-determination for the Sudanese people. The parties to the Southeast Asia Treaty Organization "uphold the principle of equal rights and self-determination of peoples," and declare that "they will earnestly strive by every means to promote self-government and to secure the independence of all countries whose peoples desire it and are able to undertake its responsibilities."[49] One of the most universalist treaties in the world—the United Nations Charter—reflects broadly the practice of the parties. By ratifying the Charter, states have undertaken under Articles 1 and 55 "to develop friendly relations among nations based on respect for the principle of equal rights and self-determination of peoples." Under Article 56 "all Members pledge themselves to take joint and separate action in cooperation with the Organisation for the achievement of the purposes set forth in Article 55." The pledge to respect the prin-

---

46.   YILC (1963), 2:199. *See also* the comments by the Philippines at YILC (1966), 2:22 and Ukraine at 2:23. Brownlie considers self-determination to be an "aspect of *jus cogens*;" Brownlie, p. 75. Without going so far, Fawcett describes it as "a right of a second order: it stands behind the human rights set out in the Universal Declaration and Covenants as a precondition of their full exercise by individuals as members of collectivities . . ." "The Role of the United Nations in the Protection of Human Rights: Is it Misconceived?" in Eide and Schou, eds. *International Protection of Human Rights* (Uppsala, 1968) pp. 95, 97. M. Schreiber, however, considers self-determination to be "an incontestable legal principle of our time." Ibid., p. 283.

47.   *AJIL* (1962) p. 716 *et seq.*

48.   Agreement Between Egypt and Britain Concerning Self-Government and Self-determination for the Sudan, Cairo, 1953; 161 *UNTS*, p. 157.

49.   United States Treaties, 81, 209 UNTS, p. 28; 60 *AJIL* (1966), p. 646. The parties are Australia, France, New Zealand, Pakistan, Philippines, Thailand, United Kingdom and the United States.

ciple of self-determination is in relation to all peoples under a state's jurisdiction, whether in mandated, trusteeship, colonial, or metropolitan territories. It lies within the competence of states to assume obligations in the exercise of sovereignty.[50]

The principle has received express mention in the constitutions of states like the Soviet Union, France (1958), Congo (Brazzaville), and Central African Republic, where it is supposed to be an operative principle of state policy in the relations between those governments and their subjects.

By advancing dependent peoples to independence, the major administering powers have given firm recognition to the principle in regard to colonial peoples. Earlier resentment at the concern shown by the United Nations gave way to compliance with the resolutions which demanded that independence should be granted to colonial peoples at an early date unless they chose some other status. The great majority of the states listed as administering powers in 1945 now agree on the principle of self-determination for dependent peoples who regard their emergence from dependent status as a matter of right, not favour.

5. The Status and Range of Self-determination

The question arises: Has self-determination become a principle of customary international law? Custom is a "usage felt by those who follow it to be an obligatory one."[51] It is "a general practice accepted as law."[52] In the *Asylum* case the court said: "The Colombian Government must prove that the rule invoked by it is in accordance with a constant and uniform usage practised by the States in question, and that this usage is the expression of a right appertaining to the State granting asylum, and a duty incumbent on the territorial State."[53]

The principal source of custom is state practice. The practice of the major colonial powers confirms that they regard the principle of self-determination for colonial peoples as binding. The inclusion of the principle in treaties and in constitutions is further evidence of its recognition in state practice. A general practice results from the repetition of the same conduct by states. It is not necessary that there should be no dissentient state; otherwise a single state or a group of states could stall the development of international customary law. No particular duration of

50. The Wimbledon case, PCIJ (1923), ser. A, no. 1.
51. Brierly, *The Law of Nations* (1963), p. 59.
52. Statute of the International Court of Justice, Article 38(1) (b).
53. *ICJ Rep.* (1950), p. 276.

time is essential for the development of custom; although usage over a long period provides good evidence. The customs relating to the use of airspace and the continental shelf have developed over comparatively short periods. The United Nations has not only facilitated the ascertainment of the views of states on the question of self-determination, it has also through its declarations, resolutions, and its own practice accelerated the emergence of the principle as one of international customary law. H. Bokor-Szego draws the following conclusion:

> While the right of self-determination has become a rule of positive international law through its incorporation in the UN Charter, the particular rules on the content of this right and the resulting responsibilities of States have been evolved, through custom, by state practice observing the Charter and making up in this way for the deficiency originating from the *lex imperfecta* character of the relevant provisions of the United Nations Charter.[54]

The opinions of eminent jurists from the world's main legal systems confirm in a subsidiary way the legal status of the principle.

Few legal concepts, if any, have the virtue of easy definition. Self-determination, like other international legal principles, has political implications and therefore is open to a subjective interpretation in which case the end in view may influence the exposition of the legal concept. As Nanda puts it, "the main problem was not the dichotomy between the ideal and the practicable . . . but a clarification of the major issues involved in the concept of self-determination."[55] The principle can only be described as "[v]ague in its statement as in its application, and dangerous in its anarchic consequences"[56] when it is viewed as unbridled and undisciplined. If a similar uncontrolled interpretation is given to other acknowledged principles of international law, like domestic jurisdiction and sovereignty, they would be no less pernicious than the universal "breaking up of allegiances, followed by a series of plebiscites to settle new units of government."[57]

Since there is almost complete unanimity that self-determination applies to colonial peoples, the reluctance in some quarters to examine its implications in the right perspective only serves the purpose of those who,

54. H. Bokor-Szego, *New States and International Law* (Budapest, 1970), pp. 26–27.

55. Proceedings of American Society of International Law (1966), p. 148.

56. de Visscher, *Theory and Reality in International Law*, translated by P. E. Corbett (1957), p. 80.

57. Professor Gilbert, quoted by Wambaugh, *Plebiscites Since the World War* (1933), 1:488.

for obvious reasons, wish to confine it to the colonial context with a view to excluding international concern from oppressed peoples within sovereign states. Piet-Hein Houben regrets this tendency:

> It is indeed seriously distressing that the majority of the United Nations membership is so little interested in the universal application of the principle of self-determination—a blatant example of the supremacy of narrow self-interest over the demands of world-wide justice. The doctrine now current serves only the cause of "colonially defined" territories and the Communist interest in maintaining a limited interpretation of its meaning. Precisely to counteract this limited interpretation, it is of the utmost importance that Western countries should not resign themselves to the vagueness of the principle contained in the Charter on the ground that "almost insuperable practical difficulties might be caused by the words: all peoples have the right to self-determination."[58]

The task of the international lawyer is to regulate the competing claims of sovereignty, to reconcile them in the light of the changing world on the basis of the rule of law, and to enhance the status of the individual wherever and whoever he may be. States were once the exclusive, and still remain the primary, subjects of international law. This emphasis is now shifting toward greater respect for the right of individuals. Rights accrue to collections of individuals as peoples or nations without regard to race, colour, or sex.

At San Francisco in 1946, the *rapporteur* of Commission 1 reported as follows:

> The Committee understands that the principle of equal rights of peoples and that of self-determination are two complementary parts of one standard of conduct; that the respect of that principle is a basis for the development of friendly relations and is one of the measures to strengthen universal peace; that an essential element of the principle in question is a free and genuine expression of the will of the people. . . .[59]

This assessment remains good today; so too does President Wilson's rough-and-ready dictum—"peoples may now be dominated and gov-

---

58. He said further, "Admittedly the principle does not contain a precise and complete definition covering all possible and doubtless complex situations in which it might be invoked. However difficult it may be to agree on a definition, efforts should at least be made to establish criteria for and characteristics of situations to which the legitimate question of the principle's implementation may arise. Such efforts, imperfect though the results may be, constitute the only way of making the universal applicability of the concept of self-determination a concern for the international Community as a whole." 61(2) *AJIL* (1967), pp. 724–5.

59. 6 UNCIO Docs. 396.

erned only by their own consent."[60] The *rapporteur* of the Committee on Friendly Relations remarked:

> Nearly all representatives who participated in the debate emphasised that the principle was no longer to be considered a mere moral or political postulate; it was rather a settled principle of modern international law. Full recognition of the principle was a prerequisite for the maintenance of international peace and security, the development of friendly relations and cooperation among States, and the promotion of economic, social and cultural progress throughout the world.[61]

The basic characteristics of self-determination are (1) government according to the will of the people;[62] (2) the absence of internal or external domination; (3) the free pursuit of economic, social, and cultural development; (4) the enjoyment of fundamental human rights and equal treatment; and (5) the absence of discrimination on grounds of race, colour, class, caste, creed, or political conviction.

The absence of internal or external domination connotes the recognition of the rights of the majority and of the minority within a state and not the domination of one by the other. Commenting on the claim that the whites of Rhodesia exercised their right to self-determination by the unilateral declaration of independence, McDougal and Reisman said:

> [I]t would be a travesty upon the most basic notion of "self-determination" [which they describe as "an important feature of contemporary international law"] to speak of it, in regard to a claim of 6% of a population, when the goal of the claim is to gain absolute political control over the majority and powerless citizenship. It would be completely contrary to the very purposes for which the contemporary right of self-determination has been created to employ it to justify the systematic suppression of the human rights of the vast majority of the population for no other reason than to maintain the social, political, and economic superiority of a mere 6% of the occupants of the area.[63]

60. Baker and Dodd, ed., *The Public Papers of Woodrow Wilson: War and Peace* (1927), p. 180.

61. UN Doc. A/AC.125/L.53 add. 3, p. 9 (1967).

62. *See also* E. Luard, "The Origins of International Concern over Human Rights," *The International Protection of Human Rights* (1967), p. 10: "The right to 'self-government'—the contemporary equivalent of 'self-determination' today ..." *See also* 20 *Encyclopaedia Britannica* (1960): "Self-determination has become, since the American and French revolutions, a political, if not a legal principle expressing the right of a nation to form a government of its own choice." (p. 306).

63. McDougal and Reisman, "Rhodesia and the UN," 62 *AJIL* (1968), pp. 1–19, 18.

The principle ensures that every group with a legitimate interest—geographical, national, traditional, cultural, or any other kind—enjoys full democratic rights.[64]

The most spectacular manifestation of this principle in recent times has been the eradication of colonialism in many countries and the coming to independence of many former colonies. The exercise of the principle has led to mergers with the metropolitan states, as in the case of Hawaii and Alaska with the United States, Surinam with Holland, and Greenland with Denmark. It has led to associations, as in the case of Puerto Rico with the United States, and West Samoa and Cook Islands with New Zealand. The principle has been fulfilled through the free choice of local autonomy, as in the case of French Somaliland within the French Community. In all these cases the wishes of the people were ascertained before the new relations were created.

Levin defines self-determination as "the right of the people of a nation freely, without outside pressure, to determine their State affiliation, including the right to form an independent State, and also to determine the forms of their internal political, economic, social and cultural life, which is guaranteed by international organisations and bodies."[65] He states correctly that a nation may, in the exercise of the right of self-determination, join another state. If however the conditions of the compact are breached, the acceding nation may secede "because all-member-states of the United Nations are obliged to observe the principle of self-determination of nations and the United Nations has the duty of combating violations."[66] He unconvincingly defines the legitimate "self" that is entitled to determine as "A nation, a people, a nationality . . . possessing a common territory, and most often a common language, who are united by the community of aims in the struggle for liberation." He excludes national minorities "because they do not live in any compact masses on a definite territory, but are scattered among the population belonging to another or other nations."[67] Levin seems to be wrong in his requirement

---

64. Thomas and Thomas define self-determination as "the deciding, the coming to a conclusion of one's acts or condition of being, or condition of mind without external compulsion. This would include, among other things, the right of a people to determine, freely and without compulsion, the form of their government, the people who shall administer their government, the governmental machinery, and the rules to which their government must conform." Thomas and Thomas, *Non-Intervention* (1956), p. 369.

65. D. B. Levin, *"Self-determination of Nations in International Law,"* Soviet *YBIL* (1962), p. 46.

66. Ibid., p. 46.

67. Ibid., p. 47.

that they must occupy some territory where they form the majority. In his definition, self-determination is the prerogative of the majority in a geographical area. There is in this analysis a danger of the dictatorship. not necessarily of the proletariat in the Marxist sense, but of the majority. The undesirable effect of this comes out clearly in the cultural aspect of self-determination, as with reference to the Jews in the Soviet Union who may be "legitimately" denied the right to practice their own culture, being a minority dispersed among a majority of non-Jews in the Soviet Union.[68]

Higgins defines self-determination as "the right of the majority within an accepted political unit to exercise power." Consequently "there can be no such thing as self-determination for the Nagas. The Nagas lie within the political unit of India, and do not constitute the majority therein."[69] This definition ignores the fact that the principle set out in the Charter of the United Nations, and later in the Covenant on Human Rights, refers to "peoples," which may constitute majorities or minorities.

In the view of Hans Kelsen "peoples" in Articles 1(2) and 55 of the Charter refers to states, since they have "equal rights" in international law.[70] This interpretation is however unacceptable, for it contradicts the ordinary meaning of the word. We have moved away from the era when states were almost exclusively the subjects of international law.

In his recent study of the plebiscite as an instrument of self-determination, H. S. Johnson defines self-determination as "the process by which a people determine their own sovereign status. . . . In consequence, national self-determination implies the right of each nation to be sovereign."[71] The equation of self-determination with independence ignores the fact that the principle is also expressed through local autonomy, association, self-government, merger, or other form of participation in government. He denies, by implication, that peoples within a metropolitan state who have no wish to secede have a right to self-determination. In fact, the principle is relevant to all peoples, whether dependent or

68. *See*, e.g., an advertisement covering a page of the *London Times*, 21 January 1968 by British dons protesting against the denial of cultural rights, *inter alia*, to Jews in the Soviet Union. Writing in the *London Times*, Joel Cang states, "One of the biggest grievances is that Russian Jews alone, out of 150 national minorities and ethnic groups are denied facilities to enable them to preserve their national culture." Nor is Yiddish, the Jewish tongue, taught in any school even though Article 121 of the constitution of the Soviet Union guarantees instructions in schools "in the native tongue." *London Times* 11 April 1968.

69. Higgins, p. 105.

70. Kelsen, pp. 51–3.

71. H. S. Johnson, *Self-determination Within the Community of Nations* (Leyden, 1967), p. 200.

independent. Although the right was usually regarded as belonging to nations exclusively, as in the First World War Peace Conference, it now belongs to peoples which may in some cases represent nations. The correct definition of nations on which so much effort was expended is not now absolutely necessary for the application of self-determination. Higgins in fact concedes that, in principle, self-determination could refer to a racial, religious, or political party group.[72]

The legitimate "self" that "determines" is now not so difficult to pinpoint. The "self" that the Minorities Treaties sought to protect was defined in the *Greco-Bulgarian* case as

> a group of persons living in a given country or locality, having a race, religion, language and traditions of their own and united by this identity of race, religion, language and traditions in a sentiment of solidarity, with a view to preserving their traditions, maintaining their form of worship, ensuring the instruction and upbringing of their children in accordance with the spirit and traditions of their race and rendering mutual assistance to each other.[73]

The modern principle of self-determination is the right, not only of groups that fall within the above definition, but in fact groups that may be non-racial, non-national, and that may form majorities. The legitimate "self," therefore, is a collection of individuals having a legitimate interest which is primarily political, but may also be economic, cultural, or of any other kind.[74] When it is identified with the whole population of a state there is no doubt at all that they are entitled to exercise the right. But it may also represent part of the population of a state, in that case the more substantial the "self" the easier it is to recognise its right to determine. It may under certain circumstances represent the population of more than one state. The central figure is the individual combining with other individuals to form peoples, nations, minorities, or majorities, in the exercise of legitimate rights, as opposed to when he is acting alone. Individuals, as peoples, are entitled to exercise democratic rights and enjoy a commensurate share in determining their political, cultural, and economic future.

The effect of the right's being recognised in international law is that its exercise may be a matter of international concern. It is not that every

---

72. Higgins, p. 106.

73. PCIJ (1930), ser. B., no. 17, p. 21.

74. Self-determination is "the right of a group to adapt their political position in a complicated world to reflect changing capabilities and changing opportunities." R. Fisher, "The Participation of Microstates in International Affairs," *American Society of International Law* (April 1968), pp. 164, 166.

slight infringement or claim of the right qualifies as a matter of international concern but that a legal, political, social, economic, or cultural situation that seriously reflects a claim or negation of the right is a proper concern for the community of nations. The political principle of self-determination may operate internally within domestic jurisdiction to regulate relations between the parts of a state. The mere claim of a particular form of self-determination, such as independence, does not *ipso facto* make it a question of self-determination in international law. The action of the government complained of must amount, in the words of the committee of jurists, to "a manifest and continued abuse of sovereign power, to the detriment of a section of the population."[75] There must be a serious contravention of one or more of the characteristics set out above.[76] It is a matter of degree. What constitutes such a situation depends on all the circumstances of the case. Thus the denial of independence to a colonial people who demand and deserve it, the massacre of a people who in an attempt to safeguard their existence, as by reaction against genocide, assert the right to independence, and the denial of democratic rights to a people, as such, constitute such a situation, particularly if these actions result from state policy. On the other hand, the refusal to grant independence to a town or village and denying to a minority the right to dominate the majority, as in Rhodesia, do not constitute a denial of self-determination.

A situation involving the international legal principle of self-determination cannot be excluded from the jurisdiction of the United Nations by a claim of domestic jurisdiction. International customary law is binding on all states regardless of consent; and in any event, states have bound themselves under the Charter to respect the principle.

The plebiscite has become an important instrument of self-determination. Invented during the French Revolution, it was applied to specific territories under certain circumstances.[77] It was applied in the territorial settlements of Central Europe after the First World War, though not as a general principle, and in boundary settlement between Soviet Russia and some of its neighbors in the years immediately following the October Revolution of 1917.[78] More recently the future of some trust territories was decided in plebiscites.[79] If a people are not to be tossed about from sovereignty to sovereignty as if they were chattel, the transfer or cession

75. *LNOJ* no. 3 (October 1920), p. 5.
76. *See* p. 192.
77. *See* p. 10.
78. *See* p. 164.
79. *See* p. 104.

of territory must be subject to a plebiscite so that the people most directly concerned may have the opportunity to decide their future. Where a boundary cannot be satisfactorily ascertained or where the issue is simply that of the future of a dependent territory, such as Gibraltar, the Falkland Islands, or the minute territories dotted in the oceans of the world, the principle of self-determination is a relevant factor. Such territories may find that it is in their best interests to maintain close relations with the nearest mainland. It follows that the cession or transfer of territory today against the wishes of the inhabitants is contrary to the principal of self-determination.[80]

Attempts have been made to exclude the application of the principle to metropolitan territories. It was argued by Kenya that "the principle has relevance where foreign domination is the issue. It has no relevance where the issue is territorial disintegration by dissident citizens."[81] Some representatives at the Seminar on Human Rights in Developing Countries maintained that once independence was attained, no more question could arise on self-determination. They insisted that the right applied exclusively to a dependent territory seeking independence from a colonial power. While recognising the right of a people to change their government if they so desire, they were opposed to the idea of self-determination for a particular group, as this could lead to the destruction of the political unity of new states having minorities.[82] This anxiety reveals a basic democratic weakness and is intended to exclude from international concern situations created by the denial of self-determination. The principle applies equally to dependent and independent peoples, including those who have recently emerged from dependence.

The importance of attaching the right to peoples as against states lies in the fact that a government may be wholly unrepresentative as by a rigged election or an unpopular military coup. A geographical section of a state may maintain an absolute dominance over the rest while forming a majority-government at the centre. A government may act in disregard, and without consultation with its people. Thus in their quest

---

80. *See also* Jennings, *The Acquisition of Territory in International Law* (Manchester, 1963), pp. 8–9. According to him the plebiscite principle may be useful in determining title to "certain kinds of territory."

Article 52 of the Constitution of Gabon, 38 of Mali, and 44 of Mauretania require referenda of the people concerned before the cession, exchange or acquisition of territory. In the case of Gabon, a referendum of the Gabonese people is also required. *See* Peaslee, vol. 1; R. R. Wilson, "International Law in New Constitutions," 58 *AJIL* (1964), nn. 3, 432–3.

81. Pan-African Unity and the Northern Frontier District Question (Mogadishu, May 1963).

82. ST/TAO/HR, 21 May 1964, pp. 12–13.

for national states without national minorities the Turkish and Greek governments in the Lausanne Treaty of 20 January 1923 agreed to "a compulsory exchange of Turkish nationals of the Greek Orthodox religion established in Turkish territory, and of Greek nationals of Moslem religion in Greek territory."[83] This involved the compulsory movement of 450,000 Greeks and 145,000 Turks who were not formally consulted, as in plebiscites, about their future. Similarly Nazi Germany concluded a series of treaties involving the exchange of populations with Italy, Estonia, Latvia and USSR in 1939, Hungary and Roumania in 1940, Croatia in 1941, and Bulgaria in 1943. A Bulgarian-Roumanian treaty of 1940 necessitated the exchange of 62,000 Bulgarians for 110,000 Roumanians. The exercise of sovereignty in such cases would today be subject to the principle of self-determination of peoples.

The principle of self-determination seeks to impose certain minimum standards of administration and to secure the participation of all sections of the population in the government of a state. Governments have no inherent right to deny democratic rights to their subjects, not even in the years of "teething difficulties" in the case of new states. Windass maintains quite correctly: "The attention of the world. . . . is focussed on another dimension of the principle of self-determination—not so much on the breakaway of remaining colonies, as on internal self-determination, the free interaction of all political groups within a State, and racial equality."[84] Far from being a spent force, an unwarranted intrusion, or an ebbing tide, the principle is bound to assume increasing importance in international as well as in municipal law.[85]

Self-determination supplements other principles of international law, such as sovereignty, domestic jurisdiction, equality, and nondiscrimination. Its main impact is that they should be applied with due regard to the wishes of the people most directly concerned. The exercise of sovereignty in accordance with the wishes of the people prevents autocratic

---

83.   32 LNTS, p. 77.

84.   G. S. Windass, "Power Politics and Ideals: The Principle of Self-determination," 3 *International Relations* (1967) (David Davis Memorial Institute of International Affairs), p. 186. Further "it remains as true as it was in 1945 or in 1918 that rights emerge as a fine distillation from the cauldron of power conflicts, and do not fall gently to earth from the haven of intellectual contemplations." (Ibid.)

85.   *See also* W. O'Connor, "Self-determination: The New Phase," 1 *World Politics* (October 1967), p. 53; Mattern, *The Employment of the Plebiscite in the Determination of Sovereignty*: "There can be no denial of the fact that constitutional and municipal law have come to recognise almost universally the principle of self-determination in all matters which lie within their sphere." (p. 192.)

government. A proper act of recognition ensures that the wishes of the people are carried into effect at the international level. A policy of non-discrimination according with the wishes of the people ensures harmony and the proper development of the capabilities of the peoples concerned. An action that may otherwise constitute a breach of the above principles may be justified on the basis of the wishes of the people—consent.

One of the supposed dangers of self-determination is that it might encourage secession. There is no rule of international law that condemns all secessions under all circumstances. The principle of fundamental human rights is as important, or perhaps more so, as that of territorial integrity. Neither a majority nor a minority has the legal right to secede, without more, since secession may jeopardise the legitimate interests of the other part. If, for instance, a majority or minority insists on committing an international crime, such as genocide, or enforces a wholesale denial of human rights as a deliberate policy against the other part, it is submitted that the oppressed party, minority or majority, may have recourse to the right of self-determination up to the point of secession.[86] On the other hand, a majority or minority accorded its normal democratic rights cannot legally request the international community to help it to secede.[87] The existence of a right and the form it takes must have regard to other principles of international law, such as sovereignty, and to the particular circumstances of each case including strategic considerations and political viability. Modern requirements for political and economic viability are connected with larger political and economic units, rather than smaller ones; these considerations must influence the manifestations of self-determination. The protection of fundamental human rights must, however, be the main objective of all political systems.

The law takes note of a situation that results from existing facts. Thus a *de facto* state, resulting from the exercise of self-determination in the form of secession, but which the international community could not have legally helped to create, may be recognised *de jure*. A secession that would have been justifiable but which is rendered ineffective by the

---

86. *See also* D. W. Bowett, "Self-Determination and Political Rights in Developing Countries," *American Society of International Law* (April, 1966): "No one would advocate the right to secession of a township, standing in splendid isolation but making no economic sense. Equally, no one could advocate the right of the wealthy part of a territory to secede from the rest of the territory so as to deprive the remainder of its economic base: this was one of the dangers in the Katangese secession." (p. 131.) He suggested two negative pre-conditions, "that it cannot result in a miniscule without economic or political viability, and that it cannot deprive a State of its economic base." (Ibid.)

87. This applies to Scottish and Welsh nationalists in the present circumstances of the United Kingdom.

superior force of the state from which it is intended to secede, may remain a dormant issue. International law should, however, protect the justifiable exercise of the right, while preventing its abuse. The possibility of the abuse of a right does not, however, invalidate it in law.

If a *de facto state* has crystallised, refusal to recognise it may be tantamount to a denial of self-determination.[88] The refusal to recognise the separate existence of East Germany, Communist China, Bangladesh, or Israel amounts to such a denial, regardless of the use of force in their original establishment.

An issue of self-determination is involved when an external power is invited by a government to help in the suppression of a revolt. The intervening power, usually a strong military one, normally pleads consent in justification of its intervention. This was the case in the intervention of the Soviet Union in East Germany in 1953 and in Hungary in 1956. The United States intervened in Lebanon in 1958 on the invitation of President Chamoun to protect him from being overthrown. On the same basis and about the same time Britain intervened in Jordan. The American involvement in Vietnam is justified by the American government on the ground, *inter alia*, that it was invited by the legal government of a *de facto* state. The Geneva agreement[89] which ended the French-Vietnamese War in 1954 provided that elections were to be held in 1956 and were to be followed by the unification of the two "zones" separated by the cease-fire line. The Diem government, with the military and economic support of the United States, rejected the holding of elections because the probability of communist victory was great. The breach of the agreement has brought down upon the two "zones" a whole series of violent consequences.[90] Without going deeply into the legality of the use of force, outside intervention may seriously hamper the realisation of the wishes of the people as against their government's. A corrupt and unpopular government may hang on to power by the use of force and may only be removed by the use

---

88.   It is correctly stated with regard to civil war, "After the international requirements for the recognition of belligerency have been fulfilled, a duty of recognition of belligerency necessarily follows, and refusal of recognition is interference with the right of political self-determination of the people of a State, and therefore constitutes illegal intervention." Thomas and Thomas, p. 220.

89.   For full text, *see* 60 *AJIL* (1966), p. 629.

90.   Among the ever-growing juristic writings on Vietnam, *see* Q. Wright, "Legal Aspects of the Vietnam Situation," 60 *AJIL* (1966), p. 750; J. H. Norton, "The Lawfulness of Military Assistance for the Republic of Vietnam," 61 *AJIL* (1967), p. 1; Wolfgang Friedmann, "Law and Politics in the Vietnamese War: A Comment," 61 *AJIL* (1967), p. 776; F. B. Schick, "Some Reflections on the Legal Controversies Concerning America's Involvement in Vietnam," 17 *ICLQ* (1968), p. 953.

of force by the subjects. The prohibition of the use of force in international law is not extended to these situations; for a discredited government to stay in power by leaning on outside support spurns the self-determination of the people.

External support against a dissident section of the army whose activities do not reflect the wishes of the people does not offend their right to self-determination. Such was the limited intervention by Britain in Tanzania, Kenya, and Uganda, and France in Gabon in 1964. These were situations calling for a short and precise "police action." A large-scale revolt representing a fundamental cleavage within the population and involving defined peoples, territories, or authorities calls for non-intervention from outsiders even in respect of the supply of arms. Intervention by outsiders may have the effect of influencing the political solution and may hamper the right of the people to self-determination. It may contradict with Article 2(4) of the Charter which provides: "All Members shall refrain in their international relations from the threat or use of force against the territorial integrity or political independence of any State, or in any other manner inconsistent with the Purposes of the United Nations."[91] (These include respect for the principle of self-determination.)

Quincy Wright formulates the following test where consent is pleaded for intervention: "The validity of this justification depends in law upon whether, under the circumstances, that government was competent to speak for the State."[92]

External aggression violates the right of a people to self-determination. A recent example of this is the invasion of Czechoslovakia in 1968 by the members of the Warsaw Pact (with the exception of Roumania). Outside support for self-defence against aggression is legal under Article 51 of the Charter "until the Security Council has taken the measures necessary to maintain international peace and security." The Czechoslovakians did not want to defend themselves militarily, so the question of outside intervention on invitation did not arise.

The situation is complicated when the intervention is defended on the ground of "indirect aggression." Aggression is not justifiable because it is indirect but there is also the danger that the situation may be given a subjective assessment in order to justify a given policy. It could not be

91. In the Essentials for Peace Resolution of 1 December 1949 the assembly called upon every state "to refrain from any threats or acts direct or indirect, aimed at impairing the freedom, independence or integrity of any State, or at fomenting civil strife and subverting the will of the people of any State."

92. Q. Wright, "United States Intervention in the Lebanon" 53 *AJIL* (1959), pp. 112, 125. For a different view, *see* P. B. Potter, "Legal Aspects of the Beirut Landing," 52 *AJIL* (1958), p. 727.

said of some of the situations characterised as "indirect aggression" in the past that "the necessity of that self-defence is instant, overwhelming, and leaving no choice of means and no moment for deliberation."[93] Elihu Lauterpacht provides the following working formula in cases calling for intervention: "The policy which must guide those entrusted with the solution of these problems should have as its starting point the acknowledgment of the principle of self-determination—the idea that the majority will must prevail, coupled with the acknowledgment that the position of the minority must not be abused and must, if necessary, be specifically protected."[94]

Persistent disregard of the resolutions of the United Nations on a question of self-determination for a territory is a matter of international concern. The disregard of the principle by a state in dealing with its own subjects may be sufficiently serious to be the concern of the organisation. A threat to world peace and stability resulting from the assertion or denial of the right is, *a fortiori*, a matter for the United Nations requiring the urgent attention of the Security Council under Chapter 7 of the Charter.

The principle of self-determination does not necessarily imply a uniform system of government; it accommodates centralized, as well as decentralised systems, provided the choice accords with the wishes of the people; the techniques of democracy are far from being completely explored. The principle, however, excludes the imposition from outside of an alien form of government that has no roots in the desires of the people. Thus a political theory that seeks to impose a pattern of government on a people, contrary to their wishes, conflicts with the principle, though a popular revolution in order to install a political system is consistent with it.

Self-determination has important cultural and economic aspects. Culturally it ensures the unimpeded development of a people's cultural heritage. A people are entitled to safeguard their culture even when they are a minority, but they are also free to subordinate it to a superior culture or in the interest of uniformity. Economically, a people are entitled to determine their economic future and to exploit all the opportunities for their economic development within the limits of the law. The people of a state are entitled to full sovereignty over their natural resources and to exploit them in accordance with the rules of international law.[95]

93. The Caroline case (2), *Moore's Digest of International Law* (Washington, 1908), p. 412.
94. E. Lauterpacht, "Some Concepts of Human Rights," XI *Howard LJ* (1965), p. 272.
95. *See* chapter 9.

The *raison d'être* for the principle of self-determination is the enjoyment by all peoples, regardless of race, religion, or sex, of full democratic rights within the law, free from internal or external domination. It seeks to provide the opportunities for the political, economic, social, and cultural development of all peoples. These *desiderata* will guide the future development of the principle of self-determination.

IX Economic Self-Determination

1. The Meaning of Economic Self-determination

Economic self-determination concerns the right of states and peoples to determine their economic future. The regulation by a state of its economic affairs is a legitimate exercise of sovereignty. The League of Nations Economic Committee remarked in 1937 that [e]very country seeks, and seeks rightly, to protect its own economy.[1] In the *Austrian-German Customs Union*[2] which dealt with the interpretation of the Treaty of St. Germain and the separation of Austria from Germany as a means of weakening the latter, the court indicated the essential nature of economic independence:

> [T]he independence of Austria, according to Article 88 of the Treaty of St. Germain, must be understood to mean the continued existence of Austria within her present frontiers as a separate State with sole right of decision in all matters economic, political, financial or other with the result that the independence is violated, as soon as there is any violation thereof, either in the economic, political, or any other field, these different aspects of independence being in practice one and indivisible.[3]

The importance of economic independence is well demonstrated by Georg Schwarzenberger, who noted: "Without a minimum of political,

1. *Survey of International Affairs* (1937), pp. 1, 73.
2. PCIJ, ser. A/B, no. 41.
3. Ibid., p. 45.

economic or military *de facto* independence, *de jure* independence is meaningless."[4] Nothing, however, stops a state from surrendering its economic independence voluntarily to another state.[5] An example of this is the tiny state of Liechtenstein, independent since 1866, but which has been a member of the Swiss Customs Union since 1924 and uses Swiss currency. In the absence of such voluntary surrender of power, a state reserves the right to organise its economic future, otherwise what appears to be sovereignty on the surface becomes, in the words of Judge Hudson, "a ghost of a hollow sovereignty" or "a sovereignty shorn of the last vestige of power."[6]

2. The United Nations and Sovereignty over Natural Resources

The United Nations has passed resolutions concerning the recognition of the sovereignty of peoples over their natural resources and wealth as well as cooperation in the economic development of the underdeveloped countries.[7] Thus in Resolution 626(VII) of 12 December 1952 the assembly acknowledged that the right of peoples to exploit freely their natural resources and wealth is inherent in them and recommended international cooperation in the exercise of that right. It also recommended restraint from "acts direct and indirect, designed to impede the exercise of the sovereignty of State over its natural resources." This resolution was relied upon by the Japanese and Italian high courts in upholding the Iranian Nationalisation Laws.[8] The Italian court held that it was "evident that the decision of the United Nations at that meeting, taking into consideration the date when it was taken and the international situation to which it related, constituted a clear recognition of the international lawfulness of the Persian Nationalisation Law."[9]

In formulating the economic objectives of the United Nations and the

---

4. "The Principles of International Economic Law," 117 *Recueil de Cours* (1966), pp. 1, 31.

5. *The Alabama* (1872) 1, Moore, International Arbitration, 653. The practical effect of this type of surrender is participation in a large economic sovereignty.

6. *Lighthouses in Crete and Samos*, ser. A/B 71 (1937), p. 127.

7. The United Nations has passed resolutions on full employment, e.g., 308(IV) of 25/11/49 and 405(V) of 12/12/50; land reform: 401(V) of 20/11/50 and 1424 (XIV) of 5/12/59; industrialisation and productivity: 521(VI)· of 12/1/52 and 1425(XIV) of 12/4/60; primary commodities and international trade: 623(VII) of 21/12/52 and 1423(XIV) of 5/12/54; financing of economic development: 400(V) of 20/11/50; private capital: 824(IX) of 11/12/54; public capital: 724(VIII) of 7/12/53 and 1240(XIII).

8. *Anglo-Iranian Oil Coy* v. *Idemitsu Kosa, K. K. ILR* (1953), p. 309, and *Anglo-Iranian Coy* v. *SUPOR Coy, ILR* (1955), p. 19.

9. *ILR* (1955), p. 41.

principle of international economic cooperation, especially in the under-developed countries and in order to safeguard their independence, the assembly resolved that *inter alia*: "the sovereign right of every State to dispose of its wealth and its natural resources should be respected in conformity with the rights and duties of States under international law."[10]

In 1958 the assembly set up a commission of nine[11] "to conduct a full survey of the status of the basic constituent of the right to self-determination" and where necessary make recommendations for strengthening that right. It was to have due regard for the rights and duties of states under international law and the importance of international cooperation in the development of underdeveloped countries. The assembly acknowledged that "the right of peoples and nations to self-determination as affirmed in the two draft Covenants . . . includes permanent sovereignty over their natural wealth and resources.[12] On the request of the commission, the secretariat prepared a preliminary study which dealt with, *inter alia*, national measures affecting ownership or use of natural resources by foreigners, state controls over resources and their exploitation, international agreements for the exploitation of resources, acquired rights, concession agreements, the extent of foreign investment, and the flow of capital.[13]

The United Nations Commission on Permanent Sovereignty over Natural Resources recommended a draft resolution of eight principles to the Economic and Social Council in 1961. During the discussion of the principles in the Second Committee of the General Assembly (Economic and Financial) many delegates pointed out that the main problem was the reconciliation of the respect for the sovereignty of the under-developed countries with the protection of foreign-owned investments. Among the amendments that were adopted was one jointly proposed by the United Kingdom and the United States preserving the rights and obligations of successor states and governments in respect of property acquired before the accession to independence of former colonies. Their second amendment noted that the subject of state succession was being examined by the International Law Commission. Algeria thereupon withdrew its own amendment which would have declared that international law did not protect alleged rights acquired before independence

10. Res. 1515(XV) of 15 December 1960.

11. Afghanistan, Chile, Guatemala, the Netherlands, the Philippines, Sweden, USSR, UAR, and United States.

12. Res. 1314(XII) of 12 December 1958. *See also UNYB* (1958), pp. 212–214.

13. The Status of Permanent Sovereignty over Natural Wealth and Resources (1962), A/AC. 97/5/Rev. 2.

but subjected such claims to renegotiation by the parties who were equal as sovereign states.

Two amendments proposed by the Soviet Union were not adopted: one subjected compensation to the law of the expropriating state, the other confirmed the inalienable right of peoples and nations to the unobstructed execution of nationalisation and other means aimed at strengthening their sovereignty over their natural wealth and resources. Another amendment by which the assembly unreservedly supported measures taken by peoples and states to re-establish or strengthen their sovereignty over their natural wealth and resources and condemned acts aimed at obstructing that right was adopted in the Second Committee but failed in the plenary session. The United States proposed an amendment that provided for "prompt, adequate and effective compensation" but later withdrew it.

The final resolution was adopted in the form of eight principles:

(1) The right of peoples and nations to permanent sovereignty over their natural wealth and resources must be exercised in the interest of the national development and of the well-being of the people of the State concerned.

(2) The exploration, development and disposition of such resouices, as well as the import of the foreign capital required for these purposes, should be in conformity with the rules and conditions which the peoples and nations freely consider to be necessary or desirable with regard to the authorisation, restriction or prohibition of such activities.

(3) In cases where authorisation is granted, the capital imported and the earnings on that capital shall be governed by the terms thereof, by the national legislation in force, and by international law. The profits derived must be shared in the proportions freely agreed upon, in each case, between the investors and the recipient State, due care being taken to ensure that there is no impairment, for any reason, of that State's sovereignty over its natural wealth and resources.

(4) Nationalisation, expropriation or requisitioning shall be based on grounds or reasons of public utility, security or national interest which are recognised as overriding purely individual or private interests, both domestic and foreign. In such cases the owner shall be paid appropriate compensation, in accordance with the rules in force in the State taking such measures in the exercise of its sovereignty and in accordance with international law. In any case where the question of compensation gives rise to a controversy, the national jurisdiction of the State taking such measures shall be exhausted. However upon agreement by sovereign States and other parties concerned, settlement of the dispute should be made through arbitration or international adjudication.

(5) The free and beneficial exercise of the sovereignty of peoples and nations over their natural resources must be furthered by the mutual respect of States based on their sovereign equality.

(6) International cooperation for the economic development of developing countries, whether in the form of public or private capital investments, exchange of goods and services, technical assistance, or exchange of scientific information, shall be such as to further their independent national development and shall be based upon respect for their sovereignty over their natural wealth and resources.

(7) Violation of the rights of peoples and nations to sovereignty over their natural wealth and resources is contrary to the spirit and principles of the Charter of the United Nations and hinders the development of international cooperation and the maintenance of peace.

(8) Foreign investment agreements freely entered into by or between sovereign States shall be observed in good faith; States and international organisations shall strictly and conscientiously respect the sovereignty of peoples and nations over their natural wealth and resources in accordance with the Charter and the principles set forth in the present resolution.[14]

Professor Schwarzenberger has subjected the resolution to scathing criticism. He describes it as

a circumlocution, couched in a terminology intended to make it respectable, of the outright denial of the rule of international customary law that the legality of expropriation depends on the payment of full, prompt and effective compensation. In short, it is a pseudo-legal ideology of international lawlessness, the naturalist counterpart to the equally fallacious natural-law doctrine of the absolute sancrosanctity of private property. . . . It is amusing in its self contradictions and, if it puts anything on record, it is the alienable character of sovereignty.[15]

The resolution was in fact a carefully drawn-up compromise intended to protect both capital-importing and capital-exporting countries. It protects the sovereignty of the importing states which are mostly poor, and encourages their economic development through technical assistance and loans. It affirms their right to regulate and control the exploitation of their natural resources for the well-being of their peoples and emphasizes that political independence without economic freedom is a negation of sovereignty. Investment agreements should be freely entered into and in the event of a dispute local remedies should first be exhausted before

14. Res. 1803(XVII) of 14 December 1962.
15. 117 *Recueil des Cours* (1966), 1:32.

resort to international remedies.[16] It seeks to avoid the sort of interventions that typified American policy in the South American states during the later part of the nineteenth century and the beginning of the twentieth, a situation which today would undoubtedly be treated as "contrary to the spirit and principles of the Charter of the United Nations and hinders the development of international cooperation and the maintenance of peace." The resolution guarantees for the capital-exporting countries the enjoyment of the legitimate fruits of their investment. Investment contracts are subjected to national laws and the terms of the contracts as well as to international law which ensures that the last shall prevail in the event of a dispute. Without such protection, hopes for international cooperation in the economic development of undeveloped countries will remain a dream. The assembly urged the secretary-general to continue his study of aspects of permanent sovereignty over natural resources.[17]

Nationalisation or expropriation is not to be embarked upon arbitrarily but only on the grounds of "public utility, security or national interest." In that event, "appropriate compensation" must be paid. This differs from the standard of "prompt, adequate and immediate compensation." "Appropriate" compares with "just" or "reasonable" and represents the current trend. What is appropriate will depend upon all the circumstances of the case, such as the terms of the contract, the nature of the terms, the circumstances of the contract, the nature of the resource, the amount of capital involved, the interest so far recouped, the effect of the existing arrangements on the people, and the ability to pay compensation.

An expropriation which involves a large amount of money will require a longer time to pay than one that is small. The expropriation of a resource on which the whole economy depends is readily justifiable as being in the public interest than one that is less strategic; in fact for the former, a state runs a risk if such a resource is left in the hands of foreigners or if they are allowed more than a minor participation. If the original right was acquired through an unequal contract, or if it was obtained through force, the threat of force or deceit, expropriation, as pointed out above, will have the effect of restoration. This invariably effects the amount of compensation, if any. The foreign firm may have made profits wholly disproportionate to the amount of investment which amounts to depriving the people of wealth that rightly belongs to them. In such circumstances, there is no reason why in principle, expropriation

16.   For a contrary view, see K. N. Gess, "Permanent Sovereignty over Natural Wealth and Resources," *ICLQ* (1964), 398 at 449.

17.   See also *UNYB* (1961), pp. 498–504.

may not involve the payment of extra amount by the foreign firm even after the property has been taken over. The meaning of the word "appropriate compensation" in Resolution 1803(XVII) may involve a difficult interpretation and a delicate balance between the rights and wrongs of the parties over a period of time.

In the view of W. Friedmann, the resolution "neither endorses the claim for 'prompt, full and adequate' compensation usually made by Western Lawyers nor the claim made by some representatives of the less-developed countries that compensation is purely a matter of internal discretion and not an obligation of International Law. Again, the resolution goes some way towards affirming the contractual character of international concession agreements."[18]

In Resolution 2158(XXI) of 25 November 1966 the assembly reiterated the principle of permanent sovereignty over natural resources with particular reference to developing countries with a view to securing for them greater participation in exploiting natural resources.

In his report to the International Law Commission on State Succession in Respect of Rights and Duties Resulting from Sources Other Than Treaties, M. Bedjaoui made the following relevant comment:

[I]n Moslem law, according to the views of the Imam Malek, whose school of thought predominates in North Africa, all mines, even those of freehold land, are the property of the community (Umma) and can only be worked by the State through a concession, which is granted in return for the payment of either a fixed sum or part of the yield. The portion of the yield retained by the concessionaire should in no case exceed a fair recompense for the work and effort involved in operating the mine. The concessionaire's role is thus reduced to that of a mere operator."[19]

The principle of economic self-determination is given prominence in the Covenant on Human Rights, the first articles of which include:

18. W. Friedmann, *The Changing Structure of International Law* (London, 1964), p. 138. The resolution was supported by many states including Australia, Canada, Denmark, Greece, Israel, Italy, Japan, the Netherlands, New Zealand, Sweden, United Kingdom and United States and was opposed only by France and South Africa. The following abstained: Bulgaria, Burma, Bylorussia, Cuba, Czechoslovakia, Ghana, Hungary, Mongolia, Poland, Roumania, Ukraine, and USSR. In the light of this pattern, it seems difficult to justify the assertion that "such a resolution does not reflect the small voting strength of the world's capital-exporting countries; rather, it reflects the position of a majority of the capital-importing and undeveloped countries in enlightened self-interest." Gess, *ICLQ* (1964), p. 448. *See* J. H. Hyde, "Permanent Sovereignty over Natural Wealth and Resources," 50 *AJIL* (1956), pp. 854–867; V. I. Sapozhnikov, "Sovereignty over Natural Wealth and Resources," *Soviet YBIL* (1965).

19. UN Doc. A/CN 4/204 of 5 April 1968.

(1) All peoples have the right of self-determination. By virtue of that right they freely determine their political status and freely pursue their economic, social and cultural development.

(2) All peoples may, for their own ends, freely dispose of their natural resources without prejudice to any obligations arising out of international economic cooperation based upon the principle of mutual benefit, and international law. In no case may a people be deprived of its means of subsistence.

The question may be asked: How can a people be deprived of their own means of existence? The experience of the people of some of the new states, as in a few of the old, has shown that a people may have to be protected against their own government. To give a hypothetical example: If a corrupt government of the independent state of X whose means of subsistence is phosphate deposits sold the resource to a foreign company in consideration that ten percent[20] of the purchase price should go into the private pockets of the leaders of government, there would be a good case for the application of the articles of the Covenants. There have been governments that were not persuaded that their primary duty was the welfare of the governed.

In the Committee on Friendly Relations Among States some delegates, while condemning the use of force against the independence of states, defined force as including "all forms of pressure including those of a political and economic character, which have the effect of threatening the territorial integrity or political independence of any State."[21] Although this may be stretching the meaning of "force" too far, yet it reveals the fear in some of the weaker states of losing their economic self-determination.

The Convention on the Settlement of Investment Disputes Between States and Nationals of Other States, which entered into force on 14 October 1966, is an important development in the settlement of disputes that could arise from the abuse of, or threat to, the principle of economic self-determination.[22] It provides for the setting up of a centre which is "to provide facilities for the conciliation and arbitration of investment disputes between Contracting States and nationals of other Contracting States in accordance with the provisions of the Convention."[23] The centre

---

20. "Ten percent" became a notorious phrase in some of the new states, for it represented the portion of the value of investments that corruptly went into the pockets of the ministers or their political parties.

21. AC/125.L 48 of 27 July 1967 sponsored by Algeria, Cameroon, Ghana, India, Madagascar, Nigeria, Syria, UAR, and Yugoslavia.

22. For full text see 4 International Legal Materials (1965), pp. 532–544.

23. Article 1(2).

itself is not directly engaged in conciliation and arbitration but in providing facilities for settlement. Nor does it so much enunciate the substantive law regarding investment as provide means of arbitration and conciliation. The jurisdiction of the centre is based on the consent of the parties to a dispute; thus nothing stops a state from seeking other means of redress, such as judicial settlement. The convention applies to a dispute between a state, its subdivision (approved by it), and a national of another member state.[24] A company that is registered in a state may be treated as foreign by reason of foreign control.

The adjudication is limited to a "legal dispute arising directly out of investment" and does not extend to disputes of a political nature. While the convention is invoked, other remedies are barred. Parties agree to carry out an award under the convention as if it were a judgment of their own courts.[25] Disputes are decided in accordance with "rules of law" as may be agreed upon by the parties or, failing that, in accordance with the law of the contracting states and applicable rules of international law.[26] The chief aim of the convention is to stimulate the flow of international private capital while at the same time to guarantee the rule of law in the field of international investment. The activities of the centre should provide some guidelines to the development of the principle of economic self-determination.[27]

24. Article 25(3).

25. Article 54.

26. See also Mann, "The Proper Law of Contracts Concluded by International Persons," 35 *BYBIL* (1959), p. 49; Friedmann, *The Changing Structure of International Law* (1964), p. 175; Delaume, "The Proper Law of Loans Concluded by International Persons: A Restatement and a Forecast," 56 *AJIL* (1962), p. 62; J. F. Lalive, "Contracts Between a State or State Agency and a Foreign Company—Theory and Practice: Choice of Law in a New Arbitration Case," 13 *ICLQ* (1964), p. 987; Suratgar, "Considerations Affecting Choice of Law Clauses in Contracts Between Governments and Foreign Nationals," 2 *Indian JIL* (1962), p. 273; Jennings, "State Contracts in International Law," 37 *BYBIL* (1961), p. 156.

27. See G. R. Delaume, "The Convention on the Settlement of Investment Disputes Between States and Nationals of Other States," 1 *International Lawyer* (1967), pp. 64–80; "The Convention on the Settlement of Investment Disputes Between States and Nationals of Other States," 1 *Israel Law Review* (1966), p. 27; Bourquin, "Arbitration and Economic Development Agreement," 15 *Business Lawyer* (1966), p. 860; Ray, "Law Governing Contracts Between States and Foreign Nationals," *Proceedings of the 1960 Institute on Private Investment Abroad* (1960), p. 5; A. Broaches, "The Convention on the Settlement of Investment Disputes," *Columbia Journal of Transnational Law* (1966); N. S. Rodley, ·Some Aspects of the World Bank Convention on the Settlement of Investment Disputes," *Canadian YBIL* (1966), p. 43; R. G. Atkey, "Foreign Investment Dispute: Access of Private Individuals to International Tribunals," *Canadian YBIL* (1967), p. 229; G. Schwarzenberger, *Foreign Investments and International Law* (London, 1969).

3. Economic Self-determination and Nationalisation[28] of Foreign-Owned Property

The principle of economic self-determination sometimes comes into conflict with the protection of foreign-owned property. Nationalisation was first carried out in the Soviet Union under the communist system and has since spread to the capitalist world (as in the United Kingdom 1949–1950) and to the underdeveloped countries.

Normally the property rights of foreigners are protected and any actions affecting them are required to comply with certain minimum standards. Yet, respect for foreign-owned property may perpetuate an undesirable status quo that originated in graft, bribery, and corruption. The requirements of social reorganisation may be so pressing as to amount to an emergency situation requiring special provisions that may impinge on the right to property.[29]

The Latin-American states after the 1930s presented such a situation. According to one author, "the [Mexican] peasants, and majority of the population, lived in the most abject state of servitude. Such [Red] Indian communal lands which survived Spanish exploitation found their way into [the] hands of the large landowners, with the aid of Diaz' new laws."[30] The oil industry was wholly in the hands of American firms as a result of the new petroleum laws passed by the Diaz regime, reversing the Spanish and Mexican tradition which left the properties of the subsoil in the hands of the state. The Mexican nationalisations in 1938 were

---

28. There is a wealth of literature on the subject. *See* e.g., Friedmann, *Expropriation in Public International Law* (1953); Wortley, *Expropriation in Public Internationl Law* (1959); Moller, "Compensation for British-Owned Foreign Interests," 44 *Grotius Transactions* (1958–9); K. Jansma, "International Legal Consequences of Nationalisation," 41 *Grotius Transactions* (1956); Chia-yi Liu, "Competence of a State To Deprive Aliens' Property In International Law," *Chinese Annals of International Law* (July 1966), no. 3; P. D. Weinstein, "The Attitude of the Capital-Importing Nations Towards the Taking of Foreign-Owned Private Property," 5 *Indian JIL* (1965), p. 113; S. Petren, "Confiscation of Foreign Property and International Claims Arising Therefrom," 109 *Recueil des Cours* (1963), p. 2; *Indian Proceedings of International Law* (1964), p. 55; Martin Domke, "Foreign Nationalisations," 55 *AJIL* (1961), p. 585.

29. Thus in *E. R. Kelley v. The United Mexican States*, the Mexican–American arbitration said, "As is shown by precedents that have been cited and others that might be mentioned, there is a wide range of defensive measures in time of hostilities. Undoubtedly the justification for such measures must be found in the nature of the emergency in each given case and the methods employed to meet the situation.

With reference to matters more directly connected with actual military affairs, there are interesting illustrations of property losses for which those who have suffered such losses have not been considered entitled to compensation." (25 *AJIL* (1931), pp. 388, 391.)

30. C. N. Ronning, *Law and Politics in Inter-American Diplomacy* (1963), p. 37.

therefore necessary to ensure a fair redistribution of the natural resources of the country.[31]

In Guatemala the United Fruit Company dominated the economy as did the oil companies in Mexico. It acquired lands on ninety-nine-year leases and paid less than 10 percent of its profits in taxes. Although the 1953 nationalisations of the Arbenz government were not precisely carried through, some readjustments were made to the benefit of the people in the form of land redistribution.

In Bolivia three expatriate firms controlled the tin mines which produced 80 percent of the country's foreign exchange. They had in the past financed revolutions and made substantial contributions to the political parties opposed to the National Liberation Movement. The nationalisation decree of 1952 placed certain mines under state ownership.

The Cuban Agrarian Reform Law of 1959 provided for the expropriation of property over a certain size depending on the yield and size. The United States was not satisfied with the nature and amount of compensation and a legislation was passed authorising the president to reduce the sugar quota for Cuba. The reaction was a new Cuban decree giving the Cuban president and prime minister "full powers to proceed with the nationalisation of all concerns and properties of natural and juridical persons of the United States of America or of concerns in which said persons have a majority interest or share." Subsequently the United States oil firms—Texaco and Esso—refused to refine oil obtained from sources other than their own, a move directed against the crude oil from the Soviet Union. The Cuban government then confiscated the remaining properties owned by United States citizens.[32]

In all the Latin American cases, expropriation followed bitter controversy over labour conditions, taxes, profit sharing, or land ownership.

The principle of nationalisation is now universally acknowledged provided it is in the public interest, a characteristic of which a state is itself the best judge. There is controversy over the other conditions for nationalisation. The Soviet writers maintain that a state has the unrestricted right to nationalise foreign-owned private property within its territory.[33] Western writers however subject nationalisation to two more conditions: (a) there must be full compensation and (b) the nationalisation must not be discriminatory against foreigners.

31. Wortley, "The Mexican Oil Dispute," *Transactions of the Grotius Society* (1957), 43:15–37.

32. The Sabbatino case, 58 *AJIL* (1964), p. 779 arose out of the Cuban nationalisations.

33. *See*, e.g., Sapoztinikov, "Neocolonialist Doctrines of International Protection of Foreign Concessions," *Soviet YBIL* (1966–7), p. 98.

In the Mexican nationalisations, the United States Secretary of State Cordell Hull, in a note of 22 August 1938 to the Mexican government demanded the payment of "prompt, effective and adequate compensation." The Mexican government, however, asserted earlier that "there is in international law no rule universally accepted in theory nor carried out in practice, which makes obligatory the payment of immediate compensation nor even of deferred compensation, for expropriations of a general and impersonal character like those which Mexico has carried out for the redistribution of land."[34] As for the oil nationalisations, Mexico was willing to settle "in justice and equity" for money actually put into the industry but the whole matter was to be treated under domestic law, thus excluding diplomatic intervention or discussion.

The rationale of compensation is stated by Bin Cheng to be

the fact that certain individuals in a community, or certain categories of individuals, without their being in any way at fault, are being asked to make a sacrifice of their property for the general welfare of the community, when other members of the community are not making corresponding sacrifices. The compensation paid to the owners of the property taken represents precisely the corresponding contributions made by the rest of the community in order to equalise the financial incidence of this taking of private property.[35]

Thus the cost of nationalisation in an ordinary case should be borne by the society as a whole and so the owner of the property is compensated for the special loss he suffers. This does not apply to a situation where the owner of property has been at fault, as in a case where he obtained the property through force, corruption, threats, or deceit. Nationalisation may in fact be the restoration to the people of property illegally taken away from them with resultant effects on the mode and *quantum* of compensation.[36]

Even though the Italian court upheld the legitimacy of the expropriation in the *Anglo-Iranian Company* v. *SUPOR* it made it clear that it would not have done so if there had been a breach of international law:

Italian Courts must refuse to apply in Italy any foreign law which

34.   Note of 3 August 1938 reproduced in U.S. Dept. of State, Compensation for American-Owned Lands Expropriated in Mexico, Inter-American Series 16.

35.   "The Rationale of Compensation for Expropriation," 44 *Grotius Transactions*, 267 at 297.

36.   An important development commenced in Latin America with its first freely-elected Marxist President of Chile, Dr. Allende who toward the end of 1970 nationalised copper mines and promised to pay compensation. Banks were nationalised early in 1971 and there are plans to take over saltpetre, steel, insurance, and automobile industry. The foreign investors affected are mainly Americans.

decrees an expropriation, not for reasons of public interests but for purely political, persecutory, discriminatory, racial, and confiscatory motives. Furthermore, the Italian Courts must refuse to apply in Italy such foreign Laws as may, even for non-political and non-persecutory motives, decree the expropriation of the property of any foreign national without compensation.[37]

This broadly represents the situation in international law.[38]

Some national constitutions provide for the payment of compensation for expropriation.[39] The Kenyan Foreign Investments Protection Act (1964)[40] provides for investment certificates for approved investments and these are issued by the minister if he is satisfied that "the enterprise would further the economic development of, or would be of benefit to, Kenya." A certificate may also be issued for a previous investment that satisfied the conditions. The act guarantees the transfer of profits, proceeds of sale, and the capital (plus interest) of investments specified in the certificate. Such investments may not be compulsorily acquired except in accordance with Article 75(1) of the constitution, which provides for such acquisitions in specified circumstances:

(1) the taking of possession or acquisition is necessary in the interest of defence, public order, public morality, public health, town or country planning or the development or utilization of any property in such manner as to promote the public benefit; and

(2) the necessity therefor is such as to afford reasonable justification for the causing of any hardship that may result to any person having an interest in or right over the property; and

(3) provision is made by a law applicable to that taking of possession or acquisition for the prompt payment of full compensation.[41]

37. *ILR* (1955), p. 42.

38. *Anglo-Iranian Co.* v. *SUPOR, ILR* (1955), p. 23; *Anglo-Iranian Co.* v. *Idemitsu Kosan Kabushiki, ILR* (1953), p. 305. On the contrary, the Aden Supreme Court in *Anglo-Iranian Co.* v. *Jaffrate and Others, ILR* (1953), p. 316 found that the Iranian nationalisations were carried out in disregard of international law since no effective compensations were paid and were therefore void. In the Sabbatino case, 58 *AJIL* (1964), p. 779, the U.S. District Court and Court of Appeals found that a Cuban expropriation decree violated international law in that it was discriminatory, motivated by a retaliatory and not a public purpose and failed to provide adequate compensation. The decision was reversed by the U.S. Supreme Court which held that the U.S. courts were precluded from inquiring into the validity of expropriation of property within its own territory by a foreign government that was recognised by the U.S.

39. E.g., Article 3 of the Republican Constitution of Nigeria 1963; Article 31 of the Indian Constitution; 30 of Columbian Constitution, 18 of Zambian Constitution 1964.

40. 4 *International Legal Materials* (1965), pp. 241–254. *See also* Foreign Investment Protection Act, Cap. 533, Revised Laws of Tanganyika, 1963.

41. Peaslee, p. 267.

A foreigner who is aggrieved by expropriation is entitled to seek compensation from the expropriating state. His own state may not intervene, however, to seek remedies on the international plane until he has first exhausted local remedies or if there are no local remedies at all.[42] Some opinions favour direct individual access to international tribunals but this involves procedural difficulties.[43]

The requirement that nationalisation must not be discriminatory against foreigners must now be interpreted to mean that it must not be "unreasonably discriminatory against foreigners." In many new states the most important sectors of the economy such as banking, mining, and transport were dominated by foreigners. Any nationalisations in those sectors necessarily affected foreigners almost exclusively but cannot for that reason alone be held to be invalid in international law.[44] The recent nationalisations in Tanzania and Zambia deserve special mention.

A. *Tanzanian Nationalisations.*[45] In February 1967 the Tanganyikan political party—Tanganyika African National Union (TANU)—took a decisive step toward Socialism with the adoption of the Arusha Declaration.[46] It proclaims that national policy shall be based on the twin base of socialism and self-reliance (*Ujamaa na Kujitegemea*). Economic self-reliance is in fact an aspect of economic self-determination. The princi-

---

42. *Ambatielos Arbitration (1956)*, 23 *ILR*, p. 306; The Inter-Handel case, *ICJ Rep.* (1959), p. 6.

43. *See*, e.g., J. H. Hyde (U.S. rep.) in the 49th Session of the International Law Association (1960), pp. 185–7. For a contrary view, *see* P. Kalesky (Czechoslovakia), p. 183 and Khalfinn (USSR), p. 187.

44. The question of expropriation has received the attention of the International Commission of Jurists. In the Congress of Athens 1955, it resolved:
> In the case of expropriation or restrictions on the use of private property, adequate compensation, of which the persons entitled may freely dispose, should be awarded. Confiscation of property through Court judgments should not be used as a means of expropriation.
This was elaborated in the Congress of Bangkok 1965:
> Nationalisation of private enterprises by a democratically elected government when necessary in the public interest is not contrary to the Rule of Law. However, such nationalisation should be carried out in accordance with principles laid down by the legislature and in a manner consistent with the Rule of Law, including the payment of fair and reasonable compensation as determined by an independent tribunal. The same consideration should apply to other governmental action with similar purpose and effect.

45. Considered in greater detail by A. W. Bradley in 3 *EALJ* (1967), pp. 149–176. Previous successful nationalisations in Africa are the Suez Canal and the Algerian oil industry. Subsequent nationalisations (full or partial) have since been carried out in the following African states—Congo (Brazzaville), Congo (Kinshasha), Libya, Sierra-Leone, Somalia, Sudan, and Uganda and more may be expected.

46. Published by the Publicity Section, TANU and printed by the Government Printer (Dar es Salaam, 1967).

ples of the Arusha Declaration include the vesting of "[m]ajor means of Production . . . under Control of Peasants and Workers" and the eradication of the exploitation of man by man. Included in the major means of production are "forests; mineral resources; water; oil and electricity; communications; transport; banks; insurance; import and export trade; wholesale business; the steel machine tools, arms, motorcar, cement, and fertilizer factories; the textile industry; and any other big industry upon which a large section of the population depends for its living, or which provides essential components for other industries; large plantations; especially those with essential raw materials."[47] Some of these were already under the control of the government.[48]

Following the declaration, the government nationalised all banking and took over the minority shares in insurance which belonged to private companies (it already had the majority holding). A number of firms were nationalised in an assortment of trade, including tourism and merchandise, and two public corporations were created—the State Trading Corporation for external and wholesale trade, and the National Bank of Commerce.

Private firms not included in the list of those to be nationalised were allowed to continue their operations. In another list of firms, the government merely took over the majority holdings while determined to avoid the dislocation of economic production. In others it retained its minority or 50 percent holdings. Thus, while rejecting private enterprise as a national policy, the government continues to welcome it in specific areas where "we no longer have any cause to fear the effect of [private investors'] activities on our social purpose."[49]

With regard to nationalisations, the government promised to pay "full and fair compensation for the assets acquired" and to act "honestly and fairly" toward the foreign property owners. These pledges seem to have been carried out to a large extent as evidenced from the absence of disputes—legal or diplomatic—with a few exceptions.

B. *The Zambian Copper Takeover.* On 11 August 1969 the Zambian government announced the takeover of 51 percent of the shares of the copper mining companies. The main reason was described by President

47. Ibid., p. 3.
48. *See also* on the Arusha Declaration, L. Cliffe, "Arusha Declaration: Challenge to Tanzanians," *EALJ* (March 1967); K. E. Svendson, "Socialism Problems after the Arusha Declaration" *EALJ* (May 1967).
49. Per President Mwalimu Nyerere on Public Ownership in Tanzania, published in the *Sunday News* 12 February 1967. *See also* P. Temu, "Nationalisation in Tanzania," *EALJ* (June 1967).

Kaunda as "the virtual lack of mining development since Independence.[50] The economy of Zambia is heavily dependent on the copper mines— 95 percent of the export earnings and 66⅔ percent of the government revenues are derived from the copper mines, which are imbedded in an area thirty miles by seventy miles skirting the border of the Congo. The area probably contains about a quarter of the world's reserve of copper. Detail arrangements for the takeover include the formation of a new company—Roan Consolidated Mines—in which the government has 51 percent of the shares, Roan Selection Trust (mainly United States holders) has 37 percent, and Anglo-American Trust (mainly South African holders) has the bulk of the remainder. The shares expropriated from the companies are to be paid out of future profits in negotiable external bonds fully guaranteed by the government and payable in American dollars. A total of $150 million is to be paid to RST in sixteen equal annual installments and $102 million to Anglo-American in twelve equal annual installments. The Industrial Development Corporation (INDECO) managed the government shares and was entitled to appoint six out of the eleven directors, including the chairman. On 1 April 1970 a new corporation—Mineral Development Corporation (MINDECO)—took over the administration of the state's investment interests.

Most of the mining rights had been given in perpetuity by Cecil Rhodes and by the British South African Company, which owned the mines until 1964 and received royalties and rents. The new law reverts the mineral rights to the state which grants a lease for twenty-five years. If the holder of a special grant has discovered a mineral deposit, he has the option of applying for a lease or for an exploration licence which gives him three years to prepare a programme for mining development. The state has 51 percent of the shares in any new mining company.

A number of small firms were affected in addition to the big firms, namely, the North Charterland Concessions, Rhodesia Katanga Concessions, African Gold and Base Metal Holdings, Bechuanaland Exploration Company, Kafue Development Company, and the London Missionary Society. The president expressed his admiration for some of the small-scale miners, most of whom lived outside Zambia, who paid rent to the holders of the special grant. The small miners often "slaved away and sometimes are unable to make a living out of a small mine and yet they have to pay a percentage to the holders of the special grant. . . ." They are now given the right to apply directly to the government for a lease without passing through middlemen.

50. *See* "Toward Complete Independence," address by President Kaunda to the UNIP Council held at Matero Hall, Lusaka, on 11 August 1969.

A tax amounting to 51 percent of the profits replaces the royalties and the export tax and this is in accordance with the demands of the mining companies themselves. Income is nevertheless paid on the 49 percent. The remittance of dividends is not subject to any other control.

It is significant that the foreign companies have not complained against the partial nationalisations; in fact they readily announced their intention to cooperate with the government. That the present arrangement is a very fair deal for the companies is best explained by reference to the manner the rights were acquired and the profits made by the companies over the years. The rights were obtained from illiterate Zambian chiefs through a combination of force, threats of force, deceit, and downright robbery. For articles of little value, the chiefs were made to give away rights over their natural resources. In fact there was no legal authority for the chiefs to give away the patrimony of the people to foreigners of any race.

The British South African Company founded by Cecil Rhodes ruled Zambia from 1889 until the 1920s but the company continued to own the mines until 1964, during which time it received rents and royalties totalling about £80 million. Up to 1964 the main capital consisted of £30 million invested at the initial stages, profits ploughed back as capital, as well as £13 million borrowed from the United States government and £66.5 million borrowed from Japan.[51] At the time of the takeover, the mines were given an asset value of £240 million. Taxes had been paid partly to the Rhodesias, Nyasaland, and to the United Kingdom, where the headquarters of the companies were situated and where half of the total tax was paid. In all, Sonny Bolden estimates that over £400 million had left Zambia as profits and another £400 million as taxes since the 1920s—a "fantastic return on the original investment of £30 million. It is enough to make the pirates of the sixteenth century blush."

A very considerable amount of wealth left Zambia, where the per capita income is £50 and where many people in the rural areas earn only £10 per year. During this period, gifts from outside amounted to about £100 million and most of these came in since 1964 as part of the British-sponsored but ineffective sanctions against Rhodesia. Far from being a beggar receiving aid from the developed countries, Zambia has been a donor, the beneficiaries being the developed nations, principally the United Kingdom, the United States, and South Africa.

The British press did not fail to express their fury at Zambia's attempt to assert its right to economic self-determination. Thus the influencial *Financial Times* warned President Kaunda against killing the goose that

51. Sonny Bolden on "Zambia's Lost Millions" in the *Nationalist* (Tanzania), 1 September, 1969.

laid the country's golden eggs. The *Daily Telegraph* requested Britain to suspend further aid to Lusaka until the expropriated mining shares are fully paid for. The *Guardian* feared that the move demonstrated that President Kaunda was losing grip on his own party and that he was the best guarantee against extremism, which the paper held could be Zambia's worst enemy. The *Express* seized the opportunity to urge that sanctions against Rhodesia should be dropped to enable the United Kingdom to develop the copper resources of Southern Africa, especially Rhodesia.[52] The measures were however hailed by the All-African Trade Union Federation (AATUF) in Dar es Salaam as an assertion of the "inalienable right of the people of Zambia."[53] The *Tanzanian Nationalist* hailed the announcement as the "Voice of Hope."[54]

The Zambia nationalisation measures are extremely favourable to the foreign investors. Zambia's philosophy of humanism and the desire to retain the services of the skilled foreign miners have contributed to the respect for rights illegally acquired. If a strict view is taken about the circumstances of the acquired rights and the extraordinary profits made over the years at the expense of the people, the nationalisation could, in fact, have been carried out without material compensation, since the investors would be deemed to have more than compensated themselves.

4. Conclusion

Economic self-determination is now a recognised principle of international law and is relevant both to developing and developed countries. The principle is of special significance to those states that have recently emerged from colonialism, since their economy was invariably linked with the metropolitan states. It was usual to subordinate the economy of the colonies to that of the metropolitan states: while the former were the producers of raw materials, the latter were the manufacturers of finished products. This has been one of the main contributory factors to the disparity between the rich industrial states and the former colonial territories.[55]

The emphasis in the United Nations on the economic development of the underdeveloped countries demonstrates the importance of economic self-determination as a universal principle since it is already a right

52. *See* a summary of the reactions in the *Nationalist* (Tanzania), 13 August 1969.

53. The *Nationalist* (Tanzania), 12 August 1969.

54. The *Nationalist* (Tanzania), 12 August 1969.

55. *See* e.g., P. Jalée, *The Pillage of the Third World* (New York and London, 1968).

enjoyed and exercised by the developed states. The right of a state to have full control over its economic development may understandably affect the sacrosanctity of acquired rights.

Some international lawyers claim that the rule of nationalisation with compensation was created by the imperialist states and therefore, insofar as other states are concerned, it is *res inter alios acta*. Sovereignty is said by that school of thought to include the taking of foreign property within state territory without compensation.

The basic weakness of this approach is the implied denial of the fact that international society is becoming increasingly organised, requiring unified rules and principles. A distinction must be drawn between rights acquired under equal treaties and those acquired under unequal treaties. Whereas the latter may be voidable, the former should be respected under the principle of *pacta sunt servanda*. Unequal treaties are those that were forced on the weaker party through the use of force or threat of force. This is true of many of the old concession agreements during the colonial days.[56]

The better approach to the question of compensation for nationalisation is to adopt the general outlines of the existing law in a progressive manner. The principle of reasonable compensation for nationalisation can be related to particular circumstances to produce a just result.

The social need to readjust the benefits from the natural resources of a state may necessitate the nationalisation of certain sectors of the national economy, whether or not they are foreign-controlled. When such steps become necessary, international law requires payment, in the ordinary case, of reasonable compensation. What is reasonable depends on all the circumstances of the case; where the property was unjustly taken away by the person who controls it, he may be required to restore it to the rightful owners. The amount of investment ploughed into a natural resource and the profits so far recouped are important elements in determining the amount of compensation.

There is an inherent danger in a state's economy being dominated by outsiders. A state has not the same control over foreigners as it has over its own nationals. Moreover, foreigners may be guided principally

---

56.   *See also* A. N. Talalayev and V. G. Boyarshinov, "Unequal Treaties, a Mode of Prolonging Colonial Dependence of the New States of Asia and Africa," *Soviet YBIL* (1961), p. 156; S. A. Osnitskaya, "Colonialist Concepts of Equal and Unequal Subjects of International Law in the Theory and Practice of Imperialist States," *Soviet YBIL* (1962), p. 49; Sinha, "Perspectives of the Newly Independent States on the Binding Quality of International Law," 14 *ICLQ* (1965), p. 121; A. Lester, "Bizerta and the Unequal Treaty Theory," 11 *ICLQ* (1962), p. 847; G. Schwarzenberger, "Decolonisation and the Protection of Foreign Investment," 20 *CLP* (1967), pp. 213–231.

by their own national interests rather than those of the host state, especially in the event of conflict. While controlled and limited foreign investment can be beneficial in the economic development of a state, its preponderance may militate against its interest. With a view to strengthening British control over the British economy, James McMillan and Bernard Harris have pointed out the dangers of the domination of the Canadian economy by United States companies. They estimate that

> more than 50 per cent of Canada's entire production economy is American-owned. Twenty-five per cent of Canada's fuel companies (oil and coal) are American; 60 per cent of Canada's gas industry, 62 per cent of her mining and smelting, 25 per cent of her railways, 13 per cent of her utilities are in American hands.[57]

Where there is "the same ready acquiescence in letting someone else do the saving, the investing, the working and the thinking"[58] there is a danger that economic self-determination might be threatened. The undesirable effect of this situation is demonstrated by the fate of a contract won by Canadian car manufacturers to supply tractors to Communist China. Detroit, the seat of American car manufacture, immediately declared that the transaction was contrary to the national interests of the United States (not Canada) and effectively stopped the Canadian firms, which were American-dominated, from proceeding with it. As Conservative leader, John Diefenbaker, once declared:

> Canada's economy is altogether too vulnerable to sudden changes in the trading policy of Washington. Canadians do not wish to have their economic, any more than their political, affairs determined outside Canada. Moreover we have become dependent on the U.S.A. which now largely controls our iron, petroleum, copper, and the like.[59]

In contrast, Japan has made great economic strides since the end of the Second World War while retaining economic control and self-determination. It avoids foreign control in important areas of industry but admits foreign capital on an associate basis. In designated areas foreigners may own up to 50 percent of the share capital of firms but in a few areas, such as steel, textile, and motorcycles, they may own up to 100

---

57.   James McMillan and Bernard Harris, *The American Takeover of Britain* (Leslie Frewen, London, 1968). This is a contrast to the situation in 1911 when 72 percent of overseas investment were British (now 15 percent) and 25 percent were American (now 80 percent).

58.   Ibid., p. 196.

59.   Ibid., pp. 194–5.

percent. In these the Japanese are already firmly entrenched but in others such as computers, electronics, and aviation, where foreigners could dominate if given the opportunity, they are firmly kept out.

On foreign aid, the Arusha Declaration warns:

> Independence cannot be real if a Nation depends upon gifts and loans from another for its development. Even if there was a Nation, or Nations, prepared to give us all the money we need for our development, it would be improper for us to accept such assistance without asking ourselves how this would affect our independence and our very survival. Gifts which start off or stimulate our own efforts are useful gifts. But gifts which weaken our own efforts should not be accepted without asking ourselves a number of questions.[60]

The inability of a state to control any aspect of its national activity leads to resentment and frustration. The training of local cadres and the creation of opportunities for them to take over eventually is one way of promoting good relations between states.

The principle of economic self-determination does not exist in isolation. It must be exercised with due regard to other principles of law, such as respect for fundamental human rights, the sovereignty of other states, and *pacta sunt servanda*. Political self-determination is, however, incomplete without economic self-determination.

60. Arusha Declaration, p. 9.

X Claims of Self-Determination in Metropolitan Territories

There is virtually universal agreement that the principle of self-determination applies to dependent peoples and colonies. Finding themselves on the defensive, the colonial powers have taken pains to point out that the principle is also relevant to peoples in metropolitan territories who may not have a government of their choice. They emphasize that colonialism need not be confined to territories separated from the metropolitan section by the seas but may in fact apply to contiguous territories where colonial conditions exist.[1] ˙

The application of the principle of self-determination to peoples in metropolitan territories raises more controversial and difficult problems. Differences in race, language, or religion may be used in support of the claim to self-determination. States are unduly sensitive to suggestions that their peoples are entitled to self-determination, for they fear that the result may be disintegration. The principle need not result in independence or secession for it may also be expressed through association, merger, or local autonomy, provided the choice reflects the wishes of the people.

The questions then arise: Is the principle of self-determination relevant to groups within metropolitan states? Are they entitled to exercise the right of self-determination up to the point of secession? Is the demand for secession a matter for the exclusive jurisdiction of the state concerned? When, if at all, is the exercise of self-determination within

1. For the mutual disagreements over colonialism, *see* the debate on the Declaration on Independence to Colonial Countries and Peoples, p. 69 *et seq.*

a metropolitan state a matter of international concern? Since it is not possible to consider here all claims to self-determination, we shall examine the claims of the Somalis, the Kashmiris, the Nagas, the Afro-Americans, the French Canadians, and the Biafrans.

1. The Somalis

A. *Somaliland.* There are very few nation-states in Africa in the sense that the population has a common cultural background. Most African states are a hotchpotch of subnations at varying stages of development and undergoing a process of forming modern nations. The Republic of Somaliland, with a population of two million is one of the very few exceptions, for it has a population that has a common language (with different dialects), a common religion, and cultural background. The Republic was formed by the union of the British protectorate of Somaliland and the trust territory of Italian Somaliland in 1961.

The Somalis are also found in the Northern Frontier District of Kenya—in the districts of Mandera, Wajir, Garissa, Isiolo, Marsabit, and Moyola, which together comprise about a fifth of the country. In 1962 they numbered about 240,000 out of a total population of 388,000 in the area.[2] In Ethiopia they number about a million and occupy the southeast District of Ogaden; their migratory population increases during the grazing season. In French Somaliland they form 43 percent of the population of about 100,000 and constitute the bulk of the population of Djibouti. They have had long contact with Europeans and are very politically conscious. Somali areas make up the triangular Somali Plateau of about 370,000 square miles, but the Republic covers two-thirds of it.

B. *Somali Nationalism.* The Somali nation, though having a common culture, language, and religion, has never come under a central authority. Before the colonial partition, the important unit was the clan and clan-segment in which all males played a prominent role. They exhibited a fierce individualism that laid them open to partitioning by the colonial powers.

In 1884–86 they entered into treaties of protection with the British. The Anglo-Ethiopian Treaty of 1897 demarcated the boundary between Ethiopia and British Somaliland. The treaty which was concluded during the unsettled conditions of the Anglo-Egyptian campaign in the Sudan and after the defeat of the Italians at Adowa in 1896, was, not un-

2. Report of the Northern Frontier District Commission (1962), Cmd. 1900.

naturally, rather favourable to Ethiopia for it conceded to it grazing lands frequented by Somali nomads. The treaty however secured for them the right to graze and use the wells. Somalis within Ethiopia were to be well treated.

The boundary with Kenya was drawn in the Anglo-Italian Treaty of 1894[3] demarcating British East Africa, Italian East Africa, and the Sudan from Ethiopia. In 1896 Major Nerazini, for Italy, came to agreement with Emperor Menelik of Ethiopia over the boundary between Italian Somaliland and Ethiopia. The maps drawn then have since disappeared. A convention between Italy and Ethiopia in 1908 made the boundary clear in certain areas but vague in others. An attempt to demarcate it in 1959 failed because the two could not agree on the arbitration commission's term of reference.[4]

After the conquest of Ethiopia by Italy in 1935, the Ogaden was incorporated as part of Italian Somaliland. With the outbreak of the Second World War, the Italians conquered British Somaliland and incorporated the territory. Fortunes reversed in 1941 when the Italians were driven out of Somaliland and Ethiopia. Within a few years, the Somalis witnessed the successive defeat of their foreign rulers. The British administration divided all Somali lands into Italian Somaliland (including the Ogaden), British Somaliland, and the Reserved Area of Ethiopia. At the Foreign Ministers Conference of 1946, in what was known as the Bevin Plan, the British foreign secretary proposed, with Ethiopia's consent, a trusteeship of all Somali lands.[5] The French, however, favoured the return of Italian Somaliland to the Italians and so the plan failed. The reserved Area and the Ogaden were returned to Ethiopia in 1948 and this arrangement was confirmed in the Anglo-Ethiopian Agreement of 1954.[6] The agreement preserved the rights of the Somalis to graze their cattle and use the water wells. It was to operate for fifteen years, after which it could be terminated by either party by six months notice; such termination could not, however, affect the grazing rights.

The government of Ethiopia encountered great difficulties in keeping the Somalis under control. They proved unruly and some of them formed gangs to raid cattle. The increased population of Somalis during the grazing months complicate the issue of which Somali is Ethiopian, a

3. 86 *BFSP* (1893–94), p. 73.
4. *See also* Drysdale, *The Somali Dispute* (London, 1964), chapter 1.
5. Foreign Ministers of Great Britain, France, United States, and USSR.
6. Treaty Series No. 1 (1955), Cmd. 9348: 191 *UNTS*, p. 65.

status invested on them by Ethiopian law after six months consecutive residence.[7] Administrative officers are allowed to migrate with them in the performance of their duties. The conflict between the authorities often resulted in "a Protectorate (British Somaliland) tribal policeman being arrested by an Ethiopian policeman, and tried for arresting a Protectorate clansman whom the Ethiopian authorities claimed as an Ethiopian subject."[8]

The Northern Frontier District (NFD) of Kenya was not effectively policed until recently. The desire to secede from Kenya and join the Somali Republic came into the open during the constitutional talks for Kenya's independence in 1962. Their special status was recognised when they were given separate representation at the talks. The colonial secretary gave an undertaking that a commission of inquiry would be set up to ascertain the wishes of the people before independence.[9] The Somalis argued that they had always been governed as a separate entity; they were not amenable to African native courts but had their own laws administered by special courts; they needed a pass to enter Kenya and were culturally affiliated with their kinsmen across the border.[10]

A commission consisting of G. C. Onyuike, Q. C. of Nigeria and Major M. P. Bogart, D. S. O. of Canada was set up "[t]o ascertain and report on public opinion in the Northern Frontier District (comprising the districts of Isiolo, Garissa, Mandera, Marsabit, Moyale, and Wajir) regarding arrangements to be made for the future of the area in the light of the likely course of constitutional development in Kenya."[11]

The commission found the following shades of opinion: (a) areas of "Somali Opinion" which are "the biggest in total population and size and are in fact one. They extend from Somali-Galla line and beyond to include the grazing lands of the Ajuran"[12] and (b) areas of "Kenya Opinion"—"the grazing lands of the Gabra in Marsabit District, of the non-Moslem Boran in the Moyola District and the riverine tribes on the banks of the Tana in Garissa District." It found that the two opinions

7. The General Assembly passed a number of resolutions before the independence of Somalia urging Ethiopia and Italy to negotiate a peaceful demarcation of their boundaries: Res. 392(V) of 15/12/54, 854(IX) of 14/12/54, 947(X) of 15/12/55, 1068(XI) of 26/2/57, 1213(XII) of 14/12/57, and 1345(XIII) of 13/12/58.

8. D. J. L. Brown, "The Ethiopian-Somali Frontier Dispute," *ICLQ* (1956), p. 245.

9. Statement made by Mr. Maudling at a press conference on 6 April 1962 at Lancaster House, London.

10. The Issue of the NFD White Paper by the Government of the Somali Republic, (Mogadishu, May 1963), pp. 15–16.

11. Report of the NFD Commission, Cmd. 1900 (London 1962).

12. *Ibid.*, p. 18.

were expressed with vigour and conviction and defied compromise. There were in addition: (c) areas of "Mixed Opinion"—Moyola Township and the grazing area of the Sakuye to the east as far as Boran-Ajuran Line, Marsabit Township, Isiolo District, Garissa Township, and the grazing area of the Orma south and west of the Tana River," and (d) areas of "Incoherent Opinion"—the Gelubba.

The commission rejected the opinion of the Rendille as it was not "an accurate reflection of the opinion of the people."[13]

A Regional Boundaries Commission that visited Garissa, Wajir, Mandera, and parts of Moyola Districts found that the delegations favoured union with the Somali Republic, although one wished that the area should continue to be under the guidance of the British in the meantime. The commission would have favoured the creation of a seventh region, but its terms of reference restricted it to six. It therefore joined the area east of the Somali line to the coast region and the rest of the eastern region.

On 8 March 1963 Mr. Sandys made an announcement on Kenya radio:

> Her Majesty's Government have now decided that, as part of the constitutional arrangements for internal self-government in Kenya, the predominantly Somali areas referred to in the Report of the Regional Boundaries Commission . . . should be formed into a separate seventh region enjoying a status equal to that of other regions in Kenya. The creation of the new region will give its inhabitants greater freedom in the management of their own affairs and more effective means of safeguarding their interests and maintaining their way of life.[14]

The discontent resulting from the refusal to grant secession led to the disruption of diplomatic relations between Britain and the Somali Republic and these were not restored until 1968.

Italian Somaliland was put under Italian trusteeship in 1950 and independence was set for 1960. In the meantime the decolonising atmosphere of the time was affecting British Somaliland. The main impetus for Greater Somalia came with the union of British and Italian Somalilands after independence into the Somali Republic on 1 July 1960. The union of all Somali lands became an official policy of the new state. The star in its flag has five points representing British Somaliland, Italian Somaliland, French Somaliland, Ethiopian Ogaden, and the Northern Frontier District of Kenya. The union of two has so far been

13. Ibid., p. 19.
14. Drysdale, pp. 140–141.

achieved and the others were to be brought in as soon as circumstances permitted. The Constitution of the Republic of Somaliland affirms "the right of self-determination of peoples" and declares that "the Somali Republic promotes, by legal and peaceful means, the union of Somali territories. . . ."[15]

Greater Somalism was directed against Kenya from 1960–63, Ethiopia from 1964–65, and French Somaliland in 1966. Between 1962 and 1967 the Kenyan government spent £5 million annually to keep down the cattle bandits who appeared to act independently of Somalian authorities. The struggle with Ethiopia resulted in violent clashes between the armies of both states and sophisticated weapons were used. In French Somaliland there was political agitation for union especially after the visit of General de Gaulle in August 1966. He threw the matter open to a referendum in which the inhabitants had one of two choices: (a) independence and an end to French aid, or (b) greater autonomy with French aid. The Somali party wanted independence, the Danakil (Afar) party opted for association, while a rival Danakil party supported the Somalis. The referendum of 19 March 1967 disclosed that 61 percent of the voters supported association with France. This was achieved by excluding nearly half of the Somalian population as transient nomads while registering all the Afars though they are equally nomadic.[16]

An interesting aspect of the Somali struggle is the use of poetry in the unification propaganda. The Somalis are rich in poetry and have poems for every occasion—war, grief, resting, peace, dancing, and even for getting the cattle to drink. Radio broadcasts from Mogadishu, and to a lesser extent from Cairo, espoused the cause of Greater Somalism.[17]

C. *Self-determination for the Somalis.* The Somalis rest their demand for unification on the principle of self-determination. They argue that, as a people of the same stock, they should be allowed to decide whether they want to join Somalia or remain within the states in which they find themselves: "those who seek the implementation of the principle for self-determination for themselves would not deny it to others."[18] The

15. Peaslee, 1:776, Art. 6.

16. See further I. M. Lewis, "Developments in the Somali Dispute," 66 *African Affairs*, no. 263 (April 1967), pp. 104–112.

17. B. W. Adrzejewski, "Poetry in Somali Society," *New Society* (London, 21 March 1963); Adrzejewski and I. M. Lewis, *Somali Poetry* (London, 1964); Colin Legum, "Somali Liberation Songs," *JMAS*, 1.4 (1963), pp. 503–19. The last deals with poems broadcast between September and December 1963 from Mogadishu; Cartherine Hoskyms, *Case Studies in African Diplomacy—The Ethiopia-Somali-Kenya Dispute* (Dar es Salaam, 1969).

18. *The Issue of the NFD* (Mogadishu, May 1963), p. 10.

demand, it is stressed, is not territorial aggrandizement but respect for the wishes of the people affected. Rejecting the assertion that Pan-Somalism was contrary to Pan-Africanism, President Abdullah said in a state dinner for Dr. Kenyatta of Kenya on 28 July 1962:

> [T]he principle of self-determination, when used properly to unify and enlarge an existing state with a view towards its absorption in a federal system of government is neither balkanisation nor fragmentation. It is a major contribution to unity and stability, and totally consistent with the concept of Pan-Africanism.[19]

The union of British Somaliland with Italian Somaliland, Dr. Ali Shermarke (prime minister) maintained, was neither colonialism, expansionism, nor annexation, but a "positive contribution to peace and unity in Africa and was made possible by the principle of the right to self-determination." The Somali Youth League told the Four Power Commission of 1948 how totally committed they were to their aspirations:

> The union of Italian Somaliland with the other Somali lands was their primary objective, for which they were prepared to sacrifice any other demand standing in the way of the achievement of Greater Somalia.[20]

In its bid to incorporate French Somaliland, the Somali Parliament resolved that aggression against Djibouti (which was threatened by Ethiopia) was aggression against Somalia and requested the government to recognise the "freedom fighters," who in Kenya and Ethiopia were known as "shiftas" or cattle bandits.[21]

Support for Greater Somalia has been limited. The Russians supplied arms and pledged their support. This appears more to be an effort to establish their influence in the Horn of Africa as a counterpoise to American presence in Ethiopia than an expression of genuine support for the Somali cause.

The first Afro-Asian Solidarity Conference in Cairo (1957) accepted a Somali resolution condemning all forms of colonialism, impliedly including Ethiopian rule in Ogaden. A resolution of the All African Peoples Conference in Accra in December 1958 "denounces artificial frontiers drawn by imperialist powers to divide peoples of the same stocks; calls for the abolition or adjustment of such frontiers at an early

---

19. Drysdale, p. 114.
20. Report of the Four Power Commission (London, 1949), 2:10–11.
21. *See also London Times* 30 March 1967; R. Lewis, "African Border War at Stalement," *JMAS* (1964), p. 13; the *Times Leader* of 12 May 1967 on "Britain, Kenya and the Somalis."

date; calls upon the independent states of Africa to support a permanent solution to this problem founded upon the wishes of the people."[22]

The Second All African Peoples Conference of Tunis (1960) "salutes and applauds the Somali struggle for independence and for the unity which will give birth to a greater Somalia."[23]

After the visit of President Abdullah to Ghana in October 1961, both countries issued a communique which acknowledged that "outstanding frontier problems inherited from colonial regimes" could be solved through federalism and stressed "the imperative need to restore the ethnic, cultural and economic links arbitrarily destroyed by colonialism." This public support must be understood in the light of Ghana's desire to incorporate territory from the Ivory Coast on the basis of tribal affinity with part of its own population. Ghana had earlier, through a United Nations plebiscite, incorporated British Togoland but French Togoland stoutly resisted any invitation to a merger. Egypt has been another supporter of the Somali cause but this can be explained as a display of Muslim brotherhood since success would ensure the adherence of a large number of people to a state whose official religion is Islam.

Greater Somalism is opposed primarily by those who stand to lose parts of their territories. It was argued by the Kenyan African National Union (KANU) delegates at the 1962 Constitutional Conference that the NFD had been cut off from the mainstream of Kenyan affairs and should therefore share participation in the conduct of affairs in order to express a reasoned opinion, and further that the secessionists did not in fact represent the people.

Dr. Kenyatta in 1962 thought that the problem could be solved by a federation embracing Kenya, Ethiopia, and Somaliland, since boundaries separating them would no longer be very important. The Somalis, though welcoming the idea, insisted that unification of Somali lands was a necessary prerequisite to federation.

Ethiopia bases its sovereignty over the Ogaden on the treaty of 1897, confirmed by the 1954 agreement. Beyond this, it argues that from ancient times, its borders extended to the Red Sea and the Indian Ocean, thus including the Somali Republic and French Somaliland. Ethiopia also offers the prospect of federation with it but rules out the possibility of losing its acquired rights.

22. Quoted by Emerson, "Pan-Africanism," 16 *International Organisation* (1962), p. 278.
23. Quoted by A. A. Castagno, "Somali-Kenyan Controversy: The Future" 2 *JMAS* (1964), 165–88 at 182.

The Somalis argue that they took no part in the 1897 treaty, which to them is *res inter alios acta*, nor did they mandate any power to dispose of their lands. The 1897 Treaty reserved for them grazing rights and so did the 1954 agreement, the termination of which would not affect the rights. If there is any conflict between the 1897 treaty and the treaties of protection of 1884–86, the latter would be ineffective since they were concluded with entities that were later colonised. It may be argued that protection, which the Somalis bargained for, could be given by any power, not necessarily Britain.[24] On 5 June 1960 Addis Ababa denounced the 1954 agreement but did not expressly abrogate the grazing rights conceded by the 1897 treaty. Its effect seems to be the acceptance of the boundaries but rejection of grazing rights. The emperor later modified Ethiopia's stand by offering the rights on a *quid pro quo* basis of recognising the boundaries. On independence the Somali Republic renounced the 1897 treaty.[25] It would appear that in spite of the denunciations, both the grazing rights and the frontiers are still binding on the parties.

The African heads of state meeting in Addis Ababa in 1963 viewed support for Greater Somalism as prejudicial to African unity. The Addis Ababa Conference of Pan-African Freedom Movement for East and Central Africa of February 1962 recommended a peaceful solution. In 1964 the OAU formally accepted existing boundaries as a basis for African unity.[26] When serious border clashes occurred between Ethiopia and Somaliland in November 1963, the OAU promptly called for a cease-fire, an end to provocations, and a resumption of negotiations. It helped to bring peace in 1964.

African states have developed understandable sensitivity to threats affecting their territorial boundaries even though colonially defined and having little regard for ethnic affiliations. Inviolability of boundaries, however defective, has become an important principle of inter-African relations in spite of earlier hopes that there would be adjustments after

24. *See also* D. J. L. Brown in *ICLQ* (1961), p. 167.

25. The British secretary of state in fact regretted the conclusion of the 1897 Treaty "but like much that has happened before, it is impossible to undo it." (23 February 1955). *Hansard Parl. Deb.*, Fifth Series, vol. 539, (1954–55), col. 1258.

26. *See* Legum, *Pan-Africanism, a Short Political Guide* (1962), pp. 229–233. The resolution
   (1) solemnly reaffirms strict respect by all Member States of the Organisation for the principles laid down in paragraph 3 of Article III of the Charter of the OAU (respect for the territorial integrity and the independent existence of States),
   (2) solemnly declares that all Member States pledge themselves to respect the borders existing on their achievement of national independence.

independence. The declaration of the Senegalese foreign minister speaks the minds of many African statesmen:

(1) No consideration of a historic, geographic or ethnic order can permit an African state to claim sovereignty over another African state or territory.

(2) The frontiers established between the different African territories at the time of colonisation are recognised as valid and have been consolidated. When an African territory accedes to independence, its new sovereignty extends to the totality of the territory which had been delimited as such by the colonial power.

(3) The only principle which can decide the destiny of a people is that of self-determination. A territory can merge with another, or federate itself with it if the majority of its population so decides, following the rules and the procedures which it has fixed for itself.[27]

Without going into the merits and demerits of these propositions, it must be emphasised that the ultimate purpose of territorial integrity is to safeguard the interest of the peoples of a territory. The concept of territorial integrity is therefore meaningful so long as it continues to fulfill that purpose to all the sections of the people.

Somali nationalism comes into open conflict with the doctrine of sovereignty and territorial integrity.[28] A correct appreciation of the principle of self-determination reveals that there need be no conflict between the exercise of the right and territorial integrity. Kenya's argument that the principle is inapplicable to peoples of independent states cannot be sustained. The principle applies, with equal vigour, to all peoples, dependent or independent. The exercise of the right may take the form of independence but it may also take the form of association, merger, or local autonomy which accords with the wishes of the people. If the preponderance of opinion in the NFD and the Ogaden seeks union with the Somali Republic, there is no legal weapon to achieve that end, however politically desirable it may be for Greater Somalism. Action may lie on the political plane but the United Nations Charter requires that disputes should be settled by peaceful means.[29] A sufficient degree of self-determination would be accorded to the Somalis in Kenya and Ethiopia if they are given a commensurate share in government. Special arrange-

27. Doudou Thiam, *La Politique Etrangere des Etats Africains* (Paris, Presses Universitaires de France, 1963) pp. 101–2.

28. See also Rupert Emerson in his foreword to S. Touval, *Somali Nationalism* (1963): "The normative postulates of national self-determination challenge the positive law which safeguards the maintenance of the established order." (p. VI)

29. Article 2(3).

ments for the protection of minorities may be provided but the minimum is one-man-one-vote.[30] In the absence of a denial of fundamental human rights, including political, economic, and cultural rights, the Somalis cannot claim to be denied the right of self-determination. The mere assertion of a denial by the Somali Republic or any other state does not establish the wrongful act. An arrangement that ensures the free exercise of these rights would satisfy the international standard. Though the people of French Somaliland are not independent, they have exercised their right to self-determination by freely choosing to be associated with the Republic of France.

It is however essential that, in the interests of peace and stability, the demands of all sections of the population should be carefully looked into. Federal relations for the East African states may be the answer to the problem since they would diminish the importance of artificial boundaries and promote the mobility of the population.[31] Most African states contain heterogeneous peoples with different religious and cultural backgrounds.[32] Allowing people to secede merely because they are culturally or religiously different from others would result in a multiplicity of mini-states in a continent that already abounds with too many states. If the Somalis are denied fundamental human rights or if relations with Kenya and Ethiopia clearly prove unworkable, the Somalian case may then receive a different consideration, for the sanctity of territorial boundaries must not be carried to the extent that it contradicts with human dignity.[33]

30. See Y. Ghai, "Independence and Safeguards in Kenya," 3 *EALJ* p. 177.

31. The coastal plains are "Lowlands to her (Ethiopia's) mountains, burning hot to her coolness, semi-desert to her verdure, and scant nomads' pasture to her rich agriculture." Margery Perham: *The Government of Ethiopia* (1948), p. 435. *See also* Mesfin Wolde Miriam, "The Background of the Ethiopian-Somalian Boundary Dispute," 2 *JMAS* (1964), pp. 189–219.

32. *See also* M. Mushkat, "African Concepts of Problems Relating to International Law," *International Problems of the Israeli Institute of International Affairs* (1967) vol. 5, no. 1–2. "Africa, more than any other Continent, is a mosaic of States, peoples and tribes, with diverse economic, social, religious, and political systems."

33. The OAU meeting of heads of state held in Congo (Kinshasha) in 1967 appointed a committee to effect a reconciliation between Kenya and Somali Republic over the boundary dispute. Following a meeting of the two heads of state, an agreement was announced which "recognises the existence a major dispute and lends itself to a solution for its settlement, whilst Somalia on its part undertakes to respect the sovereignty of Kenya." *See* Haji Ibrahim Egal, "Somalia: Nomadic Individualism and the Rule of Law" 67 *African Affairs* (1968), pp. 219, 225. The reaffirmation of the self-determination of Somali peoples by the Somalian Military Regime in 1969 led to speculations that the border disputes would be reopened. Tension was, however, eased by a subsequent proclaimed intention to maintain good relations with neighbours.

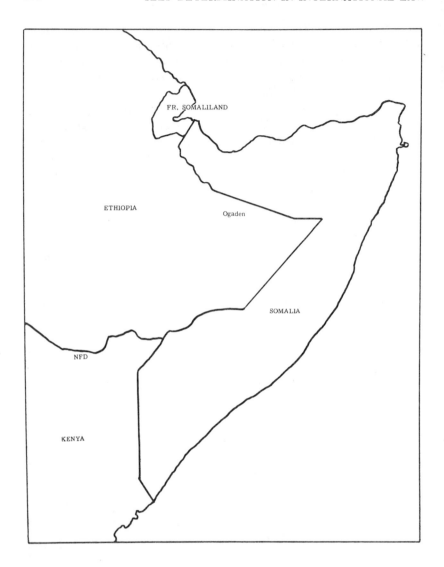

2. Kashmir

A. *The Nature of Kashmir.* Kashmir and Jammu are a composite state that occupies a strategic position in the extreme northwest of India. It shares borders with India, Pakistan, China, Afghanistan and is only fifty miles from the USSR in the extreme northwest. Its 84,000 square miles inhabited by 4 million people is not a homogenous unit but consists of peoples having different languages, religions, cultures, and traditions. There are Muslims (about 80 percent of the population), Hindus, Buddhists, and Sikhs and the topography varies from the high mountains and deep valleys of the east, north and northeast to the Vale of the west-central.

The state may be divided into six regions: (1) the Vale, the most important area with over half of the population, is the main tourist centre and produces the bulk of the wealth. It has agriculture, carpet manufacture, silk weaving, and timber. Srinigar, the capital of Kashmir has a predominantly Muslim population (about 93 percent); (2) Jammu is the mountainous home of the Dogra Dynasty which bought the region from the British for £.5 million in the Treaty of Armitsar, 1846.[34] About 59 percent of the population are Hindus; (3) Poonch, where 90 percent of the population are Muslim; (4) Ladakh, sparsely populated and once a Buddhist Kingdom, has ethnic ties with Tibet. The population is overwhelmingly Buddhist; (5) Baltistan, which is overwhelmingly Muslim; and (6) Gilgit, which contains peoples whose languages belong to the Dardic group but are quite distinct from Iranian and Indo-Aryan.

B. *Accession to India.* About a third of India consisted of 562 princely states which acknowledged British suzerainty but had a large measure of autonomy. The relations between them and the British government were governed by what was known as the doctrine of paramountcy.

> The princely States were allies of the British Crown rather than subjects of the British Government. Their rulers of course, were not exactly equals of the British monarch, and their status could not be compared to that of any of the major European kings. Yet they were not precisely subjects of the British monarch either. The relationship between Indian prince and British monarch was described as one in which the Prince recognised British Paramountcy, an act which certainly differed in some significant ways from the recognition of British sovereignty.[35]

By the doctrine of lapse, the kingdom of a ruler who left no heir at the time of his death escheated to the British government. Disturbances usually followed such events or their probabilities so Lord Dalhousie in 1858 decided to drop the doctrine of lapse and substitute instead the doctrine of paramountcy. This prevailed until independence on the eve of which the rulers were given the option to join India or Pakistan.

---

34. 38 *BFSP* 1 (1849–50), p. 800.
35. Alastair Lamb, *Crisis in Kashmir* (1966), p. 4.

Three of the rulers failed to make up their minds promptly. The declaration of the Muslim ruler of Junagadh, with a Hindu majority, for Pakistan was rejected. India's occupation was later confirmed in a plebiscite of February 1948. The Nizam of Hyderabad's desire for independence was met with India's economic blockade and subsequent military occupation. Both states are within India.

The Maharaja of Kashmir and Jammu signed a standstill agreement with Pakistan to keep services running in the interim period. It became clear to his subjects, a majority of whom were Muslims, that he was negotiating to accede to India. Disturbances broke out in July 1947 and gained such strength that the maharaja was forced to move to his winter capital in Jammu. The rising started in Poonch and spread to Jammu, where bands of Hindus and Sikhs massacred Muslims and provoked retaliatory attacks from others. Muslims from Rajasthan flowed into Kashmir to help the protesting Muslims; they burned and looted their opponents' property. The Muslims formed the Azad government which gained control over a large part of Kashmir. Supported by the biggest popular organisation headed by Sheikh Abdullah, the maharaja appealed for Indian help in order to repel the invaders but India refused to act in the absence of accession. On 26 October 1947 the maharaja signed the letter of accession. In his letter of acceptance, Lord Mountbatten, the governor-general stated: "Consequently with this policy that in the case of any State where the issue of accession has been the subject of dispute, the question of accession should be decided in accordance with the wishes of the people of the State, it is my Government's wish that as soon as law and order have been restored in Kashmir and her soil cleared of the invader the question of the State's accession should be settled by reference to the people."[36] In the same letter he welcomed the fact that Sheikh Abdullah was being invited to join the new government, the government of Pandit Kak having been dismissed from office for pro-Pakistan sympathies. The actual instrument of accession, however, contained no conditions subsequent, such as a referendum. India moved troops into Kashmir and found that some of the invaders were in fact regular troops of the Pakistani army.

India's right to Kashmir has been based mainly on the instrument of accession. It is argued that the accession was within the letter and the spirit of the Indian Independence Act (1947) and that India succeeded to the sovereign powers that belonged to Britain. Pakistan's presence in Kashmir is considered to be "aggression," which has existed since the state was invaded.

36. P. L. Lakhanpal, *Essential Documents and Notes on Kashmir Dispute* (New Delhi, 1965), p. 57.

At the early stages, India repeatedly defined its presence in terms of the defence of Kashmir and only for as long as the invader committed aggression. In a meeting at Lal Chow, Srinigar in November 1947, Nehru asserted:

> It must be remembered that the struggle in Kashmir is a struggle of the people of Kashmir under popular leadership against the invader. We have come to defend your country against raiders, and as soon as Kashmir is free from the invader our troops will have no further necessity to remain here and you will be free to determine your future in accordance with your wishes.[37]

A few days earlier on 2 November 1947, he said in a broadcast in Delhi:

> We are anxious not to finalise anything in a moment of crisis and without the fullest opportunity to be given to the people of Kashmir to have their say. It was for them ultimately to decide. And let me make it clear that it has been our policy all along that where there is a dispute about accession of a State to either Dominion, the accession must be made by the people of that State. It was in accordance with this policy that we have added a proviso to the instrument of Accession of Kashmir.[38]

In 1952, still affirming his stand, Mr. Nehru said in Parliament:

> While the accession was complete in law and fact, the other part which has nothing to do with law also remains, namely our pledge to the people of Kashmir—if you like to the people of the world —that this matter can be affirmed again or cancelled by the people of Kashmir according to their wishes. We do not want to win people against their will and with the help of armed forces; and, if the people of Kashmir and Jammu State wish to part company with us, they can go their way and we shall go ours. We want no forced marriages, no forced unions. . . .[39]

India's attitude has however changed in the course of time. Pakistan's membership of CENTO and SEATO is seen, not as opposition to communism and in defence of the "free world," but as preparation for aggression on India. In 1956 Nehru argued: "The American military aid to Pakistan and Pakistan's membership in military pacts . . . destroyed the roots and foundations of the plebiscite proposal in Kashmir."[40]

Chinese threat to India adds a new dimension to the strategic importance of Kashmir in the defence of the subcontinent. Fearing that it

37. Quoted in Sheikh Abdullah, "Kashmir Issue: Statement to the Press," (17 February 1958), pp. 4–5.
38. Ibid., p. 5.
39. Ibid., p. 15.
40. *Asian Recorder*, 24–30 March 1956, no. 65, 746.

might lose in the event of a plebiscite, India now argues that four general elections on the basis of universal adult suffrage, since independence, confirm the desire of the people to remain part of India. The Indo-Pakistan war of 1965, which India claims was started by Pakistan, the suspected collusion with China, and the giving away by Pakistan of 2,000 square miles of Kashmiri territory in a "corrective" border treaty with China have hardened India's reluctance to apply the plebiscite principle.[41] It has instead proceeded with steps to integrate Indian-held Kashmir with India. Thus the Kashmir Constituent Assembly declared on 17 November 1965 that Kashmir was an integral part of India. The delegation of members from the Kashmiri Parliament to the Indian Parliament was abolished in 1960 in favour of elected members to bring it in line with other Indian states. By a 1965 legislation, the president of India could take over the administration if the administrative machinery failed; in that event the Indian Parliament could promulgate laws for Kashmir. Its special autonomy is now lost.

C. *Link with Pakistan.* Pakistan's main argument for wishing to incorporate Kashmir is that the bulk of the population is Muslim. Pakistan was itself founded on the need to create a state for Muslims where they may live according to Muslim law. Kashmir is part of the problem of Pakistan itself which India tried desperately to stop from being created. Pakistan believes that if a plebiscite is held, the great majority of the population would vote in favour of union with it. It also argues that India incorporated Hyderabad and Junagadh precisely for the reason that the bulk of the population were Hindus. If that principle was meaningful, it also had to be applied in Kashmir. Pakistan resents being considered a foreign power, for it too inherited from Britain.

The legality of the instrument of accession is brought into question because the maharaja acted contrary to the wishes of the majority of his subjects. He was then in "flight" while the Azad government was in *de facto* control of a large part of the state. While the Standstill Agreement of 10 October 1947 was in force, it is argued, the maharaja had no right to accede to India.[42] In any case, the acceptance of the accession was provisional and conditional to the holding of a plebiscite to

41.   During the Indo-Pakistan war, China warned India to vacate certain military outposts which it claimed were on its side of the border or "bear full responsibility for all the grave consequences." *Times* of London, 18 September 1965. The Pakistan Foreign Minister claimed that China played a decisive role in getting the United Nations to link a cease-fire with a settlement of the Kashmir problem. *Washington Post*, 7 October 1965.

42.   For the text, *see* Lakhanpal, p. 45.

confirm it. Further, Kashmir is a natural part of Pakistan, having a common river system, transport, and communications. In a luncheon speech at the National Press Club in Washington on 3 July 1961, President Ayub Khan disclosed that 32 million acres of irrigated lands in Pakistan depended on rivers whose upper courses are in Kashmir.[43] Mr. Bhutto, the Pakistani foreign minister, emphasised that: "Pakistan can never be complete without self-determination in Kashmir. This is the demand of the Muslims of the sub-continent."[44]

It is further stressed that the security of Pakistan demands that Kashmir should be part of it. It may be added that Pakistan may also be trying to redress the imbalance between it and India in size and population. Like India, it has adopted measures that further integrate Pakistan-held Kashmir with Pakistan.

D. *United Nations Involvement.* The Kashmir question was first referred to the Security Council by India on 1 January 1948 after the failure of Lord Mountbatten's attempt to arrive at a solution with Pakistan's first prime minister. On 20 January 1948 the United Nations Commission for India and Pakistan was set up to investigate the matter. It recommended that the dispute should go to arbitration but this was rejected by India.

A Security Council resolution of 21 April 1948 noted: "Both India and Pakistan desire that the question of the accession of Jammu and Kashmir to India or Pakistan should be decided through the democratic method of a free and impartial plebiscite." Pakistan was to withdraw all its soldiers including those Muslims who had entered for the purpose of fighting and deny them aid that might sustain their fighting capacity. India was to withdraw the bulk of its troops "when it is established to the satisfaction of the Commission . . . that the tribesmen are withdrawing and that arrangements for the cessation of the fighting have become effective. . . ." It was then to "put into operation in consultation with the Commission a plan for withdrawing their own forces from Jammu and Kashmir and reducing them progressively to the minimum strength required for the support of the civil power in the maintenance of law and order. . . ."

In the resolution of 13 August 1948, the Security Council called for immediate cease-fire and the withdrawal of troops as laid down in earlier resolutions. It reiterated:

43. *Pakistan Times,* 14 July 1961.
44. M. C. Chagla: *Kashmir 1947–1965* (Govt. of India publication, 1965) p. 83.

The Government of India and the Government of Pakistan re-affirm their wish that the future status of the State of Jammu and Kashmir shall be determined in accordance with the will of the people and to that end, upon the acceptance of the truce agreement, both Government's agree to enter into consultations with the Commission to determine fair and equitable conditions whereby such free expression will be assured.

The commission achieved a cease-fire for 1 January 1949 but was not satisfied with India's scheme of withdrawal and felt unable to carry on. In its resolution of 14 March 1950, the Security Council reaffirmed the commission's resolution of 5 January 1949, which spelled out the following principles: "The question of accession of the State of Jammu and Kashmir to India or Pakistan will be decided through the democratic method of a free and impartial plebiscite."

It then appointed Sir Owen Dixon of Australia to go into the matter. He favoured partition but found no basis for effecting it. India insisted on the "vacation of aggression" before a plebiscite and Pakistan would not trust a plebiscite held behind its back.

Sheikh Abdullah convened a constituent assembly of the part of Kashmir under Indian control and it resolved that "the State of Jammu and Kashmir is and shall be an integral part of the Union of India." The Security Council however considered that a disposition that was not in accord with agreed principles was ineffective. The president of the Security Council, Gunnar Jerring of Sweden and later F. P. Graham of the United States, tried to mediate but failed. Pakistan's offer to withdraw its troops provided United Nations forces took their place was also rejected by India. In 1962 Pakistan brought India's bellicose statement on the "liberation" of Azad Kashmir to the Security Council but a decision was made impossible by the USSR's one hundreth veto. The disappearance of the relic of Mohammed's hair from the Hazratbel shrine in Srinigar in 1963 followed by a retaliatory disappearance of holy Hindu relics from a temple in Jammu was occasion for serious disturbances. Pakistan brought the matter to the Security Council but a decision was postponed *sine die* for fear that it might prejudice the cordial atmosphere that seemed to be emerging. War broke out in 1965 but a cease-fire was achieved by a Security Council resolution. The crux of the matter remains unsolved. The Tashkent Agreement of 10 January 1966 merely acknowledged the existence of the problem. Both sides agreed to withdraw to positions held before August 1965, re-establish diplomatic relations, discourage hostile propaganda, and continue peaceful discussions of problems affecting them.[45]

45. For the full text of the Tashkent Treaty *see Indian JIL* (1966), 560 *UNTS,* p. 39.

E. *Self-determination for Kashmir*. It is not proposed here to offer a panacea to a problem that has defied the wisdom of the United Nations and of many world statesmen. The relevance of self-determination in the Kashmir dispute will be examined and posited as a possible mode of settlement that takes into consideration the wishes of the people most intimately affected—the Kashmiris.

Indian reliance on the instrument of accession is not entirely without blemish. Though it provides for no plebiscites or referenda, the ruler was expected to act in his capacity as the custodian of his subjects. The very circumstances of the accession cast some blur on it. There was an insurrection in which a rival government was set up over parts of the state. The instrument was signed in a moment of stress between parties that were hardly equal when the state of Kashmir faced imminent collapse. In recognition of this fact and the fact that the majority of the population was Muslim and might prefer union with Pakistan, the governor-general indicated that the whole issue would be referred to the people in a plebiscite. This was repeatedly confirmed by Mr. Nehru.

Pakistan s claim based on religion has some merit in that that very principle led to the creation of Pakistan as a separate state. If the option had been thrown directly to the people instead of the Hindu maharaja, Kashmir might have joined Pakistan. It is however dangerous to rest on religion alone. India has 65 million Muslims and is the third largest Muslim state, next to Indonesia and Pakistan. Should all the Indian Muslims move to Pakistan, or have another state carved out of India? India is a secular state, although with Hindu overtones, but other religious adherents enjoy equal rights of citizenship. It is therefore wrong in principle and potentially explosive to join Kashmir with Pakistan solely on the ground of religious affinity. About 20 percent of the population of Kashmir are non-Muslims; they are entitled not to join a Muslim state if they so desire.

Economic considerations alone are not enough. The fact that much of Pakistan's irrigation relies on waters whose upper reaches are in Kashmir is not by itself a determining factor. There are today many international rivers and there is no question of their exclusive appropriation by particular states for their economic aggrandizement. Nor must the importance of communication links be exaggerated at the expense of other legitimate interests.

Each side claims that Kashmir is of strategic importance to it. Indeed the further the borders of a state are extended the better for strategic reasons. It is a weak argument that smacks of expansionism.

In these circumstances the best deciding factor would be the wishes of the people most directly concerned. They should be free to exercise their right to self-determination. The principle of self-determination is the lowest common denominator between the United Nations, India, and Pakistan. None would claim to deny it to the Kashmiris. It could be exercised through independence, merger, association, or local autonomy within India or Pakistan or in any form that ensures full participation in government provided it accords with the wishes of the people. The question then is, How best can self-determination be applied to Kashmir? The six units enumerated above could decide in plebiscites based on universal adult suffrage in which the following questions are put: (1) Do you wish to have an independent Kashmir? (2) Do you wish to join Pakistan? (3) Do you wish to join India?

If a majority in all the regions are in favour of independence, then it should be granted. If the majority in a region votes to join India or Pakistan, provided it is contiguous to it, it should be free to do so. If some regions vote to join but others opt for independence, those wishing to join either side should first be counted out, subject to the principle of contiguity. The rest should choose between independence or joining any side after possible accessions. The result will be that the regions that are contiguous might form an independent state after at least one plebiscite. Alternatively the questions should be put to the two units—Indian-held Kashmir and Pakistan-held Kashmir—in recognition of the de facto authorities that control the state of Kashmir and Jammu. The armed forces of both sides should be replaced by United Nations forces in order to ensure a free vote.[46] Whatever the choice, the rights of minorities should be guaranteed. A scheme such as this would place the wishes of the people over and above the pride in territorial integrity and remove the issue from the chessboard of international politics. The Security Council should effectively avert the frustration by any state of a solution based on self-determination, which should be imposed with force, if necessary.[47]

46. Peter Lyon, *Kashmir*, 3 *International Relations*, no. 2 (David Davis Memorial Institute of International Studies, 2 October 1966). Lyon suggests one of the following solutions: (a) accession to India or Pakistan, (b) partition, (c) confederation, (d) independence.

47. *See* on Kashmir, Chagla, *Kashmir 1947–1965* (Delhi, 1965); Josef Korbel, *Danger in Kashmir* (Princeton Univ. Press, 1966); *Mr. Nehru Answers Critics of Kashmir* (Indian House, London); *Aggression in Kashmir* (Delhi, 1964); *India's Aggression Against Pakistan* (Pakistan High Commission, London, 1965); *The Kashmir Crisis, Speeches at the Security Council* by S. M. Zafar, Law Minister of Pakistan, September 18 and 20, 1965 (Karachi, Din Muhammadi Press); *Kashmir in Agony, Impartial Reports* (Karachi, 1966); *The Kashmir Issue and Indian Aggression: News and Views* (Karachi, 1965); P. B. Potter, "The Principal Legal and Political Problems Involved in the Kashmir Case" 44 *AJIL* (1959), p. 361.

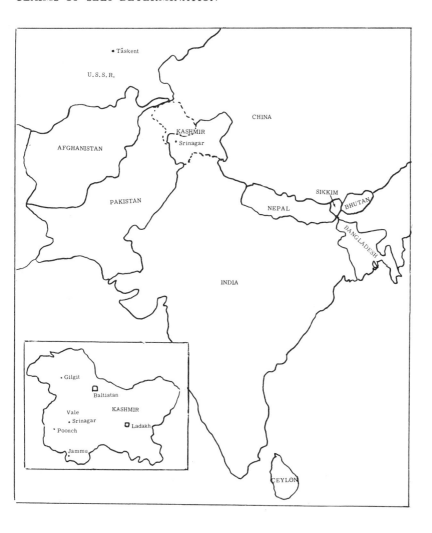

3. The Nagas

A. *Nagaland.* Nagaland is divided into three administrative districts
—Kohima, Mokokchung and Tuensang. It covers 6,366 square miles
and has a population of over 4 million. The land consists of long narrow
strips of hills on the left bank of the river Brahmaputra, east of the
Assam Plains. The people belong to the Indo-Mongolian group and are
divided into about fourteen major tribes. The Nagas were notorious for

headhunting; the cutting of heads was an important symbol that determined social status, including eligibility for marriage.

Naga villages are perched on hilltops between 3,000 and 4,000 feet above sea level. Whenever a village became too crowded, part of the population broke off and founded another village on another hilltop. In this way the tribes multiplied but they came from a common stock. The Nagas are noted for their handicraft. Their culture has many interesting aspects, such as the equality of men and women and a casteless society unlike most of India. They have a strong love for freedom and this explains their resort to the use of force to secure what they consider to be their right against a much greater opponent.[48]

B. *Relations with India.* The Nagas were politically and culturally independent of India before the advent of the British, whose penetration of the Naga Hills did not begin until 1849. In the thirty years that followed, not less than twelve battles were fought against the Nagas until they were finally defeated at Kohima in 1879. For a long time after that, they were left alone, for their headhunting was not yet a menace to commercial enterprise. However in 1902 the Tuensang villages were brought under the control of the governor of Assam and civil administration was gradually extended to other areas. Headhunting was then proscribed in the wake of greater governmental control.

When the Simon Commission visited Kohima in 1929, the Nagas were already sensing that the impending grant of home rule to India might work against their traditional ways of life. One of their leaders is reported to have told the commission: "You [the British] are the only people who have ever conquered us; when you go we should be as we were."[49]

When the Government of India Act (1935) was discussed in Parliament, doubts were expressed by some members as to whether the Nagas would receive fair treatment in the hands of the rest of the Indians. The act made the region a "tribal area" instead of the "backward tract" as stipulated in the Government of India Act (1919). The reforms of 1937 which followed the suggestions of the commission made the backward regions "excluded area" and "partially excluded area" within the province of Assam.

> The main point of distinction between these two types of area was that, while both classes were excluded from the competence of the Provincial and Federal Legislatures, the administration of the

48. *See also* S. R. Johri, *Our Borderlands* (Lucknow, 1964), chapter 3.
49. Verrier Elwin, *Nagaland* (Shillong, 1961), p. 49.

Excluded Areas was vested in the Governors acting in their discretion and that of the Partially Excluded Areas in the control of the Ministers subject, however, to the Governor exercising his individual judgment.[50]

The term "excluded" was used where the population was compact, and "partially excluded" where it was less homogeneous. The governor could in his discretion suspend the application of general law in favour of simpler law, including customary law, in the area. The main objective was to preserve tribal law, customs, and traditions. The Inner Line Regulation was made in 1873 to check the commercial activities of the tea planters and others such as money lenders among the hill tribes. No outsider could carry on business beyond the Inner Line without official permit. Business men were also protected by this law, for it minimised provocations and the consequent wrath of the tribesmen. This policy unfortunately kept the Nagas apart from the rest of Indians, with whom they were to be compatriots.

During the Second World War Nagaland was briefly overrun by the Japanese. Hopes for the restoration of their independence were revived but the Japanese were driven out by the Allies. The desire for independence grew as Indian independence approached after the war. In order to prevent the possibility of the Nagas' standing in the way of Indian independence, the Congress Government of Assam began negotiations with Naga leaders in 1946. A draft agreement was produced but the Indian government was reluctant to sign it while the governor maintained that Nagaland should remain part of India.

A Naga delegation met Gandhi on 19 July 1947 to inform him about their intention to declare the independence of Nagaland on 14 August 1947, a day before Indian independence. Gandhi allegedly admitted the justice of their cause and reportedly told the delegation:

> Nagas have every right to be independent. We do not want to live under the domination of the British and they are now leaving us. I want you to feel that India is yours. I feel that the Naga Hills are mine just as much as they are yours. But if you say they are not mine, the matter must stop there. I believe in the brotherhood of man, but I do not believe in force or forced unions. If you do not wish to join the Union of India, nobody will force you to do that.[51]

50. Ibid., p. 36.

51. A report of the meeting given by Phizo, a Naga leader. A reference is made to it by Bipinpal Das, "The Naga Problem," 5 *Socialist Tract* (Hyderabad, 1956), p. 42.

The Hydari Agreement[52] was signed on 22 June 1948 by the Naga leaders on the one side and by Sir Akbar Hydari, governor of Assam on the other and on behalf of India. The agreement recognised "the right of the Nagas to develop themselves according to their free[ly] expressed wishes." It conceded to them a large measure of autonomy, including the right to develop their customs and traditions. Civil and criminal cases were to be dealt with in their customary courts and land could be alienated to a non-Naga only with the approval of the Naga National Council. Article 9 evoked much controversy.

> The Governor of Assam as agent of the Government of the Indian Union will have a special responsibility for a period of ten years to ensure the due observance of this agreement; at the end of this period, the Naga National Council will be asked whether they require the above agreement to be extended for a further period or a new agreement regarding the future of the Naga people to be arrived at.

Naga leaders interpreted this to mean that they could opt for independence at the end of the period if they chose and that the agreement would be incorporated in the Indian Constitution. The governor did not, however, attach so much importance to it and a year later insisted that secession was out of the question. A Naga delegation met Governor-General Sri. C. Rajagopalachari to express its fears. The Nagas feared that the new constitution reduced their autonomy and that their lands might be taken away from them. The Hindustan Standard of Calcutta gave the following report of the governor-general's reaction:

> His Excellency, who gave the deputation a quiet hearing, replied that the Government also wanted to be friendly with them. They did not want to deprive them of their lands. They were at full liberty to do as they liked, either to become part of India or to be separate if they felt it would be best in their interests to be isolated and that he would convey their fears to the Government of India.[53]

Mr. Nehru as prime minister laid down five principles in dealing with the backward peoples of India, of which the Nagas were one, a tribal Panch Shila[54]: (1) They should develop their own culture and traditions along their own lines without hinderance from outside. (2) Their land patrimony should be respected. (3) Their skills should be developed

52. For the full text, see Das, pp. 15–17.
53. *Hindustan Standard* of Calcutta, 30 November 1949.
54. A Hindu derivative from Sanskrit meaning "Five Principles." The term *Panch Shila* was first used by Nehru in the Indian Parliament in 1954 to describe the principles of coexistence enunciated in his joint statement with the Chinese Foreign Minister, Chou En-Lai during the latter's visit to India that year. These

for their own services and only a minimum number of skilled personnel from outside should be introduced. (4) Development should be effected through local institutions and a multiplicity of development schemes was to be avoided. (5) Results should be judged only from the quality in human development, regardless of costs.

The Indian Constitution makes special provisions for backward areas. By Article 46 "the State shall promote with special care the educational and economic interests of the weaker sections of the people, and, in particular of the Scheduled Castes and the Scheduled Tribes, and shall protect them from social injustice and all forms of exploitation." Article 275 provides that money should be made available from the Consolidated Fund for their development, regardless of their own income. Part 16 provides that the backward areas should be given reserved seats in the Lok Sabha and in state legislatures. Under Article 335 they are entitled to special consideration in state and Union appointments. The Union may give directions to states regarding the administration of the scheduled areas and the president may appoint an officer to investigate their administration. The constitution provides that the governors should be advised by Tribes Advisory Councils, three-quarters of whose membership are tribesmen.[55] The Naga Hill District had representation in the Assam legislature and was to some extent under its administration, but the Naga Tribal Area, later the Naga Hills Tuensang Area, was administered directly by the president through the governor, although the area could be brought under the provisions of the Sixth Schedule, which grants a measure of autonomy.

In spite of the provisions of the Indian Constitution and Mr. Nehru's tribal Panch Shila, the relations between the Nagas and the government of India deteriorated. The resentment over the Hydari Agreement did much harm. If the governor of Assam could go back on his words, so it seemed to the Nagas, there was no hope that any guarantee in favour of the Nagas could be respected by the government. Elections into the Assam legislature were boycotted while a plebiscite conducted by the Naga National Council (NNC), to which Indian officials were invited as observers, produced an overwhelming support for independence. The lack of sympathy and understanding for the Naga cause, ill-considered official statements, and a number of unfortunate incidents further

---

are (1) mutual respect for each other's territorial integrity and sovereignty, (2) non-aggression, (3) non-interference in each other's internal affairs, (4) equality and mutual benefit, (5) peaceful coexistence. (Press information Bureau, New Delhi, 28 June 1954). See also C. J. Chacko, "Peaceful Co-existence as a Doctrine of Current International Affairs," 4 Indian YBIA (1955), pp. 13–41.

55. For the Indian Constitution, see Peaslee, 2:308.

worsened the situation.[56] In one such incident in March 1953, a crowd of 5,000 Nagas had gathered in Kohima to hear Prime Minister Nehru. The officials refused to allow the secretary-general of the NNC to present a memorandum to him, whereupon the crowd was signalled to disperse. When Nehru realised what had happened he ordered that the Nagas should be invited to return, but the crowd could not be persuaded. A series of repressive and high-handed measures followed the incident which the officials considered to be a gross disrespect to the leader of government. Armed resistance broke out in 1954 and the Indian army was ordered to restore order.

In 1957 an All Naga Tribes Peoples Convention convened in Kohima sued for an end to the insurrection and a return to peace. The Naga Peoples Convention was founded and Nagaland was constituted a single administrative district under the External Affairs Ministry. It is curious that this ministry was entrusted with Naga affairs and raises the doubt as to whether the government intended to acquiesce in secession at some time in the future. A second convention was held the following year in Mokokchung, a pro-rebel village, and a committee was set up to draft the terms of relations with India. A third convention held in the same village in 1959 demanded a separate state and legislature, a council of ministers, village councils, range councils, and tribal councils.

On 1 August 1960 Nehru announced that the demand for a separate state would be granted. He said: "Our policy has always been to give the fullest autonomy and opportunity of self-development to the Naga people, without interfering in any way in their internal affairs or way of life." He said further: "India achieved her independence. . . . and the Nagas are as independent as other Indian citizens."[57] A separate statehood was granted in 1963 but that did not satisfy the separatists who kept up sporadic guerrilla activities in spite of a cease-fire. Elections held in February 1969 returned the Naga Nationalist Organisation, which supports the Indian government policy. Whether this justifies the hope that the extremists are being isolated is yet to be confirmed.[58]

C. *Self-determination for the Nagas.* When the Japanese overran Burma and Nagaland during the Second World War, they claimed to have "liberated" them from colonialism. They were subsequently driven

56. See also the views expressed by Bipinpal Das, a Socialist member of Parliament in his pamphlet *supra*.

57. Quoted in Elwin, p. 1.

58. See C. P. Ramachandran on "Nagaland Travel Ban May End" in the *London Observer* of 23 February 1969.

out from both territories. Britain concluded a treaty recognising the independence of Burma,[59] but this was not the case with Nagaland, which remained part of India. The boundaries of India as set out in Section 2 of the Indian Independence Act (1947), by implication, include Nagaland within India.[60] On the attainment of independence, India inherited its colonial boundaries from the British and these include Nagaland even though the latter was independent of the former before colonial administration. The situation raises the question as to what extent a colonial boundary created by a colonial power for its own convenience and in agreement with other colonial powers but without consultation with the colonial peoples should be regarded as sacrosanct. An attempt to grant separate independence to Nagaland would no doubt have been strongly resented in some quarters.

After independence, Nagaland formed part of the state of Assam and was entitled to representation in the state legislature, although the seats were never filled. As a backward region, it was entitled to special treatment under the constitution. It has since gained separate statehood.

Whether Gandhi would have granted sovereignty to the Nagas if he survived Indian independence is speculative but there would have been no legal remedy against India if Gandhi refused to honour a pledge that was only morally binding. It was an undertaking given by the leader of a political party to a part of the population of a colonial territory and outside the realms of international law. The promise made by the governor-general to the Nagas had a similar status.

The Indian government had probably not displayed political sagacity in dealing with the Nagas but this has not seriously affected their position on the question of Naga secession in international law. The principle of self-determination is manifested, not only through independence, but also through autonomy, association, or self-government. In order to discard the principle of territorial integrity in favour of secession pursuant to the principle of self-determination, a strong case must be made by those demanding it. Such a case could be made if, for instance, the Nagas were denied fundamental human rights or discriminated against by official policy to the detriment of their political, economic, and cultural development. In the absence of such a situation, the greater autonomy guaranteed by separate statehood and a commensurate share in the Union government appear to protect the right of the Nagas to self-determination. They should be encouraged to avail themselves of their rights under the Indian Constitution which guarantees "Justice, social,

59. 70 *UNTS*, p. 183.
60. Statutes of England (1947) 10 & 11, Geo. 6, 237–238.

economic, and political; Liberty of thought, expression, belief, faith, and worship; Equality of opportunity." The constitution also seeks to promote among all the peoples of India "fraternity assuring the dignity of the individual and the unity of the Nation."[61]

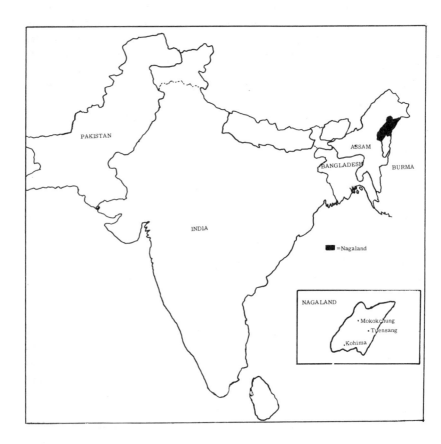

4. The Afro-Americans

A. *Historical Background.* One of the longest-oppressed minorities of the world is the Afro-Americans of the United States, whose struggle for human rights dates back to the seventeenth century. The first Africans who arrived in the United States in 1619 were indentured servants,

61. *See also* "Nagaland," *The March of India*, vol. 12 (October 1960); G. D. Means and I. N. Means, "Nagaland: The Agony of Ending a Guerrilla War," *Pacific Affairs*, vol. 39, nos. 3 and 4 (1966–67), pp. 290–313.

some of whom actually regained their freedom. They were followed by slaves who were widely used in the North American colonies, particularly in the South. On the eve of abolition in 1860, there were about 4 million black slaves and less than 500,000 free black people. The attitude of the whites toward the black slaves was characterized by the denial of humanity, segregation, and restriction to a low standard of living. This differed from the attitude in Spanish-Portuguese colonies with a dominant Catholic influence. Unlike the Protestants of North America, the Spanish and Portuguese recognised the equality of men before God. A slave was, to them, an unfortunate human being whose material conditions did not affect his spiritual quality before God.

The North of the United States, with a smaller slave population, was more liberal than the South, which felt threatened by the large number of slaves. Hatred for the blacks in the South increased immediately after the Civil War but ameliorating factors included the presence of federal troops and the change of the state governments of the South. There were twenty black representatives in the House of Representatives and two in the Senate. White extremists reacted by forming the Ku Klux Klan and White Citizen Councils with the avowed aim of intensifying white supremacy. Attacks and lynchings of blacks were on the increase.

The reign of the Democratic party during the last twenty-five years of the nineteenth century brought a deterioration in the position of the blacks. The Civil Rights Act of 1875 that sought to secure equal rights for all citizens at hotels, theatres, and other public places were struck down by the Supreme Court in 1883.[62] In *Plessey* v. *Ferguson* (1896)[63] the Supreme Court upheld a Louisiana law calling for separate facilities on railroads. It held that segregation did not deny the blacks of equal protection under the law. The separate-but-equal doctrine was thereafter developed. Segregation was thus legally practised by the provision of separate facilities that were invariably unequal. The black Americans were excluded from the electorate by tactics like "literacy" or "understanding" tests administered by whites, and "grandfather clauses" restricting the vote to those whose grandfathers had it.

One of the prominent groups formed to protect civil rights for the blacks was the National Association for the Advancement of Colored People (NAACP). Founded in 1909, its basic aim was "to make 11,000,000 Americans physically free from peonage, mentally free from ignorance, politically free from disenfranchisement, and socially free

62. The Civil Rights cases, 109 U.S., p. 3.
63. 163 U.S., p. 537.

from insult." It was a multiracial organisation whose original national officers were whites, with the exception of W. E. B. Du Bois.

The First World War encouraged the urbanisation of the blacks, for opportunities which were previously closed to them were opened in the industrial towns. The Second World War had the same effect and also encouraged emigration to the North with greater opportunities. Urbanisation facilitated coordination in political action and a greater awareness among the black population. The mutual opposition of black and white Americans to Nazism served to accentuate opposition to white racism at home. President Roosevelt's New Deal increased the powers of the federal government and the opportunities for blacks to acquire training in skilled and professional jobs. President Truman declared in 1948 that "there shall be equality of treatment and opportunity for all persons in the armed services without regard to race, color, religion, or national origin."

More organisations were formed with the aim of winning civic rights for the black Americans. The Congress of Racial Equality had its origins in the Chicago Committee of Racial Equality founded in 1942 by James Farmer with the help of the Fellowship of Reconciliation. It grew into a national organisation in 1946 when the headquarters were also moved to New York. The Southern Christian Leadership Council was founded in 1956 by one hundred clergymen who thought the church should play a dominant role in the battle for civil rights. This organisation was dominated by Dr. Martin Luther King, who was murdered by a white extremist in 1968. The Black Muslims, founded by Elijah Mohamed, believe that strength lies in the acquisition of economic power and in segregation from the whites.

Meanwhile, the emphasis on human rights in the United Nations, the Universal Declaration of Human Rights, and the crumbling of colonialism had their effects on the United States, for the clamour for equality by the Afro-Americans was intensified. Under the influence of this "wind of change" the United States Supreme Court handed down decisions that curtailed racial discrimination and promoted human rights. In *Morgan* v. *Virginia*[64] it decided that a black passenger in interstate transport was not obliged to conform with the segregation laws of the states he passed through. In *Shelley* v. *Kraemer*[65] it held that the restrictive covenants excluding persons of a designated race or colour could not be enforced by the courts. In *Sipuel* v. *Board of Regents*,[66]

64.   328 U.S. (1946), p. 373.
65.   334 U.S. (1948), p. 1.
66.   332 U.S. (1948), p. 631.

a district court held that the state of Oklahoma had the duty to provide a black student with legal education and to "provide it as soon as it does for any other group." Oklahoma and certain other states consequently opened the doors of white schools to blacks for courses that were not available in black schools. In *McLaurin* v. *Oklahoma State Regents*[67] the appellant, who possessed a masters degree and was admitted by the university to work toward a doctorate in education, was required to sit apart at a designated desk in an anteroom adjoining the classroom; to sit at a designated desk in the mezzanine of the library, but not to use the desks in the regular reading room; and to sit at a designated table and to eat at a different time from the other students in the school cafeteria. The section of the classroom in which the appellant sat was surrounded by a rail with the marking "Reserved For Colored." The district court held that the restrictions did not violate the Constitution but the Supreme Court struck the decision down. In *Sweatt* v. *Painter*[68] the Supreme Court decided that a black applicant should be admitted to the University of Texas Law School since it was superior to a hastily organized law school set up by the university for blacks. The culminating decision was *Brown* v. *Board of Education*[69] in which the Supreme Court held unanimously that segregation was inherently unequal since it denied the segregated person full participation in the educational process guaranteed by the Fourteenth Amendment.[70]

B. *Self-determination for Afro-Americans.* Self-determination relates to the right of a group to determine its political, economic, cultural, and social future. An issue of self-determination may be sufficiently serious to be a matter of international concern, but it may also be of such a low level of intensity as to fall within exclusive domestic jurisdiction. The question may then be asked: Are the Afro-Americans as a people freely determining their future? The brief historical background given establishes that they have been persistently, and as a matter of policy, denied human rights in a country to which they belong. Despite this history of denial, the issue has not come before the United Nations or other international organisations. This may be explained by the fact that the victims may have lost faith in internationalism as a means of redress-

---

67. 339 U.S. (1950).

68. 339 U.S. (1950), p. 629.

69. 347 U.S. (1954), p. 483.

70. *See* articles on Equal Protection of the Laws in *Selected Essays on Constitutional Law* (St. Paul, Minn., 1963) edited by a Committee of the Association of American Law Schools, section 6.

ing their wrongs. They may also be satisfied with the progress they have achieved within local remedies. The most likely reason is probably that they have been unable or unwilling to get third states to champion their cause at the international level.

There is no substantial demand for carving out part of the United States for a black independent state or a state in federal relations with the rest.[71] What is reasonably demanded (and possible of attainment) is that the Afro-Americans should play a commensurate role in the political, economic, cultural, and social life of the United States. A fair representation in the legislatures, judiciary, and executive is a measure of the attainment of self-determination as an integral part of the state. Substantial representation in local authority will go a long way in removing some of the local disabilities. The American educational system should be oriented toward respect for the different communities and a fair treatment of their historical background should be a guiding policy. Respect for human rights could be usefully inculcated in the minds of all citizens, not least the young ones. The victims of oppression must themselves, in a spirit of self-reliance, be able to identify and press for their rights. International instruments like the Charter of the United Nations, the Universal Declaration of Human Rights, the International Covenants on Human Rights, whether or not they are ratified by the United States, indicate that the struggle of the Afro-Americans within municipal law should be supplemented by pressure at the international level. Such combined efforts will persuade the leader of what the West calls "the free world" to give its democracy a legal content that ensures rights for all its citizens regardless of colour or race.[72]

5. The French Canadians

A section of the French Canadians demands independence for Quebec. The separatists occasionally receive good publicity as by the open sympathy of the late President de Gaulle and the kidnapping in 1970 of a

71. In their "Message to America" on the 107th anniversary of the Emancipation Proclamation, the Black Panther Party issued the following statement: "If we are to remain a part of the United States, then we must have a new Constitution that will strictly guarantee our Human Rights to Life, Liberty, and the Pursuit of Happiness which is promised but not delivered by the present Constitution. We shall not accept one iota less than this, our full unblemished Human Rights. If this is not to be, if we cannot make a new arrangement with the United States, then we have no alternative but to declare ourselves free and independent of the United States." *Africa and the World* (London, November 1970), p. 18.

72. *See also* C. Wagley and M. Harris, *Minorities in the New World* (New York, London, 1958); B. Quarles, *The Negro in the Making of America* (New York, London 1967); S. M. Scheiner, *Negro Mecca* (New York, 1965).

Canadian cabinet minister and a British diplomat. The former was murdered but the latter was released.

The French Canadians constitute 30 percent of the Canadian population but constitute a much smaller proportion of skilled, professional, or managerial workers. They consider themselves underprivileged, exploited, and discriminated against. Even in Quebec, technical and financial control is in the hands of the English Canadians. Since English is a requirement for some business or professional positions, bilingualism is a necessity for the French. The two groups are mutually suspicious and paint an adverse and exaggerated picture of the other. Thus the English are pictured as "barbarians—more interested in dogs than in children, in sports than in religion, in money than in arts" and the French as "a backward peasant, a papist fanatic, a narrow-minded Catholic, and a medieval fossil clinging rigidly to an outmoded way of life."[73]

A. *Historical Background.* Official French colonisation of Canada dates back to 1534 when Jacques Cartier dispossessed the Indians in the name of the French king. The colony proved to be more of a liability, for there was neither gold nor spices nor did it provide the route to the Indies. The Indians proved unsuitable as a work force and so the colonists had to rely on their extended families for cultivation and fur collection. A high birthrate was encouraged in order to provide the much needed labour.

New France was conquered by the English in 1760. The absence of strong economic links with old France and the latter's preoccupation with internal problems were factors that secured an easy victory for the English. In 1763 Louis XV formally ceded Canada to Britain in the Treaty of Paris. The representatives of the French civil authorities and the middle class departed, leaving behind the priests and the farmers. The influence of the priests thus outlasted that of the civil authorities.

In an attempt to stem the rising tide of anti-colonialism in the North American colonies and to deny it the support of the French Canadians, the Quebec Act of 1774 was passed restoring the French religion, culture, and some of their laws and institutions. This act was crucial to the survival of the French as a distinct group. They resisted attempts to draw them into active participation either on the side of the American colonists or of the British; at the end of the war, Canada was firmly in British hands. The emigration of American royalists into Canada increased the numerical strength of the English, who were soon to demand

73. Wagley and Harris, op. cit., p. 185.

representative government in the hope of dominating despite their numerical inferiority.

The Canada Act, 1791 divided the country into Upper Canada with a population of 10,000, mostly English, and Lower Canada with a population of 150,000, mostly French. Nova Scotia and New Brunswick were separate colonies. Despite the predominantly French population in Lower Canada, their representation in the Lower House decreased steadily to nine out of twenty-seven members in 1827. Three out of the ten judges were French and only ten of the thirty judicial appointments between 1800 and 1827 were French. Although the French constituted three-quarters of the population in 1834, only a quarter of the public places were occupied by them. Mutual suspicion and hatred were on the ascendancy and culminated in 1837 in a French-led rebellion which was crushed. Lord Durham was appointed to investigate the disturbances. His report was remarkably biased against the French whom he considered as having "no history and no literature." On the other hand he was confident that the English were "sure to predominate even in Lower Canada, as they predominate already in knowledge, energy, enterprise, and wealth."[74] The Union Act of 1840 abolished the dual division of Canada. Sustained immigration from the British Isles reduced the French numerical strength and made them more concerned about their language and culture. The British North America Act of 1867 united Quebec (Lower Canada) and Ontario (Upper Canada) with Nova Scotia and New Brunswick; six other provinces were later to join.

Powers are divided between the federal government and the provinces, each of which exercises executive powers with elected legislature. Education falls within provincial authority and this power is jealously guarded by Quebec. Increased immigration from the British Isles, Northwest Europe, the Balkans, Western and Southern Russia has facilitated the opening of the prairies and of the west and has diminished further the French proportion of the total population despite their prolific birthrate. Whereas other national groups have been largely assimilated, the French tenaciously remain a distinct group.

B. *Self-determination for French Canadians.* Tension still exists between the French Canadians and the English Canadians. Although industrialism and urbanisation have had centripetal tendencies, language, religion and culture have produced centrifugal effect. Self-determination for the French has centred around self-determination for Quebec, where the French still predominate.

74. Ibid., p. 181.

Suggested solutions range from outright secession to a unitary government for the whole of Canada with varying proposals inbetween. One
compromissary suggestion is the transfer to Quebec, but not to the other
provinces, of certain federal powers.[75]
Inasmuch as the political machinery of Canada has adopted a flexible
approach to the problem of the French Canadians, it is maintained that
it remains an internal affair of Canada and not one of international concern. The French Canadians are comparatively a privileged minority.
The special facilities provided for them serve as a pointer to the way
other minorities who refuse to be assimilated may be treated. The well-
publicised French demand should not, however, blur the claims of the
Indians whose racial difference may produce more problems. They too
are entitled to self-determination.[76]

75.   A. W. Johnson, "The Dynamics of Federalism in Canada," *Canadian Journal
of Political Science*, vol. 1, no. 1. (March 1968), pp. 18–39.
76.   *See also* P. M. Leslie, "The Role of Political Parties in Promoting the
Interest of Ethnic Minorities," *Canadian Journal of Political Science*, vol. 2, no. 4.
(December 1969), pp. 419–433; H. Guidon, "Two Cultures: An Essay on Nationalism, Class, and Ethnic Tension," in R. H. Leach, ed., *Contemporary Canada*
(Duke University Press, Durham 1967).

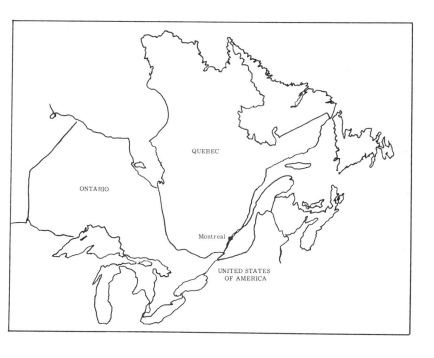

6. Biafra

The Eastern Region of Nigeria seceded from Nigeria on 30 May 1967 as the Republic of Biafra. The state existed with a diminishing territory until 12 January 1970 when it finally crumbled. It was one of the most outstanding claims of the principle of self-determination on the part of a metropolitan territory in recent times. It is not intended to conduct more than a cursory and tentative study of the situation at this stage, since more time is needed for Nigerians to be able to see the issues in their proper perspective.

A. *Historical Background*. The name Biafra was derived from an ancient kingdom that flourished in the hinterland of the bight that bears the name, though lying farther east of the territory it lately represented. The peoples of the Eastern Region of Nigeria consist of the Ibos, the Ibibios, the Ekois, the Efiks, the Ijaws, and the Ogonis. About 60 percent of the 14 million people of Biafra were Ibos. The territory had been continuously inhabited for more than three thousand years and was unaffected by large-scale immigrations or emigrations that affected other parts of Nigeria.[77]

Although the Portuguese were the first Europeans to visit, by the second half of the nineteenth century British traders gained a dominant influence over the coasts. The colonial era commenced with the appointment of a British consul for Calabar in 1849. In 1893 the Niger Coast protectorate was proclaimed and in 1900 the protectorate of Southern Nigeria, but most of Biafra was not effectively administered until after the First World War.[78]

In 1914 Northern and Southern Nigeria were joined to form the colony and protectorate of Nigeria under Sir Frederick Lugard as governor-general. There had been no attempt to get the consent of the Northern rulers for the merger. It was carried out principally for administrative convenience and in order to offset the losses that were incurred in the administration of Northern Nigeria.[79] In fact, the merger was unpopular in the North. In his autobiography, A. Bello, the Sardauna of Sokoto, wrote: "Lord Lugard and his Amalgamation were

---

77. *See* Thurstan Shaw, "The Mystery of the Buried Bronzes," *Nigeria Magazine*, no. 92 (March 1967), pp. 55–74.

78. *See* K. O. Dike, *Trade and Politics in the Niger Delta* (Oxford, 1956); G. I. Jones, *The Trading States of the Oil Rivers* (London, 1963); O. I. Odumosu, *The Nigerian Constitution: History and Development* (London, 1963), pp. 7–8.

79. *See* British Foreign Office Handbook, Africa, 1920 prepared under the direction of the historical division, no. 94.

far from being popular amongst us at that time."[80] The semi-official Hausa language newspaper, *Gaskiya Ta Fi Kwobo*, reflected the view of the North when it wrote "We on reflection, consider that a mistake was made in 1914 when the North and South were joined together."[81]

However, as much as the amalgamation was detested in the North, it opened avenues for the Eastern Nigerians, who spread to the North as clerks, mechanics, traders, businessmen, etc. While the Southerners in the North forged ahead, the Northerners were encouraged to lag behind by the colonial administration with the aim of using them as a brake in the political progress of the whole country. Feudalism was thus encouraged to the extent that it was compatible with colonial administration. Indirect Rule was rigidly enforced and it offered the excuse to exclude the north from the stream of progress. Thus the first legislative council set up in 1922 could only pass laws for the South while the governor-general ruled the North through proclamations. The South was subsequently divided into three parts and later into two, the Eastern and Western Provinces.

The Richards Constitution introduced in 1946 hardened regionalism that had been nurtured by the colonial administration. It gave Nigeria a federal constitution with strong regional powers. It further provided the North with a House of Chiefs to preserve the hereditary autocracy. The Northern region alone contained three-quarters of the land area and about half of the population. The calculated imbalance within the federation preserved Northern political domination and provided the colonial power with a lever for political manipulation.

A constitutional crisis erupted in 1953 over the timing of self-government. The Action Group wanted it "as soon as possible" while the Northern Peoples Congress desired it "as soon as practicable." The Sardauna of Sokoto regretted that "the mistake of 1914 had come to light"—a reference to the amalgamation.[82] The North contemplated secession but refrained because of (a) the future loss of customs duties that were only collected at the ports, and (b) the possibility that the South could deny the use of the ports to the North.

The dispute between the Action Group and the Northern Peoples Congress led to riots in Kano in which 52 persons, mostly Eastern Nigerians, were killed and wounded. A Commission of Inquiry found that the riots were "so spontaneous, so violent, and so widespread that

80.   A. Bello, *My Life* (Cambridge, 1962), p. 135.
81.   11 February 1950.
82.   House of Representative Debates, 1 April 1953, p. 1053.

no right-thinking person could assign to them short-term causes." It added that the influx of Ibos into Hausaland had changed the landscape of Kano into a community which "represents the meeting place of two contending cultures." It then added:

> The seeds of the trouble which broke out in Kano on May 16 (1953) have their counterparts still in the ground. It could happen again, and only a realization and acceptance of the underlying causes can remove the danger of re-occurrence.[83]

The Action Group–Northern Peoples Congress dispute resurfaced the hatred for the Eastern Nigerians, for they had earlier been massacred on a small scale in riots in Jos in 1945.

The 1954 constitution conferred more powers on the regions. The West threatened to secede over the separation of Lagos from it and was only deterred by a strict warning from Oliver Lyttelton, the British colonial secretary. At the 1957 Constitutional Conference, the East and West demanded self-government for 1958 but the North wanted it in 1959. Independence was granted in 1960.[84]

Nigeria attained independence with high hopes that the sleeping giant of Africa was finally awake. Regrettably, political debates were never directed to the widening gap between the foreign businessmen and the local people, the local elites and the ordinary people (the workers and peasants), the towns and the villages. Debates centred around the accumulation of power by a particular region or a particular national group. The Willinck Minorities Commission appointed by the colonial government to investigate the fears of the minorities in 1958 recommended the creation of the Middle Belt and of the Midwest states. The latter was created but not the former and the Northern regional government had to use troops and the police to suppress the demand for a Tiv state.

A dispute within the Action Group in 1962 led to the declaration of a state of emergency and the taking over of the regional government by the federal government.[85] An attempt to take a census in 1962 ended in controversy. A repeat performance that produced the figures 30 million, 12 million, and 10 million respectively for the North, East, and West

83.   Report of the Kano Disturbances, para. 109, p. 21.

84.   *See* A. H. M. Kirk-Green, "The Peoples of Nigeria: The Cultural Background for the Crisis," 66 *African Affairs*, no. 262, (January 1967), pp. 3–11; P. Amber, "Modernisation and Political Disintegration: Nigeria and the Ibos," 2 *JMAS* (1967), pp. 163–79.

85.   *See* Federal Supreme Court decision 187/1962; Davis, "Nigeria, Some Recent Decisions on the Nigerian Constitution," 11 *ICLQ*. (1962), pp. 912–936; *Akintola v. Aderemi*, AC (1963), pp. 614–633.

(including the Midwest) was even more controversial and increased the fear and resentment of "Northern domination," a threat that was supported by loose statements from certain Northern leaders that the North would rule the country forever. A suit brought by the Eastern Region which rejected the figures was dismissed on a technicality.[86] The federal elections of 1964, which were a straight fight between the Nigerian National Alliance (the Northern Peoples Congress and the Nigerian Democratic party) and the United Progressive Grand Alliance (the National Convention of Nigerian Citizens and the Action Group) brought more confusion. The harassment of UPGA candidates in the North led to the boycott of the elections by the UPGA and this only served to entrench the NPC more firmly in the North. The Nigerian President, N. Azikiwe, refused to invite the NNA to form the government at the centre but later compromised when the prime minister promised to form a broadly based government. The president was also motivated by the desire to maintain the unity of the country.

In 1965 the replacement of Professor Eni Njoku, an Eastern Nigerian, as vice-chancellor of the Lagos University by a Western Nigerian, Professor Biobaku, led to the resignation of Eastern Nigerian members of staff as well as most of the staff from the Western countries. It was seen as an unwarranted display of tribalism.

The Western regional elections of the same year were marked by the most glaring abuses that could be witnessed anywhere in parliamentary elections. The elections were openly rigged; some results were announced before the ballot papers were counted; some "pregnant" women delivered themselves of ballot papers in the voting booths and some boxes in predictable areas were destroyed.

Such was the discontent by the end of 1965 that most people prayed for a military takeover and wondered if the Nigerian army had become "an army of women." The Western Region, in particular, was in turmoil. This was the situation when the Commonwealth Prime Ministers Conference met early in Lagos in January 1966 to discuss the illegal seizure of independence by a white minority and racist regime in Southern Rhodesia. The last of the delegates, Archbishop Makarios, had not left when the army removed the civilian regime from power on 15 January 1966. Prime Minister T. Balewa, Premier S. L. A. Akintola, Premier A. Bello, Federal Finance Minister Okotie-Eboh and nine military officers (one from the East, three from the West, and five from

---

86.   *A. G. (Eastern Nigeria)* v. *A. G. (Federal Nigeria)* Journal of the Supreme Court 29 June 1964. *See also* S. A. Aluko, "How Many Nigerians? An Analysis of Nigeria's Census Problems 1901–63" 3 *JMAS* (1965), pp. 371–392.

the North) were killed.[87] The organisers who talked of "true Nigerianism in the Army" did not succeed in coming to power, having been out-maneuvered by Major-General Aguiyi-Ironsi who had them detained. The coup was however welcomed throughout the length and breadth of the country and by the major political parties and the national papers as an opportunity for a fresh start.[88]

Meanwhile, discontent was stirred up in the North by certain local and foreign elements who insinuated that the takeover was an Ibo coup and that the civilian victims were almost entirely from the North. The stage was set for the massacre of 3,000 Eastern Nigerians in Northern Nigeria in May 1966. In July, Northern military officers staged a coup in which 224 Eastern Nigerian officers and other ranks were killed over a period of two weeks. Lieutenant Colonel Gowon, as he then was, came to power in Lagos and although he initially saw no basis for unity decided subsequently to maintain the unity of the country.

An *ad hoc* constitutional conference met on 12 September 1966 and came close to agreeing on a loose form of association. The Northern delegation advocated a "number of autonomous states." The west and Lagos proposed a "Commonwealth of Nigeria . . . completely sovereign in all matters except those with respect to which responsibility is dele-gated to the Council of State," if there was no agreement on federalism. The midwest stuck to federalism. The North, however, withdrew its memorandum within a few weeks and the conference was brought to an end. During the weekend starting on 29 September 1966 and for a fort-night after, there were wholesale massacres of Eastern Nigerians, par-ticularly Ibos, in Northern Nigeria. Colin Legum, a Commonwealth correspondent for the *Observer* newspaper wrote:

> After a fortnight, the scene in the Eastern Region continues to be reminiscent of the in-gathering of exiles into Israel after the end of the last war. The parallel is not fanciful. Men, women and children arrived with arms and legs broken, hands hacked off, mouths split open. Pregnant women were cut open and the unborn children killed.[89]

About 2 million Eastern Nigerians returned to Eastern Nigeria to

---

87. *See* January 15, 1966, *Before and After* (Government Printer, Enugu, 1967) appendix IV being the list of officers killed as released by the Federal Government.

88. *See*, e.g., *West African Pilot* (19 January 1966), *Daily Times* (18 January 1966) and *Morning Post* (19 January 1966); D. I. O. Ewelukwa, "The Constitu-tional Aspects of the Military Takeover in Nigeria," *The Nigerian Law Journal*, vol. 2(1) (1967).

89. *The Observer* (London), 16 October 1966. *See also Time Magazine* (USA), 7 October 1966.

seek refuge and had to be cared for by their near and distant relations and the government of the Eastern Region. Centrifugal tendencies were, for the first time, set in motion in the Eastern Region by the in-gathering of the returnees.

A meeting of the military governors held in Ghana on 4-5 January 1967 arrived at an agreement to preserve confederal links but this was later repudiated by Lagos, which favoured closer links. The federal budget for April 1967 made no special provisions for the increased population of the Eastern Region, which replied by appropriating federal revenues emanating from the East in order to care for the refugees.

In May 1967 the military leaders of the Western and Midwestern Regions and their "leaders of thought" came out in support of a confederal arrangement but the East continued to drift toward secession. A joint meeting of the Consultative Assembly and the Advisory Committee of Chiefs and Elders authorised the military governor, Lieutenant Colonel Ojukwu, on 27 May 1967 to secede at "the earliest practicable date." On 28 May 1967 Lieutenant Colonel Gowon assumed supreme command, declared a state of emergency, divided the country into twelve states, and imposed a total blockade on the Eastern Region. On 30 May, Eastern Nigeria seceded and declared itself Biafra and on 6 July, Nigeria commenced a war of reunification which was successfully concluded on 12 January 1970 when the rump of the Biafran leadership surrendered.[90]

B. *Self-determination for the Biafrans.* The Biafrans are, as a people, entitled to self-determination. The crucial question is: What sort of self-determination are they entitled to in international law?

90.   See the resolution of the joint assembly and the Declaration of Independence in appendices A and B, reproduced in the Republic of Biafra, Proclamations (Enugu 1968); International Legal Materials Vol. 6, 665. For a short summary of events from January 1966–December 1967 see G. Birch and D. S. George: *Biafra, the Case for Independence* (London 1967). See further on the historical background: *The Problem of Unity, the Case for Eastern Nigeria* (Enugu 1966); *Nigeria Crisis* Vol. 7 (Enugu 1967); *The Meeting of the Supreme Military Council* (Enugu 1967); A. Nwankwo and S. U. Ifejika: *The Making of a Nation,* Biafra (London 1969); F. Foresythe: *The Biafra Story* (Penguin 1969); J. D. Chick, "Nigeria at War" *Current History,* February 1968; W. A. E. Skurnik, "Nigeria in Crisis", *Current History,* March 1967; B. J. Dudley, "Nigeria's Civil War" *The Round Table,* January 1968; C. O. Ojukwu: *Random Thoughts, Biafra* (Harper and Row, New York etc. 1969): "Nigeria/Biafra, Armed Conflict with a vengeance," *The Review of the International Commission of Jurists,* No. 2, June 1969; S. K. Panter-Brick, "The Right of Self-determination, Its Application to Nigeria" 44, *International Affairs,* April 1968; K. W. Post, "Is there a Case for Biafra?" 44 *International Affairs* (1968) 28; Conor C. O'Brien, "The Tragedy of Biafra," the *New York Times Review of Books,* 21 December, 1967; C. O. Ojukwu; *Biafra, Selected Speeches with Journals of Events* (New York, 1969); C. O. Ojukwu, *The Ahiara Declaration* (Geneva, 1969); T. N. Tamuno, "Separatist Agitations in Nigeria," 8(4) *JMAS,* December 1970), pp. 563–604.

We have already pointed out that the manifestation of self-determination should take other principles of international law, such as sovereignty, into account. It should also have regard to the factual situation. As far back as May through October 1966 the relevant manifestation of the principle to the Biafrans could have been independence if it accorded with the wishes of the people. Denied human rights in other parts of the country, including the right to live, the Biafrans were entitled to secure their very existence if they could do so by secession. A complicating element is a possible finding that the massacres were not authorised and were in fact condemned by the authorities. The fact that the culprits were never tried indicates that, if the massacres were not actually authorised, they were out of control. The large number of persons affected (over 30,000 killed and 2 million refugees created) could have been a proper concern of the international community. The justification for the independence of Biafra at the time could have been the finding that the Biafrans appear to have been rejected by the country to which they belonged.

As time elapsed and after the Eastern Nigerians were cleared from Northern Nigeria, the federal government once again asserted its authority over the whole country. On the eve of secession, Lagos warned that stern measures would be taken to quell any rebellion; this it was entitled to do. How could self-determination for Biafra be manifested in view of Enugu's determination to secede and Lagos's even greater determination to maintain the country's territorial integrity?

Had Biafra succeeded, it would have been hardly worthwhile arguing that it ought not to have succeeded, just as it is hardly worthwhile to maintain now that it ought not to have been crushed. A state is entitled to preserve its territorial integrity by the use of reasonable force. Secession is generally frowned upon especially in Africa, whose modern states contain different national groups with the possible exception of Somalia. The independence variant of self-determination for these nationalities would only lead to increased confusion and weakness. Africa needs greater unity and integration, not disintegration. Such unity and integration must, however, be based on a foundation of strict respect for fundamental human rights and not a denial of them.

The recognition of Nigeria's right to maintain territorial integrity is bound up with its responsibility to respect the human rights of its subjects. The secession of Biafra was the consequence of the gross violation of the human rights of Eastern Nigerians who had been the foremost advocates of national unity. The irreconcilable views of Lagos and Enugu set the stage for the interplay of force. The duty of third states in such a situation was not to increase the yield of force but to minimise it by maintaining strict neutrality. The prohibition in the Charter of the United Nations against "the threat or use of force against the territorial integrity or political independence of any State, or in any manner inconsistent with the Purposes of the United Nations"[91] extends to the infusion of arms by third states into a domestic conflict. Furthermore, the obligation that "All Members shall settle their international disputes by peaceful means in such manner that international peace and security, and justice, are not endangered"[92] implies that third states should encourage a member state to settle its internal disputes by peaceful rather than violent means. External involvement was made more questionable by the apparent racial bias, for the suppliers were whites while the victims were blacks. Had they belonged to the same race, the suppliers might have brought their weight firmly in favour of a peaceful, rather than military, settlement regardless of their economic or ideological interests. A limited police action may call for reasonable aid from third states but a conflict deeply rooted in political cleavages calls for their strict neutrality.

The law takes note of a *fait accompli* such as has been brought about by the Nigerian Civil War. The Biafrans must reconcile themselves to an exercise of self-determination that is compatible with the existing situation in Nigeria and Africa generally.

It is desirable to remove the causes that impel a people to wish to secede. The need to have a constitutional arrangement that accords with the wishes of the people cannot be exaggerated. Once a constitution has been agreed upon, it should be strictly respected and provisions made for the changes that a fast-developing society may need. Greater political integration, desirable as it may be, calls for specific measures that promote it and condemns actions that negate it. The right to integrity must be considered strictly in terms of the responsibility that accompanies it. The justification for the forcible reintegration of the former Biafrans must include their enjoyment of full rights of citizenship. The great needs have been correctly identified as rehabilitation, reconciliation, and reconstruction. The considerable natural and human resources of Nigeria could, under a leadership that encourages hard work and self-reliance and eschews external or internal exploitation of the people, provide the material for building a just society. The inventiveness and ingenuity of the Biafrans in their adversity are examples

91. Article 1(4).
92. Article 1(3).

of self-reliant efforts that can bring the full benefits of independence to African states.

The Nigerian Civil War underlines both the desirability for African states to ensure strict respect for the fundamental human rights of the people and the risks of secession by a minority against the determined opposition of the majority. For the principle of territorial integrity to be meaningful, it must prevent the gross violations of the human rights of any section of the population.

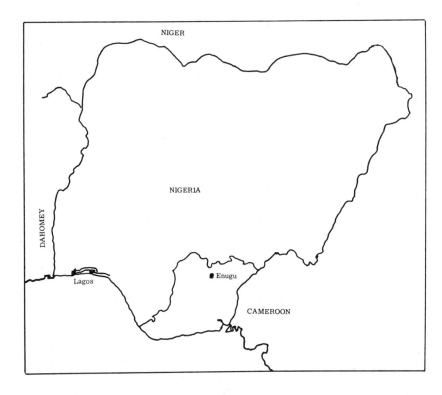

7. Conclusion

For all groups within states clamouring for self-determination, the question is: Are the members of the said group enjoying the rights of full citizens in a way fully to enhance their political, economic, and cultural development? Are the members of the group enjoying fundamental human rights?

A people whose development is stultified by the official policy of the state to which they belong do not enjoy the right of self-determination. A good example of such a people is the non-white population of South Africa who are discriminated against and denied basic human rights.

A people who are threatened with extermination and are cabined and confined within unreasonable limits in a country to which they are supposed to belong cannot be said to be enjoying self-determination. Such a group may exercise self-determination up to the point of secession if they are able and willing to do so. The justification for this extreme step rests both on the denial of human rights and the dim prospects for their future development.

As repeated above, self-determination does not necessarily involve independence. It is when considered from this limited standpoint that the principle is condemned for its fissiparous effect. Self-determination is also exercised through merger, association, local autonomy, self-government, or other form of participation that reflects the wishes of the people. Universal adult suffrage is an important attribute and remains the cornerstone of modern democracy.

In Cyprus the only constitution that was acceptable to the Greek and Turkish communities was one that shared representation, appointments, and other benefits in the proportion of 3:7 between the Turks and Greeks corresponding roughly to the population ratio. In the armed forces the ratio is 4:6. The population of 600,000 is made up of 80 percent Greeks and 18 percent Turks. The constitution provides for a Greek president and a Turkish vice-president; in departments and corporations, the head and his assistant must come from different communities. The official languages are Greek and Turkish and Greek and Turkish flags may be flown alongside the Cypriot on national holidays. Either the Greek-Cypriot president or the Turkish-Cypriot vice-president may veto a decision of the Council of Ministers.[93] Although Professor de Smith describes the arrangement as "an appropriate setting for the Constitutionalist in Wonderland"[94] yet it points to the manner in which communities may participate in the exercise of self-determination. Partition is wholly unacceptable to the Greeks and *enosis* (union with Greece) is rejected by the Turks. The stringent guarantes given to the Turks and the constitution itself broke down in 1964 and for a period the Turks played no effective part in government. This emphasises the importance of harmony between different communities in a state besides

93. *See also* Cmd. 679, the memorandum setting out the Agreed Foundation for the Final Settlement of the Problem of Cyprus (London, 19 February 1959).
94. de Smith, "Constitutionalism in The Commonwealth Today," 4 *Malaya Law Reports* (1962), p. 210.

constitutional guarantees. The best solution is not one that hamstrings the majority and concretises the minority but one that ensures that the minority plays a fair role as part of the whole.

Self-determination, however, constitutes a threat to irresponsible majorities that have scant regard for the rights of the minorities. It is also a threat to reckless minorities that seek to exercise rights wholly disproportionate to their numbers and to those who wish to contravene territorial integrity without having adequate reasons for doing so, for the principle is in a way complementary to sovereignty.

Not every slight issue of self determination within a state is a matter of international concern; it has to be of a magnitude sufficient to attract the attention of the international community, such as a demand or denial that affects world's peace and stability. In such circumstances, a claim of domestic jurisdiction will not avail to exclude legitimate international concern.

The basic objective of the principle of self-determination is the achievement of good government without discrimination as to race, colour, creed, or sex. It is recognised that force may be a potent factor in its realisation, denial, or abuse within states but the wish of the international lawyer is the approximation of international right to international might so that no nation or people, dependent or independent, are denied the right of self-determination.[95]

95.　See also chapter 8.

Conclusions

The principle of self-determination developed from a philosophical to a political concept in international relations and has now matured into a fundamental principle of positive international law. It has developed recently as an aspect of human rights belonging to the group rather than to the individual. The Covenant of the League of Nations made no express provision for it but the idea was embodied in the mandate system and in the minority treaties. In the *Aaland Islands* case[1] the committee of jurists, though denying that self-determination was then a legal principle, held that an international dispute arising from it might be taken out of the sphere of domestic jurisdiction.

Any doubt that might have persisted about the legal nature of the principle under the League was removed by the Charter of the United Nations which made express reference to it in Articles 1 and 55. It further embodied the idea in the provisions for non-self-governing territories. Taking note of this and other developments in international law, Judge Moreno Quintana referred in his dissenting judgment in the *Right of Passage* case[2] to "the age of independence"[3] and to the fact that "the Charter made legal provision to cover the independence of non-self-governing territories."[4] In the *South-West Africa* cases,[5] Judge Nervo,

1. *LNOJ*, no. 3 (October 1920).
2. *ICJ Rep.* (1960), p. 6.
3. Ibid., p. 95.
4. Ibid., p. 96.
5. *ICJ Rep.* (1966).

dissenting, expressed the belief that the concept of equality and freedom "will inspire the vision and the conduct of peoples the world over until the goal of self-determination and independence is reached."[6] He views the mandate system as "a gradual process of self-determination" intended to enable the peoples to stand by themselves in the modern world.

Whereas in 1920 the principle could be found only in a few treaties, the practice of many states now confirms its legal nature. Thus the Anglo-Egyptian Treaty (1953), the Franco-Algerian Treaty of Evian (1962), the Southeast Asia Treaty Organisation, and more especially the Charter of the United Nations recognise the principle of self-determination. It is also embodied in the constitutions of states such as the Soviet Union (1936), France (1958), the Congo (Brazzaville, 1963), and the Central African Republic (1962). It has been affirmed in resolutions of the Organisation of African Unity, by the conferences of non-aligned states, the World Conference of Lawyers on World Peace Through Law, and the International Commission of Jurists.

The recognition of the principle as one of law in recent times has come about principally in the context of decolonisation in which the United Nations has played a pre-eminent role. Under the pressure of self-determination, many former colonies have since 1945 gained independence and joined the ranks of sovereign states; others have voluntarily associated themselves with the former colonial power. The major colonial powers have, as a matter of policy, devised and developed techniques to accommodate the desire of the peoples for self-determination. The pace was accelerated both by the United Nations and by the pressure from the dependent peoples themselves who claimed to be entitled, as of right, to a government of their choice.

Communist writers, as well as those from the non-aligned states, most of which are former colonies, treat self-determination as a fundamental principle of international law, although there may not be unanimity on its definition. An increasing number of Western writers subscribe to the view that self-determination has developed into a principle of international law. The main legal problems connected with it are the definition of the legitimate "self" that determines and the solutions involved in the principle. The "self" represents an identifiable group of people having common legitimate aims. Clearly, a group that covers the population of a state is entitled to self-determination. But it may also represent the populations of two or more states. It may even represent part of the population of a state; in this case, however, the more substantial the

6.   Ibid., p. 465.

group, the easier it may be to recognise their right to self-determination. The activities covered by the principle are primarily political but they may also have other characteristics, such as economic or cultural. As to the solutions covered by the principle, it is important to note that politically, it need not lead irresistibly to independence or secession, for it may also be manifested through association, self-government, merger, local autonomy, or other form of participation in government that accords with the wishes of the people. It follows that the moment a territory achieves self-determination is not necessarily when it gains independence, though this is the case in many instances, but when the government accords with the wishes of the people and they desire no alternative. Such a moment in international relations arrives on the attainment of the relations stated above.

Economic self-determination guarantees the right of states to control their economic future but subject to the rules of international law. The advantages of large units become more evident in this sphere for the concept is more meaningful to them than to small or weak ones. The emphasis in the United Nations on interdependence and the economic development of underdeveloped countries demonstrates the importance of economic self-determination. The European Community is an expression of the principle among Western European states. Although it now covers the economic field mainly, it is hoped that the community will develop political links as well, which would be a more significant manifestation of self-determination.

The basic objective of the principle is to guarantee that all peoples have a government of their choice that responds to their political, economic, and cultural needs. The principle aims at the elimination of external or internal domination and the creation of the proper atmosphere in which individuals have the possibility of enjoying fundamental human rights. It seeks to impose certain minimum standards of administration in all states regardless of race, creed, colour, or sex.

Self-determination is not a juggernaut that tramples upon all other principles of international law. Far from being an absolute right, its exercise must have due regard for other principles, such as sovereignty, territorial integrity, and fundamental human rights. There may be borderline cases but the wishes of the people and good government should dominate. The manifestation must also have due regard to factual situations, such as economic viability, geographical position, strategic considerations, political consequences, and divergencies or similarities among peoples.

As colonies and dependent territories fade away, the principle will continue to be relevant to peoples in metropolitan territories. Discontent with governments resulting from the deprivation of human rights, discrimination or underdevelopment may lead to claims for self-determination in the form of independence or to changes in constitutional relations. Provided the conditions for international concern are satisfied, the community of nations should not be inhibited from intervention by the domestic-jurisdiction principle. There is a case for the setting up of an international committee to investigate serious claims of, or denials of, self-determination worthy of international concern. Such a committee should then advise the United Nations on proper cases for intervention and the possible remedies. If the International Covenant on Civil and Political Rights becomes effective, the Human Rights Committee could be usefully vested with this special responsibility.

Self-determination need not be viewed as having ominous and disruptive implications, for it may lead to wider unity such as the merger or close association of neighbouring states in accordance with the wishes of the people. Indeed, the continuing improvement in the standards of administration is likely to diminish differences and facilitate closer relations between states. States having a common cultural, religious, or other background, particularly common ideas of human rights and the rule of law, will find that it is in their own interest to draw closer to one another. Many of the excolonial states are weak and poor. An exercise of self-determination that creates wider unity will be in their best interests.

The fact that self-determination is now an international legal principle does not mean that every minor claim or denial of the right is a matter for international concern. Rather a situation that seriously reflects the denial or claim of the right, particularly if international peace and security are thereby threatened, is the proper concern of the international community. In such situations the United Nations should, in the words of Article 1(2) of the United Nations Charter, endeavour "[t]o develop friendly relations among nations based on respect for the principle of equal rights and self-determination of peoples, and to take other appropriate measures to strengthen universal peace."

Appendixes

Article 22 of the Covenant of the League of Nations

To those colonies and territories which as a consequence of the late war have ceased to be under the sovereignty of the States which formerly governed them and which are inhabited by peoples not yet able to stand by themselves under the strenuous conditions of the modern world, there should be applied the principle that the well-being and development of such peoples form a sacred trust of civilisation and that securities for the performance of this trust should be embodied in this Covenant.

The best method of giving practical effect to this principle is that the tutelage of such peoples should be entrusted to advanced nations who by reason of their resources, their experience or their geographical position can best undertake this responsibility, and who are willing to accept it, and that this tutelage should be exercised by them as Mandatories on behalf of the League.

The character of the mandate must differ according to the stage of development of the people, the geographical situation of the territory, its economic conditions and other similar circumstances.

Certain communities formerly belonging to the Turkish Empire have reached a stage of development where their existence as independent nations can be provisionally recognised subject to the rendering of administrative advice and assistance by a Mandatory until such time as they are able to stand alone. The wishes of these communities must be a principal consideration in the selection of the Mandatory.

Other peoples, especially those of Central Africa, are at such a stage that the Mandatory must be responsible for the administration of the territory under conditions which will guarantee freedom of conscience and religion, subject only to the maintenance of public order and morals, the prohibition of abuses such as the slave trade, the arms traffic and the liquor traffic, and the prevention of the establishment of fortifications or military and naval bases and of military training of the natives for other than police purposes and the defence of the territory, and will also secure equal opportunities for the trade and commerce of other Members of the League.

There are territories such as South-West Africa and certain of the South Pacific islands, which, owing to the sparseness of their population, or their small size, or their remoteness from the centres of civilisation, or their geographical contiguity to the territory of the Mandatory, and other circumstances, can be best administered under the laws of the Mandatory as integral portions of its territory, subject to the safeguards above mentioned in the interests of the indigenous population.

In every case of mandate, the Mandatory shall render to the Council an annual report in reference to the territory committed to its charge.

The degree of authority, control, or administration to be exercised by the Mandatory shall, if not previously agreed upon by the Members of the League, be explicitly defined in each case by the Council.

A permanent Commission shall be constituted to receive and examine the annual reports of the Mandatories and to advise the Council on all matters relating to the observance of the mandates.

APPENDIX B
Mandate for German South-West Africa (C-Mandate)

The Council of the League of Nations:

WHEREAS by Article 119 of the Treaty of Peace with Germany signed at Versailles on June 28th, 1919, Germany renounced in favour of the Principal Allied and Associated Powers all her rights over her overseas possessions, including therein German South-West Africa; and

WHEREAS the Principal Allied and Associated Powers agreed that, in accordance with Article 22, Part A (Covenant of the League of Nations) of the said Treaty, a Mandate should be conferred upon His Britannic Majesty to be exercised on his behalf by the Government of the Union of South Africa to Administer the territory afore-mentioned, and have proposed that the Mandate should be formulated in the following terms; and

WHEREAS His Britannic Majesty, for and on behalf of the Government of the Union of South Africa, has agreed to accept the Mandate in respect of the said territory and has undertaken to exercise it on behalf of the League of Nations in accordance with the following provisions; and

WHEREAS, by the afore-mentioned Article, paragraph 8, it is provided that the degree of authority, control or administration to be exercised by the Mandatory not having been previously agreed upon by the Members of the League, shall be explicitly defined by the Council of the League of Nations:

Confirming the said Mandate, defines its terms as follows:

Article 1
The territory over which a Mandate is conferred upon His Britannic Majesty and on behalf of the Government of the Union of South Africa (hereinafter called the Mandatory) comprises the territory which formerly constituted the German Protectorate of South-West Africa.

Article 2
The Mandatory shall have full power of administration and legislation over the territory subject to the present Mandate as an integral portion of the Union of South Africa, and may apply the laws of the Union of South Africa to the territory, subject to such local modifications as circumstances may require.

The Mandatory shall promote to the utmost the material and moral well-being and the social progress of the inhabitants of the territory subject to the present Mandate.

Article 3

The Mandatory shall see that the slave trade is prohibited, and that no forced labour is permitted, except for essential public works and services, and then only for adequate remuneration.

The Mandatory shall also see that the traffic in arms and ammunition is controlled in accordance with principles analogous to those laid down in the Convention relating to the control of the arms traffic, signed on September 10, 1919, or in any convention amending the same.

The supply of intoxicating spirits and beverages to the natives shall be prohibited.

Article 4

The military training of natives, otherwise than for purposes of internal police and the local defence of the territory, shall be prohibited. Furthermore, no military or naval bases shall be established or fortifications erected in the territory.

Article 5

Subject to the provisions of any local law for the maintenance of public order and public morals, the Mandatory shall ensure in the territory freedom of conscience and the free exercise of all forms of worship, and shall allow all missionaries, nationals of any State Member of the League of Nations, to enter into, travel and reside in the territory for the purpose of prosecuting their calling.

Article 6

The Mandatory shall make to the Council of the League of Nations an annual report to the satisfaction of the Council, containing full information with regard to the territory, and indicating the measures taken to carry out the obligations assumed under Articles 2, 3, 4 and 5.

Article 7

The consent of the Council of the League of Nations is required for any modification of the terms of the present mandate.

The Mandatory agrees that, if any dispute whatever should arise between the Mandatory and another Member of the League of Nations relating to the interpretation or the application of the provisions of the Mandate, such dispute, if it cannot be settled by negotiation, shall be submitted to the Permanent Court of International Justice provided for by Article 14 of the Covenant of the League of Nations.

The present declaration shall be deposited in the archives of the

League of Nations. Certified copies shall be forwarded by the Secretary-General of the League of Nations to all Powers signatories of the Treaty of Peace with Germany.
Made at Geneva the 17th day of December, 1920.

APPENDIX C
Declaration Regarding Non-Self-Governing Territories
(United Nations Charter)

Article 73
Members of the United Nations which have or assume responsibilities for the administration of territories whose peoples have not yet attained a full measure of self-government recognize the principle that the interests of the inhabitants of these territories are paramount, and accept as a sacred trust the obligation to promote to the utmost, within the system of international peace and security established by the present Charter, the well-being of the inhabitants of these territories, and, to this end:

a) to ensure, with due respect for the culture of the peoples concerned, their political, economic, social, and educational advancement, their just treatment, and their protection against abuses;

b) to develop self-government, to take due account of the political aspirations of the peoples, and to assist them in the progressive development of their free political institutions, according to the particular circumstances of each territory and its peoples and their varying stages of advancement

c) to further international peace and security;

d) to promote constructive measures of development, to encourage research, and to cooperate with one another and, when and where appropriate, with specialized international bodies with a view to the practical achievement of the social, economic and scientific purposes set forth in this Article; and

e) to transmit regularly to the Secretary-General for information purposes, subject to such limitations as security and constitutional considerations may require, statistical and other information of a technical nature relating to economic, social and educational conditions in the territories for which they are respectively responsible other than those territories to which Chapters XII and XIII apply.

Article 74

Members of the United Nations also agree that their policy in respect of the territories to which this Chapter applies, no less than in respect of their metropolitan areas, must be based on the general principle of good-neighbourliness, due account being taken of the interests and well-being of the rest of the world, in social, economic, and commercial matters.

APPENDIX D
International Trusteeship

Article 75

The United Nations shall establish under its authority an international trusteeship system for the administration and supervision of such territories as may be placed thereunder by subsequent individual agreements. These territories are hereinafter referred to as trust territories.

Article 76

The basic objectives of the trusteeship system, in accordance with the Purposes of the United Nations laid down in Article 1 of the present Charter, shall be:

a) to further international peace and security;

b) to promote the political, economic, social, and educational advancement of the inhabitants of the trust territories, and their progressive development towards self-government or independence as may be appropriate to the particular circumstances of each territory and its peoples and the freely expressed wishes of the peoples concerned, and as may be provided by the terms of each trusteeship agreement;

c) to encourage respect for human rights and for fundamental freedoms for all without distinction as to race, sex, language, or religion, and to encourage recognition of the interdependence of the peoples of the world; and

d) to ensure equal treatment in social, economic, and commercial matters for all Members of the United Nations and their nationals, and also equal treatment for the latter in the administration of justice, without prejudice to the attainment of the foregoing objectives and subject to the provisions of Article 80.

Article 77

(1) The trusteeship system shall apply to such territories in the following categories as may be placed thereunder by means of trusteeship agreements:

a) territories now held under mandate;

b) territories which may be detached from enemy states as a result of the Second World War; and

c) territories voluntarily placed under the system by states responsible for their administration.

(2) It will be a matter for subsequent agreement as to which territories in the foregoing categories will be brought under the trusteeship system and upon what terms.

Article 78

The trusteeship system shall not apply to territories which have become Members of the United Nations, relationship among which shall be based on respect for the principle of sovereign equality.

Article 79

The terms of trusteeship for each territory to be placed under the trusteeship system, including any alteration or amendment, shall be agreed upon by the states directly concerned, including the mandatory power in the case of territories held under mandate by a member of the United Nations, and shall be approved as provided for in Articles 83 and 85.

Article 80

(1) Except as may be agreed upon in individual trusteeship agreements, made under Articles 77, 79 and 81, placing each territory under the trusteeship system, and until such agreements have been concluded, nothing in this Chapter shall be construed in or of itself to alter in any manner the rights whatsoever of any states or any peoples or the terms of existing international instruments to which Members of the United Nations may respectively be parties.

Article 81

The trusteeship agreement shall in each case include the terms under which the trust territory will be administered and designate the authority which will exercise the administration of the trust territory. Such authority, hereinafter called the administering authority, may be one or more states or the Organization itself.

Article 82

There may be designated, in any trusteeship agreement, a strategic area or areas which may include part or all of the trust territory to which the agreement applies, without prejudice to any special agreement or agreements made under Article 43.

Article 83

(1) All functions of the United Nations relating to strategic areas, including the approval of the terms of the trusteeship agreements and of their alteration or amendment, shall be exercised by the Security Council.

(2) The basic objectives set forth in Article 76 shall be applicable to the people of each strategic area.

(3) The Security Council shall, subject to the provisions of the trusteeship agreements and without prejudice to security considerations, avail itself of the assistance of the Trusteeship Council to perform those functions of the United Nations under the trusteeship system relating to political, economic, social, and educational matters in the strategic areas.

Article 84

It shall be the duty of the administering authority to ensure that the trust territory shall play its part in the maintenance of international peace and security. To this end the administering authority may make use of volunteer forces, facilities, and assistance from the trust territory in carrying out the obligations towards the Security Council undertaken in this regard by the administering authority, as well as for local defence and the maintenance of law and order within the trust territory.

Article 85

(1) The functions of the United Nations with regard to trusteeship agreements for all areas not designated as strategic, including the approval of the terms of the trusteeship agreements and of their alteration or amendment, shall be exercised by the General Assembly.

(2) The Trusteeship Council, operating under the authority of the General Assembly, shall assist the General Assembly in carrying out these functions.

APPENDIX E

The Universal Declaration of Human Rights
Adopted by the General Assembly of the United
Nations on 10 December 1948

PREAMBLE

WHEREAS recognition of the inherent dignity and of the equal and inalienable rights of all members of the human family is the foundation of freedom, justice and peace in the world,

WHEREAS disregard and contempt for human rights have resulted in barbarous acts which have outraged the conscience of mankind, and the advent of a world in which human beings shall enjoy freedom of speech and belief and freedom from fear and want has been proclaimed as the highest aspiration of the common people,

WHEREAS it is essential, if man is not to be compelled to have recourse, as a last resort, to rebellion against tyranny and oppression, that human rights should be protected by the rule of law,

WHEREAS it is essential to promote the development of friendly relations between nations,

WHEREAS the peoples of the United Nations have in the Charter reaffirmed their faith in fundamental human rights, in the dignity and worth of the human person and in the equal rights of men and women and have determined to promote social progress and better standards of life in larger freedom,

WHEREAS Member States have pledged themselves to achieve, in co-operation with the United Nations, the promotion of universal respect for and observance of human rights and fundamental freedoms,

WHEREAS a common understanding of these rights and freedoms is of the greatest importance for the full realization of this pledge,
Now, therefore,

THE GENERAL ASSEMBLY PROCLAIMS

THIS UNIVERSAL DECLARATION OF HUMAN RIGHTS as a common standard of achievement for all peoples and all nations, to the end that every individual and every organ of society, keeping this Declaration constantly in mind, shall strive by teaching and education to promote respect for these rights and freedoms and by progressive measures, national and international, to secure their universal and effective recognition and observance, both among the peoples of Member States themselves and among the peoples of territories under their jurisdiction.

Article 1
All human beings are born free and equal in dignity and rights. They are endowed with reason and conscience and should act towards one another in a spirit of brotherhood.

Article 2
Everyone is entitled to all the rights and freedoms set forth in this Declaration, without distinction of any kind, such as race, colour, sex, language, religion, political or other opinion, national or social origin, property, birth or other status.

Furthermore, no distinction shall be made on the basis of the political, jurisdictional or international status of the country or territory to which a person belongs, whether it be independent, trust, non-self-governing or under any other limitation of sovereignty.

Article 3
Everyone has the right to life, liberty and security of person.

Article 4
No one shall be held in slavery or servitude; slavery and the slave trade shall be prohibited in all their forms.

Article 5
No one shall be subjected to torture or to cruel, inhuman or degrading treatment or punishment.

Article 6
Everyone has the right to recognition everywhere as a person before the law.

Article 7
All are equal before the law and are entitled without any discrimination to equal protection of the law. All are entitled to equal protection against any discrimination in violation of this Declaration and against any incitement to such discrimination.

Article 8
Everyone has the right to an effective remedy by the competent national tribunals for acts violating the fundamental rights granted him by the constitution or by law.

Article 9
No one shall be subjected to arbitrary arrest detention or exile.

Article 10
Everyone is entitled in full euality to a fair and public hearing by an independent and impartial tribunal, in the determination of his rights and obligations and of any criminal charge against him.

Article 11
(1) Everyone charged with a penal offence has the right to be presumed innocent until proved guilty according to law in a public trial at which he has had all the guarantees necessary for his defence.

(2) No one shall be held guilty of any penal offence on account of any act or omission which did not constitute a penal offence, under national or international law, at the time when it was committed. Nor shall a heavier penalty be imposed than the one that was applicable at the time the penal offence was committed.

Article 12
No one shall be subjected to arbitrary interference with his privacy, family, home or correspondence, nor to attacks upon his honour and

reputation. Everyone has the right to the protection of the law against such interference or attacks.

Article 13

(1) Everyone has the right to freedom of movement and residence within the borders of each state.

(2) Everyone has the right to leave any country, including his own, and to return to his country.

Article 14

(1) Everyone has the right to seek and to enjoy in other countries asylum from persecution.

(2) This right may not be invoked in the case of prosecutions genuinely arising from non-political crimes or from acts contrary to the purposes and principles of the United Nations.

Article 15

(1) Everyone has the right to a nationality.

(2) No one shall be arbitrarily deprived of his nationality nor denied the right to change his nationality.

Article 16

(1) Men and women of full age, without any limitation due to race, nationality or religion, have the right to marry and to found a family. They are entitled to equal rights as to marriage, during marriage and at its dissolution.

(2) Marriage shall be entered into only with the free and full consent of the intending spouses.

(3) The family is the natural and fundamental group unit of society and is entitled to protection by society and the State.

Article 17

(1) Everyone has the right to own property alone as well as in association with others.

(2) No one shall be arbitrarily deprived of his property.

Article 18

Everyone has the right to freedom of thought, conscience and religion; this right includes freedom to change his religion or belief, and freedom, either alone or in community with others and in public or private, to manifest his religion or belief in teaching, practice, worship and observance.

Article 19

Everyone has the right to freedom of opinion and expression; this right includes freedom to hold opinions without interference and to seek, receive and impart information and ideas through any media and regardless of frontiers.

Article 20

(1) Everyone has the right to freedom of peaceful assembly and association.

(2) No one may be compelled to belong to an association.

Article 21

(1) Everyone has the right to take part in the government of his country, directly or through freely chosen representatives.

(2) Everyone has the right of equal access to public service in his country.

(3) The will of the people shall be the basis of the authority of government; this will shall be expressed in periodic and genuine elections which shall be by universal and equal suffrage and shall be held by secret vote or by equivalent free voting procedures.

Article 22

Everyone, as a member of society, has the right to social security and is entitled to realization, through national effort and international co-operation and in accordance with the organisation and resources of each State, of the economic, social and cultural rights indispensable for his dignity and the free development of his personality.

Article 23

(1) Everyone has the right to work, to free choice of employment, to just and favourable conditions of work and to protection against unemployment.

(2) Everyone, without any discrimination, has the right to equal pay for equal work.

(3) Everyone who works has the right to just and favourable remuneration ensuring for himself and his family an existence worthy of human dignity, and supplemented, if necessary, by other means of social protection.

(4) Everyone has the right to form and to join trade unions for the protection of his interests.

Article 24

Everyone has the right to rest and leisure, including reasonable limitation of working hours and periodic holidays with pay.

Article 25

(1) Everyone has the right to a standard of living adequate for the health and well-being of himself and of his family, including food, clothing, housing and medical care and necessary social services, and the right to security in the event of unemployment, sickness, disability, widowhood, old age or other lack of livelihood in circumstances beyond his control.

(2) Motherhood and childhood are entitled to special care and assistance. All children, whether born in or out of wedlock, shall enjoy the same social protection.

Article 26

(1) Everyone has the right to education. Education shall be free, at least in the elementary and fundamental stages. Elementary education shall be compulsory. Technical and professional education shall be made generally available and higher education shall be equally accessible to all on the basis of merit.

(2) Education shall be directed to the full development of the human personality and to the strengthening of respect for human rights and fundamental freedoms. It shall promote understanding, tolerance and friendship among all nations, racial or religious groups, and shall further the activities of the United Nations for the maintenance of peace.

(3) Parents have a prior right to choose the kind of education that shall be given to their children.

Article 27

(1) Everyone has the right freely to participate in the cultural life of the community, to enjoy the arts and to share in scientific advancement and its benefits.

(2) Everyone has the right to the protection of the moral and material interests resulting from any scientific literary or artistic production of which he is the author.

Article 28

Everyone is entitled to a social and international order in which the rights and freedoms set forth in this Declaration can be fully realized.

Article 29

(1) Everyone has duties to the community in which alone the free and full development of his personality is possible.

(2) In the exercise of his rights and freedoms, everyone shall be subject only to such limitations as are determined by law solely for the purposes of securing due recognition and respect for the rights and freedoms of

others and of meeting the just requirements of morality, public order and the general welfare in a democratic society.

(3) These rights and freedoms may in no case be exercised contrary to the purposes and principles of the United Nations.

Article 30

Nothing in this Declaration may be interpreted as implying for any State, group or person any right to engage in any activity or to perform any act aimed at the destruction of any of the rights and freedoms set forth herein.

APPENDIX F

I. Programme of Action for the Full Implementation of the Declaration on the Granting of Independence to Colonial Countries and Peoples (Resolution 2621 (XXV))

THE GENERAL ASSEMBLY,

Having decided to hold a special commemorative session on the occasion of the tenth anniversary of the Declaration on the Granting of Independence to Colonial Countries and Peoples,

Considering that, by arousing world public opinion and promoting practical action for the speedy liquidation of colonialism in all its forms and manifestations, the Declaration has played and will continue to play an important role in assisting the peoples under colonial domination in their struggle for freedom and independence,

Conscious of the fact that, although many colonial countries and peoples have achieved freedom and independence in the last ten years, the system of colonialism continues to exist in many areas of the world,

Reaffirming that all peoples have the right to self-determination and independence and that the subjection of the peoples to alien domination constitutes a serious impediment to the maintenance of international peace and security and the development of peaceful relations among nations,

1. *Declares* the further continuation of colonialism in all its forms and manifestations a crime which constitutes a violation of the Charter of the United Nations, the Declaration on the Granting of Independence to Colonial Countries and Peoples and the principles of international law;

2. *Reaffirms* the inherent right of colonial peoples to struggle by all necessary means at their disposal against colonial Powers which suppress their aspiration for freedom and independence;

3. *Adopts* the following programme of action to assist in the full implementation of the Declaration on the Granting of Independence to Colonial Countries and Peoples:

(1) Member States shall do their utmost to promote, in the United Nations and the international institutions and organizations within the United Nations system, effective measures for the full implementation of the Declaration on the Granting of Independence to Colonial Countries and Peoples in all Trust Territories, Non-Self-Governing Territories and other colonial Territories, large and small, including the adoption by the Security Council of effective measures against Governments and régimes which engage in any form of repression of colonial peoples, which would seriously impede the maintenance of international peace and security.

(2) Member States shall render all necessary moral and material assistance to the peoples of colonial Territories in their struggle to attain freedom and independence.

(3) (*a*) Member States shall intensify their efforts to promote the implementation of the resolutions of the General Assembly and the Security Council relating to Territories under colonial domination.

(*b*) In this connexion, the General Assembly draws the attention of the Security Council to the need to continue to give special attention to the problems of southern Africa by adopting measures to assure the full implementation of General Assembly resolution 1514 (XV) of 14 December 1960 and its own resolutions, and in particular:

(i) To widen the scope of the sanctions against the illegal régime of Southern Rhodesia by declaring mandatory all the measures laid down in Article 41 of the Charter of the United Nations;

(ii) To give careful consideration to the question of imposing sanctions upon South Africa and Portugal, in view of their refusal to carry out the relevant decisions of the Security Council;

(iii) To give urgent consideration, with a view to promoting the speedy elimination of colonialism, to the question of imposing fully and unconditionally, under international supervision, an embargo on arms of all kinds to the Government of South Africa and the illegal régime of Southern Rhodesia.

(iv) To consider urgently the adoption of measures to prevent the supply of arms of all kinds to Portugal, as such arms enable that country to deny the right of self-determination and independence to the peoples of the Territories under its domination.

(c) Member States shall also intensify their efforts to oppose collaboration between the régimes of South Africa and Portugal and the illegal racist régime of Southern Rhodesia for the preservation of colonialism in southern Africa and to end the political, military, economic and other forms of aid received by the above-mentioned régimes, which enables them to persist in their policy of colonial domination.

(4) Member States shall wage a vigorous and sustained campaign against activities and practices of foreign economic, financial and other interests operating in colonial Territories for the benefit and on behalf of colonial Powers and their allies, as these constitute a major obstacle to the achievement of the goals embodied in resolution 1514 (XV). Member States shall consider the adoption of necessary steps to have their nationals and companies under their jurisdiction discontinue such activities and practices; these steps should also aim at preventing the systematic influx of foreign immigrants into colonial Territories, which disrupts the integrity and social, political and cultural unity of the peoples under colonial domination.

(5) Member States shall carry out a sustained and vigorous campaign against all military activities and arrangements by colonial Powers in Territories under their administration, as such activities and arrangements constitute an obstacle to the full implementation of resolution 1514 (XV).

(6) (a) All freedom-fighters under detention shall be treated in accordance with the relevant provisions of the Geneva Convention relative to the Treatment of Prisoners of War of 12 August 1949.

(b) The specialized agencies and international institutions associated with the United Nations shall intensify their activities related to the implementation of resolution 1514 (XV).

(c) Representatives of liberation movements shall be invited, whenever necessary, by the United Nations and other international organizations within the United Nations system to participate in an appropriate capacity in the proceedings of those organs relating to their countries.

(d) Efforts shall be intensified to provide increased educational opportunities for the inhabitants of Non-Self-Governing Territories. All States shall render greater assistance in this field, both individually through programmes in the countries concerned and collectively by contributions through the United Nations.

(7) All States shall undertake measures aimed at enhancing public awareness of the need for active assistance in the achievement of complete decolonization and, in particular, creating satisfactory conditions for activities by national and international non-governmental organizations in support of the peoples under colonial domination.

(8) The United Nations as well as all States shall intensify their efforts in the field of public information in the area of decolonization through all media, including publications, radio and television. Of special importance will be programmes relating to United Nations activities on decolonization, the situation in colonial Territories and the struggle being waged by colonial peoples and by the national liberation movements.

(9) The Special Committee on the Situation with regard to the Implementation of the Declaration on the Granting of Independence to Colonial Countries and Peoples shall continue to examine the full compliance of all States with the Declaration and with other relevant resolutions on the question of decolonization. The questiton of territorial size, geographical isolation and limited resources should in no way delay the implementation of the Declaration. Where resolution 1514 (XV) has not been fully implemented with regard to a given Territory, the General Assembly shall continue to bear responsibility for that Territory until such time as the people concerned had had an opportunity to exercise freely its right to self-determination and independence in accordance with the Declaration. The Special Committee is hereby directed:

(a) To continue to assist the General Assembly in finding the best ways and means for the final liquidation of colonialism;

(b) To continue to give special consideration to the views expressed orally or in written communications by representatives of the peoples in the colonial Territories;

(c) To continue to send visiting missions to the colonial Territories and to hold meetings at places where it can best obtain first-hand information on the situation in colonial Territories, as well as to continue to hold meetings away from Headquarters as appropriate;

(d) To assist the General Assembly in making arrangements, in co-operation with the administering Powers, for securing a United Nations presence in the colonial Territories to participate in the elaboration of the procedural measures for the implementation of the Declaration and to observe the final stages of the process of decolonization in the Territories;

(e) To prepare draft rules and regulations for visiting missions for approval by the General Assembly.

Resolution 2621 (XXV) was adopted by the General Assembly on 12 October 1970 by a vote of 86 in favour to 5 against (Australia, New Zealand, South Africa, United Kingdom, United States), with 15 abstentions (Austria, Belgium, Canada, Denmark, Finland, Iceland, Italy, Japan Luxembourg, Malawi, Netherlands, Norway, Spain, Swaziland, Sweden).

APPENDIX G

Declaration on Principles of International Law Concerning Friendly Relations and Co-operation Among States in Accordance with the Charter of the United Nations.
(Resolution 2625 (XXV) of 24 October 1970.)

The Principle of equal rights and self-determination of peoples.

By virtue of the principle of equal rights and self-determination of peoples enshrined in the Charter, all peoples have the right freely to determine, without external interference, their political status and to pursue their economic, social and cultural development, and every State has the duty to respect this right in accordance with the provisions of the Charter.

Every State has the duty to promote, through joint and separate action, the realization of the principle of equal rights and self-determination of peoples, in accordance with the provisions of the Charter, and to render assistance to the United Nations in carrying out the responsibilities entrusted to it by the Charter regarding the implementation of the principle in order:

(a) To promote friendly relations and co-operation among States; and

(b) To bring a speedy end to colonialism, having due regard to the freely expressed will of the peoples concerned;

and bearing in mind that subjection of peoples to alien subjugation, domination and exploitation constitutes a violation of the principle, as well as a denial of fundamental human rights, and is contrary to the Charter of the United Nations.

Every State has the duty to promote through joint and separate action universal respect for and observance of human rights and fundamental freedoms in accordance with the Charter.

The establishment of a sovereign and independent State, the free association of integration with an independent State or the emergence into any other political status freely determined by a people constitute modes of implementing the right of self-determination by that people.

Every State has the duty to refrain from any forcible action which deprives peoples referred to above in the elaboration of the present principle of their right to self-determination and freedom and independence. In their actions against and resistance to such forcible action in pursuit of the exercise of their right to self-determination, such peoples are entitled to seek and to receive support in accordance with the purposes and principles of the Charter of the United Nations.

The territory of a colony or other non-self-governing territory has, under the Charter of the United Nations a status separate and distinct from the territory of the State administering it; and such separate and distinct status under the Charter shall exist until the people of the colony or non-self-governing territory have exercised their right of self-determination in accordance with the Charter, and particularly its purposes and principles.

Nothing in the foregoing paragraphs shall be construed as authorizing or encouraging any action which would dismember or impair, totally or in part, the territorial integrity or political unity of sovereign and independent States conducting themselves in compliance with the principle of equal rights and self-determination of peoples as described above

and thus possessed of a government representing the whole people belonging to the territory without distinction as to race, creed or colour.
Every State shall refrain from any action aimed at the partial or total
disruption of the national unity and territorial integrity of any other
State or country.

POSTSCRIPT

*The Relevance of the World Court decision on
Namibia, 1971, to the principle of self-determination.*

In the *Legal Consequences for States of the Continued Presence of
South Africa in Namibia (South West Africa) Notwithstanding Security
Council Resolution 276(1970),*[1] the World Court reviewed the previous
Opinions and Judgments on Namibia and re-stated the international law
of mandates.

It re-affirmed the Opinion of 1950 that "two principles were considered to be of paramount importance: the principle of non-annexation
and the principle that the well-being and development of such peoples
form 'a sacred trust of civilisation'.[2] The trust was intended to be
exercised for the benefit of the peoples concerned "who were admitted
to have interests of their own and to have a potentiality for independent
existence on the attainment of a certain stage of development."[3] This
confirms our view in chapter 2 that the tutelage over mandated territories
was not intended to be permanent but temporary, pending the attainment of a sufficient degree of development. The Court denied that the
Mandate Agreement on South West Africa allowed the annexation of
the territory, an idea that had been decidedly rejected at the Paris Peace

1. I.C.J. Rep. 1971 p. 16.
2. I.C.J. Rep. 1950 p. 131.
3. I.C.J. Rep. 1971 p. 28-9.

Conference 1919. It found that "the subsequent development of international law in regard to non-self-governing territories, as enshrined in the Charter of the United Nations, made the principle of self-determination applicable to all of them."[4] The Charter of the U.N. thus carried the principle of the sacred trust further by extending it to colonies. Resolution 1514(XV) of 14 December 1960 on the Granting of Independence to Colonial Territories and Peoples was a further milestone in the development of the principle of unimpeded right to independence for subject peoples. The fact that only two of the fifteen original mandated territories are still dependent is a manifestation of the trend that led to the birth of many new States.

Re-affirming the principle of inter-temporal law discussed in chapter 6, the Court found that the Mandate Agreement was not only to be interpreted in accordance with the intention of the parties. It embodied evolutionary concepts—"the strenuous conditions of the modern world", "the well-being and development" of the peoples concerned and "the sacred trust". The Court, thus, had to consider the half-century of developments in international law. "Moreover, an international instrument has to be interpreted and applied within the frame-work of the entire legal system prevailing at the time of the interpretation."[5] The ultimate objective of the sacred trust was "the self-determination and independence" of the peoples concerned.[6] It did not vary according to the class of mandates: the designation of C-Mandates did not make them "the objects of disguised cessions."[7] On South Africa's argument that the demise of the League of Nations was fatal to the survival of mandates, the Court affirmed that the responsibilities of mandatory and supervisor (the League Council) were complementary; the disappearance of the one could not affect the survival of the institution. All the mandatories, with the exception of South Africa, had heeded the request of the U.N. that the mandates should be submitted to the Trusteeship System. Prolonged negotiations over the demand proved abortive because "one side (South Africa) adamantly refused to compromise"[8] leading ultimately to the termination of the mandate by the General Assembly.

Rejecting South Africa's request for further information concerning the purposes and objectives of the policy of *apartheid*, the Court found that it was contrary to the principle of respect for human rights en-

4. Ibid. 31.
5. Ibid 31.
6. Ibid 31.
7. Ibid 32.
8. Ibid 44.

shrined in the Charter of the U.N. "To establish instead, and to enforce distinctions, exclusions, restrictions and limitations, (on the Namibians) exclusively based on grounds of race, colour, descent or national or ethnic origin which constitute a denial of fundamental human rights is a flagrant violation of the purposes and principles of the Charter."[9]

South Africa also requested that a plebiscite should be held under the joint supervision of the Court and itself to determine whether the people wished to be ruled by South Africa or by the U.N. This was rejected. A determination by the people in a plebiscite would be in accord with the principle of self-determination. It is clear that South Africa will not co-operate in preparing the grounds for a meaningful plebiscite which will be preceded by a release of political prisoners, return of political refugees, abolition of restrictions on human rights, and, more especially, withdrawal of the repressive regime in the interest of a fair and free choice. Holding a plebiscite under the ruthless regime might, indeed, produce a result that would be a travesty of the wishes of the people.

The Court considered *obiter dicta*, the legality of General Assembly Resolution 2145(XXI) which terminated the mandate. It quoted the decision of 1962 that the Mandate Agreement was in fact and in law "an international agreement having the character of a treaty or convention"[10] The General Assembly of the U.N. considered earlier that South Africa had, in its conduct of the mandate, contradicted the principles of the Mandate Agreement, the Charter of the U.N. and the Universal Declaration of Human Rights. It was unnecessary to call for fresh evidence of the breach for it had been given on previous occasions. Moreover, South Africa refused to render reports and to submit to supervision. The inescapable conclusion was that South Africa had committed a serious breach of the mandate. Considering this in light of the Vienna Convention on the Law of Treaties which in many respects is a codification of customary law, the Court found that the right of termination had been properly exercised in view of South Africa's deliberate and persistent violation of treaty obligations. This right exists whether or not it was included in the treaty for it is rooted in general international law and is independent of the instrument.

The Court then considered the legal effect of Security Council Resolutions 264(1969), 269(1969) and 276(1970). The first called on South Africa to withdraw its administration from the territory forthwith. The second set 4th October 1969 as the date-line for the withdrawal. The third declared that the continued presence of South Africa in Namibia

9. Ibid 57.
10. I.C.J. Rep. 1962 p. 330.

was illegal and that its defiant attitude undermines the authority of the U.N. The Court held that the Security Council acted within its primary responsibility of maintaining peace and security under Article 24 of the Charter and that Member States were under Article 25 bound to accept and carry out its decisions.

The consequence of the illegal situation, the Court found, was that South Africa was bound to end its illegal occupation of Namibia. It also incurred international responsibilities arising from the continuing violation of international obligations or of the rights of the people. Member States of the U.N. were obliged to recognise the invalidity and illegality of South Africa's continued presence and refrain from lending assistance to its occupation of Namibia. The precise determination of the actions to be taken was a matter for the organs of the U.N. Non-recognition of the acts of South Africa was not, however, to deny the Namibian people the advantages of international co-operation. The Court also found that the declaration of the illegality of South Africa's presence in Namibia and the termination of the mandate were opposable to all States, members or non-members of the U.N.

In an important passage the Court held:

"all States should bear in mind that the injured entity is a people which must look to the international community for assistance in its progress towards the goals for which the sacred trust was instituted."[11]

It was left to Judge Ammoun to expatiate, in his Separate Opinion, on the theme of support for colonial people. He re-stated the modern view that a people forcibly colonised retained their international legal personality though deprived of the right to exercise sovereignty. Thus, South West Africa, under the Germans, constituted "a subject of law that was distinct from the German State, possessing national sovereignty but lacking the exercise thereof."[12]

Sovereignty, Judge Ammoun held, is in every people, just as liberty is inherent in every individual. The legitimacy of the colonial struggle against domination emanated from the right of self-defence and is confirmed by Article 51 of the Charter. He saw O.A.U. support for African freedom fighters as a right of collective self-defence. He, then, traced the philosophical and historical background of the right of equality, and hence of self-determination, to Natural Law as taught by Zeno of Sidon, founder of the Stoic School of thought in ancient Greece. The right of

11. Ibid p. 56.
12. Ibid p. 68.

equality, he reaffirmed, was the most important of all human rights. The 1971 Opinion and the Separate Opinion of Judge Ammoun confirm our views on the present international law on subject territories. Colonial peoples have an inherent right to independence; sovereignty, forcibly denied them remains their imprescriptible right. Colonialism, maintained and prolonged by the use of force, is a violation of human rights and calls for adequate means of eradication. Present international law recognises the legitimacy of the struggle of colonised people to free themselves and the international community is obliged to give them all necessary support. The gross violation of the right of a people to self-determination, particularly by a UN member, attracts the whole gamut of sanctions under the Charter for a breach of peace or threat thereof. Support for resistance to colonial rule given by a regional organisation or by sympathetic states is proper in international law.

It may be said that both the Court's Opinion and Separate Opinion bring judicial reasoning up to date on colonialism and freedom fighting. The debate, whether or not colonial peoples are entitled to self-determination, as a legal right, is closed. Attention is now shifted to the legitimate means of attaining this right expeditiously with minimum sacrifice.

Bibliography

Books and Articles

Abdullah, S. Kashmir Issue, Statement to the Press, 17 February 1958.

Acton, Lord. *Lectures on the French Revolution.* London, 1916.

Adrzejewski, B. W. and Lewis, I. M. *Somali Poetry.* London, 1964.

Allen, P. M. "Self-determination and Independence." *International Conciliation*, 1966.

Aluko, S. A. "How Many Nigerians? An Analysis of Nigeria's Census Problems 1901–63." 3 *JMAS* (1965).

Amber, P. "Modernisation and Political Disintegration: Nigeria and the Ibos." 2 *JMAS* (1967).

Amuzar, J. "Nationalism vs. Economic Growth." 44 *Foreign Affairs* (1965–1966).

Aristotle. *Politics.*

Arzinger, R. *Das Selbstbestimmungsrecht Un Allgemeinen Volkerrecht der Gegenwart. (Staatsverlag Der Deutschen Demokratischen Republic)* Berlin, 1966.

Asamoah, O. Y. "The Legal Effect of Resolutions of the General Assembly." 3 *Columbia Journal of Transnational Law* (1965).

———. *The Legal Significance of the Declaration of the General Assembly of the United Nations.* Hague, 1966.

Asbeck, V. "International Law and Colonial Administration." 29 *Transactions of the Grotius Society* (1954), p. 23.

Association of American Law Schools. *Selected Essays on Constitutional Law* (1963).

Atkey, R. G. "Foreign Investment Disputes." *Canadian YBIL* (1967).

Bailey, S. D. "The Future Composition of the Trusteeship Council." 13 *International Organisation* (1959), no. 3, pp. 412–421.

Baines, J. S. "Angola, the United Nations, and International Law." 3 *Indian JIL* (1963).

Baker, R. S. *Woodrow Wilson and World Settlement.* vol. 1. London and New York, 1923.

Baker and Dodd, eds. *The Public Papers of Woodrow Wilson: War and Peace.* vols. 1 and 2.

———. *The New Democracy.* vol. 1.

Baratashvili, D. I. *International Law and the States of Asia and Africa.* Moscow, 1968.

Barnes, L. *The Duty of Empire.*

Barsegov, Y. Y. "The Durand Line and the Question of Self-determination of Pushtunistan in Afganistan-Pakistan Relations." *Soviet YBIL* (1959), p. 398.

Batsell, W. R. *Soviet Rule in Russia.* New York, 1929.

Baynes, N. H. *The Speeches of Adolf Hitler, April 1922–August 1939.* vol. 1. (1942).

Bello, A. *My Life* Cambridge, 1962.

Bentwich, N. *The Mandates System.* London, 1930.

———. "Colonial Mandates and Trusteeship." 32 *Transactions of the Grotius Society* (1945).

Birch, G. and George, D. S. *Biafra, The Case for Independence.* London, 1967.

Bissell, T. St. G. "Negotiations by International Bodies and the Protection of Human Rights." 7 *Columbia Journal of Transnational Law* (1968), p. 90.

Blair, P. W. *The Ministate Dilemma.* Carnegie Foundation for International Peace, Occasional Paper no. 6, October 1967.

Bohan, R. T. "The Dominican Case: Unilateral Intervention." 60 *AJIL* (1966), p. 809.

Bourquin, M. "Arbitration and Economic Development Agreements." 15 *Business Lawyer* (1966), p. 860.

Bowett, D. W. *et al.* "Self-determination and Political Rights in Developing Countries." *American Society of International Law* (April 1966).

———. *Self-defence in International Law* (1958).

Bradby, E. D. *The French Revolution.* Oxford, 1926.

Brierly, N. "The Mandate for Jordan." *BYBIL* (1929).

———. *Law of Nations.* Oxford, 1963.

Broches, A. "The Convention of the Settlement of Investment Disputes." *Columbia Journal of Transnational Law* (1966).

Broderick, M. "Associated Statehood—A New Form of Decolonisation." 17 *ICLQ* (April 1968).

Brown, D. J. L. "The Ethiopian-Somali Frontier Dispute." *ICLQ* (1956), p. 245.

Brown, P. M. "Self-determination in Central Europe." 14 *AJIL* (1920).

Brownlie, I. *Basic Documents in International Law*. Oxford, 1967.

———. *Principles of International Law*. Oxford, 1966.

Buell, R. L. *The Native Problem in Africa*. vol. 1. New York, 1928.

Burlamaqui, J. J. *Principes du Droit Naturel*. Geneva, 1748.

Calvocoressi, P. "South-West Africa." 65 *African Affairs* (1966), pp. 223–232.

Castagno, A. A. "Somalia-Kenyan Controversy: The Future." 2 *JMAS* (1964), pp. 165–188.

Cefkin, J. L. "The Rhodesian Question at the United Nations." XXI *International Organisation* (1968), pp. 649–669.

Cervenka, Z. "Legal Effects of Non-recognition of Southern Rhodesia's Unilateral Declaration of Independence in International Law." *Casopis pro mezinarodni pravo Rocnik*. vols. 2 and 3 (1967).

Chacko, C. J. "Peaceful Co-existence as a Doctrine of Current International Affairs." 4 *Indian YBIA* (1955).

Chagla, M. C. *Kashmir 1947–1965*. Government of India publication, 1965.

Cheng, B. "The Rationale of Compensation for Expropriation." 44 *Transactions of the Grotius Society*, p. 267.

Chick, J. D. "Nigeria at War." *Current History*. February 1968.

Claude, I. L. *National Minorities: An International Problem*. Cambridge, 1955.

Cobban, A. *National Self-determination*. London, 1945.

Commanger, H. S. ed. *Documents of American History*. London and New York, 1948.

Coret, A. "La Declaration de l'Assembles Generale de l'ONU sur l'octroi de l'independence aux pays et aux peuples coloniaux." 15 *Revue Juridique et Politique d'Outre* (October–December 1961).

Crawford, J. F. "South-West Africa: Mandate Termination in Historical Perspective." 6 *Columbia Journal of Transnational Law*. no. 1 (1967).

Crocker, W. R. *Self-government for the Colonies*. London, 1948.

D'Amato, A. A. "The Bantustan Proposals for South-West Africa." 4 *JMAS*. no. 2 (1966), pp. 177–192.

Das, B. "The Naga Problem." 5 *Socialist Tract*. Hyderabad, 1956.

Davies, S. G. "Some Recent Decisions on the Nigerian Constitution." 11 *ICLQ* (1962).

Delaume, G. R. "The Convention on the Settlement of Investment Disputes Between States and Nationals of Other States." 1 *International Lawyer* (1967), pp. 64–80.

Delaume, G. R. "The Proper Law of Loans Concluded by International Persons: A Restatement and a Forecast." 56 *AJIL* (1962), p. 62.

Dike, K. O. *Trade and Politics in the Niger Delta*. Oxford, 1956.

Dinestein, H. S. "Soviet Policy in Latin America." *The American Political Science Quarterly*, vol. 61, no. 1 (March 1967).

Domke, M. "Foreign Nationalisations." 55 *AJIL* (1961).

Drysdale, J. G. S. *The Somali Dispute*. London, 1964.

Dudley, B. J. "Nigeria's Civil War." *The Round Table* (January 1968).

Dugard, C. J. R. "The South-West Africa Cases." *South African Law Journal* (1966).

————. "The OAU and Colonisation: An Inquiry into the Plea of Self-determination as Justification for the Use of Force in the Eradication of Colonialism." 16 *ICLQ* (1967).

————. "The Revocation of the Mandate for South-West Africa." 62(1) *AJIL* (1968), p. 78.

————. "The Legal Effect of UN Resolutions on Apartheid." 83 *South African LJ* (1966), p. 44.

Duverger, M. *Droit Constitutional et Institutions Politiques*. Paris, 1955.

Egal, H. I. "Somalia: Nomadic Individualism and the Rule of Law." 67 *African Affairs* (1968), p. 219.

Eide, A. and Schou, A., eds. *International Protection of Human Rights*. Uppsala, 1968.

Elwin, V. *Nagaland*. Shillong, 1961.

Emerson, R. "Self-determination Revisited in the Era of Decolonisation," *Occasional Papers in International Affairs*, Harvard Center of International Affairs, no. 9 (December 1964).

————. *From Empire to Nation*. Cambridge, Massachusetts 1960.

————. "Pan-Africanism." 16 *International Organisation* (1962).

————. "Colonialism, Political Development, and the United Nations." *International Organisation* (Summer 1965).

Eppstein, J. *The Catholic Tradition of the Law of Nations*. (1935).

Ewelukwa, D. I. O. "The Constitutional Aspects of the Military Takeover in Nigeria." *The Nigerian Law Journal*, vol. 2 (1) (1967).

Ezejiofor, G. *Protection of Human Rights Under the Law*. London, 1964.

Fabunmi, L. A. The Sudan *in Anglo-Egyptian Relations*. London, 1960.

Falks, R. A. *"The South-West Africa Cases: An Appraisal"* 21 *International Organisation* (1967), no. 1.

Fawcett, J. E. S. *The British Commonwealth in International Law.* London, 1963.

——. "The Commonwealth and the United Nations." *Journal of Commonwealth Political Studies,* vols. 1 and 2 (1961–4), p. 123.

——. *The Inter-se Doctrine in Commonwealth Relations.* London, 1958.

——. "Gibraltar: The Legal Issues." 43 *International Affairs.* Royal Institute, 1967.

——. "Security Council Resolutions on Rhodesia." 41 *BYBIL* (1965–66).

Feit, E. "Military Coups and Political Development." 20 *World Politics,* no. 2 (January 1968).

Fenwick, C. G. "The Dominican Republic: Intervention or Collective Self-defense" 60 *AJIL* (1966), p. 64.

Ferguson, C. C. "The United Nations Human Rights Covenants: Problems of Ratification and Implementation." *Proceedings of American Society of International Law* (April 1968).

Fisher, R. "The Participation of Microstates in International Affairs." *American Society of International Affairs* (April 1968).

Fleming, B. "South-West Africa Cases." *Canadian YBIL* (1967).

Fletcher-Cooke, J. "Some Reflections on the International Trusteeship, with Particular Reference to Its Impact on the Governments and Peoples of the Trust Territories." 13 *International Organisation* (1959), pp. 422–437.

Ford, P. L., ed. *The Writings of Thomas Jefferson,* vols. 1, 6, 9.

Foresythe, F. *The Biafra Story.* Penguin, 1969.

Friedmann, S. *Expropriation in Public International Law.* London, 1953.

Friedmann, W. G. "Law and Politics in the Vietnamese War." 61 *AJIL* (1967), p. 776.

——. *The Changing Structure of International Law.* London, 1964.

——. "The Jurisprudential Implications of the South-West Africa Case." 6 *Columbia Journal of Transnational Law* (1967).

Ganji, M. *International Protection of Human Rights.* Geneva, 1962.

George, D. L. *The Truth About the Peace Treaties.* London, 1938.

Gess, K. N. "Permanent Sovereignty over Natural Wealth and Resources." *ICLQ* (1964).

Ghai, Y. "Independence and Safeguards in Kenya." 3 *EALJ,* p. 177.

Ginsburgs, G. "A Case Study of Soviet Use of International Law." 52 *AJIL* (1958).

Godwin, R., ed. *Readings in American Foreign Policy* (1959).

Golder, F. A. ed. *Documents of Russian History 1914–1917*. New York, 1927.

Goodman, E. "The Cry of National Liberation: Recent Soviet Attitudes Toward National Self-determination." 14 *International Organisation* (1960).

Goodrich, L. M. *The United Nations*. New York, 1959.

Goodrich and Hambro. *The Charter of the United Nations*. London, 1949.

Green, L. C. *International Law Through the Cases*. London, 1951.

———. "The United Nations, South-West Africa, and the World Court." 7 *Indian JIL* (1967), p. 491.

Gross, E. A. "The South-West Africa Cases: What happened." *Foreign Affairs* (October 1966).

Haight, G. W. "The Special Committee on Friendly Relations and Co-operation among States." 1 *International Lawyer* (1967), pp. 122–126.

Hales, J. C. "The Creation and Application of the Mandate System." 25 *Transactions of the Grotius Society* (1939), pp. 185–204.

———. "Some Legal Aspects of the Mandate System: Sovereignty, Nationality, Termination, and Transfer," 23 *Transactions of the Grotius Society* (1937), pp. 85–126.

Hall, H. D. *Mandates, Dependencies and Trusteeship*. London, 1948.

Hass, E. "Reconciliation of Conflicting Colonial Policy Aims: Acceptance of the League of Nations System." 6 *International Organisation* (1952), pp. 521–536.

Heasman, D. J. "The Gibraltar Affair." *International Journal*, vol. 22, no. 2. Canadian Institute of International Affairs, 1967.

Higgins, R. "The International Court of Justice and South-West Africa." 42 *International Affairs*. Royal Institute, 1966.

———. *The Development of International Law Through the Political Organs of the United Nations*. London, 1963.

Hill, N. *Claims to Territory in International Law and Relations*. London, 1945.

Hitler, A. *Mein Kampf*. Munich, 1925.

Hobbes, T. *The Leviathan*. Oxford, 1881.

Hodgkin, T. *Nationalism in Colonial Africa*. London, 1956.

Hobson, J. A. *Imperialism*. London, 1902.

———. *Towards International Government*. London, 1915.

Holmes, J. "The Impact on the Commonwealth of the Emergence of Africa." *International Organisation* (1962).

Horowitz, D. *From Yalta to Vietnam*. Penguin Edition, 1967.

Hoskyns, C. *Case Studies in African Diplomacy: The Ethiopia-Somali-Kenya Dispute*. Dar es Salaam, 1969.

Houben, R. "Principles of International Law Concerning Friendly Relations and Cooperation among States." 61 *AJIL* no. 2 (1967).

Hudson, M. O., ed. *International Legislation*. New York, 1950.

Hull, C. *The Memoirs of Cordell Hull*. vol. 2. New York, 1948.

Hurst, C. *Great Britain and the Dominions*. Chicago, 1928.

Hyde, J. H. "Permanent Sovereignty over Natural Wealth and Resources." 50 *AJIL* (1950), pp. 854–867.

Inman, H., Hynning, C. J., and Carey, J. "The World Court's Decision on South-West Africa." 1 *International Lawyer* (1966).

Jacobson, H. K. "The United Nations and Colonialism: A Tentative Appraisal." *International Organisation* (1962).

James, A. "Legal Aspects of the Transfer of Power to Dependent Territories in Tropical Africa." Unpublished thesis, B. Litt., Oxford Univ., 1966.

Jansma, K. "International Consequences of Nationalisation." 41 *Transactions of the Grotius Society* (1956).

Jefferson, T. *Summary View of the Rights of British America, 1794*. New York, 1943.

Jenks, C. W. *The Prospects of International Adjudication*. London and New York, 1964.

Jennings, R. Y. "State Contracts in International Law." 37 *BYBIL* (1961), p. 156.

―――. *The Acquisition of Territory in International Law*. Manchester, 1963.

Jessup, P. C. "The Palmas Island Case." 22 *AJIL* (1928), p. 740.

―――. *A Modern Law of Nations*. New York, 1949.

Johnson, A. W. "The Dynamics of Federalism in Canada." *Canadian Journal of Political Science*, vol. 1, no. 1. (March 1968).

Johnson, D. H. N. "The Effect of Resolutions of the General Assembly." 32 *BYBIL* (1955–56).

―――. "The Case Concerning the Northern Cameroons." *ICLQ* (1964).

Johnson, H. S. *Self-determination Within the Community of Nations*. Leyden, 1967.

Johri, S. R. *Our Borderlands*. Lucknow, 1964.

Jones, G. I. *The Trading States of the Oil Rivers*. London, 1963.

Jones, W. T. *Masters of Political Thought*. London, 1960.

Jones, M. G. "National Minorities: A Case Study in International Protection." 14 *Law and Contemporary Problems* (1949).

Joubert, de M. G. *L'Empire Colonial Francais.*

Kaekenbeeck, G. *"Territories Non Autonomous Tutelle."* 1 *Recueil des Cours* (1947).

Kay, D. A. "The Politics of Decolonisation: The New Nations and the United Nations Political Process. 21 *International Organisation,* no. 4 (1967), pp. 786–811.

Kelsen, H. *The Law of the United Nations.* London, 1950.

Khan and Kaur. "The Deadlock over South-West Africa," 8 *Indian JIL* (1968), p. 179.

Kilbride, P. E. "The Cook Islands Constitution." 1 *New Zealand Universities Law Review* (1965), pp. 571–6.

Kirk-Green, A. H. M. "The Peoples of Nigeria: The Cultural Background for the Crisis." 66 *African Affairs,* no. 262 (January 1967).

Korbel, J. *Danger in Kashmir.* New Jersey, 1966.

Korey, W. "The Key to Human Rights Implementation," *International Conciliation* (November 1968).

Korowicz, M. St. *Introduction to International Law.* Hague, 1959.

Krylov, S. B. *Materials for the History of the United Nations,* vol. 1 (1949).

Kunz, J. L. "The United Nations Declaration of Human Rights." 43 *AJIL* (1949), pp. 316–323.

———. "The Present Status of International Law for the Protection of Minorities." 48 *AJIL* (1954).

Lachs, M. "The Law in and of the United Nations Organisation." *Indian JIL* (1961).

———. "Some Reflections on the Problems of Self-determination." *Review of Contemporary Law* (1957).

Lakhanpal, P. L. *Essential Documents and Notes on Kashmir Dispute.* New Delhi, 1965.

Lalive, J. "Contracts Between a State or State Agency and a Foreign Company—Theory and Practice: Choice of Law in a New Arbitration Case. 13 *ICLQ* (1964), p. 987.

Lamb, A. *Crisis in Kashmir.* London, 1966.

Lansing, R. *The Peace Negotiations: A Personal Narrative.* London, 1921.

Lasserson, M. M. "The Development of Soviet Foreign Policy in Europe 1917–1942." *International Conciliation* (1943).

Lauterpacht, E. "Some Concepts of Human Rights." 11 *Howard Law Journal* (1965).

Lauterpacht, H. *International Law and Human Rights*. London, 1950.
Leach, R. H., ed. *Contemporary Canada*. Durham, 1967.
Legum, C. *Pan-Africanism, A Short Political Guide*. New York, 1962.
———. "Somali Liberation Songs." *JMAS*, vol. 1, no. 4 (1963), pp. 503–519.
Lenin, N. *Marx, Engels, Marxism*. London, 1951.
———. *Selected Works*, vol. 1. London, 1936.
———. *The Right of Nations to Self-determination*. New York, 1951.
———. *Collected Works*, vol. 22. London, 1960.
Leslie, P. M. "The Role of Political Parties in Promoting the Interest of Ethnic Minorities," *Canadian Journal of Political Science*, vol. 2, no. 4. (December 1969).
Levin, D. B. "The Principle of Self-determination of Nations in International Law," *Soviet YBIL* (1962).
Lewis, I. M. "Developments in the Somali Dispute," *African Affairs*, vol. 66, no. 263. (April 1967), pp. 104–112.
Lewis, R. "African Border War at Stalement." *JMAS* (1964).
Lissitzyn, O. J. "International Law in a Divided World." *International Conciliation* (1963).
Liu, C. "Competence of a State to Deprive Aliens' Property in International Law." *Annals of the Chinese Society of International Law*, vol. 3. (July 1966).
Locke, J. *Treatise of Civil Government*. London, 1884.
Louis, W. R. "The South-West African Origins of the Sacred Trust." 66 *African Affairs* (January 1967).
———. "African Origins of the Mandate Idea." 19 *International Organisation* (1965).
Luard, D. E. T., ed. *The International Protection of Human Rights*. London, 1967.
Lui, P. S. "The Principle of Parity in the Trusteeship Council." *Annals of the Chinese Society of International Law*, vol. 2. (1965), pp. 28–36.
Lyon, P. "Kashmir." *International Relations*, vol. 3, no. 2. David Davis Memorial Institute of International Studies (October 1966).
Macartney, G. A. *National States and National Minorities*. Oxford and London, 1934.
Machiavelli, N. *The Prince*. London, 1958.
Malacela, J. W. S. "The United Nations and Decolonisation of Non-Self-Governing Territories." *UN Monthly Chronicle*, vol. 4, no. 8.
Mandlovitz, F. and Falk R., eds. *The United Nations*. vol. 3 (1966).

Manley, N. W. "The Role of the Opposition in a Young Nation." *The Parliamentarian IL*, no. 1 (January 1968).

Mann, F. A. "The Proper Law of Contracts Concluded by International Persons." 35 *BYBIL* (1959).

Marston, G. "Termination of Trusteeship Territories." 18 *ICLQ* (1969).

Mason, P. "Some Aspects of the Odendaal Report." *Race*, vol. 5. London, 4 April 1964.

Mattern, J. *The Employment of the Plebiscite in the Determination of Sovereignty*. Baltimore: The Johns Hopkins Press, 1920.

McDougal, M. S. and Reisman, W. M. "Rhodesia and the UN." 62 *AJIL* (1968), p. 1.

McMillan, J. and Harris, B. *The American Takeover of Britain*. Leslie Frewen: London, 1968.

McNair, A. D. *The Law of Treaties*. Oxford, 1961.

Means, G. D. and Means, I. N. "Nagaland: The Agony of Ending a Guerrilla War." *Pacific Affairs*, vol. 39, nos. 3 and 4 (1966–67), pp. 290–313.

Meek, C. K. *Law and Authority in a Nigerian Tribe*. Oxford, 1937.

Mensah, T. *Self-determination under the United Nations Auspices* (1963).

Merle, M. *"Les Plēbiscites Organises Par Les Nations Unies." Annuaire Francaise de Droit International* (1961), pp. 425–445.

Millar, T. B. "The Commonwealth and the United Nations." *International Organisation* (1962).

Miller, D. H. *Diary*, 19.

———. *The Drafting of the Covenant*. vols. 1 and 2. London and New York, 1928.

Minoque, K. R. *Nationalism*. London, 1967.

Mirriam, M. W. "The Background of the Ethiopian-Somalian Boundary Dispute." 2 *JMAS* (1964), pp. 189–219.

Moller, N. H. "Compensation for British-Owned Foreign Interests." 44 *Transactions of the Grotius Society* (1958–59).

Moore, M. *Digest of International Law*, vol. 2.

Morris, C. *Great Legal Philosophers*. Philadelphia, 1959.

Murray, J. N. *The UN Trusteeship System*. Urbana, Illinois, 1957.

Mushkat, M. "African Concepts of Problems Relating to International Law." *International Problems*, vol. 5., nos. 1 and 2. Israeli Institute of International Affairs, 1967.

———. "The Process of African Decolonisation." 4 *Indian JIL* (1966).

Nawaz, M. K. "The Meaning and the Range of the Principle of Self-determination." *Duke University LJ* (1965).

Nawaz, M. K. "Colonies, Self-government, and the United Nations." *Indian YB IA* (1962).

Nicolson, H. *Peacemaking 1919*. London, 1933.

Nkrumah, K. *Class Structure in Africa*. London, 1970.

Northey, J. F. "Self-determination in the Cook Islands." 74 *Journal of the Polynesian Society*.

Norton, J. H. "The Lawfulness of Military Assistance for the Republic of Vietnam." 61 *AJIL* (1967), p. 1.

Nussbaum, A. *A Concise History of the Law of Nations*. New York, 1962.

Nwabueze, B. O. *Constitutional Law of the Nigerian Republic*. London, 1964.

Nwankwo, A. and Ifejika, S. U. *The Making of a Nation: Biafra*. London, 1969.

Nye and Morpugo. *A History of the United States of America*. Hammondswoth & Co., 1955.

O'Brien, C. C. "The Tragedy of Biafra," *The New York Times Book Review* (21 December, 1967).

O'Connell, D. P. O. *International Law*. vol. 1. London, 1965.

O'Connor, W. "Self-determination: The New Phase." 1 *World Politics* (October 1967).

Odumosu, O. I. *The Nigerian Constitution, History and Development*. London, 1963.

Ojukwu, C. O. *Random Thoughts*. New York, 1969.

————. *Selected Speeches*. New York, 1969.

————. *The Ahiara Declaration*. Geneva, 1969.

Oppenheim, L. F. "The Science of International Law." *AJIL* (1908).

————. *International Law*. London, 1963.

Padelford, N. J. "The Aaland Islands Question," 33 *AJIL* (1939).

Padover, S. K., ed. *The Complete Jefferson*. (1943).

————. *Thomas Jefferson and the Foundations of American Freedom*. Saul Kusiel, 1965.

Panhuys, V. "The International Aspect of the Reconstruction of the Kingdom of the Netherlands in 1954." *Netherlands International Law Review* (1958).

————. "The Netherlands Constitution and International Law." 47 *AJIL* (1953).

Panter-Brick, S. K. "The Right to Self-determination; Its Application to Nigeria." 44 *International Affairs*. United Kingdom, April 1968.

Peaslee, A. J., ed. *Constitutions of Nations*. vols. 1 and 2. Netherlands, 1965, 1966.

Perham, M. *The Government of Ethiopia.* London, 1948.

Petren, S. "Confiscation of Foreign Property and International Claims Arising Therefrom." 109 *Recueil des Cours*, no. 11 (1963).

Phinney, A. "Racial Minorities in the Soviet Union." 8 *Pacific Affairs*, no. 3 (September 1935).

Pickles, D. M. *The Fifth Republic.* London, 1965.

Post, K. W. "Is There a Case for Biafra?" 44 *International Affairs.* United Kingdom, 1968.

Potter, P. B. "Legal Aspects of the Beirut Landing." 52 *AJIL* (1958), pp. 727–30.

———. "The Principal Legal and Political Problems Involved in the Kashmir Case." 44 *AJIL* (1959), p. 361.

Quaison-Sackey, A. "Progress Toward Charter Aims in the World's Dependent Territories." 6 *UN Review* (5 May 1960).

Quarles, B. *The Negro in the Making of America.* New York and London, 1967.

Quintanilla, L. *A Latin American Speaks.* (1943).

Rajan, M. S. *The United Nations and Domestic Jurisdiction.* New York, 1961.

Rao, P. C. "The Rhodesian Imbrioglio." 6 *Indian JIL* (1966).

———. "South-West Africa Cases: Inconsistent Judgment from the International Court of Justice." 6 *Indian JIL* (1966).

Rapport, J. G. "The Participation of Ministates in International Affairs." *American Society of International Law* (April 1968).

Rarua, O. O. "Will New Guinea Be the Last Colonial Country?" *Australian Quarterly*, vol. 39 (4) (1967), pp. 21–35.

Ray, G. W. "Law Governing Contracts Between States and Foreign Nationals." *Proceedings of the 1960 Institute on Private Investments Abroad* (1960).

Reisman, W. M. "Revision of the South-West Africa Cases." 7 *Virginia JIL* (1968), p. 3.

Robinowitz, C. "UN Sanctions and Rhodesia," 7 *Virginia JIL* (1967).

Robinson, J. "From Protection of Minorities to Promotion of Human Rights, 1948." *Jewish YBIL* (1949).

Robinson, K. *The Public Law of Overseas France Since the War.*

———. "Constitutional Reform in French Tropical Africa." *Political Studies*, vol. 6, no. 1 (February 1955).

———. "Constitutional Autochthony in Ghana." *Journal of Commonwealth Political Studies*, vols. 1 and 2 (1961–4), p. 41.

Rodley, N. S. "Some Aspects of the World Bank Convention on the Settlement of Investment Disputes." *Canadian YBIL* (1966) 43.

Roling, B. V. A. *International Law in an Expanded World*. Amsterdam, 1960.

Rosenne, S. *The Law and Practice of the International Court of Justice*. Leyden, 1965.

Ross, A. *The Constitution of the United Nations*. 1950.

Rousseau, J. *Les contrat social*. Paris, 1955.

Russel, F. M. *Theories of International Relations*. London and New York, 1936.

Russel and Muther. *A History of the United Nations Charter*. Brookings and Washington, D.C., 1958.

Sady, E. *The United Nations and Dependent Peoples*. Washington, 1956.

Sapozhnikov, V. I. "Sovereignty over Natural Wealth and Resources." *Soviet YBIL* (1965).

Sarraut, A. *La Mise-en-Valeur des colonies Francaises*. Paris and Payout, 1923.

Sassoon, D. M. "The Convention on the Settlement of Investment Disputes Between States and Nationals of Other States." *Israel Law Review* (1967).

Sayre, F. B. "Legal Problems Arising from the UN Trusteeship System." 42 *AJIL* (1948).

Scheiner, S. M. *Negro Mecca*. New York, 1965.

Schick F. B. "Some Reflections on the Legal Controversies Concerning America's Involvement in Vietnam." 17 *ICLQ* (1968), p. 953.

Schwarz, S. *The Jews of the Soviet Union*. Syracuse University Press: Syracuse, 1951.

Schwarzenberger, G. *A Manual of International Law*. London, 1967.

———. "The Principles of International Economic Law." 117 *Recueil des Cours* 1 (1966).

———. *Foreign Investments and International Law*. London, 1969.

Schwelb, E. "Trieste Settlement and Human Rights." 49 *AJIL* (1956).

Scott, D. J. R. *Russian Political Institutions*. London, 1965.

Scott, J. B. *Official Statements of War Aims and Peace Proposals*. Washington, 1921.

Shaheen, S. *The Communist Bolshevik Theory of National Self-determination*. The Hague, 1956.

Shapiro, L., ed. *Soviet Treaty Series*, vol. 1 Washington, 1950.

Shaw, T. "The Mystery of the Buried Bronzes." *Nigeria Magazine*, no. 92 (March 1967).

Sinha, S. C. "Role of President Woodrow Wilson in the Evolution of the Mandate System." *Indian Journal of Political Science*, vol. 3 (1941–42).

Sinha, S. P. *New Nations and the Law of Nations*. Leyden, 1967.

Skurnik, W. A. E. "Nigeria in Crisis." *Current History* (March 1967).

Sloan, F. B. "The Binding Force of a 'Recommendation' of the General Assembly of the United Nations." *BYBIL* (1948).

de Smith, S. A. "The Cook Islands." *Annual Survey of Commonwealth Law*, vol. 1 (1965).

————. *The Vocabulary of Commonwealth Relations*. London, 1965.

————. "Constitutionalism in the Commonwealth Today." 4 *Malaya Law Reports* (1962).

Smuts, J. C. *The League of Nations: A Practical Suggestion*. (1918).

Snyder, E. "Protection of Private Foreign Investment: Examination and Appraisal." *ICLQ* (1961).

Sobakin, V. K. *Public International Law*. Moscow, 1962.

Sorensen, M., ed. *Manual of Public International Law*. New York, 1968.

Stahl, K. M. *British and Soviet Colonial Systems*. London, 1951.

Stalin, J. *Marxism and the National Colonial Question*. London, 1936.

————. *Collected Articles on the National Question*. Moscow and Leningrad, 1925.

Starke, J. B. *An Introduction to International Law*. London, 1967.

Starr, R. " 'Friendly Relations' in the United Nations." 2 *International Lawyer*. (1968).

Starunshenko, G. *The Principle of National Self-determination in Soviet Foreign Policy*. Moscow, 1963.

Stone, D. "The Rise of the Cook Island Party 1965." 74 *Journal of the Polynesian Society*.

————. "Self-determination in the Cook Islands." 1 *Journal of Pacific History* (1966).

Sukovic, O. "The Colonial Question in the Charter and the Practice of the UN." *International Problems of the Institute of Politics and Economy*, Belgrade, 1966.

Suratgar, D. "Considerations Affecting Choice of Law Clauses in Contracts Between Governments and Foreign Nationals." 2 *Indian JIL* (1962).

Sydenham, M. J. *The French Revolution*. London, 1965.

Tamuno, T. N. "Separatist Agitations in Nigeria." 8 (4) *JMAS* (December 1970), pp. 563–604.

Taracouzio, T. A. *The Soviet Union in International Law*. New York, 1935.

Temperley, H. W. V. *A History of the Peace Conference of Paris*, vols. 1, 2, 4, 6 London, 1920–24.

Thiam, D. *La Politique Etrangers des Etats Africains.* Paris: Presses Universitaires de France, 1963.

Thomas and Thomas. *Non-intervention.* Dallas, 1956.

Thorton, A. P. "Colonialism." 17 *International Journal.* Canadian Institute of International Affairs, 1961–2.

Toussaint, C. E. "The Colonial Controversy in the UN." *YBWA* (1956).

Touval, S. *Somali Nationalism.* Cambridge, Mass., 1963.

Tunkin, G. I. *Droit International Public; Problems Theoriques.* Paris, 1965.

———, ed. *Contemporary International Law.* Moscow, 1969.

Tuzmukhamedov, R. A. "Charter of the OAU in the Light of International Law." *Soviet YBIL* (1963).

Twitchett, K. J. "The American National Interest and the Anti-colonial Crusade." *International Relations.* David Davis Memorial Institute of International Studies, vol. 3, no. 4 (October 1967).

Umozurike, U. O. "International Law and Colonialism in Africa" 3(1) *EALR* (1970).

Vallat, F. A. "The Competence of the United Nations General Assembly." 97 *Recueil des Cours* (1959).

Verdross, A. "Protection of Private Property Under Quasi-International Agreements." 6 *Nederlands Tijdschrift Voor International Recht* (1959).

de Visscher, C. *Theory and Reality in International Law.* London, 1957. (Translated by P. E. Corbett.)

———. *Problemes d'Interpretation Judiciare en Droit International Public* (1966).

Vyshinsky, A. Y. *The Law of the Soviet State.* New York, 1948.

Wagley, C. and Harris, M. *Minorities in the World.* New York and London, 1958.

Waldock, H. *Human Rights in Contemporary International Law.* British Institute of International and Comparative Law (1963).

———. "General Course in Public International Law." 106 *Recueil des Cours* 2 (1962).

Wambaugh, S. *Plebiscites Since World War.* Washington, 1933.

Weinstein, P. D. "The Attitude of the Capital-Importing Nations Toward the Taking of Foreign-Owned Private Property." 5 *Indian JIL* (1965).

Welsh, R. S. "The Constitutional Case in Southern Rhodesia." 83 *LQR* (January 1967).

Wheare, K. C. *Constitutional Structure of the Commonwealth.* Oxford, 1960.

White, F. *Mandates.* London, 1926.

Whiteman, M. M., ed. *Digest of International Law*, vols. 1 and 5. Washington, 1965.

Williams, J. F. *Some Aspects of the Covenant of the League of Nations.* London, 1934.

Wilson, A. and Amery, L. S. "The African Mandates and Their Future." 28 *United Empire* (1937), pp. 204–212.

Wilson, R. R. "International Law in New Constitutions." 58 *AJIL* (1964).

———. "International Law in the Commonwealth." 60 *AJIL* (1966).

———. "The Commonwealth as Symbol and Instrument." 53 *AJIL* (1959).

Windass, G. S. "Power Politics and Ideals: The Principle of Self-determination." *International Relations*, vol. 3, no. 3. David Davis Memorial Institute of International Studies (April 1967).

Winter, R. C. *Blueprints for Independence.* Djabbatan and Netherlands, 1961.

Wolfe, G. V. "The States Directly Concerned: Article 79 of the UN Charter." 42 *AJIL* (1948).

Wortley, B. A. *Expropriation in International Law.* Cambridge, Mass., 1959.

Wright, Q. *Mandates under the League of Nations.* Chicago: University of Chicago Press, 1930.

———. "Self-determination and Recognition." 98 *Recueil des Cours* (1959).

———. *The Role of International Law.* Manchester, etc., 1961.

———. "Proposed Termination of the Iraq Mandate." 25 *AJIL* (1931), p. 436.

———. "The Goa Incident." 56 *AJIL* (1962), p. 617.

———. "United States Intervention in the Lebanon," 53 *AJIL* (1959), p. 112.

———. "Legal Aspects of the Vietnam Situation." 60 *AJIL* (1966), p. 750.

Yturriaga, J. A. "Non-Self-Governing Territories: The Law and the Practice of the UN." *YBWA* (1964).

Zafar, S. M. *The Kashmir Crisis: Speeches at the Security Council,* 18 and 20 September 1965. Karachi: Din Muhammadi Press.

Documents

INTERNATIONAL LAW ASSOCIATION
Report of the Conference (1956).
Report of the Conference (1960).
Rule of Law and Human Rights: Principles and Definition, Geneva, 1966.

INTERNATIONAL LAW COMMISSION
Conclusion, entry into force and registration of treaties ILC Doc. A/CN. 4/148 of 3 July 1962.

LEAGUE OF NATIONS
The Mandates System—Origin, Principles, Application.
Survey of International Affairs I (1937).
Report of the 1st Comm., Doc. A3 (1946) on mandates.
Special suppl. no. 194, 21st ord. sess. on mandates.
6 PMC minutes (1925) on mandates.
22 PMC minutes (1932) on mandates.
26 PMC minutes (1934) on mandates.
31 PMC minutes (1937) on mandates.
Minutes of 20th sess. (4 September 1931) on mandates.

UNITED NATIONS
Security Council Official Record of 7 March 1947 on strategic territories.
Doc. S/PV/124 of 2 April 1948—US draft of mandate agreements for strategic territories.
Doc. A/C. 4/SR. 38 of 7 October 1967 on UN resolutions.
Doc. A/CN 4/L117 Add. I—Draft Law of Treaties.
Doc. A/C 4/385 on colonial territories.
Doc. A/334—South African statement on South-West Africa.
Doc. A/3625—Possible legal action on South-West Africa. Prepared by the Committee on South-West Africa.
Doc. A/6640 of 7 April 1967 on South-West Africa.
Report on Tanganyika, Trusteeship Council, 15th sess., suppl. no. 3.
ST/DP. 1/Set. A/73 Rev. I—background paper on chapter 11 of the Charter.
E/3325 of 26 February 1960 on the promotion of international flow of capital.
E/3492 of 18 May 1961 on the international flow of capital.
A/AC. 97/5/Rev. 2—Status of Permanent Sovereignty over Natural Wealth and Resources (1962).

Doc. A/4519 of 29 September 1960—Communication from the governor of Puerto Rico.

ST/TAO/HR of 21 May 1964—Seminar on human rights in developing countries.

A/AC. 125/L Part VI (1967)—Committee on Friendly Relations Cooperation Among States.

Doc. 109/L108—Secretariat Working Paper on South-West Africa.

A/AC. 109/SR 491 on the associated states on the West Indies.

Doc. A/6640—Report of *ad hoc* committee on South-West Africa, 7 April 1967.

Doc. A/CN. 4/204 of 5 April 1968 on state succession.

Miscellanea (Articles, Books, and Documents)

Africa Report 1963

Proceedings of Summit Conference of Independent African States (Addis Ababa, 1963).

Bandung: Selected Documents of Bandung Conference 26 May 1955, Institute of Pacific Relations.

Colonial Problem (London: Royal Institute of International Affairs, 1937).

Conference de la Paix (1919–20) *Recueil des Actes de la Conference, partie* 4B (1).

Cook Islands: A Report to Members of the Legislative Assembly of the Cook Islands on Constitutional Development by Aikman, Davidson, and Wright (Karatoga, 1963).

Cyprus: Memorandum Setting out the Agreed Foundation for the Final Settlement of the Problem of Cyprus. (London, 19 February 1959.)

Encouragement and Protection of Investment in Developing Countries, Report of the conference held on 28–29 September 1961, *ICLQ* (1962), suppl. no. 3.

Encyclopaedia Britannica, vol. 20 (1960).

Encyclopedie Politique de la France et du Mond, 2nd ed. (Paris, 1948).

Great Britain: British State and Foreign Papers Commonwealth Association in Brief, British Information Services (1958).

Cmd. 151—Commentary on the League of Nations Covenant.

Cmd. 2397 of 1925 on East Africa.

Cmd. 2768 on the Imperial Conference of 1962.

Cmd. 3234 of 1929 on Kenya.

Foreign Office Handbook; Africa.

Parl. Deb., (HC) on colonial territories, col. 984, 12 November 1951.

Parl. Deb., 5th ser., vol. 593, col. 1258 (1954–55) on the Somalis.

Parl. Deb., 374 (HC) cols. 67–69 (1942) on colonies.

Harvard Research in International Law.
India: *India and the World*. Indian Institute of International Affairs, 1957.
(The) *March of India*. vol. 12. India, October 1960.
Proceedings of International Law (1964), discussion on nationalisation.
International Labour Organisation
Official Bulletin, vol. 45, no. 2, Suppl. 2 of April 1962.
Official Bulletin, vol. 46, no. 2, Suppl. 2 of April 1963.
International Commission of Jurists, Review of, no. 2, June 1969.
International Legal Materials.
Kashmir: Aggression in Kashmir (New Delhi, 1964).
Kashmir in Agony, Impartial Reports (Karachi, 1966).
Kashmir Issue and Indian Aggression, News and Views (Karachi, 1965).
India's Aggression Against Pakistan (Pakistan High Commission). London, 1965.
Mr. Nehru Answers Critics on Kashmir (India House, London).
Kenya: Report on the Northern Frontier District Commission (1962) Cmd. 1900.
The Somali Republic and African Unity (Mogadishu, 1962).
The Issue of the Northern Frontier District of Kenya (Mogadishu, May 1963).
League of Nations Treaty Series.
New York Times Current History, vols. 2, 7, 8.
Nigeria: House of Rep. Debates, 1 April (1953), 1053.
January 15 (1966), Before and After (Enugu, 1968).
Meeting of the Supreme Military Council (Enugu, 1967).
Nigeria Crisis, vol. 7 (Enugu, 1967).
Problem of Unity, the Case for Eastern Nigeria (Enugu, 1968).
Report of the Kano Disturbances, 1953.
Republic of Biafra, Proclamations (Enugu, 1968).
Press Information Bureau (New Delhi, 28 June 1954).
Proceedings of the Institute on Private Investment Abroad (1960).
Round Table, no. 9 (1918).
Recuiel de Decisions de Tribunaux Mixtes institutes par les Traites de Paix (Paris 1922–1930).
Report on the treatment of Armenians in the Ottoman Empire by Bryce.
Report on the Near East by King-Crane.
Report on the Annual Conference of the Independent Labour Party April 1917 and April 1918.
Report of the Four Power Commission on Somaliland (London, 1949).

Service de Presse et d'Information, New York, French Affairs, no. 108, December 1960.
South Africa
    Parl. Deb. (Lords) cols. 2893-4 of 1951 on the Bantus.
    Col. 5481 of 1965 on Bantustans.
    Odendaal Report on South-West Africa.
    South-West Africa Survey (Pretoria, 1967).
    South Africa: Racial Affairs, Integration or separate development? (Stellensbosch, 1952)
    Fact Paper (1961).
Sudan: Revolution in Action, Regional Autonomy for the South (Khartoum, 1970).
United Nations:
    Monthly Chronicle
    Repertory of Practice of UN Organs.
    Treaty Series.
    United Nations Conference on International Organisation
    Year-books
    The Charter of the UN
    Statute of the International Court of Justice.
United States:
    Department of State Bulletins:
        volumes 6 and 7 on colonialism.
        20 April 1953 on Puerto Rico.
        26 April 1954 on international communism.
        21 June 1954 on colonialism.
        no. 31 of 1954 on the Pacific Charter.
        30 April 1956 on colonialism.
        15 October 1956 on colonialism.
        2 March 1960 on Tibet.
        24 August 1960 on international communism.
        Press release no. 121 of 8 March 1954, and no. 486 of August 1960
        M.S. Department of State File 371 0418-2660 CS/MDR on Puerto Rico.
        Report of the International American Conference, Washington 1889–90, vol. 2.
        Foreign Relations of the United States, vols. 1 and 5.
USSR: Gazette of the temporary worker-peasant government (January 18/31 1918).

Index